Thomas Jefferson

Thoughts on War and Revolution

Thomas Jefferson

Thoughts on War and Revolution

Annotated Correspondence

Edited and Annotation by

Brett F. Woods

Algora Publishing
New York

© 2009 by Algora Publishing.
All Rights Reserved
www.algora.com

No portion of this book (beyond what is permitted by
Sections 107 or 108 of the United States Copyright Act of 1976)
may be reproduced by any process, stored in a retrieval system,
or transmitted in any form, or by any means, without the
express written permission of the publisher.

Library of Congress Cataloging-in-Publication Data —

Jefferson, Thomas, 1743-1826.
    Thomas Jefferson : thoughts on war and revolution / edited and annotation by Brett
F. Woods.
        p. cm.
    Includes bibliographical references and index.
    ISBN 978-0-87586-636-9 (soft cover: alk. paper) — ISBN 978-0-87586-637-6
(hard cover: alk. paper) — ISBN 978-0-87586-638-3 (ebook) 1. Jefferson, Thomas,
1743-1826—Correspondence. 2. War. 3. Revolutions. I. Woods, Brett F. II. Title.

    U22.J43 2009
    973.4'6092—dc22
                        2008053097

Front Cover: Portrait of Thomas Jefferson by Gilbert Stuart
Image: © Burstein Collection/CORBIS
Creator Name: Gilbert Stuart
Date Created: ca. 1805-1807

Printed in the United States

I have sworn upon the altar of God eternal hostility against every form of tyranny over the mind of man.

- Thomas Jefferson, Letter to Benjamin Rush, September 23, 1800

TABLE OF CONTENTS

Table of Contents

Editor's Note

> All honor to Jefferson, the man who, in the concrete pressure of a struggle for national independence by a single people, had the coolness, forecast, and capacity to introduce into a merely revolutionary document an abstract truth, applicable to all men and all times, and so to embalm it there that today, and in all coming days, it shall be a rebuke and a stumbling block to the very harbingers of reappearing tyranny and oppression!
> — Abraham Lincoln, April 6, 1859[1]

From a historical perspective, it can be argued that Thomas Jefferson continues to capture the collective imagination because, quite simply, the United States continues to echo his ideals. In 1776, as a young lawyer from Virginia, he drafted the *Declaration of Independence* for the Continental Congress, therein articulating what would emerge as a fundamental, if bold statement of revolutionary principles — that all men are created equal and meant to be free.

Thomas Jefferson was born in 1743 in Albemarle County, Virginia, inheriting from his father, a planter and surveyor, some 5,000 acres of land, and from his mother, a Randolph, high social standing. He studied at the College of William and Mary and then read law. In 1772, he married Martha Wayles Skelton, a widow, and took her to live in his partly constructed mountaintop home, Monticello. Freckled and sandy haired, he was rather tall and awkward. And while eloquent as a correspondent, he was certainly no public speaker and in the Virginia House of Burgesses and the Continental Congress, he contributed his pen rather than his voice to the patriot cause. Still, as the "silent member" of the Congress, at 33 Jefferson drafted the *Declaration of Independence*. Then, in following years, he worked to make its words a real-

---

1 Malone 1948, 226.

ity in Virginia, most notably crafting a bill establishing religious freedom that was enacted in 1786.[1]

Jefferson was also a principal figure in early American diplomacy. During the era that followed the actual attainment of American independence, he occupied positions of critical importance in the conduct of foreign policy, serving as minister to France (1784–89), secretary of state (1790–93), and president of the United States (1801–9). America, he believed, was the bearer of a new diplomacy, founded on the confidence of a free and virtuous people that would secure its ends based on the natural and universal rights of man: innate means that escaped war and its multiple corruptions. This new diplomacy broke radically, Jefferson thought, from the practices and principles of the old European tradition of reason of state, with its settled belief in the primacy of foreign over domestic policy. That the security and even aggrandizement of the state ought to have priority over domestic welfare, and that the actions of the state ought to be judged according to a different moral calculus than the conduct of individuals, were ideas that Jefferson found utterly antithetical to human progress and enlightenment.[2]

While in Europe, Jefferson's sympathy for the French Revolution led him into conflict with Alexander Hamilton. This eventually prompted Jefferson to resign as Secretary of State in President Washington's Cabinet in 1793. But sharp political conflict developed and remained, with two separate parties, the Federalists and the Democratic–Republicans, began to form. Jefferson gradually assumed leadership of the Republicans, who sympathized with the revolutionary cause in France. Attacking Federalist policies, he opposed a strong centralized government and championed the rights of states.

As a reluctant candidate for president in 1796, Jefferson came within three votes of election. Through a flaw in the Constitution, he became vice president, although an opponent of President Adams. In 1800, the defect caused a more serious problem. Republican electors, attempting to name both a president and a vice president from their own party, cast a tie vote between Jefferson and Aaron Burr. The House of Representatives settled the tie. Hamilton, disliking both Jefferson and Burr, nevertheless urged Jefferson's election. When Jefferson assumed the presidency, the crisis in France had passed. He slashed Army and Navy expenditures, cut the budget, eliminated the tax on whiskey so unpopular in the West, yet reduced the national debt by a third. He also sent a naval squadron to fight the Barbary pirates, who were harassing American commerce in the Mediterranean. Further, although the Constitution made no provision for the acquisition of new land, Jefferson suppressed his qualms over constitutionality when he had the opportunity to acquire the Louisiana Territory from Napoleon in 1803.

During Jefferson's second term, he was increasingly preoccupied with keeping the nation from involvement in the Napoleonic wars, though both England and France interfered with the neutral rights of American merchant-

1 White House 2008.
2 Tucker 1992, iix-ix.

men. Jefferson's attempted solution, an embargo upon American shipping, worked badly and was unpopular. Jefferson retired to Monticello to ponder such projects as his grand designs for the University of Virginia. The Marquis de Chastellux, a visiting French nobleman, observed that he had placed his house and his mind "on an elevated situation, from which he might contemplate the universe."[1]

A word regarding methodology. While there are any number of texts that, to greater or lesser degrees, touch on various interludes in Jefferson life, I have elected to approach his career from more of a documentary perspective and focus my efforts to his writings on war and revolution, an interesting journey, to say the least. Whether he is writing to peers such as James Madison, Patrick Henry, and George Washington; to French associates such as the Marquis de Lafayette and Hector St. John de Crevecoeur; or even to British adversaries such as the American traitor. Benedict Arnold, and Sir Guy Carleton, Governor of Canada, Jefferson demonstrates a remarkable understanding of the issues. And whether the subject might be an argument for national retaliation, the treatment of prisoners of war, or the application of blockades in naval engagements, he writes with remarkable clarity, insight, and eloquence.

I have long believed that the most comprehensive portrait of the founding fathers can be seen in their personal letters and journal entries. Jefferson is no exception, and those he wrote concerning war and revolution — through many of the most critical episodes in early American history — are of singular importance. This is particularly true when one reviews them in their entirety, as opposed to selected excerpts that, if indeed they have been reprinted at all, have been available only in part, reduced to excerpts, citations, or references which, in many instances, have been repeatedly cited as the foundation for a particular interpretation of events, or conclusion of fact. Accordingly, in this selection of a comparatively few letters from the voluminous body of Jefferson correspondence that has been preserved, my intention is twofold: first, to add to the body of literature exploring early American colonial history; and secondly, and perhaps more importantly, to provide an additional glimpse into the character and thought processes of Jefferson the revolutionary.

The source material for this compilation is the twenty-volume reference *The Writings of Thomas Jefferson,* edited by Andrew Adgate Lipscomb and Albert Ellery Bergh, which was issued in 1903 under the auspices of the Thomas Jefferson Memorial Association of the United States. The format of the letters, as Jefferson wrote them, has been preserved whenever possible, while my efforts have been directed to refining the presentation, identifying the addressees, many of whom have been lost to history, and, where indicated, providing explanatory notes so as to assist the reader in placing the correspondence in its particular historical, political, or conceptual context. This methodology, I believe, serves to make the material more palatable to a gen-

---

1 Berman 1947, 152.

---

eral readership, as well as to students of military, diplomatic, or political history. Additionally, it will also permit — or, at a minimum, encourage — readers to arrive at their own conclusions as to the intention of a particular piece of correspondence.

Any errors in selection, fact, transcription, and interpretation remain, of course, my responsibility.

Brett F. Woods, Ph.D.

THOMAS JEFFERSON — CHRONOLOGY[1]

1743 – Born in Shadwell, Virginia
1762 – Leaves College of William and Mary to study law with George Wythe
1767 – Admitted to Virginia bar
1768 – Elected to Virginia House of Burgesses
1769 – Begins building Monticello
1772 – Marries Martha Wayles Skelton
1774 – Writes *A Summary View of the Rights of British America*
1775 – Chosen as delegate to Second Continental Congress
1776 – Drafts *Declaration of Independence*
1779 – Wins election as governor of Virginia
1782 – Martha Jefferson dies
1783 – Virginia delegate to Confederation Congress
1784 – Journeys to France on diplomatic mission
1785 – Succeeds Franklin as American minister to France
1787 – Publishes *Notes on the State of Virginia*
1789 – Leaves France for United States
1790 – Appointed Secretary of State
1793 – Retires as Secretary of State
1795 – Begins detailed remodeling of Monticello
1796 – Republican candidate for President, becomes John Adams' Vice President
1798 – Drafts Kentucky Resolutions calling for nullification of Alien and Sedition Acts
1800 – Republican candidate for President, defeats John Adam
1801 – House of Representatives declares Jefferson elected as third President
1802 – Seeks acquisition of New Orleans from France
1803 – Negotiates Louisiana Purchase
1804 – Reelected President
1809 – Retires from public life at Monticello
1815 – Congress purchases Jefferson's library to rebuild Library of Congress
1818 – Writes *Rockfish Gap Commission Report* proposing creation of University of Virginia
1821 – Writes *Autobiography*
1825 – Serves as Rector of the University of Virginia
1826 – Dies at Monticello

---

1 Library of Congress 2008; Thomas Jefferson Foundation 2008.

John Adams, 1777, 4:286[1] - Our people, even under the
Monarchical Government, had learnt to consider it as the last
of all oppressions.

To John Adams[2]
Williamsburg, May 16, 1777

Matters in our part of the continent are too much in quiet to send you
news from hence. Our battalions for the Continental service were some time
ago so far filled as rendered the recommendation of a draught from the militia hardly requisite, and the more so as in this country it ever was the most
unpopular and impracticable thing that could be attempted.[3] Our people,
even under the monarchical government, had learnt to consider it as the last

---

1 NOTE: 4:298 refers to Volume 4, Page 286, of *The Writings of Thomas Jefferson* (1903). This methodology is applied to the identification of all correspondence.

2 Boyd suggests that this is the "earliest known letter exchanged" between Jefferson and John
Adams; further "that [the correspondence] continued, with some intervals, for forty-nine
years and that remains unrivaled, in the United States at least, for its revelation of the writers' minds and characters, its literary distinction, and its historical importance" (Boyd 1950,
19).

3 In this context, "draught" refers to the concept of a draft or forced enlistment. While Jefferson
was clearly against the implementation of a "draught" — or forced service in the military —
the matter was a pressing concern at the time, for Washington, anticipating that he could
not depend on having enough trained men, had concluded that he needed an army that was
enlisted for the duration of the war. In response, and after a number of modifications in
troop levels, by December 1776, Congress had authorized a strength of some 110 battalions
for the Continental Army. Of course, in reality, these numbers were mostly on paper, and
the Continental Army never had as many as 30,000 men at any one time. By the winter of
1777-78, the effort to enlist men for three years or the duration collapsed, and the following
spring, with the sanction of Washington, Congress reverted to a system of one-year enlistments and recommended to the states that they institute a system of drafting men from
the militia for one year's service. However, this first American wartime draft was applied

of all oppressions. I learn from our delegates that the confederation is again on the carpet, a great and a necessary work, but I fear almost desperate. The point of representation is what most alarms me, as I fear the great and small colonies are bitterly determined not to cede. Will you be so good as to collect the proposition I formerly made you in private, and try if you can work it into some good to save our union? It was, that any proposition might be negatived by the representatives of a majority of the people of America, or of a majority of the colonies of America. The former secures the larger, the latter, the smaller colonies. I have mentioned it to many here. The good Whigs, I think, will so far cede their opinions for the sake of the Union, and others we care little for.

The journals of Congress not being printed earlier, gives more uneasiness than I would wish ever to see produced by any act of that body, from whom alone I know our salvation can proceed. In our Assembly, even the best affected think it an indignity to freemen to be voted away, life and fortune, in the dark. Our House has lately written for a manuscript copy of your journals, not meaning to desire a communication of any thing ordered to be kept secret. I wish the regulation of the post-office, adopted by Congress last September, could be put in practice. It was for the travel night and day, and to go their several stages three times a week. The speedy and frequent communication of intelligence is really of great consequence. So many falsehoods have been propagated that nothing now is believed unless coming from Congress or camp. Our people, merely for want of intelligence which they may rely on, are become lethargic and insensible of the state they are in. Had you ever a leisure moment, I should ask a letter from you sometimes, directed to the care of Mr. Dick, Fredericksburg, but having nothing to give in return, it would be a tax on your charity as well as your time.[1] The esteem I have for you privately, as well as for your public importance, will always render assurances of your health and happiness agreeable. I am, dear sir, your friend and servant.

THEODORICK BLAND, JR., 1779, 4:295 - *[THE] OBJECT IN WAR IS TO EXTINGUISH HUMAN NATURE.*

To Theodorick Bland, Jr.[2]

---

irregularly in the various states and succeeded no better than had earlier methods in filling the Continental ranks (Matloff 1996, 54).

1 Major Charles Dick, of Fredericksburg, Virginia, had been appointed during the old French and Indian War by Governor Dinwiddie to be Commissary of the forces. During the Revolution, he was a member of a board which operated a powder factory at Fredericksburg and manufactured small arms (Wilson 1916, 565).

2 Theodorick Bland was a prominent Virginia antifederalist. A physician, planter, patriot, soldier, and legislator, his entire career was influenced by a devotion to — and the preservation of — the world of the tobacco aristocracy. Bland was perhaps best known for his command of a June 1775 theft of prominently displayed weapons from the front hall of Governor's Palace. The weapons, over two hundred pistols and muskets and several swords, were removed and distributed to those who would need weapons in the event of an armed clash with the forces of Lord Dunmore, then quartered aboard ship in the Chesapeake. While other members of the group included such aristocratic individuals as James Monroe and

Williamsburg, June 8, 1779

Sir, Your letter to Governor Henry, of the 1st instant, came to hand yesterday, and I immediately laid it before the council. It gave them pain to hesitate on any request from General Phillips, whose polite conduct has disposed them to every indulgence consistent with the duties of their appointment. The indiscriminate murder of men, women and children with the horrid circumstances of barbarity practiced by the Indian savages, was the particular task of Governor Hamilton's employment; and if anything could have aggravated the acceptance of such an office, and have made him personally answerable in a high degree, it was that eager spirit with which he is said to have executed it, and which, if the representations before the council are to be credited, seems to have shown that his own feelings and disposition were in unison with his employment. The truth of these representations will be the subject of their inquiry shortly, and the treatment of Governor Hamilton will be mild or otherwise, as his conduct shall appear to merit, upon a more intimate examination. We trust it must furnish contemplation highly pleasing to the generous soldier, to see honorable bravery respected, even by those against whom it happens to be enlisted, and discriminated from the cruel and cowardly warfare of the savage, whose object in war is to extinguish human nature.

By a letter dated May 27th, you were desired to discharge the militia under your command as soon as you judged it proper; lest that letter should have miscarried, I now enclose you a copy. Colonel Finnie informs me he has written to you to apply for clothes at Winchester, for the use of your regiment of guards, and of the horse now with you. He yesterday showed me a letter from the continental board of war, giving the same directions; he says also that he had lately written to you on the subject of the articles desired for your particular use, and that he is not enabled to procure them more fully.

As to putting the horse now with you on the same pay-roll with the regiment of guards, the council is of opinion that either your own powers are competent to it, or at least that it may be done in concert with the continental paymaster. The regiment of guards is recognized as continental; the duty they are jointly engaged in is continental; they, therefore, wish that this matter should go into the continental line altogether, rather than be controlled by their interference, where it is not absolutely necessary. I am your most obedient servant, etc.

PATRICK HENRY, 1779, 4:45 - *IS AN ENEMY SO EXECRABLE THAT, THOUGH IN CAPTIVITY, HIS WISHES AND COMFORTS ARE TO BE DISREGARDED AND EVEN CROSSED?*

To His Excellency Patrick Henry

Benjamin Harrison, Jr., it was Bland who was placed in charge of the cache of weaponry and was responsible for its distribution. Bland's leadership role in this event, which evolved into one of the watershed events in the coming of revolution to Virginia, shows his growing acceptance of the likelihood of open conflict with Britain rather than a peaceful reconciliation (Hagy 1996, 3-11).

Albemarle, March 27, 1779

Sir, A report prevailing here, that in consequence of some powers from Congress, the Governor and Council have it in contemplation to remove the Convention troops, either wholly or in part, from their present situation, I take the liberty of troubling you with some observations on that subject.[1] The reputation and interest of our country, in general, may be affected by such a measure: it would, therefore, hardly be deemed an indecent liberty in the most private citizen, to offer his thoughts to the consideration of the Executive. The locality of my situation, particularly in the neighborhood of the present barracks, and the public relation in which I stand to the people among whom they are situated, together with a confidence which a person-al knowledge of the members of the Executive gives me, that they will be glad of information from any quarter on a subject interesting to the public, induce me to hope that they will acquit me of impropriety in the present representation.

By an article in the Convention of Saratoga, it is stipulated, on the part of the United States, that the officers shall not be separated from their men. I suppose the term officers, includes *general* as well as *regimental* officers. As there are general officers who command all the troops, no part of them can be separated from these officers without a violation of the article: they can-not, of course, be separated from one another, unless the same general officer

---

1 General Horatio Gates' defeat of the forces led by British General John Burgoyne at Saratoga, New York, in the fall of 1777, is considered to be one of the pivotal moments in the American Revolution. However, the actual terms of the British surrender would soon spawn one of the more troublesome issues of the day. According to the language memorialized in a docu-ment entitled the *Convention of Saratoga*, the prisoners were to be marched to Boston and ultimately returned to England. But the issue, at least from the American perspective, was that under the convention, it was possible to send Burgoyne's army back to England for garrison duty, which could then release fresh troops for service in America. Gates seems not to have originally seen this possibility, but George Washington grasped it the moment he read the document. The matter presently came up in Congress, and that body resolved that the embarkation should not take place until the convention was explicitly ratified by the court of Great Britain. It also argued that Burgoyne had not surrendered all his "arms," because he had concealed his cartridge-boxes and colors. Further, in response to British complaints that the prisoners were suffering for food and shelter, Congress insisted that the British should pay for the provisions, and in gold, not Continental currency. It was an unseemly controversy and many of the positions taken by Congress were admittedly not tenable; but it all arose from the trick by which Burgoyne tried to outwit Gates by a sur-render which would result in bringing an equal number of fresh troops from England as fast as ships could cross the ocean and back. In any event, the controversy dragged on for nearly four years, during which the subject of "convention troops" was in controversy both in and out of Congress, while the British and Americans charged the other with bad faith and a breach of the convention. The majority of the troops, some four thousand in number — six English regiments, five regiments of Brunswick dragoons, in addition to Hessian artil-lery and a battalion of grenadiers — ended up in Virginia, where their arrival in Albemarle attracted Jefferson's attention and protection. When an attempt was made to effect their removal from Albemarle County, it was largely a question of politics and Jefferson was quick to take up the prisoners' cause, not for personal reasons, but seemingly because it embraced a certain sense of humanity that marked his conduct on similar occasions. This March 27, 1779 letter to the Patrick Henry, then Governor of Virginia, clearly shows the im-portance he attached to the matter and the careful thought he gave to resolving the matter in a humanitarian fashion (Kimball 1947, 32-25; Greene 1911, 128-130).

---

could be in different places at the same time. It is true, the article adds the words, "as far as circumstances will admit." This was a necessary qualification; because, in no place in America, I suppose, could there have been found quarters for both officers and men together; those for the officers to be according to their rank. So far, then, as the circumstances of the place where they should be quartered, should render a separation necessary, in order to procure quarters for the officers, according to their rank, the article admits that separation. And these are the circumstances which must have been under the contemplation of the parties; both of whom, and all the world beside (who are ultimate judges in the case), would still understand that they were to be as near in the environs of the camp, as convenient quarters could be procured; and not that the qualification of the article destroyed the article itself, and laid it wholly at our discretion. Congress, indeed, have admitted of this separation; but are they so far lords of right and wrong as that our consciences may be quiet with their dispensation? Or is the case amended by saying they leave it optional in the Governor and Council to separate the troops or not? At the same time that it exculpates not them, it is drawing the Governor and Council into a participation in the breach of faith. If indeed it is only proposed, that a separation of the troops shall be referred to the consent of their officers; that is a very different matter. Having carefully avoided conversation with them on public subjects, I cannot say, of my own knowledge, how they would relish such a proposition. I have heard from others, that they will choose to undergo anything together, rather than to be separated, and that they will remonstrate against it in the strongest terms. The Executive, therefore, if voluntary agents in this measure must be drawn into a paper war with them, the more disagreeable, as it seems that faith and reason will be on the other side. As an American, I cannot help feeling a thorough mortification, that our Congress should have permitted an infraction of our public honor; as a citizen of Virginia, I cannot help hoping and confiding, that our Supreme Executive, whose acts will be considered as the acts of the Commonwealth, estimate that honor too highly to make its infraction their own act. I may be permitted to hope, then, that if any removal takes place, it will be a general one; and, as it is said to be left to the Governor and Council to determine on this, I am satisfied that, suppressing every other consideration, and weighing the matter dispassionately, they will determine upon this sole question, Is it for the benefit of those for whom they act, that the Convention troops should be removed from among them? Under the head of interest, these circumstances, viz., the expense of building barracks, said to have been £25,000, and of removing the troops backwards and forwards, amounting to, I know not how much, are not to be pretermitted, merely because they are Continental expenses; for we are a part of the Continent; we must pay a shilling of every dollar wasted. But the sums of money which, by these troops, or on their account, are brought into, and expended in this State, are a great and local advantage. This can require no proof. If, at the conclusion of the war, for instance, our share of the Continental debt should be twenty millions of dollars, or say that we are called on to furnish an annual quota of two millions four hundred thousand dollars, to Congress, to be raised by tax, it is obvious that we should raise these given sums with greater or less ease, in proportion to the greater or less quantity of money found in circulation among us. I expect that our circulating money is, by the presence of these troops, at the rate of $30,000 a week, at the least. I have heard, indeed, that an objection arises to their being kept within this State, from the information of the commissary that they cannot be subsisted here. In attending to the information of that officer, it should be borne in mind that the county of King William and its vicinities are one thing, the territory of Virginia another. If the troops could be fed upon long letters, I believe the gentleman at the head of that department in this country, would be the best commissary upon earth. But till I see him determined to act, not to write; to sacrifice his domestic ease to the duties of his appointment, and apply to the resources of this country, wheresoever they are to be had, I must entertain a different opinion of him. I am mistaken if, for the animal subsistence of the troops hitherto: we are not principally indebted to the genius and exertions of Hawkins, during the very short time he lived after his appointment to that department, by your board. His eye immediately pervaded the whole State, it was reduced at once to a regular machine, to a system, and the whole put into movement and animation by the fiat of a comprehensive mind. If the Commonwealth of Virginia cannot furnish these troops with bread, I would ask of the commissariat, which of the thirteen is now become the grain colony? If we are in danger of famine from the addition of four thousand mouths, what is become of that surplus of bread, the exportation of which used to feed the West Indies and Eastern States, and fill the colony with hard money? When I urge the sufficiency of this State, however, to subsist these troops, I beg to be understood, as having in contemplation the quantity of provisions necessary for their real use, and not as calculating what is to be lost by the wanton waste, mismanagement, and carelessness of those employed about it. If magazines of beef and pork are suffered to rot by slovenly butchering, or for want of timely provision and sale; if quantities of flour are exposed, by the commissaries entrusted with the keeping it, to pillage and destruction; and if, when laid up in the Continental stores, it is still to be embezzled and sold, the land of Egypt itself would be insufficient for their supply, and their removal would be necessary, not to a more plentiful country, but to more able and honest commissaries. Perhaps the magnitude of this question, and its relation to the whole State, may render it worth while to await the opinion of the National Council, which is now to meet within a few weeks. There is no danger of distress in the meantime, as the commissaries affirm they have a great sufficiency of provisions for some time to come. Should the measure of removing them into another State be adopted, and carried into execution, before the meeting of Assembly, no disapprobation of theirs will bring them back, because they will then be in the power of others, who will hardly give them up.

Want of information as to what may be the precise measure proposed by the Governor and Council, obliges me to shift my ground, and take up the subject in every possible form. Perhaps, they have not thought to remove the troops out of this State altogether, but to some other part of it. Here, the objections arising from the expenses of removal, and of building new barracks, recur. As to animal food, it may be driven to one part of the country as easily as to another: that circumstance, therefore, may be thrown out of the question. As to bread, I suppose they will require about forty or forty-five thousand bushels of grain a year. The place, to which it is to be brought to them, is about the centre of the State. Besides, that the country round about is fertile, all the grain made in the counties adjacent to any kind of navigation, may be brought by water to within twelve miles of the spot. For these twelve miles, wagons must be employed; I suppose half a dozen will be a plenty. Perhaps, this part of the expense might have been saved, had the barracks been built on the water; but it is not sufficient to justify their being abandoned now they are built. Wagonage, indeed, seems to the commissariat an article not worth economizing. The most wanton and studied circuity of transportation has been practiced: to mention only one act, they have bought quantities of flour for these troops in Cumberland, have ordered it to be wagoned down to Manchester, and wagoned thence up to the barracks. This fact happened to fall within my own knowledge. I doubt not there are many more such, in order either to produce their total removal, or to run up the expenses of the present situation, and satisfy Congress that the nearer they are brought to the commissary's own bed, the cheaper they will be subsisted. The grain made in the western counties may be brought partly in wagons, as conveniently to this as to any other place; perhaps more so, on account of its vicinity to one of the best passes through the Blue Ridge; and partly by water, as it is near to James river, to the navigation of which, ten counties are adjacent above the falls. When I said that the grain might be brought hither from all the counties of the State adjacent to navigation, I did not mean to say it would be proper to bring it from all. On the contrary, I think the commissary should be instructed, after the next harvest, not to send one bushel of grain to the barracks from below the falls of the rivers, or from the northern counties. The counties on tide water are accessible to the calls for our own army. Their supplies ought, therefore, to be husbanded for them. The counties in the northwestern parts of the State are not only within reach for our own grand army, but peculiarly necessary for the support of Macintosh's army; or for the support of any other northwestern expedition, which the uncertain conduct, of the Indians should render necessary; insomuch, that if the supplies of that quarter should be misapplied to any other purpose, it would destroy, in embryo, every exertion, either for particular or general safety there. The counties above tide water, in the middle and southern and western parts of the country, are not accessible to calls for either of those purposes, but at such an expense of transportation as the article would not bear. Here, then, is a great field, whose supplies of bread cannot be carried to our army, or rather, which will raise no supplies of bread, because there is nobody to eat them. Was it not, then, wise in Congress to remove to that field four thousand idle mouths, who must otherwise have interfered with the pasture of our own troops? And, if they are removed to any other part of the country, will it not defeat this wise purpose? The mills on the waters of James river, above the falls, open to canoe navigation, are very many. Some of them are of great note, as manufacturers. The barracks are surrounded by mills. There are five or six round about Charlottesville. Any two or three of the whole might, in the course of the winter, manufacture flour sufficient for the year. To say the worst, then, of this situation, it is but twelve miles wrong. The safe custody of these troops is another circumstance worthy consideration. Equally removed from the access of an eastern or western enemy; central to the whole State, so that, should they attempt an irruption in any direction, they must pass through a great extent of hostile country; in a neighborhood thickly inhabited by a robust and hardy people, zealous in the American cause, acquainted with the use of arms, and the defiles and passes by which they must issue: it would seem, that in this point of view, no place could have been better chosen.

Their health is also of importance. I would not endeavor to show that their lives are valuable to us, because it would suppose a possibility, that humanity was kicked out of doors in America, and interest only attended to. The barracks occupy the top and brow of a very high hill, (you have been untruly told they were in a bottom.) They are free from fog, have four springs which seem to be plentiful, one within twenty yards of the piquet, two within fifty yards, and another within two hundred and fifty, and they propose to sink wells within the piquet. Of four thousand people, it should be expected, according to the ordinary calculations, that one should die every day. Yet, in the space of near three months, there have been but four deaths among them; two infants under three weeks old, and two others by apoplexy. The officers tell me, the troops were never before so healthy since they were embodied.

But is an enemy so execrable, that, though in captivity, his wishes and comforts are to be disregarded and even crossed? I think not. It is for the benefit of mankind to mitigate the horrors of war as much as possible. The practice, therefore, of modern nations, of treating captive enemies with politeness and generosity, is not only delightful in contemplation, but really interesting to all the world, friends, foes, and neutrals. Let us apply this: the officers, after considerable hardships, have all procured quarters, comfortable and satisfactory to them. In order to do this, they were obliged, in many instances, to hire houses for a year certain, and at such exorbitant rents, as were sufficient to tempt independent owners to go out of them, and shift as they could. These houses, in most cases, were much out of repair. They have repaired them at a considerable expense. One of the general officers has taken a place for two years, advanced the rent for the whole time, and been obliged, moreover, to erect additional buildings for the accommodation of part of his family, for which there was not room in the house rented.

Independent of the brick work, for the carpentry of these additional buildings, I know he is to pay fifteen hundred dollars. The same gentleman, to my knowledge, has paid to one person three thousand six hundred and seventy dollars for different articles to fix himself commodiously. They have generally laid in their stocks of grain and other provisions, for it is well known that officers do not live on their rations. They have purchased cows, sheep, &c., set in to farming, prepared their gardens, and have a prospect of comfort and quiet before them. To turn to the soldiers: the environs of the barracks are delightful, the ground cleared, laid off in hundreds of gardens, each enclosed in its separate paling; these well prepared, and exhibiting a fine appearance. General Riedesel alone laid out upwards of two hundred pounds in garden seeds for the German troops only.[1] Judge what an extent of ground these seeds would cover. There is little doubt that their own gardens will furnish them a great abundance of vegetables through the year. Their poultry, pigeons and other preparations of that kind, present to the mind the idea of a company of farmers, rather than a camp of soldiers. In addition to the barracks built for them by the public, and now very comfortable, they have built great numbers for themselves, in such messes as fancied each other; and the whole corps, both officers and men, seem now happy and satisfied with their situation. Having thus found the art of rendering captivity itself comfortable, and carried it into execution, at their own great expense and labor, their spirits sustained by the prospect of gratifications rising before their eyes, does not every sentiment of humanity revolt against the proposition of stripping them of all this, and removing them into new situations, where, from the advanced season of the year, no preparations can be made for carrying themselves comfortably through the heats of summer; and when it is known that the necessary advances for the conveniences already provided, have exhausted their funds and left them unable to make the like exertions anew. Again, review this matter, as it may regard appearances. A body of troops, after staying a twelvemonth at Boston, are ordered to take a march of seven hundred miles to Virginia, where, it is said, they may be plentifully subsisted. As soon as they are there, they are ordered on some other march, because, in Virginia, it is said, they cannot be subsisted. Indifferent nations will charge this either to ignorance, or to whim and caprice; the parties interested, to cruelty. They now view the proposition in that light, and it is said, there is a general and firm persuasion among them, that they were marched from Boston with no other purpose than to harass and destroy them with eternal marches. Perseverance in object, though not by the most direct way, is often

1 One of the articles of the Saratoga Convention provided that the officers were not to be separated from their captured men. This proved advantageous, for the officers not only cared for the needs of the troops but provided assistance to the Virginia regiment of guards in the enforcement of discipline. Major General William Phillips, the British commanding officer, lived at Blenheim, Colonial Colonel Landon Carter's estate, while Major General Friederich von Riedesel, commander of the German troops, along with his family, rented quarters from Philip Mazzei, a middle-aged Italian immigrant, who lived adjacent to Jefferson (Peterson 1975, 163).

more laudable than perpetual changes, as often as the object shifts light. A character of steadiness in our councils is worth more than the subsistence of four thousand people.

There could not have been a more unlucky concurrence of circumstances than when these troops first came. The barracks were unfinished for want of laborers, the spell of weather the worst ever known within the memory of man, no stores of bread laid in, the roads, by the weather and number of wagons, soon rendered impassable: not only the troops themselves were greatly disappointed, but the people in the neighborhood were alarmed at the consequences which a total failure of provisions might produce. In this worst state of things, their situation was seen by many and disseminated through the country, so as to occasion a general dissatisfaction, which even seized the minds of reasonable men, who, if not affected by the contagion, must have foreseen that the prospect must brighten, and that great advantages to the people must necessarily arise. It has, accordingly, so happened. The planters, being more generally sellers than buyers, have felt the benefit of their presence in the most vital part about them, their purses, and are now sensible of its source. I have too good an opinion of their love of order to believe that a removal of these troops would produce any irregular proofs of their disapprobation, but I am well assured it would be extremely odious to them.

To conclude. The separation of these troops would be a breach of public faith, therefore I suppose it is impossible; if they are removed to another State, it is the fault of the commissaries; if they are removed to any other part of the State, it is the fault of the commissaries; and in both cases, the public interest and public security suffer, the comfortable and plentiful subsistence of our own army is lessened, the health of the troops neglected, their wishes crossed, and their comforts torn from them, the character of whim and caprice, or, what is worse, of cruelty, fixed on us as a nation, and, to crown the whole, our own people disgusted with such a proceeding.

I have thus taken the liberty of representing to you the facts and the reasons, which seem to militate against the separation or removal of these troops. I am sensible, however, that the same subject may appear to different persons, in very different lights. What I have urged as reasons, may, to sounder minds, be apparent fallacies. I hope they will appear, at least, so plausible, as to excuse the interposition of Your Excellency's most obedient and most humble servant,

GOVERNOR OF CANADA, 1777, 5:301 - *WE THINK OURSELVES JUSTIFIED IN GOVERNOR HAMILTON'S STRICT CONFINEMENT ON THE GENERAL PRINCIPLE OF NATIONAL RETALIATION.*

To The Governor of Canada (Sir Guy Carleton)[1]

---

1 General Sir Guy Carleton was, of all available British generals, perhaps the most qualified to head the British forces in Canada. He was a professional soldier of the best type, with some of the qualities of a great statesman, and those qualities were especially needed in Canada during the American war. The British task in Canada was not only to defend it

Williamsburg, July 22, 1777

Sir, Your letter on the subject of Lieutenant Governor Hamilton's con-finement came safely to hand. I shall with great cheerfulness explain to you the reasons on which the advice of Council was founded, since after the sat-isfaction of doing what is right, the greatest is that of having what we do approved by those whose opinions deserve esteem.[1]

We think ourselves justified in Governor Hamilton's strict confinement on the general principle of national retaliation. To state to you the particular facts of British cruelty to American prisoners, would be to give a melancholy history from the capture of Colonel Ethan Allen, at the beginning of the war to the present day, a history which I will avoid, as equally disagreeable to you and to me. I with pleasure do you the justice to say that I believe these facts to be very many unknown to you, as Canada has been the only scene of your service in America, and, in that quarter, we have reason to believe that Sir Guy Carleton, and the three officers commanding there, have treated our prisoners (since the instance of Colonel Allen) with considerable lenity. What has been done in England, and what in New York and Philadelphia, you are probably uninformed; as it would hardly be made the subject of epis-tolary correspondence. I will only observe to you, Sir, that the confinement and treatment of our officers, soldiers and seamen, have been so rigorous and cruel, as that a very great portion of the whole of those captured in the course of this war, and carried to Philadelphia while in possession of the British army and to New York, have perished miserably from that cause only; and that this fact is as well established with us, as any historical fact which has happened in the course of the war. A Gentleman of this Commonwealth in public office, and of known and established character, who was taken on the sea, carried to New York and exchanged, has given us lately a particular information of the treatment of our prisoners there. Officers taken by land, it seems, are permitted to go on parole within certain limits of Long Island, till suggestions shall be made to their prejudice by some Tory refugee, or other equally worthless person, when they are hurried to the Provost in New York, without enquiring "whether they be founded upon positive facts, be matter of hearsay, or taken from the reports of interested men." The example of en-quiring into the truth of charges of this nature according to legal principles

---

against American attack, or even to use it as a base for aggressive action, but also to hold the Canadians to loyalty to a Crown to which they had been attached for only a decade (Valentine 1962, 149).

1 Lieutenant Governor Henry Hamilton was of Irish birth and had served in the British army since 1754. He was appointed lieutenant-governor of Detroit in 1775 and assumed his new duties in November of that year. In the autumn of 1778, he advanced upon and captured Vincennes, only to be taken in turn, with his whole garrison, by Lieutenant Colonel George Rogers Clark, of Virginia. Hamilton was despised by the Americans, owing to the belief that he was active in fomenting Indian scalping parties against them, and was known as the "hair buying general." Clark sent him a prisoner to Virginia where he was closely confined and endured great hardship. On being exchanged in 1780, he visited England, returning to Canada as lieutenant-governor in 1782. He later served as governor of the Bermudas and of Dominica, where he died in 1796 (Clark 2001, 57).

of evidence has surely not been set us by our enemies. We enquired what these Provosts were and were told they were the common miserable jails, built for the confinement of malefactors. Officers and men taken by sea were kept in prison ships infested with [ ]¹...ought on by the crowd [ ] from five to ten a day. When, therefore, we are desired to the possible consequence of treating prisoners with rigor, I need only ask when did those rigors begin? Not with us assuredly. I think you, Sir, who have had as good opportunities as any British officer of learning in what manner we treat those whom the fortune of war has put in our hands can clear us from the charge of rigor as far as your knowledge or information has extended. I can assert that Governor Hamilton's is the first instance which has occurred in my own country, and, if there has been another in any of the United States, it is unknown to me; these instances must have been extremely rare, if they have ever existed at all, or they could not have been altogether unheard of by me, when a uniform exercise of kindness to prisoners on our part has been returned by as uniform severity on the part of our enemies. You must excuse me for saying it is high time, by other lessons, to teach respect to the dictates of humanity, in such & case retaliation becomes an act of humanity.

But suppose, Sir, we were willing still longer to decline the drudgery of general retaliation, yet Governor Hamilton's conduct has been such as to call for exemplary punishment on him personally. In saying this, I have not so much in view his particular cruelties to our Citizens, prisoners with him (which though they have been great, were of necessity confined to a small scale) as the general nature of the service he undertook at Detroit and the extensive exercise of cruelties which they involved. Those who act together in war are answerable for each other. No distinction can be made between principal and ally by those against whom the war is waged. He who employs another to do a deed makes the deed his own. If he calls in the hand of the assassin or murderer, himself becomes the assassin or murderer. The known rule of warfare of the Indian savages is an indiscriminate butchery of men, women, and children. These savages, under this well known character, are employed by the British Nation as allies in the war against the Americans. Governor Hamilton undertakes to be the conductor of the war. In the execution of that undertaking, he associates small parties of the whites under his immediate command with large parties of the savages, and sends them to act, sometimes jointly, and sometimes separately, not against our forts or armies in the field, but the farming settlements on our frontiers. Governor Hamilton is himself the butcher of men, women, and children. I will not say to what length the fair rules of war would extend the right of punishment against him; but I am sure that confinement under its strictest circumstances, for Indian devastation and massacre must be deemed lenity. I apprehend you had not sufficiently adverted to the expression in the advice of the Council when you suppose the proclamation there alluded to, to be the one addressed to

---

1 Note: Brackets indicate where several lines at the bottom of the pages of this letter are missing.

the inhabitants of the Illinois afterwards printed in the public papers and to be affirmed to contain denun... [ ] ...ians [ ]. Proclamation, there alluded to, contained nothing more than an invitation to our officers and soldiers to join British arms against those whom he is pleased to call Rebels and Traitors. In order to introduce these among our people, they were put into the hands of the Indians; and in every house, where they murdered or carried away the family, they left one of these proclamations, some of them were found sticking on the breasts of the persons murdered, one under the hand and seal of Governor Hamilton came to our hands, The Indians being the bearers of proclamations under the hand and seal of Governor Hamilton (no matter what was the subject of them) there can be no doubt they were acting under his direction, and, as including this proof, the fact was cited in the advice of the Council. But if you will be so good as to recur to the address of the Illinois, which you refer to, you will find that, though it does not in express terms threaten vengeance, blood, and massacre, yet it proves that the Governor had made for us the most ample provision of all these calamities. He there gives in detail the horrid catalogue of savage nations, extending from South to North whom he had leagued with himself to wage combined war on our frontiers; and it is well known that that war would of course be made up of blood and general massacres of men, women and children. Other papers of Governor Hamilton's have come to our hands containing instructions to officers going out with scalping parties of Indians and Whites, and proving that kind of war was waged under his express orders; further proofs in abundance might be adduced, but I suppose the fact is too notorious to need them.

Your letter seems to admit an inference that, whatever may have been the general conduct of our enemies towards their prisoners, or whatever the personal conduct of Governor Hamilton, yet, as a prisoner by capitulation, you consider him as privileged from strict confinement. I do not pretend to an intimate knowledge of this subject. My idea is that the term "prisoners of war" is a generic one, the specification of which is – 1st Prisoner at discretion; and 2d prisoners on convention or capitulation. Thus in the debate of the House of Commons of the 27th November last, on the address, the minister, speaking of General Burgoyne (and in his presence) says he is "a prisoner," and General Burgoyne calls himself "a prisoner under the terms of the Convention of Saratoga," intimating that though a prisoner, he is a prisoner of a particular species entitled to certain terms. The treatment of the first class ought to be such as to be approved by the usage of polished nations; gentle and humane unless a contrary conduct in an enemy or individual, render a stricter treatment necessary. The prisoners of the second class have nothing to exempt them from a like treatment with those of the first except so far as they shall have been able to make better terms by articles of Capitulation. So far then as these shall have provided for an exemption from strict treatment so prisoners on Capitulation have a right to be distinguished from those at discretion [ ] certain causes antecedent thereto, though such instances might

be produced, from English history, too, and in one case where the King himself commanded in person, Marshal Boufflers after the taking of the castle
Namur was arrested and detained prisoner of war by King William though
by an article of capitulation it was stipulated that the officers and soldiers
of the garrison in general, and Marshal Bothers by name should be at liberty.
However, we waive reasoning on this head because no article in the Capitulation of Governor Hamilton is violated by his confinement. Perhaps not having seen the Capitulation, you were led to suppose it a thing of course that
being able to obtain terms of surrender, they would first provide for their
own treatment. I enclose you a copy of the Capitulation, by which you will
see that 2d Article declares them prisoners of war; and nothing is said as to
the treatment they were to be entitled to. When Governor Hamilton signs,
indeed, he adds a flourish, containing the motives inducing him to capitulate,
one of which was confidence in a generous enemy. He should have reflected
that generosity on a large scale would take side against him. However, these
were only his private motives and did not enter into the contract with Colonel Clarke. Being prisoners of war then, with only such privileges as their
Capitulation had provided, and that having provided nothing on the subject
of their treatment, they are liable to be treated as other prisoners. We have
not extended our order, as we might justifiably have done to the whole of
this corps. Governor Hamilton and Captain Lamothe alone, as leading offenders, are in confinement. The other officers and men are treated as if they
had been taken in justifiable war; the officers being at large on their parole,
and the men also having their liberty to a certain extent. Dejean was not
included in the Capitulation, being taken 8 days after on the Wabache 150
miles from St. Vincennes.

I hope, Sir, that being made more fully acquainted with the facts on
which the advice of Council was grounded, and exercising your own good
sense in cool and candid deliberation on these facts, and the consequences
deducible from them according to the usages and sentiments of civilized nations, you will see the transaction in a very different light from that in which
it appeared at the time of writing your letter, and ascribe the advice of the
Council, not to want of attention to the sacred nature of public conventions,
of which I hope we shall never, in any circumstances, lose sight, but to a desire of stopping the effusion of ye unoffending blood of women and children,
and the unjustifiable severities exercised on our captive officers and soldiers
in general, by proper severities on our part. I have the honor to be with much
personal respect, Sir, your most obedient and most humble servant.

GEORGE MATHEWS, 1779, ME 4:77 – *HUMANE CONDUCT ON OUR*
PART WAS FOUND TO PRODUCE NO EFFECT; THE CONTRARY, THEREFORE,
WAS TO BE TRIED.

To Colonel Mathews[1]

---

1 The imprisonment of these officers was brought to the attention of General Washington, and
on August 6 he wrote to Jefferson advising that the irons be removed. His request was at

In Council, October, 1779

Sir, The proceedings respecting Governor Hamilton and his companions, previous to your arrival here, you are acquainted with. For your more precise information, I enclose you the advice of Council, of June the 16th, of that of August the 28th, another of September the 19th, on the parole tendered them the 1st instant, and Governor Hamilton's letter of the same day, stating his objections, in which he persevered: from that time his confinement has become a voluntary one. You delivered us your letters the next day, when the post being just setting out, much business prevented the Council from taking them into consideration. They have this day attended to them, and found their resolution expressed in the enclosed advice, bearing date this day. It gives us great pain that any of our countrymen should be cut off from the society of their friends and tenderest connections, while it seems as if it was in our power to administer relief. But we trust to their good sense for discerning, and their spirit for bearing up against the fallacy of this appearance. Governor Hamilton and his companions were imprisoned and ironed, 1st. In retaliation for cruel treatment of our captive citizens by the enemy in general. 2d. For the barbarous species of warfare which himself and his savage allies carried on in our western frontier. 3d. For particular acts of barbarity, of which he himself was personally guilty, to some of our citizens in his power. Any one of these charges was sufficient to justify the measures we took. Of the truth of the first, yourselves are witnesses. Your situation, indeed, seems to have been better since you were sent to New York; but reflect on what you suffered before that, and knew others of your countrymen to suffer, and what you know is now suffered by that more unhappy part of them who are still confined on board the prison ships of the enemy. Proofs of the second charge, we have under Hamilton's own hand; and of the third, as sacred assurances as human testimony is capable of giving. Humane conduct on our part was found to produce no effect; the contrary, therefore, was to be tried. If it produces a proper lenity to our citizens in captivity, it will have the effect we meant; if it does not, we shall return a severity as terrible as universal. If the causes of our rigor against Hamilton were founded in truth, that rigor was just, and would not give right to the enemy to commence any new hostilities on their part; and all such new severities are to be considered, not as retaliation, but as original and unprovoked. If those causes were not founded in truth, they should have denied them. If, declining the tribunal of

---

once acceded to, and on September 29, 1779, the Virginia Council ordered that Governor Hamilton, Captain La Mothe, and Philip Dejean be sent to Hanover Court House to remain at large on parole. The prisoners objected to a parole which would prevent them from saying anything to the prejudice of the United States, and so they were remanded to confinement in jail until they could "determine with themselves to be inoffensive in word as well as deed." They were apparently again put into irons. Efforts in their behalf were continued, and the records of the Virginia Council for October, 1779, contain a memorandum of a letter from Governor Jefferson to Colonel Matthews, who had been a prisoner in Hamilton's power; Matthews pleaded for leniency towards Hamilton, and brought a second letter from Washington, disapproving of his being in irons. These were again taken off, and Jefferson wrote this letter to Colonel Matthews (Farmer 1890, 254).

truth and reason, they choose to pervert this into a contest of cruelty and destruction, we will contend with them in that line, and measure out misery to those in our power, in that multiplied proportion which the advantage of superior numbers enables us to do. We shall think it our particular duty, after the information we gather from the papers which have been laid before us, to pay very constant attention to your situation and that of your fellow prisoners. We hope that the prudence of the enemy will be your protection from injury; and we are assured that your regard for the honor of your country, would not permit you to wish we should suffer ourselves to be bullied into an acquiescence, under every insult and cruelty they may choose to practice, and a fear to retaliate, lest you should be made to experience additional sufferings. Their officers and soldiers, in our hands are pledges for your safety: we are determined to use them as such. Iron will be retaliated by iron, but a great multiplication on distinguished objects: prison ships by prison ships, and like for like in general. I do not mean by this to cover any officer who has acted, or shall act improperly. They say Captain Willing was guilty of great cruelties at the Natches; if so, they do right in punishing him. I would use any powers I have, for the punishment of any officer of our own, who should be guilty of excesses unjustifiable under the usages of civilized nations. However, I do not find myself obliged to believe the charge against Captain Willing to be true, on the affirmation of the British commissary, because, in the next breath, he affirms no cruelties have as yet been inflicted on him. Captain Willing has been in irons.

I beg you to be assured, there is nothing, consistent with the honor of your country, which we shall not, at all times, be ready to do for the relief of yourself and companions in captivity. We know that ardent spirit and hatred for tyranny, which brought you into your present situation, will enable you to bear up against it with the firmness which has distinguished you as a soldier, and to look forward with pleasure to the day, when events shall take place, against which, the wounded spirits of your enemies will find no comfort, even from reflections on the most refined of the cruelties with which they have glutted themselves. I am, with great respect, your most obedient, and most humble servant.

GEORGE WASHINGTON, 1780, 4:120 - *IT IS MORTIFYING TO SUPPOSE IT POSSIBLE THAT A PEOPLE, ABLE AND ZEALOUS TO CONTEND WITH THEIR ENEMY, SHOULD BE REDUCED TO FOLD THEIR ARMS FOR WANT OF THE MEANS OF DEFENSE.*

To His Excellency General Washington[1]

1 Jefferson served as Governor of Virginia from 1779 to 1781. Accordingly, during this period, his engagement with the prosecution of the war with England manifests itself in numerous pieces of correspondence. On December 9, 1780, Washington wrote to Jefferson that a British fleet carrying grenadiers, light infantrymen, Hessian grenadiers, and light dragoons had left New York moving to the south. But when word came to Richmond on December 31 that twenty-seven sail had been sighted off the Virginia capes, Jefferson refused to become alarmed. Still holding to a naive conviction that any invasion force would become bogged down in the lowland swamps, he was content to order General Thomas Nelson, head of the

Richmond, 22 October 1780.

Sir, I have this morning received certain information of the arrival of a hostile fleet in our bay, of about sixty sail. The debarkation of some light horse, in the neighborhood of Portsmouth, seems to indicate that as the first scene of action. We are endeavoring to collect as large a body to oppose them as we can arm; this will be lamentably inadequate, if the enemy be in any force. It is mortifying to suppose that a people, able and zealous to contend with their enemy, should be reduced to fold their arms for want of the means of defense. Yet no resources, that we know of, insure us against this event. It has become necessary to divert to this new object, a considerable part of the aids we had destined for General Gates. We are still, however, sensible of the necessity of supporting him, and have left that part of the country nearest him uncalled on, at present, that they may reinforce him as soon as arms can be received. We have called to the command of our forces Generals Weeden and Muhlenburg, of the line, and Nelson and Stevens of the militia. You will be pleased to make to these such additions as you may think proper. As to the aids of men, I ask for none, knowing that if the late detachment of the enemy shall have left it safe for you to spare aids of that kind, you will not await my application. Of the troops we shall raise, there is not a single man who ever saw the face of an enemy. Whether the Convention troops will be removed or not, is yet undetermined. This must depend on the force of the enemy, and the aspect of their movements. I have the honor to be your Excellency's most obedient humble servant.

BENEDICT ARNOLD, 1781, 4:399 ~ *[WE ENDEAVOR] AS FAR AS POSSIBLE TO ALLEVIATE THE INEVITABLE MISERIES OF WAR BY TREATING CAPTIVES AS HUMANITY AND NATURAL HONOR REQUIRES.*

To Major General Benedict Arnold, the Commanding Officer of the British Force at Portsmouth[1]

Virginia militia, to go to the coast, and with what he admitted later was "a fatal inattention" waited two full days before calling a meeting of the Virginia Council. It was January 2 before the order went out calling up 4,600 militiamen. The two-day delay indeed proved fatal, and was one of several evidences suggesting that Jefferson lacked the ability to serve as a leader in wartime. Benedict Arnold, the American traitor, led the invasion force that sailed up the James River to Westover and landed 1,500 men who burned and pillaged along a sixty-mile path before arriving at Richmond, where only two hundred Virginians were assembled to defend the capital. With impunity, Arnold all but sacked the city, while searching for Baron von Steuben, whom Jefferson had finally charged with Richmond's defense (Brodie 1974, 142-143). Of this episode, Ferling notes, "The devastating raid also nearly ended Jefferson's public career, as he was assailed by local critics and congressmen for his deplorable response to the emergency" (Ferling 2007, 479).

1 The business of paroles was a central concern to Jefferson. Moreover, it was a real threat to Virginia's citizens, in that the custom of immobilizing large numbers of the population, including civilians and other noncombatants, was one that the British had already put into practice in other invaded states. As Jefferson observed, it was an attempt to disarm a whole country which they could not otherwise subdue, such as in South Carolina where — at least from Jefferson's perspective — the British had seemingly conquered the entire state by paroles alone. They would, Jefferson believed, conquer Virginia as well if Virginia recognized the validity of paroles. The British commanding officer at the moment happened to

In Council, March 24, 1781

Sir, Some of the citizens of this State taken prisoners when not in arms and enlarged on parole have reported the commanding officer as affirming to them that they should be punished with death if found in arms. This has given occasion to the enclosed resolution of the General Assembly of this State. It suffices to observe at present that by the law of nations, a breach of parole (even where the validity of parole is not questioned) can only be punished by strict confinement.

No usage has permitted the putting to death a prisoner for this cause. I would willingly suppose that no British officer had ever expressed a contrary purpose. It has, however, become my duty to declare that should such a threat be carried into execution, it will be deemed as putting prisoners to death in cold blood, and shall be followed by the execution of so many British prisoners in our possession. I trust, however, that this horrid necessity will not be introduced by you and that you will on the contrary concur with us in endeavoring as far as possible to alleviate the inevitable miseries of war by treating captives as humanity and natural honor requires. The event of this contest will hardly be affected by the fate of a few miserable captives in war.

OLIVER TOWLES, 1781, 4:409 - *A COUNTRY VULNERABLE IN EVERY POINT IS OPEN TO INSULT AND DEPREDATION TO EVEN THE SMALLEST FORCE, YET IMPORTANT POINTS MAY, WE TRUST, BE GUARDED.*

To Colonel Oliver Towles
Richmond, April 14, 1781

Sir, The same very disagreeable intelligence which you have been pleased to communicate to me, of the operations of our savage enemy on the Potomac, has come to hand from several parts of that river. Colonel Skinner particularly has written on the subject of arms. The order I enclosed him, tardy as the supply may be, is the utmost it is in our power to do. From his letter we are to judge about a third of his militia have guns. These I suppose not to be very good, but they are unfortunately what we are obliged to have recourse to: the 200 stand from Annapolis, for which I gave him an order, are said to be very fine.[1] The defense at Hunter's and the public work at Fredericksburg are very important, indeed, and I hope will be very particularly attended to by the adjacent counties. No intelligence from Portsmouth gives us reason to believe that any regular forces have been sent on this expedition; so that we trust that it is less formidable than some representations make it. The worst is that a country vulnerable in every point is open to insult and depredation to even the smallest force, yet important points may we trust be guarded. In

---

be Benedict Arnold; but, as fate would have it, General William Phillips succeeded to the command on March 20, and Jefferson's letter was doubtless delivered to him. Phillips, finding the letter to be insolent, did not respond to Jefferson (Kimball 1945, 177-179).

1 A "stand of arms" generally refers to a complete set of material for one soldier, for example a musket, bayonet, cartridge box, and belt.

effecting this we rely on your exertions being added, as we are assured they will be.

COLONELS JOHN SKINNER AND WILLIAM GARRARD, 1781, 4:410 ~ *I AM EXCEEDINGLY SORRY TO LEARN THAT THE ENEMY ARE COMMITTING SUCH CRUEL DEPREDATIONS.*

To Colonels Skinner and Garrard[1],[2]

Richmond, April 14, 1781

Sirs, I am exceedingly sorry to learn that the enemy are committing such cruel depredations in your part of the country; however it may tend to produce immoveable hatred against so detestable a nation and thereby strengthen our Union. Yet in the mean time it brings afflicting distress on individuals and by diverting so great a proportion of our force from their principal object leaves achievements in their power which otherwise could not be.

We had thrown the whole burden of militia duty on the southern counties, leaving those to the north quiet till they should get through the raising of their new levies. That being done we have set the southern counties on the same business and relied on our northern citizens to constitute the opposition to the hostile army below. Thus deprived for two months of the aid of the southern counties and so many of the northern like to be diverted, our army is reduced to less than a third of the number of our enemy who, of course, may march wherever they please. Situated as you are we cannot say that the men before called for must march at all events. We wish you to consider the above circumstances and viewing at the same time your own situation, to determine yourself whether the force called for can be spared without endangering your part of the country. Every part being equally within our care we wish not to expose one for the defense of another. The very important works at and near Fredericksburg we must recommend to your particular protection, as also the saving all public tobacco within your county. Sir John Peyton for us purchased lately at Baltimore about 200 stand of arms from Isaac and Adam Van Bibber and Co. They were brought to Annapolis in the vessels which brought on the Marquis Fayette's detachment. Sir John Peyton has written to have them brought on by land, but he does not inform me to whom he has written. It is not in our power to offer you any other supply of arms but this. Were you to send some person in quest of these he would probably be able to meet with, or find them out and have them forwarded to you. His reasonable expenses and those of transportation shall be paid by the public, and the arms when you get them may be applied under your care

---

1 Brodie suggests that, although admitting to Oliver Towles (April 14, 1781) that Virginia was "open to insult and depredation to even to the smallest force," Jefferson maintained a guarded optimism in this letter to John Skinner and William Garrard, as indicated by the reference to depredations that would "tend to produce irremovable hatred against so detestable a nation and thereby strengthen our Union" (Brodie 1974, 144).

2 In response to the British incursion, Jefferson continued to receive complaints from Westmoreland, King George, Stafford, and the other counties adjacent to the Potomac. "The county lieutenants were insatiable, and remained unsatisfied, in their demand for arms. Spiritual comfort was about all the Governor had to offer" (Kimball 1947, 202).

for the defense of that part of the country instead of the 150 formerly ordered which you have not received. I enclose you an order for these arms.

COLONEL JAMES INNES, 1781, 4:411 - *ASSEMBLE IMMEDIATELY EVERY MAN ABLE TO BEAR ARMS.*

To Colonel James Innes[1]
Richmond, April 21, 1781

Sir, Within an hour after receiving your first notification that the enemy were in movement we issued orders to the militia of the counties of Chesterfield, Prince George, Dinwiddie, Powhatan, Goochland, Hanover and Henrico to assemble immediately every man able to bear arms, and one half of those of Amelia and Cumberland and to bring with them the best arms they had. They were to rendezvous at Petersburg and this place. Some volunteer cavalry were also called for. These orders were communicated to Baron Steuben and the several letters of information from you have been regularly and immediately forwarded to him.[2] And I doubt not the moment the militia

---

1 To add to Jefferson's troubles came personal tragedy. His baby daughter, Lucy Elizabeth, died on April 15; but he had little time to grieve. On April 19, he laid before his Council the alarming intelligence that the British were on the move again. Reinforced by sea, with Lafayette gone to the north and Steuben ineffective in the face of local inertia, British General William Phillips and the hated Benedict Arnold were sailing once more up the broad highway of the James River. On the 20th they had landed and were marching on Williamsburg; but Jefferson remembered the lesson of the previous invasion and immediately called out all the militia of the neighboring counties and half of those from the remoter ones. Couriers spurred with appropriate orders to the County Lieutenants, to Steuben and others. Preparations were made for removing records and stores. Yet, in spite of the orders and commands, it seemed that again all would be lost because of the failure of the militia to assemble. Jefferson's order went out on April 19 and, two full days later, not a single man had mustered. "This fatal tardiness will I fear," Jefferson fumed in this April 21 letter to Colonel James Innes, in command of the militia forces, "be as unfortunate for Williamsburg on this occasion as formerly it was for Richmond." Ultimately, Jefferson was proved correct and Virginia again seemed helpless before the show of British force (Schachner 1957, 211).

2 Friedrich von Steuben was born in 1730 and served as a staff officer in the Prussian army under Frederick the Great during the Seven Years War. He retired as a captain in 1764 in the demobilization following the Treaty of Paris. In 1777, Steuben offered his services to the Continental Congress through Benjamin Franklin and Silas Deane, who inflated Steuben's rank to lieutenant general in an effort to embellish his value to the colonial cause. In February 1778, Steuben arrived at Valley Forge to take charge of drilling the Continental Army. As acting inspector general, he standardized and greatly simplified training and tactics, and improved efficiency and morale of the Continentals troops. In May, Congress confirmed his inspector general appointment and promoted him to major general. He quickly became the Army's supreme administrator and de facto chief of staff to George Washington (Brown 2001, 453). NOTE: On September 26, 1776, the Congress's Committee of Secret Correspondence — which had been created for the purpose of procuring arms and ammunition — elected and appointed a joint commission consisting of three members to represent the new nation at the court of France. In the order they were elected, the commissioners were Benjamin Franklin, Silas Deane, and Thomas Jefferson. These three were the first full-fledged diplomatic representatives to be appointed by the U.S. Government. Jefferson declined, however, on account of his wife's health; and on October 22, 1776, the Congress elected Arthur Lee in his stead. While Franklin was in Philadelphia, Deane, of Connecticut, and Lee, of Virginia, were already in Europe, serving in their capacity as secret agents "for the purpose of ascertaining sentiment there toward the Colonies and obtaining any other information that might be useful in the Colonies' contest with England." While the com-

come in and can receive (such as are unarmed) the spare arms from the south side of the river he will order them to your assistance, now that it appears that yours is the post of their destination.

Though our orders calling out the militia went out on Thursday morning not a man is yet assembled here. I am told the Powhatan militia will be in today. Certainly those of this county will be as early. This fatal tardiness will I fear be as unfortunate to Williamsburg on this occasion as it was for Richmond.

Be assured that no effort of ours for your support shall be wanting and that the resources of the country as our powers will call them forth shall be applied to the relief of the part threatened. I must entreat you to let us hear from you daily while the scene is so interesting.

P. S. You observe we said nothing of the militia of the counties near Williamsburg because we supposed you would, of course, call for as many as you could arm.

COLONEL BENJAMIN HARRISON, 1781, 4:413 ~ *CALL INTO SERVICE ON THIS OCCASION THE MILITIA.*

To Colonel Benjamin Harrison[1]
In Council, April 22, 1781

Sir, We thought it best, as I informed you in a former letter, to call into service on this occasion the militia whose families and property were not immediately exposed. Being circumscribed in our number of arms, it still appears best, that what we have should be put into the hands of those militia. Were we to send any to Charles City we must dismiss so many militia now collected here and at Manchester. Experience has also shown it preferable for another reason to put your arms into the hands of those not exposed, because on the enemy's coming into the exposed parts of the country, the militia of the neighborhood will desert, carry off their arms and perhaps suffer them to be taken off by the enemy. We, therefore, think to retain the militia collected and collecting here, who we expect every moment will receive marching orders from Baron Steuben and that yours should be permitted to take care of their families and property. I am informed the enemy have got possession of the ship-yard and that by the most unaccountable inattention

---

missioners were to pursue a treaty with the British, Congress stipulated two nonnegotiable conditions: acknowledgment of America's independence and the continuation of the treaty with France. The rest was left to the discretion of the commissioners (Brands 2000, 599).

1 As governor, Jefferson's response to the British incursion continued to draw pointed criticism. The commander of the militia, General George Weedon, complained that Jefferson was a petty figure who was incapable of comprehending the full scope of the war. General Nathanael Greene — who commanded the southern continental army — agreed, protesting that the war could be won only if continental officials, whose national outlook superseded local interests, were empowered to direct every state militia. To Greene, who had dealt with numerous state executives, Jefferson was the least capable of understanding the depth of the American military crisis. It was a sentiment shared by von Steuben (Ferling 2002, 235).

the Lewis and safeguard galleys have withdrawn up Chickahominy instead of James River.

MAJOR GENERAL FRIEDRICH VON STEUBEN, 1781, 4:414 - *THE NEW RAISED CAVALRY OR A DUE PROPORTION OF IT MAY PERHAPS BE OF SINGULAR USE TO HIM.*

To Major General Baron Steuben
In Council, April 22, 1781

Sir, I enclose you two letters just received from Colonel Innes. We are in great anxiety for him. His force, we are told, is very considerably reduced by desertion and he has no cavalry. I make no doubt you see how far it is necessary to send him reinforcements and will order them accordingly. I have no return of the numbers of militia here. Indeed, it is changing every hour by the arrival of others. Report makes three or four hundred at this place and Manchester. The new raised cavalry or a due proportion of it may perhaps be of singular use to him. We have determined to remove our armorer's shop to the Fork of James River immediately. Colonel Davies expects they will be at work there within ten days and that he shall be able to procure a very considerable number of hands there. Considering the greater security of that place than Powhatan Courthouse and the little probability from General Muhlenberg's letter of removing the armorers from Broadwater, perhaps you will think it better that our armorers should all be employed together at the Fork under Colonel Davies's direction than to send any part of them to Powhatan Courthouse.

We made a proposition to the militia of Prince George, which we had reason to believe would have effected the immediate completion of the work at Hood's. It was that any man of that county who would go or send an able laborer to work there 12 days should have six weeks' credit on his tours of duty out of the county. Unfortunately the movements of the enemy obliged us the very next day to call every man into the field. Nevertheless, if you think it more important you will be pleased to permit such of them to quit the field, as choose to comply with the proposition. One caution may perhaps be necessary: that is to order those militia to a separate position from that of the other counties, lest the restraining the offer to the militia of Prince George might produce an idea of partiality and give dissatisfaction to the rest. One county will suffice for the execution of this work and it would be improvident to make the proposition to more. I enclose you some intelligence which at this time of depression we thought it would be well to put in hand bills and communicate to both armies. I send a parcel to Colonel Innes's and trouble you with those for General Muhlenberg's.

I received a letter from the Marquis Fayette today dated Baltimore, April 17th: he was then coming on by forced marches for Virginia.[1]

---

1 The urgency suggested by Jefferson's letters of late April 1781 is not without merit, for the British were on the move. One British column under General William Philips caused damage around Williamsburg, burned the shipyards on the Chickahominy River, and captured Petersburg, where ships, warehouses, and tobacco were torched. Some fifteen miles below

MAJOR GENERAL FRIEDRICH VON STEUBEN, 1781, 4:415 - CAN
THE OBJECT OF THE ENEMY BE OUR VESSELS AT OSBORNES?

To Major General Baron Steuben
Richmond, April 24, 1781

Sir, I have information this morning from Captain Maxwell on his own view that the enemy landed at Westover yesterday evening. If it be impossible that he should have been deceived, it is equally unaccountable that we are uninformed of it from the videttes sent.[1] The movements of the enemy up Chickataming obliged Colonel Innes, encumbered with 20 wagons with stores, and 100 sick, to cross Pamunkey at Ruffens Ferry. As soon as he has disposed of those, he will endeavor, if the movements of the enemy render it proper, to retire towards this place. There are here about 200 militia armed, and 300 unarmed. At Manchester there is, I am told, a larger number armed, but of this I have no proper information. The militia of several counties being here, I gave Colonel Wood the command till you should be able to have them arranged as you should choose. He happened to be here on business, and it will be inconvenient to him to continue any time. Can the object of the enemy be our vessels at Osbornes? There are no public stores here, and they have showed that private depredation is not within their views.

Colonel Southell showed to Colonel Wood and myself, your orders of yesterday for the militia to divide into two parties and go to the Long Bridge, and Turkey Island and to correspond with Colonel Innes. But the enemy having, as is supposed, landed at Westover, and Colonel Innes crossed Pamunkey, it was thought advisable that Colonel Wood should await your orders on those new circumstances, supposed to be unknown to you at the date of your order. As soon as it is known that the enemy are landed at Westover, and my presence here no longer necessary, I shall cross the river either here or at Tuckahoe and keep in the neighborhood on the other side. I shall be ready and happy to give you every aid from the civil power which may be necessary.

Richmond — at Coxe's Dale — a second column under Benedict Arnold destroyed nine Virginia warships, captured a dozen commercial vessels, and burned 2 million pounds of tobacco. Richmond was more fortunate. The two British columns did not join at the Virginia capital until ten days into the operation, just hours after 900 Continentals under Lafayette arrived from Baltimore in support of the 500 militiamen that had been charged to protect the city. While the British were numerically superior, they knew that von Steuben was marching on Richmond from Petersburg with about 900 militiamen. The British elected to withdraw, contenting themselves with the destruction of an additional 1 million pounds of tobacco at nearby Manchester and Warwick before sailing back down the James. In the final analysis, the raid demonstrated that the state was largely defenseless against a professional army augmented by naval power (Ferling 2002, 235-236).

1 "Videttes" is a reference to sentries mounted on horseback.

COLONEL GARRET VAN METER, 1781, 4:417 - *I AM SORRY SUCH A SPIRIT OF DISOBEDIENCE HAS SHOWN ITSELF IN YOUR COUNTY. IT MUST BE SUBDUED.*

To Colonel Van Meter[1]

Richmond, April 27, 1781

Sir, I have directed Mr. Woodrow to furnish money for the bounty of the new levies out of what was put into his hands for the removal of your militia to Pittsburg.

I am sorry such a spirit of disobedience has shown itself in your county. It must be subdued. Laws made by common consent must not be trampled on by individuals. It is very much the good to force the unworthy into their due share of contributions to the public support, otherwise the burden on them will become oppressive, indeed. We have no power by the law of raising cavalry in the counties generally, but on some similar occasions we have recommended to the County Lieutenants who have the power of forming their militia companies as they please, to form into one company such individuals of their militia as will engage to mount and equip themselves and to serve as mounted infantry, and we give commissions to the officers in the ordinary style. These may be used as effectually as cavalry; and men on horseback have been found the most certain instruments of public punishment.

Their best way, too, perhaps is not to go against the mutineers when embodied which would bring on perhaps an open rebellion or bloodshed most certainly, but when they shall have dispersed, to go and take them out of their beds, singly and without noise, or if they be not found the first time, to go again and again so that they may never be able to remain in quiet at home. This is what I must recommend to you and, therefore, furnish the bearers with the commissioners as you desire.[2]

If you find this service considerable you will, of course, give the individuals credit for it as a tour of duty.

COLONEL JAMES INNES, 1781, 4:419 - *PROSECUTION FOR TREASON OR MISPRISION OF TREASON.*

To Colonel James Innes[3]

---

1 In what, in some circles, would come to be known as "Claypool's Rebellion," on April 14, Colonel Garret Van Meter of Hampshire County had advised Jefferson that he had issued orders for the full number of men for the draught but feared they would not be complied with in view of the disaffection among the inhabitants of the county. "A certain John Claypole," Van Meter wrote, "said that if all the men were of his mind, they would not make up any clothes, beef, or men, and all that would join him should turn out." On being joined by those of his sentiments, he "got liquor and drank King George Third's health and damnation to Congress, upon which complaint was made to three magistrates." Rioters had assembled in other parts of the county "determined to stand in opposition to every measure of government. . . . Their principal object is to be clear of taxes and draughts" (Kimball 1947, 217-218).

2 This paragraph offers a particularly pointed example of Jefferson's frustration being expressed through derision and sarcasm.

3 While he was obviously troubled by the extent of civil disobedience in the state, this letter reflects an arguably important glimpse into Jefferson's attitude towards law enforcement:

Richmond, May 2, 1781

Sir, Having received information that diverse citizens of this Common-wealth in the counties of James City and York, have lately committed acts, some of which amount to high treason and others to misprision of treason, and that some though they may have been able to disguise and conceal their transactions as that legal evidence cannot be obtained by which they may be subjected to prosecution for treason or misprision of treason in a due course of law, yet have so conducted themselves as to furnish the most pregnant circumstances of suspicion that they have been guilty of those offences, or are disaffected to the independence of the United States, and will, whenever they shall have opportunity, aid or advise the measures of the public enemy, which persons, in the critical situation of this Commonwealth, it is indis-pensably necessary to punish for their crimes by way of example to others and to disable from doing mischief: I must, therefore, as you are proceeding to that part of the country, desire and authorize you to make enquiry into the premises, and where you shall have probable cause to believe that any persons have been guilty of treason or misprision of treason, that there is legal evidence to commit them thereof, and that an examining Court can be had on them in the county where the offence was committed before there shall be any danger of a rescue by the enemy, you have them delivered to the warrant of a Justice of the Peace, in order that they may be prosecuted in the usual forms of law, and be aiding in their safe conveyance to the public jail in Richmond, if they be ordered to be conveyed. But where you shall be of opinion that legal evidence cannot be obtained, that an examining Court cannot be procured in the county before there will be danger of a rescue by the enemy and that there are pregnant circumstances of suspicion that they have been guilty of the offences of treason or misprision of treason, or where there shall be pregnant causes of suspicion that persons in these counties are disaffected to the independence of the United States; and when occasion serves, aid or advise the operations of the enemy, that in those cases you ap-prehend such persons, and send them in safe custody to the jail of this county reporting to the Executive the facts and circumstances of suspicion whereon you proceed. In the executions of these powers, I must recommend to you that you have no retrospect to any fact prior to the 17th of April last, being the day the enemy embarked at Portsmouth; that you single out only those who have been foremost or most daring in their offences, and that even these be treated by those into whose hands they shall be committed with no insult or rudeness unnecessary for their safe custody.

---

the law should be swift and certain; but, too, it must be humane. Having been informed that certain citizens had been guilty of acts amounting to high treason, or misprision of treason, he writes that to deal with such persons "it is indispensibly necessary to punish for their crimes by way of example to others and to disable from doing mischief." But, he charges Colonel Innes, "single out only those who have been foremost or most daring in their of-fenses, and [let] even these be treated by those into whose hands they shall be committed with no insult or rudeness unnecessary for their safe custody" (Wiltse 1935, 169).

COLONEL ABRAHAM PENN, 1781, 4:421 ~ HE WILL BE DRIVEN BACK AND WE SHALL HAVE THE WAR ON US.

To Colonel Abraham Penn[1]
Richmond, May 4, 1781

Sir, I am exceedingly sorry that the public situation should be such as to render it necessary to call our citizens from their farms at this interesting season of the year But the enemy will not suspend their operations till we can sow or reap, so that we must have our army on foot as well at these as the other seasons of the year. We have called on eleven counties to furnish a rein-forcement to General Greene, and hope it will be the last time we shall have occasion to require our militia to go out of their 6wn country as we think it most advisable to put that distant disagreeable service on our regulars, and to send them forward as fast as raised, and to employ our militia on service in our own country. And I am confident that if the reinforcement of militia now under orders to General Greene is marched, and serves the two months with him which is intended, that by that time he will be so reinforced by regulars as to retain possession of North and the greatest part of South Carolina, and thus keep to the war at a distance from us. On the contrary, if he is not sup-ported by the militia until the regulars can get to him, he will be driven back and we shall have the war on us.

Of the eleven counties called on, seven have applied to be excused. You will immediately see, Sir, what would be the consequence of complying with their request.

The Executive have, therefore, been obliged to insist on the requisi-tion. Mr. Henry has written on the same subject, as to your county, but the grounds on which a relaxation of the order is proposed, being met as every other county has or as would, go to a perpetual exemption from military duty, we cannot withdraw the call.

Captain Baurt has engaged fifty horse to go for three months, but this is no equivalent for 250 infantry to serve two months. I must, therefore, Sir, rely on your zeal and activity to carry the former requisition into execution.

It is probable you may have among you some delinquent militia who should by law serve six months, as a punishment for their delinquency; these, if sent with the militia, might be counted as part.

---

1 Despite the challenges, Jefferson endeavored to remain engaged and did his utmost to cooper-ate with — and attempt to lead — the various militia units. But, in reality, all he could do was write letters and orders that no one seemed even to pretend to obey. Further, despite the fact that, upon receipt of news that their home counties were under threat of invasion, they deserted with their arms and returned to their families, he still justified the preserva-tion of the militia. On the other hand, he met downright disobedience with stern, if futile, reprimands. For example, when seven out of eleven counties ordered to send reinforce-ments to Greene pleaded off, alleging the necessity of attending to their crops, he declared sarcastically in this letter to Colonel Abraham Penn that "the enemy will not suspend their operations till we sow or reap" (Schachner 1957, 212).

GILBERT DU MOTIER, THE MARQUIS DE LAFAYETTE, 1781,
4:423 ~ TO MAKE A PRESENT OPPOSITION TO THE JUNCTION OF THE
TWO HOSTILE ARMIES.

To Marquis Major-General de Lafayette[1]
Richmond, May 14, 1781

Sir, I was sorry that the situation of my family had occasioned my absence from this place when you were pleased to send Captain Langhorne to
me.

I enclose you a state of the counties who have been called on to come into
the field, some of them to perform full tour of duty and others to make a present opposition to the junction of the two hostile armies. The delay and deficiencies of the first are beyond all expectation and if the calls on the latter do
not produce sufficient reinforcements to you I shall candidly acknowledge
that it is not in my power to do anything more than to represent to the General Assembly that unless they can provide more effectually for the execution
of the laws it will be vain to call on militia. I could perhaps do something by
reprimands to the County Lieutenants by repeating and even increasing the
demands on them by way of penalty. If you would be so good as to have returns made to me once a week or at any other stated periods of the particular
number of men from each county. Without these we can never know what
counties obey our calls, or how long your men are to continue with you so
as to provide in time. From Hampshire and Shenandoah we expected many
riflemen. From Berkeley and Frederick some, and a few from Culpeper, Orange, Loudoun and Fauquier, but what number may be expected I cannot
even conjecture. One tenth of the whole force (except from the counties of
Frederick, Hampshire, Berkeley, Shenandoah, and Orange, who were called
on before we had concluded on this measure) were desired to come prepared
with the horses to do duty as cavalry. The militia which were called to do a
full tour were to join the army wherever it should be. Those counties called
on to send as many men as they could send armed were to rendezvous at
Richmond, Prince Edward Court House, and Taylor's Ferry on Roanoke, as
should be most convenient, where they were given to believe orders would
be lodged from you for their future movements. These men are collecting to

1 Marie Jean Paul Joseph Roche Yves Gilbert du Motier, the Marquis de Lafayette, was a French
nobleman whose father had been killed by a British bullet at the battle of Minden. Aged two
at the time, he had inherited a fortune along with his title. He married at sixteen and was appointed a reserve captain in the French dragoons a short time later. Approaching American
representatives in Paris, Lafayette proposed that, in exchange for the rank of major general
in the American Army, he would serve for no pay, only expenses. The offer was accepted.
When he arrived in the American camp before General Howe took Philadelphia, he was
discouraged by the shacks and tents crowded with soldiers who were half naked or wear-
ing faded hunting shirts. But Lafayette was tactful when the American commander in chief
apologized to him. "We must be embarrassed," Washington said, "to show ourselves to an
officer who has just left the French Army." The marquis answered, "I am here to learn, not
to teach." George Washington had found a protégé and invited Lafayette to join his military
family and move into his headquarters. At Brandywine, Lafayette fought courageously and
took a bullet and become one of the most popular foreign officers in Washington's army
(Langguth, 1988, 468-469).

their places of rendezvous, so that they will need immediately such orders as you should be pleased to give them. I have the pleasure to enclose to you the four impress warrants, desired by Captain Langhorne.

Captain Maxwell called on me the 10th inst. And informed me he was building a few boats at the shipyard on Chickahominy. I desired him to send a good batteaux builder to Colonel Davies to superintend and direct a number of hands whom he would immediately put under him for building bateaux for the river above the Falls, and that he would set all the rest of his people to building boats for navigating the lower parts of the river, but so light and of such a form as that they might be moved on wheels, and that those should be built either here or above the Falls as safety and convenience should dictate. He left me with a promise to do so, and I expect he is engaged in the execution. His hands being to remove from the shipyard there will, of course, occasion some delay.

The General Assembly having determined to meet at Charlottesville on the 22d inst. renders it necessary for the Executive to prepare for removing there, and particularly for myself to go and see that provision be made for the reception of the Public Boards and Records. I shall leave this place this evening.

As a very frequent communication between yourself and the Executive will be necessary, I have directed the State Quartermaster to station a line of express riders from your camp to Charlottesville by whom you will be so good as to communicate your wants from time to time under a full assurance that nothing in my power shall ever be wanting to supply them. Interesting events will always be acceptable whenever you shall have time to add them to a letter or make them the subject of a special one.

P. S. Lest anything should suffer which it is in my power to prevent I have concluded to stay here this evening and to do myself the pleasure of calling on you at your quarters tomorrow morning.

JAMES MADISON, 1783, 4:430 ~ THERE IS AN IDLE REPORT HERE OF PEACE.

To James Madison[1]

---

1 In September 1782, Jefferson's wife Martha died a lingering death after the birth of their sixth child. Although he was beset with melancholy, in November 1782, Congress appointed Jefferson to the position of Minister Plenipotentiary to negotiate peace. Congress acted on the well-founded assumption that the loss of his wife had caused a change in Jefferson's sentiments toward the public service and Jefferson lost no time accepting the appointment. In little more than three weeks he was on the road to Philadelphia to embark for France. Jefferson had lost a wife; the country regained a statesman (Peterson 1975, 246-247). He was not to get to France this time, however. When he arrived in Philadelphia on the 27th he found, first, the usual delays. The French frigate *Romulus*, on which he was scheduled to sail, was locked in ice below Baltimore, and Jefferson waited in Philadelphia for almost a month anticipating news of its release. But the weather got colder and the *Romulus* was compelled to drop some miles down the bay. Jefferson set out in a small boat to board the vessel, was caught in the floating ice, and finally, after transshipment to a stouter sloop, managed to reach the frigate. Here, however, he heard for the first time that the British were cruising in strength outside the Capes to intercept the *Romulus* and her sister ship, the *Guadeloupe*. In

Baltimore, February 7, 1783

Dear Sir, I write by this post to the Minister of Foreign Affairs, but will repeat to you the facts mentioned to him and some others improper for a public letter, and some reflections on them which can only be hazarded to the ear of friendship. The cold weather having set in the evening of the 30th ult. (being the same in which I arrived here) the Chevalier de Villebrun was obliged to fall down with his ship and the *Guadeloupe* to about twelve miles below this; and the ice has since cut off all correspondence with him till yesterday, when I got a boat and attempted a passage. There having passed a small boat before us, we got about half way with tolerable ease, but the influx of the tide then happening the ice closed on us on every side and became impenetrable to our little vessel, so that we could get neither backwards nor forwards. We were finally relieved from this situation by a sloop which forced its way down and put us on board the *Romulus*, where we were obliged to remain all night. The Chevalier de Villebrun communicated to me several letters of intelligence which deserves weight; by which we are informed that the enemy, having no other employment at New York, have made our little fleet their sole object for some time, and have now cruising for us nothing less than 1 ship of 64 guns, 4 ships of 50 guns, 2 ships of 40 guns, 18 frigates from 24 to 30 guns, a most amazing force for such an object. The merchants who intended to have sent their vessels out with us, have so far declined it, that two vessels only go with us, but they are unfortunately the greatest sluggards in the world. The Minister has given Villebrun leave to remain if he thinks it expedient till the middle of March, but politely and kindly offered the *Guadeloupe* for my passage if I chose to run the risk. I find that having laid ten months under water she got perfectly sobbed, insomuch that she sweats almost continually on the inside, in consequence of which her commander and several of the crew are now laid up with rheumatism. But this I should have disregarded had it not appeared that it was giving to the enemy the ship and crew of a friend, and delaying myself in fact by endeavoring at too much haste. I, therefore, have not made use of the liberty given me by the Minister. Villebrun seems certain he shall not sail on the first of March, and I confess to you I see no reason to suppose that when that time arrives the same causes will not place our departure as distant as it now seems. What then is to be done? I will mention the several propositions which occur with some reflections on each.

1. To go to Boston and embark thence. Would to God I had done this at first. I might now have been half-way across the ocean. But it seems very late to undertake a journey of such length, through such roads and such weather: and when I should get there some delay would still necessarily intervene, yet I am ready to undertake it if this shall be thought best.

---

some perplexity, in this February 7, 1783 letter to Madison, then a Virginia delegate to the Continental Congress, he explores options (Schachner 1957, 239-249).

2. To stay here with patience till our enemies shall think proper to clear our coast. There is no certain termination to this object. It may not be till the end of the war.

3. To fall down to York or Hampton and there wait those favorable circumstances of winds and storms which the winter season sometimes presents. This would be speedier than the second but perhaps it may not be approved of by the commander for reasons which may be good though unknown to me. Should this, however, be adopted we ought to be furnished by the Marine department with, or authorized to employ one or more swift sailing boats to go out of the capes occasionally and bring us intelligence to York or Hampton wherever we should be.

4. To ask a flag for me from the enemy and charter a vessel here. This would be both quickest and most certain, but perhaps it may be thought injurious to the dignity of the States, or perhaps be thought such a favor as Congress might not choose to expose themselves to the refusal of. With respect to the last, nothing can be said: as to the first, I suppose were history sought, many precedents might be found where one of the belligerent powers has received from the other, passports for their Plenipotentiaries; and I suppose that Fitzgerald and Oswald got to Paris now under protection of a flag and passport. However, these are tender points and I would not wish the sensibility of Congress to be tried on my account, if it would be probably disagreeable.

5. To await a truce. This cannot take place till after preliminaries are signed, if then: and though these are not definitive, yet it must be evident that new instructions and new or perhaps inconsistent matter would be introduced with difficulty and discredit.

There is an idle report here of peace being actually concluded. This comes by the way of the West Indies, and must probably be founded on the settlement of preliminaries, if it has any foundation at all. Should you think that the interference of Congress might expedite my departure in any of the above ways, or any other, I have suggested these hasty reflections in hopes that you would do in it whatever you think right. I shall acquiesce in anything, and if nothing further comes to me I shall endeavor to push the third proposition with the Commander, and if I fail in that shall pursue the second; I wish to hear from you as often as you have anything new. I fear I shall be here long enough to receive many letters from you. My situation is not an agreeable one, and the less so as I contrast it with the more pleasing one I left so unnecessarily. Be so good as to present my esteem to the good ladies and gentlemen of your fireside and to accept yourself the warmest assurances of friendship from, dear Sir, your friend and servant.

Feb. 8. The preceding was written last night. Before I close my letter I will ask the favor of you to write me by the return of post and to let me have your own sentiments (whether anything be, or be not determined authoritatively) which will have great weight with me. I confess that after another night's reflection the fourth is the plan which appears to me best on the whole, and that the demand from New York is nothing more than what is made at the close of almost every war, where the one or the other power must have a passport: it is no more than asking a flag to New York. Should this, however, be disapproved, the third seems the only remaining plan which promises any degree of expedition. Perhaps the Minister may have a repugnance to venture the *Romulus* at York or Hampton, in which case if I could receive his approbation I should be willing to fall down there with the *Guadeloupe* alone and be in readiness to avail ourselves of a northwesterly snow storm or other favorable circumstance.

EDMUND RANDOLPH, 1785, 5:140 - *THE MOST SUCCESSFUL WAR SELDOM PAYS FOR ITS LOSSES.*

To Edmund Randolph[1]
Paris, September 20, 1785

Dear Sir, Being in your debt for ten volumes of Buffon, I have endeavored to find something that would be agreeable to you to receive, in return. I therefore send you, by way of Havre, a dictionary of law, natural and municipal, in thirteen volumes [also to be] called "*le Code de l'humanité.*" It is published by Felice, but written by him and several other authors of established reputation. It is an excellent work. I do not mean to say, that it answers fully to its title. That would have required fifty times the volume. It wants many articles which the title would induce us to seek in it. But the articles which it contains are well written. It is better than the voluminous "*Dictionnaire diplomatique,*" and better, also, than the same branch of the "*Encyclopedie methodique.*" There has been nothing published here, since I came, of extraordinary merit. The *Encyclopedie methodique*, which is coming out, from time to time, must be excepted from this. It is to be had at two guineas less than the subscription price. I shall be happy to send you anything in this way which you may desire. French books are to be bought here, for two-thirds of what they can in England. English and Greek and Latin authors, cost from twenty-five to fifty percent more here than in England.

I received, some time ago, a letter from Messrs. Hay and Buchanan, as Directors of the public buildings, desiring I would have plans drawn for our

---

1 Edmund Randolph was born at "Tazewell Hall", near Williamsburg, Virginia, August 10, 1753; attended the College of William and Mary; was admitted to the bar and practiced in Williamsburg; was appointed aide-de-camp to General Washington in 1775; was a member of the Virginia constitutional convention and became mayor of Williamsburg in 1776; married Elizabeth Nicholas the same year; served as Attorney General of Virginia 1776-1786; was a member of the Continental Congress 1779-1782; served as Governor of Virginia 1786-1788; was a delegate to the Annapolis Convention of 1786 and to the Federal Constitutional Convention of 1787; was a member of the Virginia convention of 1788 that ratified the Constitution; was a member of the State House of Delegates 1788-1789; served as attorney general in President Washington's Cabinet 1789-1794; was commissioned Secretary of State January 2, 1794, entered upon his duties the same day, and served until August 20, 1795; as Secretary of State, directed the negotiation of the treaty of 1795 with Spain, highly favorable to the interests of the United States; moved to Richmond and resumed the practice of law; was senior counsel for Aaron Burr in the treason trial of 1807; died in Clarke County, Virginia, September 12, 1813 (Patterson 1956, 6).

public buildings, and in the first place, for the Capitol. I did not receive their letter until within six weeks of the time they had fixed on, for receiving the drawings. Nevertheless, I engaged an excellent architect to comply with their desire. It has taken much time to accommodate the external adopted, to the internal arrangement necessary for the three branches of government. However, it is effected on a plan, which, with a great deal of beauty and convenience within, unites an external form on the most perfect model of antiquity now existing. This is the *Maison Quarrée of Nismes*, built by Caius and Lucius Caesar, and repaired by Louis XIV, which, in the opinion of all who have seen it, yields in beauty to no piece of architecture on earth. The gentlemen enclosed me a plan of which they had thought. The one preparing here, will be more convenient, give more room, and cost but two-thirds of that; and as a piece of architecture, doing honor to our country, will leave nothing to be desired. The plans will be ready soon. But, two days ago, I received a letter from Virginia, informing me the first brick of the capitol would be laid in a few days. This mortifies me extremely. The delay of this summer would have been amply repaid by the superiority and economy of the plan preparing here. Is it impossible to stop the work where it is? You will gain money by losing what is done, and general approbation, instead of occasioning a regret, which will endure as long as your building does. How is a taste for a chaste and good style of building to be formed in our countrymen, unless we seize all occasions which the erection of public buildings offers, of presenting to them models for their imitation? Do, my dear Sir, exert your influence to stay the further progress of the work, till you can receive these plans. You will only lose the price of laying what bricks are already laid, and of taking part of them asunder. They will do again for the inner walls. A plan for a prison will be sent at the same time.

Mazzei is here, and in pressing distress for money. I have helped him as far as I have been able, but particular circumstances put it out of my power to do more. He is looking with anxiety to the arrival of every vessel, in hopes of relief through your means. If he does not receive it soon, it is difficult to foresee his fate.

The quiet which Europe enjoys at present leaves nothing to communicate to you in the political way. The Emperor and Dutch still differ about the quantum of money to be paid by the latter; they know not what. Perhaps their internal convulsions will hasten them to a decision. France is improving her navy, as if she were already in a naval war, yet I see no immediate prospect of her having occasion for it.

England is not likely to offer war to any nation, unless perhaps to ours. This would cost us our whole shipping, but in every other respect we might flatter ourselves with success. But the most successful war seldom pays for its losses. I shall be glad to hear from you when convenient, and am, with much esteem, dear Sir, your friend and servant.

JAMES CURRIE, 1785, 19:11 - *FOR THE MOMENT EUROPE IS CLEAR OF WAR.*

To James Currie[1]
Paris, September 27, 1785

Dear Sir, Your favor of August 5th came to hand on the 18th instant, and I mark well what you say, "that my letters shall be punctually answered." This is encouraging, and the more so as it proves to you that in sending your letters in time to arrive at New York the middle of the month, when the French packet sails, they get to hand very speedily. The last was but six weeks from you to me. I thank you again and again for the details it contains, these being precisely of the nature I would wish. Of political correspondents I can find enough, but I can persuade nobody to believe that the small facts which they see passing daily under their eyes are precious to me at this distance; much more interesting to the heart than events of higher rank. Fancy to yourself a being who is withdrawn from his connections of blood, of marriage, of friendship, of acquaintance in all their gradations, who for years should hear nothing of what has passed among them, who returns again to see them and finds the one-half dead. This strikes him like a pestilence sweeping off the half of mankind. Events which had they come to him one by one and in detail he would have weathered as other people do, when presented to his mind all at once are overwhelming. Continue then to give me facts, little facts, such as you think every one imagines beneath notice, and your letters will be the most precious to me. They will place me in imagination in my own country, and they will place me where I am happiest. But what shall I give you in return? Political events are scarcely interesting to a man who looks on them from high ground. There is always war in one place, revolution in another, pestilence in a third, interspersed with spots of quiet. These chequers shift places but they do not vanish, so that to an eye which extends itself over the whole earth there is always uniformity of prospect.

For the moment Europe is clear of war. The Emperor and Dutch have signed articles. These are not published; but it is believed the Emperor gets ten millions of *florins*, the navigation of the Scheld to Saptinghen, and two forts, so that your conjecture is verified and the Dutch actually pay the piper. The league formed in the Germanic body by the King of Russia is likely to circumscribe the ambitious views of the Emperor on that side and there seems to be no issue for them but on the side of the Turk. Their demarkation does not advance. It is a pity the Emperor would not confine himself to internal regulation. In that way he has done much good. One would think it not so difficult to discover that the improvement of the country we possess is the surest means of increasing our wealth and power. This, too, promotes the happiness of mankind while the others destroy it and are always uncertain of their object, England seems not to permit our friendship to enter into her political calculations as an article of any value. Her endeavor is not how to

---

1 James Currie was a Virginia physician and a close confident of Jefferson

recover our affections or to bind us to her by alliance, but by what new experiments she may keep up an existence without us; thus leaving us to carry our full weight, present and future, into the scale of her enemy, and seeming to prefer our enmity to our neutrality.

The Barbary corsairs have committed depredations on us. The Emperor of Morocco took a vessel last winter which he has since restored with the crew and cargo. The Algerians took two vessels in July. These are the only captures which were known of at Algiers on the 24th of August. I mention this because the English papers would make the world believe we have lost an infinite number. I hope soon to be able to inform our countrymen that these dangers are ceased.

There is little here to communicate in the arts and sciences. The great desideratum which was to render the discovery of the balloon useful, is not absolutely desperate. There are two artists at Javel, about four miles from here, who are able to rise and fall at will without expending their gas, and to deflect 45 [degrees] from the course of the wind. The investigations of air and fire which have latterly so much occupied the chemists, have not presented anything very interesting for some time past.

I send you four books, Rolend, Sigaud de la Fond, Metherie, and Scheele, which will put you in possession of whatever has been discovered as yet on that subject. They are packed in a trunk directed to J. Madison of Orange, which will be carried to Richmond. They are in French, which you say you do not understand well. You lose infinitely by this, as you may be assured that the publications in that language at present far exceed those of England in science. With respect to the *Encyclopbdie* it is impossible for me to judge whether to send it to you or not, as I do not know your degree of knowledge in the language nor your intentions as to increasing it. Of this you must decide for yourself and instruct me accordingly.

I was unlucky as to the partridges, pheasants, hares and rabbits which I had ordered to Virginia. The vessel in which I came over was to have returned to Virginia and to Warwick. I knew I could rely on the captain's care. A fellow-passenger undertook to provide them. He did so, but the destination of the vessel was changed and the poor colonists all died while my friend was looking out for another conveyance. If I can be useful to your circulating library, the members may be assured of my zealous services. All books except English, Latin and Greek are bought here for about two-thirds of what they cost in England. They had better distribute their invoices accordingly. I must trouble you to present assurances of my friendship to Mr. and Mrs. Randolph of Tuckahoe, Mr. Cary, and their families. My attachment to them is sincere. I wish I could render them useful to them. Tell Mr. Cary I shall enjoy a very real pleasure whenever he shall carry his intentions of writing me into execution and that there is no one who more fervently wishes him well.

Accept yourself assurances of the esteem with which I am, dear Sir, your friend and servant.

JOHN JAY, 1785, 5:93 ~ *I THINK IT TO OUR INTEREST TO PUNISH THE FIRST INSULT.*

To John Jay (Private)[1]

Paris, August 23, 1785

Dear Sir, I shall sometimes ask your permission to write you letters, not official, but private. The present is of this kind, and is occasioned by the question proposed in yours of June the 14th; "whether it would be useful to us, to carry all our own productions, or none?"

Were we perfectly free to decide this question, I should reason as follows. We have now lands enough to employ an infinite number of people in their cultivation. Cultivators of the earth are the most valuable citizens. They are the most vigorous, the most independent, the most virtuous, and they are tied to their country, and wedded to its liberty and interests, by the most lasting bonds. As long, therefore, as they can find employment in this line, I would not convert them into mariners, artisans, or anything else. But our citizens will find employment in this line, till their numbers, and of course their productions, become too great for the demand, both internal and foreign. This is not the case as yet, and probably will not be for a considerable time. As soon as it is, the surplus of hands must be turned to something else. I should then, perhaps, wish to turn them to the sea in preference to manufactures; because, comparing the characters of the two lasses, I find the former the most valuable citizens. I consider the class of artificers as the panders of vice, and the instruments by which the liberties of a country are generally overturned. However, we are not free to decide this question on principles of theory only. Our people are decided in the opinion, that it is necessary for us to take a share in the occupation of the ocean, and their established habits induce them to require that the sea be kept open to them, and that that line of policy be pursued, which will render the use of that element to them as great as possible. I think it a duty in those entrusted with the administration of their affairs, to conform themselves to the decided choice of their constituents; and that therefore, we should, in every instance, preserve an equality of right to them in the transportation of commodities, in the right of fishing, and in the other uses of the sea.

---

1 John Jay was born in New York City December 12, 1745; was graduated from King's College in 1764; was admitted to the bar in 1768 and practiced law; married Sarah Van Brugh Livingston in 1774; was a member of the Continental Congress 1774-1779; aided in obtaining approval of the Declaration of Independence and in drafting the State constitution; served as Chief Justice of New York State 1777-1778; was president of the Continental Congress 1778-1779; was Minister to Spain 1779-1782; was one of the Commissioners named in 1781 to negotiate peace with Great Britain and signed the treaties of 1782 and 1783; took office as Secretary of Foreign Affairs under the Continental Congress December 21, 1784, served until the establishment of Government under the Constitution, and continued unofficially to superintend the Department until Jefferson took office as Secretary of State on March 22, 1790; during his tenure of office, treatise of commerce with Prussia and Morocco and a consular convention with France were negotiated; was Chief Justice of the United States 1789-1795; served as Minister to Great Britain 1794-1795 and negotiated and signed Jay's Treaty; was Governor of New York 1795-1801; retired to his farm at Bedford, New York City, where he died May 17, 1829 (Patterson 1956, 2).

But what will be the consequence? Frequent wars without a doubt. Their property will be violated on the sea, and in foreign ports, their persons will be insulted, imprisoned, 8x., for pretended debts, contracts, crimes, contraband, &c., &c. These insults must be resented, even if we had no feelings, yet to prevent their eternal repetition; or, in other words, our commerce on the ocean and in other countries must be paid for by frequent war. The justest dispositions possible in ourselves, will not secure us against it. It would be necessary that all other nations were just also. Justice indeed, on our part, will save us from those wars which would have been produced by a contrary disposition. But how can we prevent those produced by the wrongs of other nations? By putting ourselves in a condition to punish them. Weakness provokes insult and injury, while a condition to punish, often prevents them. This reasoning leads to the necessity of some naval force; that being the only weapon by which we can reach an enemy. I think it to our interest to punish the first insult; because an insult unpunished is the parent of many others. We are not, at this moment, in a condition to do it, but we should put ourselves into it, as soon as possible. If a war with England should take place, it seems to me that the first thing necessary would be a resolution to abandon the carrying trade, because we cannot protect it. Foreign nations must, in that case, be invited to bring us what we want, and to take our productions in their own bottoms. This alone could prevent the loss of those productions to us, and the acquisition of them to our enemy. Our seamen might be employed in depredations on their trade. But how dreadfully we shall suffer on our coasts, if we have no force on the water, former experience has taught us. Indeed, I look forward with horror to the very possible case of war with a European power, and think there is no protection against them, but from the possession of some force on the sea. Our vicinity to their West India possessions, and to the fisheries, is a bridle which a small naval force, on our part, would hold in the mouths of the most powerful of these countries. I hope our land office will rid us of our debts, and that our first attention then, will be, to the beginning a naval force of some sort. This alone can countenance our people as carriers on the water, and I suppose them to be determined to continue such.

I wrote you two public letters on the 14th instant, since which I have received yours of July the 13th. I shall always be pleased to receive from you, in a private way, such communications as you might not choose to put into a public letter.

I have the honor to be, with very sincere esteem, dear Sir, your most obedient humble servant.

JAMES MONROE, 1786, 5:383 ~ *EVERY RATIONAL CITIZEN MUST WISH TO SEE AN EFFECTIVE INSTRUMENT OF COERCION.*

To Colonel Monroe[1]

---

1 James Monroe was born in Westmoreland County, Virginia, April 28, 1758; attended the College of William and Mary 1774-1776; served as an officer in the Continental Army; stud-

Paris, August 11, 1786

Dear Sir, I wrote you last on the 9th of July; and, since that, have received yours of the 16th of June, with the interesting intelligence it contained. I was entirely in the dark as to the progress of that negotiation, and concur entirely in the views you have taken of it. The difficulty on which it hangs is a sine qua non with us. It would be to deceive them and ourselves, to suppose that an amity can be preserved, while this right is withheld. Such a supposition would argue, not only an ignorance of the people to whom this is most interesting, but an ignorance of the nature of man, or an inattention to it. Those who see but half way into our true interest will think that that concurs with the views of the other party. But those who see it in all its extent, will be sensible that our true interest will be best promoted, by making all the just claims of our fellow citizens, wherever situated, our own, by urging and enforcing them with the weight of our whole influence, and by exercising in this, as in every other instance, a just government in their concerns, and making common cause even where our separate interest would seem opposed to theirs. No other conduct can attach us together; and on this attachment depends our happiness.   The King of Prussia still lives, and is even said to be better. Europe is very quiet at present. The only germ of dissension, which shows itself at present, is in the quarter of Turkey. The Emperor, the Empress, and the Venetians seem all to be picking at the Turks. It is not probable, however, that either of the two first will do anything to bring on an open rupture, while the King of Prussia lives.

You will perceive, by the letters I enclose to Mr. Jay, that Lambe, under the pretext of ill health, declines returning either to Congress, Mr. Adams, or myself. This circumstance makes me fear some malversation. The money appropriated to this object being in Holland, and, having been always under the care of Mr. Adams, it was concerted between us that all the drafts should be on him. I know not, therefore, what sums may have been advanced to Lambe; I hope, however, nothing great. I am persuaded that an angel sent on this business, and so much limited in his terms, could have done nothing. But should Congress propose to try the line of negotiation again, I think they

ied law under Jefferson 1780-1783; was a member of the Virginia Assembly in 1782 and 1786; was a member of the Continental Congress 1783-1786; attended the Annapolis Convention of 1786; married Eliza Kortright the same year; was admitted to the bar and practiced in Fredericksburg; was a member of the State convention of 1788 that ratified the Federal Constitution; was a Senator from Virginia 1790-1794; served as minister to France 1794-1796; was governor of Virginia 1799-1802; was again minister to France in 1803; served as minister to Great Britain 1803-1807; headed a diplomatic mission to Spain 1804-1805; was again elected to the Virginia Assembly in 1810; was again governor of Virginia in 1811; was commissioned secretary of state in President Madison's Cabinet April 2, 1811, entered upon his duties April 6, 1811, and served until September 30, 1814; served as both secretary of war and secretary of state *ad interim* October 1, 1814-February 28, 1815; was again commissioned secretary of state February 28, 1815, entered upon his duties the same day, and served until March 3, 1817; during his tenure of office the War of 1812 was fought and the Treaty of Ghent, which restored peace, was negotiated; was president of the United States 1817-1825; retired to his farm in Virginia; was presiding officer of the Virginia constitutional convention of 1829; died in New York City July 4, 1831 (Patterson 1956, 16).

will perceive that Lambe is not a proper agent. I have written to Mr. Adams on the subject of a settlement with Lambe. There is little prospect of accommodation between the Algerians, and the Portuguese and Neapolitans. A very valuable capture, too, lately made by them on the Empress of Russia, bids fair to draw her on them. The probability is, therefore, that these three nations will be at war with them, and the probability is, that could we furnish a couple of frigates, a convention might be formed with those powers establishing a perpetual cruise on the coast of Algiers, which would bring them to reason. Such a convention, being left open to all powers willing to come into it, should have for its object a general peace, to be guaranteed to each, by the whole. Were only two or three to begin a confederacy of this kind, I think every power in Europe would soon fall into it, except France, England, and perhaps Spain and Holland. Of these, there is only England, who would give any real aid to the Algerians. Morocco, you perceive, will be at peace with us, were the honor and advantage of establishing such a confederacy out of the question, yet the necessity that the United States should have some marine force, and the happiness of this, as the ostensible cause for beginning it, would decide on its propriety. It will be said, there is no money in the treasury. There never will be money in the treasury, till the confederacy shows its teeth. The States must see the rod; perhaps it must be felt by some one of them. I am persuaded, all of them would rejoice to see every one obliged to furnish its contributions. It is not the difficulty of furnishing them, which beggars the treasury, but the fear that others will not furnish as much. Every rational citizen must wish to see an effective instrument of coercion, and should fear to see it on any other element than the water. A naval force can never endanger our liberties, nor occasion bloodshed; a land force would do both. It is not in the choice of the States, whether they will pay money to cover their trade against the Algerians. If they obtain a peace by negotiation, they must pay a great sum of money for it; if they do nothing, they must pay a great sum of money, in the form of insurance; and in either way, as great a one as in the way of force, and probably less effectual.

I look forward with anxiety to the approaching moment of your departure from Congress. Besides the interest of the confederacy and of the State, I have a personal interest in it. I know not to whom I may venture confidential communications, after you are gone. I take the liberty of placing here my respects to Mrs. Monroe, and assurances of the sincere esteem with which I am, dear Sir, your friend and servant.

C. W. F. Dumas, 1786, 5:310 – *The animosities of sovereigns are temporary and may be allayed.*

To Mr. Dumas[1]
Paris, May 6, 1786

---

1 C.W.F. Dumas, a man of letters, was an American secret agent based in Holland. The United States maintained secret agents in The Netherlands throughout the war and, for several years, American representatives made unsuccessful attempts to obtain a loan, but the authorities of Amsterdam finally communicated to Dumas that they desired to conclude

Sir, Having been absent in England, for some time past, your favors of February the 27th, March the 28th, and April the 11th, have not been acknowledged as soon as they should have been. I am obliged to you, for assisting to make me known to the Rhingrave de Salm and the Marquis de la Coste, whose reputations render an acquaintance with them desirable. I have not yet seen either, but expect that honor from the Rhingrave very soon. Your letters to Mr. Jay and Mr. Van Berkel, received in my absence, will be forwarded by a gentleman who leaves this place for New York, within a few days. I sent the treaty with Prussia, by a gentleman who sailed from Havre, the 11th of November. The arrival of that vessel in America is not yet known here. Though the time is not long enough to produce despair, it is sufficiently so to give inquietude lest it should be lost. This would be a cause of much concern to me; I beg the favor of you to mention this circumstance to the Baron de Thulemeyer, as an apology for his not hearing from us. The last advices from America bring us nothing interesting. A principal object of my journey to London was to enter into commercial arrangements with Portugal. This has been done almost in the precise terms of those of Prussia. The English are still our enemies. The spirit existing there, and rising in America, has a very lowering aspect. To what events it may give birth, I cannot foresee. We are young and can survive them; but their rotten machine must crush under the trial. The animosities of sovereigns are temporary, and may be allayed; but those which seize the whole body of a people, and of a people, too, who dictate their own measures, produce calamities of long duration. I shall not wonder to see the scenes of ancient Rome and Carthage renewed in our day; and if not pursued to the same issue, it may be because the republic of modern powers will not permit the extinction of any one of its members. Peace and friendship with all mankind is our wisest policy; and I wish we may be permitted to pursue it. But the temper and folly of our enemies may not leave this in our choice. I am happy in our prospect of friendship with the most estimable powers of Europe, and particularly with those of the confederacy, of which yours is. That your present crisis may have a happy issue, is the prayer and wish of him who has the honor to be, with great respect and esteem, Sir, your most obedient humble servant.

JAMES MADISON, 1786, 5:278 ~ INSULT AND WAR ARE THE CONSEQUENCES OF A WANT OF RESPECTABILITY IN THE NATIONAL CHARACTER.

To James Madison[1]

---

a treaty provided Congress would not enter into engagements with Great Britain which might prove harmful to Dutch interests (Bolton 1920, 521).

1 James Madison was born at Port Conway, Virginia, March 16, 1751; was graduated from the College of New Jersey in 1771; studied law and was admitted to the bar; was elected to the Virginia constitutional convention and was a member of the State Assembly in 1776; was a member of the State Executive Council 1778-1779; was a member of the Continental Congress 1780-1783 and 1786-1788; served in the Virginia House of Delegates 1784-1786; was a delegate to the Annapolis Convention of 1786 and to the Federal Convention of 1787, where he played a major part in the framing of the Constitution; cooperated with Hamilton

Paris, February 8, 1786

Dear Sir, My last letters were of the 1st and 20th of September, and the 28th of October. Yours, unacknowledged, are of August the 20th, October the 3d, and November the 15th. I take this, the first safe opportunity, of enclosing to you the bills of lading for your books, and two others for your namesake of Williamsburg, and for the attorney, which I will pray you to forward. I thank you for the communication of the remonstrance against the assessment. Mazzei, who is now in Holland, promised me to have it published in the Leyden gazette. It will do us great honor. I wish it may be as much approved by our Assembly, as by the wisest part of Europe. I have heard, with great pleasure, that our Assembly have come to the resolution of giving the regulation of their commerce to the federal head. I will venture to assert, that there is not one of its opposers, who, placed on this ground, would not see the wisdom of this measure. The politics of Europe render it indispensably necessary that, with respect to everything external, we be one nation only, firmly hooped together. Interior government is what each State should keep to itself. If it were seen in Europe that all our States could be brought to concur in what the Virginia Assembly has done, it would produce a total revolution in their opinion of us, and respect for us. And it should ever be held in mind, that insult and war are the consequences of a want of respectability in the national character. As long as the States exercise, separately, those acts of power which respect foreign nations, so long will there continue to be irregularities committed by some one or other of them, which will constantly keep us on an ill footing with foreign nations.

I thank you for your information as to my Notes. The copies I have remaining shall be sent over, to be given to some of my friends, and to select subjects in the College. I have been unfortunate here with this trifle. I gave out a few copies only, and to confidential persons, writing in every copy a restraint against its publication. Among others, I gave a copy to a Mr. Williams; he died. I immediately took every precaution I could, to recover this copy. But, by some means or other, a bookseller had got hold of it. He employed a hireling translator, and is about publishing it in the most injurious form possible. I am now at a loss what to do as to England. Everything, good or bad, is thought worth publishing there; and I apprehend a translation back from the French, and a publication here. I rather believe it will be most eligible to let the original come out in that country; but am not yet decided.

---

and Jay on a series of essays later published as *The Federalist*; was a member of the Virginia convention of 1788 that ratified the Constitution; was a Representative from Virginia 1789-1797; married Dolly (Payne) Todd in 1794; was again a member of the House of Delegates in 1799; served as presidential elector in 1800; was commissioned Secretary of State in President Jefferson's Cabinet March 5, 1801, entered upon his duties May 2, 1801, and served until March 3, 1809; during his tenure of office France offered and the United States accepted the Louisiana Purchase; was president of the United States 1809-1817; retired to "Montpellier" (now "Montpelier"), his estate in Virginia; became rector of the University of Virginia in 1826; was a member of the Virginia constitutional convention of 1829; died at "Montpellier", Orange County, Virginia, June 28, 1836 (Patterson 1956, 12).

I have purchased little for you in the book way, since I sent the catalogue of my former purchases. I wish, first, to have your answer to that, and your information, what parts of these purchases went out of your plan. You can easily say, buy more of this kind, less of that, &c. My wish is to conform myself to yours. I can get for you the original Paris edition of the "*Encyclopedie*," in thirty-five volumes, folio, for six hundred and twenty *livres*; a good edition, in thirty-nine volumes, 4to, for three hundred and eighty *livres*; and a good one, in thirty-nine volumes, 8vo, for two hundred and eighty *livres*.[1] The new one will be superior in far the greater number of articles; but not in all. And the possession of the ancient one has, moreover, the advantage of supplying present use. I have bought one for myself, but wait your orders as to you. I remember your purchase of a watch in Philadelphia. If it should not have proved good, you can probably sell it. In that case, I can get for you, here, one made as perfect as human art can make it, for about twenty-four *louis*. I have had such a one made by the best and most faithful hand in Paris. It has a second hand, but no repeating, no day of the month, nor other useless thing to impede and injure the movements which are necessary. For twelve *louis* more, you can have in the same cover, but on the back, and absolutely unconnected with the movements of the watch, a pedometer, which shall render you an exact account of the distances you walk. Your pleasure hereon shall be awaited.

Houdon has returned. He called on me, the other day, to remonstrate against the inscription proposed for General Washington's statue. He says it is too, I long to be put on the pedestal. I told him I was not at liberty to permit any alteration, but I would represent his objection to a friend, who could judge of its validity, and whether a change could be authorized. This has been the subject of conversations here, and various devices and inscriptions have been suggested. The one which has appeared best to me may be translated as follows: "Behold, Reader, the form of George Washington. For his worth, ask History; that will tell it, when this stone shall have yielded to the decays of time. His country erects this monument; Houdon makes it." This for one side. On the second, represent the evacuation of Boston, with the motto, "Hostibus primum fugatis." On the third, the capture of the Hessians, with "Hostibus iterum devictis." On the fourth, the surrender of York, with "Hostibus ultimum debellatis." This is seizing the three most brilliant actions of his military life. By giving out, here, a wish of receiving mottos for this statue, we might have thousands offered, from which still better might be chosen. The artist made the same objection, of length, to the inscription for the bust of the Marquis de Lafayette. An alteration of that might come in time still, if an alteration was wished. However, I am not certain that it is desirable in either case. The State of Georgia has given twenty thousand acres of land to the Count d'Estaing. This gift is considered here as very honorable to him, and it has gratified him much. I am persuaded, that a gift of lands by

1 "4to" is a reference to the size of a book whose pages are made by folding a sheet of paper twice to form four leaves.

47

the State of Virginia to the Marquis de Lafayette would give a good opinion here of our character, and would reflect honor on the Marquis. Nor, am I sure that the day will not come when it might be a useful asylum to him. The time of life at which he visited America was too well adapted to receive good and lasting impressions to permit him ever to accommodate himself to the principles of monarchical government; and it will need all his own prudence, and that of his friends, to make this country a safe residence for him. How glorious, how comfortable in reflection, will it be, to have prepared a refuge for him in case of a reverse. In the meantime, he could settle it with tenants from the freest part of this country, Bretaigne. I have never suggested the smallest idea of this kind to him; because the execution of it should convey the first notice. If the State has not a right to give him lands with their own officers, they could buy up, at cheap prices, the shares of others. I am not certain, however, whether in the public or private opinion, a similar gift to Count Rochambeau could be dispensed with. If the State could give to both, it would be better; but, in any event, I think they should to the Marquis. Count Rochambeau, too, has really deserved more attention than he has received. Why not set up his bust, that of Gates, Greene, Franklin, in your new capitol? Apropos of the capitol. Do, my dear friend, exert yourself to get the plan, begun on, set aside, and that adopted, which was drawn here. It was taken from a model which has been the admiration of sixteen centuries; which has been the object of as many pilgrimages as the tomb of Mahomet; which will give unrivalled honor to our State, and furnish a model whereon to form the taste of our young men. It will cost much less, too, than the one begun; because it does not cover one-half of the area. Ask, if you please, a sight of my letter of January the 26th, to Messrs. Buchanan and Hay, which will spare me the repeating its substance here.

Everything is quiet in Europe. I recollect but one new invention in the arts, which is worth mentioning. It is a mixture of the arts of engraving and printing, rendering both cheaper. Write or draw anything on a plate of brass, with the ink of the inventor, and, in half an hour, he gives you engraved copies of it, so perfectly like the original, that they could not be suspected to be copies. His types for printing a whole page are all in one solid piece. An author, therefore, only prints a few copies of his work, from time to time, as they are called for. This saves the loss of printing more copies than may possibly, be sold, and prevents an edition from being ever exhausted. I am, with a lively esteem, dear Sir, your sincere friend and servant.

JOHN ADAMS, 1786, 5:364 ~ WAR ON THE FAIREST PROSPECTS IS STILL EXPOSED TO UNCERTAINTIES.

To John Adams[1]

---

1 John Adams was born in what is now Quincy, Massachusetts, on October 30, 1735. He graduated from Harvard in 1755, and read law, subsequently taking up its practice in 1758. Early on adopting the patriot cause, he was elected in 1774 to the first continental congress, where two years later he was assigned to the committee given responsibility for drafting the Declaration of Independence. At the further assignment of the continental congress

Paris, July 11, 1786

Dear Sir, Our instructions relative to the Barbary States having required us to proceed by way of negotiation to obtain their peace, it became our duty to do this to the best of our power. Whatever might be our private opinions, they were to be suppressed, and the line, marked out to us, was to be followed. It has been so, honestly and zealously. It was, therefore, never material for us to consult together, on the best plan of conduct towards these States. I acknowledge, I very early thought it would be best to effect a peace through the medium of war. Though it is a question with which we have nothing to do, yet as you propose some discussion of it, I shall trouble you with my reasons. Of the four positions laid down in your letter of the 3d instant, I agree to the three first, which are, in substance, that the good offices of our friends cannot procure us a peace, without paying its price; that they cannot materially lessen that price; and that paying it, we can have the peace in spite of the intrigues of our enemies. As to the fourth, that the longer the negotiation is delayed, the larger will be the demand; this will depend on the intermediate captures: if they are many and rich, the price may be raised; if few and poor, it will be lessened. However, if it is decided that we shall buy a peace, I know no reason for delaying the operation, but should rather think it ought to be hastened; but I should prefer the obtaining it by war.

1. Justice is in favor of this opinion. 2. Honor favors it. 3. It will procure us respect in Europe; and respect is a safeguard to interest. 4. It will arm the federal head with the safest of all the instruments of coercion over its delinquent members, and prevent it from using what would be less safe. I think that so

Adams was to devote more than a decade (1777-1788) to various European diplomatic missions, only occasionally interrupting his stay there to return home. As a result of the first meeting of the Electoral College under the newly adopted Constitution, he was elected to the vice-presidency. During his two terms, Adams suffered many of the frustrations that were to burden his successors in that office. Not invited by President Washington to be an active participant in executive decision making, Adams was left to perform the one duty constitutionally assigned to vice-presidents: presiding, without benefit of vote other than to break ties, over the proceedings of the U.S. Senate. Even though Adams did on a record-setting 31 occasions cast such tie-breaking votes, he came to regard the vice-presidential role as more or less irrelevant. With Washington declining consideration of a third term Adams became, among Federalists (Alexander Hamilton's opposition notwithstanding), the anticipated choice to succeed the departing president. The presidential election of 1796, however, was to be the first characterized by competing party tickets: Adams and Thomas Pinckney of South Carolina as vice-presidential candidate for the Federalists, against Thomas Jefferson and Aaron Burr of New York as the Republican nominees. Because of the prevailing language in the Constitution with regard to the functioning of the Electoral College, the balloting resulted in the peculiarity of Adams, with 71 votes, being elected president and his Republican rival Jefferson, with 68 votes, the second highest number, winning the vice-presidency. Adams attempted to balance neutrality between and among warring European powers, and drew the fire of Hamilton and many other Federalists who preferred stronger ties with Great Britain and, from the other side, of Thomas Jefferson and the Republicans, who were equally ardent in their calls for support of revolutionary France. Despite the criticism that came from all fronts, John Adams again sought reelection in 1800. After numerous balloting issues, the outcome became clear, and not waiting for Jefferson's formal inauguration, Adams returned to Massachusetts. He died on July 4, 1826, while his son, John Quincy Adams, occupied the White House, and on the same day as the death in Virginia of his patriot colleague and sometime rival Thomas Jefferson (Binning 1999, 1-2).

far, you go with me. But in the next steps, we shall differ. 5. I think it least expensive. 6. Equally effectual: I ask a fleet of one hundred and fifty guns, the one-half of which shall be in constant cruise. This fleet, built, manned and victualled for six months will cost four hundred and fifty thousand pounds sterling. Its annual expense will be three hundred pounds sterling a gun, including everything; this will be forty-five thousand pounds sterling a year. I take British experience for the basis for my calculation: though we know, from our own experience, that we can do in this way, for pounds lawful, what costs them pounds sterling. Were we to charge all this to the Algerian war, it would amount to little more than we must pay, if we buy peace. But as it is proper and necessary that we should establish a small marine force, (even were we to buy a peace from the Algerians,) and as that force, laid up in our dock-yards, would cost us half as much annually, as if kept in order for service, we have a right to say that only twenty-two thousand and five hundred pounds sterling, per annum, should be charged to the Algerian war. 6. It will be as effectual. To all the mismanagements of Spain and Portugal, urged to show that war against those people is ineffectual, I urge a single fact to prove the contrary, where there is any management. About forty years ago, the Algerians having broke their treaty with France, this court sent Monsieur de Massiac, with one large, and two small frigates; he blockaded the harbor of Algiers three months, and they subscribed to the terms he proposed. If it be admitted, however, that war, on the fairest prospects, is still exposed to uncertainties, I weigh against this, the greater uncertainty of the duration of a peace bought with money, from such a people, from a *Dey* eighty years old, and by a nation who, on the hypothesis of buying peace, is to have no power on the sea, to enforce an observance of it.

So far, I have gone on the supposition that the whole weight of this war would rest on us. But, 1. Naples will join us. The character of their naval minister (Acton), his known sentiments with respect to the peace Spain is officiously trying to make for them, and his dispositions against the Algerians, give the best grounds to believe it. 2. Every principle of reason assures us that Portugal will join us. I state this as taking for granted, what all seem to believe, that they will not be at peace with Algiers. I suppose, then, that a convention might be formed between Portugal, Naples, and the United States, by which the burthen of the war might be quotaed on them, according to their respective wealth; and the term of it should be, when Algiers should subscribe to a peace with all three, on equal terms. This might be left open for other nations to accede to, and many, if not most of the powers of Europe, (except France, England, Holland, and Spain, if her peace be made) would sooner or later enter into the confederacy, for the sake of having their peace with the piratical States guaranteed by the whole. I suppose that, in this case, our proportion of force would not be the half of what I first calculated on.

These are the reasons which have influenced my judgment on this question. I give them to you, to show you that I am imposed on by a semblance of reason, at least; and not with an expectation of their changing your opinion. You have viewed the subject, I am sure, in all its bearings. You have weighed both questions, with all their circumstances. You make the result different from what I do. The same facts impress us differently. This is enough to make me suspect an error in my process of reasoning, though I am not able to detect it. It is of no consequence; as I have nothing to say in the decision, and am ready to proceed heartily on any other plan which may be adopted, if my agency should be thought useful. With respect to the dispositions of the State, I am utterly uninformed. I cannot help thinking, however, that on a view of all the circumstances, they might be united in either of the plans.

Having written this on the receipt of your letter, without knowing of any opportunity of sending it, I know not when it will go; I add nothing, therefore, on any other subject, but assurances of the sincere esteem and respect with which I am, dear Sir, your friend and servant.

TREASURY COMMISSIONERS, 1787, 6:303 ~ PAY MORE FOR FOREIGN PRISONERS.

To the Honorable the Commissioners of the Treasury[1]
Paris, September 18, 1787

Gentlemen, Congress having thought proper, by their vote of July the 18th, to entrust me to take measures for the redemption of our captives at Algiers, and to desire you to furnish the money necessary, it is proper to state to you some data whereby you may judge what sum is necessary. The French prisoners, last redeemed by the order of Mathurins, cost somewhat less than four hundred dollars: but the General of the order told me, that they had always been made to pay more for foreign prisoners than their own. The smallest sum then, at which we can expect ours, including redemption, clothing, feeding, and transportation, will be five hundred dollars each. There are twenty of them. Of course, ten thousand dollars is the smallest sum which can be requisite. I think a larger sum should be set apart, as so much of it as shall not be wanting for the prisoners, will remain for other uses. As soon as you shall have notified me that the money is ready, I will proceed to execute the order of Congress. I must add the injunctions of the General of the Mathurins, that it be not made known that the public interest themselves in the redemption of these prisoners, as that would induce the Algerians to demand the most extravagant price. I have the honor to be, with sentiments of the most profound respect, Gentlemen, your most obedient, and most humble servant.

---

1 One of the more complicated issues that faced the new nation was to find an effective way to deal with Morocco, Algiers, Tunis, and Tripoli, known collectively as the "Barbary States." For hundreds of years, Mediterranean commerce had been menaced by attacks committed by the pirates of the North African coast, and before the Revolutionary War the very considerable trade of the American colonies in the Mediterranean was carried on under the protection of the British. With independence, the Americans found themselves fair prey. Their ships were seized, the crews taken captive and held for high ransom, particularly by the Algerines (Kimball 1950, 27-28).

JOHN JAY, 1787, 6:304 ~ *LET IT BE KNOWN EVEN TO THE RELATIONS OF THE CAPTIVES, THAT WE MEAN TO REDEEM THEM.*

To John Jay[1]
Paris, September 19, 1787

Sir, My last letters to you were of the 6th and 15th of August; since which, I have been honored with yours of July the 24th, acknowledging the receipt of mine of the 14th and 23d of February. I am anxious to hear you have received that also of May the 4th, written from Marseilles. According to the desires of Congress, expressed in their vote confirming the appointments of Francisco, Giuseppa and Girolamo Chiappi, their agents in Morocco, I have written letters to these gentlemen, to begin a with them. To the first, I have enclosed the ratification of the treaty with the Emperor of Morocco, and shall send it either by our agent at Marseilles, who is now here, or by the Count Daranda, who sets out for Madrid in a few days, having relinquished his embassy here. I shall proceed on the redemption of our captives at Algiers, as soon as the commissioners of the treasury shall enable me, by placing the money necessary, under my orders. The prisoners redeemed by the religious order of Mathurins, cost about four hundred dollars each, and the General of the order told me, that they had never been able to redeem foreigners on so good terms as their own countrymen. Supposing that their redemption, clothing, feeding and transportation, should amount to five hundred dollars each, there must be, at least, a sum of ten thousand dollars set apart for this purpose. Till this is done, I shall take no other step than the preparatory one, of destroying at Algiers all idea of our intending to redeem the prisoners. This, the General of the Mathurins told me, was indispensably necessary, and that it must not, on any account, transpire, that the public would interest themselves for their redemption. This was rendered the more necessary, by the declaration of the *Dey* to the Spanish consul, that he should hold him responsible, at the Spanish price, for our prisoners, even for such as should die. Three of them have died of the plague. By authorizing me to redeem at the prices usually paid by the European nations, Congress, I suppose, could

---

1 While Jefferson was convinced that peace with Algiers was not an immediate prospect, he also understood that making a treaty was a different matter from securing the release of the Americans held captive. He found that an order of begging priests, the Mathurins, undertook commissions of redeeming prisoners in Algiers. Although he approached the sect leader — their "general" as Jefferson termed him — with regard to the American captives, the distance of Paris from Algiers, as well as from America, the lack of information, and most of all, the lack of money, made it difficult for Jefferson to decide on an expeditious policy. He referred it to John Jay — then serving as Secretary of Foreign Affairs, the precursor to the office of Secretary of State — for the decision of Congress, mentioning the Mathurins, and advising that the first redemption be at a low price to avoid arousing the greed of the pirates. Jefferson even assumed that it would be wise to appear to neglect the captives altogether, and to conduct all operations for their release secretly and without their knowledge. When it came up for action, Congress admitted its inability to decide and referred the redemption to Jefferson with advice to follow such measures as he deemed advisable, ordering the treasury board to furnish ways and means to meet the expense. Jefferson, therefore, assumed responsibility for solving the Barbary problem, as well as devising plans to provide subsistence to the captives until they could be released (Wollery 1927, 30-31).

not mean the Spanish price, which is not only unusual, but unprecedented, and would make our vessels the first object with those pirates. I shall pay no attention, therefore, to the Spanish price, unless further instructed. Hard as it may seem, I should think it necessary not to let it be known, even to the relations of the captives, that we mean to redeem them.

I have the honor to enclose you a paper from the admiralty of Guadaloupe, sent to me as a matter of form, and to be lodged, I suppose, with our marine records. I enclose, also, a copy of a letter from the Count de Florida Blanca to Mr. Carmichael, by which you will perceive, they have referred the settlement of the claim of South Carolina for the use of their frigate, to Mr. Gardoqui, and to the Delegates of South Carolina in Congress.

I had the honor to inform you, in my last letter, of the parliament's being transferred to Troyes. To put an end to the tumults in Paris, some regiments were brought nearer, the patrols were strengthened and multiplied, some mutineers punished by imprisonment; it produced the desired effect. It is confidently believed, however, that the parliament will be immediately recalled, the stamp tax and land tax repealed, and other means devised of accommodating their receipts and expenditures. Those supposed to be in contemplation, are a rigorous levy of the old tax of the *deux vingtiemes*, on the rich, who had, in a great measure, withdrawn their property from it, as well as on the poor, on whom it had principally fallen. This will greatly increase the receipts; while they are proceeding on the other hand, to reform their expenses far beyond what they had promised. It is said these reformations will amount to eighty millions. Circumstances render these measures more and more pressing. I mentioned to you in my last letter, that the officer charged by the ministry to watch the motion of the British squadron, had returned with information that it had sailed westwardly. The fact was not true. He had formed his conclusion too hastily, and thus led the ministry into error. The King of Prussia, urged on by England, has pressed more and more the affairs of Holland, and lately has given to the States General of Holland, four days only to comply with his demand. This measure would, of itself, have rendered it impossible for France to proceed longer in the line of accommodation with Prussia. In the same moment, an event takes place, which seems to render all attempt at accommodation idle. The Turks have declared war against the Russians, and that under circumstances which exclude all prospect of preventing its taking place. The King of Prussia having deserted his ancient friends, there remains only France and Turkey, perhaps Spain also, to oppose the two empires, Russia and England. By such a piece of Quixotism, France might plunge herself into ruin with the Turks and Dutch, but would save neither. But there is certainly a confederacy secretly in contemplation, of which the public have not yet the smallest suspicion; that is, between France and the two empires. I think it sure that Russia has desired this, and that the Emperor, after some hesitation, has acceded. It rests on this country to close. Her indignation against the King of Prussia will be some spur. She will thereby save her party in Holland, and only abandon the Turks to that fate she cannot ward off, and which their precipitation has brought on themselves, by the instigations of the English ambassador at the Porte, and against the remonstrances of the French ambassador. Perhaps this formidable combination, should it take place, may prevent the war of the western powers, as it would seem that neither England nor Prussia would carry their false calculations so far, as, with the aid of the Turks only, to oppose themselves to such a force. In that case, the Patriots of Holland would be peaceably established in the powers of their government, and the war go on against the Turks only, who would probably be driven from Europe. This new arrangement would be a total change of the European system, and a favorable one for our friends. The probability of a general war, in which this country will be engaged on one side, and England on the other, has appeared to me sufficient to justify my writing to our agents in the different ports of France, to put our merchants on their guard, against risking their property in French or English bottoms. The Emperor, instead of tracing back his steps in Brabant, as was expected, has pursued the less honorable plan of decoying his subjects thence by false pretences, to let themselves be invested by his troops, and this done, he dictates to them his own terms. Yet it is not certain the matter will end with that.

The Count de Moustier is nominated Minister Plenipotentiary to America; and a frigate is ordered to Cherbourg, to carry him over. He will endeavor to sail by the middle of the next month, but if any delay should make him pass over the whole of October, he will defer his voyage to the spring, being unwilling to take a winter passage. Monsieur de St. Priest is sent Ambassador to Holland, in the room of Monsieur de Verac, appointed to Switzerland. The Chevalier de Luzerne might, I believe, have gone to Holland, but he preferred a general promise of promotion, and the possibility that it might be to the court of London. His prospects are very fair. His brother, the Count de la Luzerne, (now Governor in the West Indies,) is appointed minister of the marine, in the place of Monsieur de Castries, who has resigned. The Archbishop of Thoulouse is appointed *ministre principale*, and his brother, Monsieur de Brienne, minister of war, in the place of Monsieur de Segur. The department of the Comptroller has had a very rapid succession of tenants. From Monsieur de Calonnes it passed to Monsieur de Forqueux, from him to Villedeuil, and from him to Lambert, who holds it at present, but divided with a Monsieur Cabarrus, (whom I believe you knew in Spain,) who is named *Directeur du tresor royal*, the office into which M. Neckar came at first. I had the honor to inform you, that before the departure of the Count de Luzerne to his government in the West Indies, I had pressed on him the patronage of our trade with the French islands; that he appeared well disposed, and assured me he would favor us as much as his instructions, and the laws of the colonies, would permit. I am in hopes these dispositions will be strengthened by his residence in the islands, and that his acquaintance among the people there, will be an additional motive to favor them. Probably they will take advantage of his appointment, to press indulgences in commerce with us. The ministry is of a liberal complexion, and well disposed to us. The war may add to the motives for opening their islands to other resources for their subsistence, and for doing what may be agreeable to us. It seems to me, at present, then, that the moment of the arrival of the Count de La Luzerne, will be the moment for trying to obtain a freer access to their islands. It would be very material to do this, if possible, in a permanent way, that is to say, by treaty. But I know of nothing we have to offer in equivalent. Perhaps the payment of our debt to them might be made use of as some inducement, while they are so distressed for money. Yet the borrowing the money in Holland will be rendered more difficult by the same event, in proportion as it will increase the demand for money by other powers.

The gazettes of Leyden and France to this date are enclosed, together with some pamphlets on the internal affairs of this country.

I have the honor to be, with sentiments of the most perfect esteem and respect, Sir, your most obedient, and most humble servant.

JOHN JAY, 1787, 6:356 ~ *THE PRESENT PACIFICATION IS CONSIDERED BY MOST AS ONLY A SHORT TRUCE.*

To John Jay[1]
Paris, November 3, 1787

Sir, My last letters to you were of the 8th and 27th of October. In the former, I mentioned to you the declaration of this country, that they would interpose with force, if the Prussian troops entered Holland; the entry of those troops into Holland; the declaration of England, that if France did oppose force, they would consider it as an act of war; the naval armaments on both sides; the nomination of the Bailli de Suffrein as Generalissimo on the ocean; and the cold reception of Mr. Granville here, with his conciliatory propositions, as so many symptoms which seemed to indicate a certain and, immediate rupture. It was indeed universally and hourly expected. But the King of Prussia, a little before these last events, got wind of the alliance on the carpet between France and the two empires; he awaked to the situation in which that would place him; he made some applications to the court of St. Petersburg, to divert the Empress from the proposed alliance, and supplicated the court of London not to abandon him. That court had also received a hint of the same project; both seemed to suspect, for the first time, that it would be possible for France to abandon the Turks, and that they were likely to get more than they had played for at Constantinople; for they had meant nothing more there, than to divert the Empress and Emperor from the affairs of the west, by employing them in the east, and at the same time, to embroil them with France as the patroness of the Turks. The court of London engaged not to abandon Prussia: but both of them relaxed a little the tone of their proceedings. The King of Prussia sent a Mr. Alvensleben here

---

1 In addition to a general observation on the political situation on Europe, toward the end of the letter Jefferson seemingly counsels against the ransom payments beginning with, "The purpose of sending you this last..."

expressly to explain and soothe; the King of England, notwithstanding the cold reception of his propositions by Granville, renewed conferences here through Eden and the Duke of Dorset. The Minister, in the affection of his heart for peace, readily joined in conference, and a declaration and counter-declaration were cooked up at Versailles, and sent to London for approbation. They were approved, arrived here at one o'clock the 27th, were signed that night at Versailles, and on the next day, I had the honor of enclosing them to you, under cover to the Count de Moustier, whom I supposed still at Brest, dating my letter as of the 27th, by mistake for the 28th. Lest, however, these papers should not have got to Brest before the departure of the Count de Moustier, I now enclose you other copies.[1] The English declaration states a notification of this court, in September, by Barthelemy, their Minister at London, "that they would send succours into Holland," as the first cause of England's arming; desires an explanation of the intentions of this court, as to the affairs of Holland, and proposes to disarm; on condition, however, that the King of France shall not retain any hostile views in any quarter, for what has been done in Holland. This last phrase was to secure Prussia, according to promise. The King of France acknowledges the notification by his Minister at London, promises he will do nothing in consequence of it, declares he has no intention to intermeddle with force in the affairs of Holland, and that

---

1 [The annexed are translations of the declaration and counter-declaration, referred to in the preceding letter.]

Declaration. The events which have taken place in the republic of the United provinces, appearing no longer to leave any subject of discussion, and still less of dispute, between the two courts, the undersigned are authorized to ask, if it be the intention of his most Christian Majesty to act in pursuance of the notification given, on the 16th of last month, by the Minister Plenipotentiary of his most Christian Majesty, which, announcing his purpose of aiding Holland, has occasioned maritime armaments on the part of his Majesty, which armaments have become reciprocal. If the court of Versailles is disposed to explain itself on this subject, and on the conduct adopted towards the republic, in a manner conformably to the desire evinced by each party, to preserve a good understanding between the two courts, it being also understood, at the same time, that no hostile view is entertained in any quarter, in consequence of the past; his Majesty, always eager to manifest his concurrence in the friendly sentiments of his most Christian Majesty, agrees forthwith that the armaments, and, in general, all preparations for war, shall be mutually discontinued, and that the marines of the two nations shall be placed on the footing of a peace establishment, such as existed on the first of January of the present year. Signed. Dorset Wm. Eden. At Versailles, the 27th of October, 1787.

Counter-Declaration. It neither being, nor ever having been, the intention of his Majesty to interpose by force in the affairs of the republic of the United provinces, the communication made to the court of London by M. Barthelemy, having had no other object than to announce to that court an intention, the motives of which no longer exist, especially since the King of Prussia has made known his resolution, his Majesty makes no difficulty in declaring, that he has no wish to act in pursuance of the communication aforesaid, and that he entertains no hostile view in any quarter, relative to what has passed in Holland. Consequently, his Majesty, desiring to concur in the sentiments of his Britannic Majesty, for the preservation of a good understanding between the two courts, consents with pleasure to the proposition of his Britannic Majesty, that the armaments, and, in general, all preparations for war, shall be mutually discontinued, and that the marines of the two nations shall be replaced upon the footing of the peace establishment, as it existed on the first day of January of the present year. Signed. Montmorin. At Versailles, the 27th of October, 1787.

he will entertain hostile views in no quarter, for what has been done there. He disavows having ever had any intention to interpose with force in the affairs of that republic. This disavowal begins the sentence, which acknowledges he had notified the contrary to the court of London, and it includes no apology to soothe the feelings which may be excited in the breasts of the Patriots of Holland, at hearing the King declare he never did intend to aid them with force, when promises to do this were the basis of those very attempts to better their constitution, which have ended in its ruin, as well as their own.

I have analyzed these declarations, because, being somewhat wrapped up in their expressions, their full import might escape, on a transient reading; and it is necessary it should not escape. It conveys to us the important lesson, that no circumstances of morality, honor, interest, or engagement, are sufficient to authorize a secure reliance on any nation, at all times, and in all positions. A moment of difficulty, or a moment of error, may render forever useless the most friendly dispositions in the King, in the major part of his ministers, and the whole of his nation. The present pacification is considered by most as only a short truce. They calculate on the spirit of the nation, and not on the agued hand which guides its movements. It is certain, that from this moment the whole system of Europe changes. Instead of counting together England, Austria, and Russia, as heretofore, against France, Spain, Holland, Prussia, and Turkey, the division will probably be England, Holland, and Prussia, against France, Austria, Russia, and perhaps Spain. This last power is not sure, because the dispositions of its heir apparent are not sure. But whether the present be truce or peace, it will allow time to mature the conditions of the alliance between France and the two empires, always supposed to be on the carpet. It is thought to be obstructed by the avidity of the Emperor, who would swallow a good part of Turkey, Silesia, Bavaria, and the rights of the Germanic body. To the two or three first articles, France might consent, receiving in gratification a well-rounded portion of the Austrian Netherlands, with the islands of Candia, Cyprus, Rhodes, and perhaps Lower Egypt. But all this is in embryo, uncertainly known, and counterworked by the machinations of the courts of London and Berlin.

The following solution of the British armaments is supposed in a letter of the 25th ultimo, from Colonel Blachden of Connecticut, now at Dunkirk, to the Marquis de Lafayette. I will cite it in his own words: "A gentleman who left London two days ago, and came to this place to-day, informs me that it is now generally supposed that Mr. Pitt's great secret, which has puzzled the whole nation so long, and to accomplish which design the whole force of the nation is armed, is to make a vigorous effort for the recovery of America. When I recollect the delay they have made in delivering the forts in America, and that little more than a year ago, one of the British ministry wrote to the King a letter, in which were these remarkable words, 'if your Majesty pleases, America may yet be yours;' add to this, if it were possible for the present ministry in England to effect such a matter, they would secure their places and their power for a long time, and should they fail in the end, they would be certain of holding them during the attempt, which it is in their power to prolong as much as they please, and, at all events, they would boast of having endeavored the recovery of what a former ministry had abandoned — it is possible." A similar surmise has come in a letter from a person in Rotterdam to one at this place. I am satisfied that the King of England believes the mass of our people to be tired of their independence, and desirous of returning under his government; and that the same opinion prevails in the ministry and nation. They have hired their news writers to repeat this lie in their gazettes so long, that they have become the dupes of it themselves. But there is no occasion to recur to this, in order to account for their arming. A more rational purpose avowed, that purpose executed, and when executed, a solemn agreement to disarm, seem to leave no doubt that the re-establishment of the Stadtholder was their object. Yet it is possible, that having found that this court will not make war in this moment for any ally, new views may arise, and they may think the moment favorable for executing any purposes they may have, in our quarter. Add to this, that reason is of no aid in calculating their movements. We are, therefore, never safe till our magazines are filled with arms. The present season of truce or peace, should, in my opinion, be improved without a moment's respite, to effect this essential object, and no means be omitted, by which money may be obtained for the purpose. I say this, however, with due deference to the opinion of Congress, who are better judges of the necessity and practicability of the measure.

I mentioned to you, in a former letter, the application I had made to the Dutch ambassadors and Prussian envoy, for the protection of Mr. Dumas. The latter soon after received an assurance, that he was put under the protection of the States of Holland; and the Dutch Ambassador called on me a few days ago, to inform me, by instruction from his constituents, "that the States General had received a written application from Mr. Adams, praying their protection of Dumas; that they had instructed their *greffier*, Fagel, to assure Mr. Adams, by letter, that he was under the protection of the States of Holland; but to inform him, at the same time, that Mr. Dumas' conduct, out of the line of his office, had been so extraordinary, that they would expect *de l'honnetete de* Mr. Adams, that he would charge some other person with the affairs of the United States, during his absence."

Your letter of September the 8th has been duly received. I shall pay due attention to the instructions relative to the medals, and give any aid I can in the case of Boss' vessel. As yet, however, my endeavors to find Monsieur Pauly, *avocat au conseil d'etat, rue Coquilliere*, have been ineffectual. There is no such person living in that street. I found a Monsieur Pauly, *avocat au parlement*, in another part of the town; he opened the letter, but said it could not mean him. I shall advertise in the public papers. If that fails, there will be no other chance of finding him. Mr. Warnum will do well, therefore, to send some other description by which the person may be found. Indeed, some friend of the party interested should be engaged to follow up this business, as it will require constant attention, and probably a much larger sum of money than that named in the bill enclosed in Mr. Warnum's letter.

I have the honor to enclose you a letter from O'Bryan to me, containing information from Algiers, and one from Mr. Montgomery, at Alicant. The purpose of sending you this last, is to show you how much the difficulties of ransom are increased since the Spanish negotiations. The Russian captives have cost about eight thousand *livres* apiece, on an average. I certainly have no idea that we should give any such sum; and, therefore, if it should be the sense of Congress to give such a price, I would be glad to know it by instruction. My idea is, that we should not ransom, but on the footing of the nation which pays least, that it may be as little worth their while to go in pursuit of us, as any nation. This is cruelty to the individuals now in captivity, but kindness to the hundreds that would soon be so, were we to make it worth the while of those pirates to go out of the Straits in quest of us. As soon as money is provided, I shall put this business into train. I have taken measures to damp at Algiers all expectations of our proposing to ransom, at any price. I feel the distress this must occasion to our countrymen there, and their connections; but the object of it is their ultimate good, by bringing down their holders to such a price as we ought to pay, instead of letting them remain in such expectations as cannot be gratified. The gazettes of France and Leyden, accompany this.

I have the honor to be, with sentiments of the most perfect esteem and respect, Sir, your most obedient humble servant.

JAMES MADISON, 1787, 6:385 - *PROTECTION AGAINST STANDING ARMIES.*

To James Madison[1]
Paris, December 20, 1787

Dear Sir, My last to you was of October the 8th, by the Count de Moustier. Yours of July the 18th, September the 6th and October the 24th, were successively received, yesterday, the day before, and three or four days before that. I have only had time to read the letters; the printed papers communi-

---

1 By December 1787, Jefferson was prepared to offer his first thoughtful analysis of the merits and shortcomings of the newly proposed American Constitution, assuring Madison that he liked very much "the general idea of framing a government which should go on of itself peaceably, without needing continual recurrence to the state legislatures." Jefferson further indicated his approval of its organization in three major branches, on the principle of checks and balances; its assignment of the power to levy taxes to the "greater house" (since this preserves inviolate "the fundamental principle that the people are not to be taxed but by representatives chosen immediately by themselves"); and its "captivating" compromise of the conflicting claims between the great and little states. He also commended the substitution of the method of voting by persons instead of by states, and the executive's veto "with a third of either house" over legislation, although he added that the judiciary should have been associated in this with the executive in some fashion, a feature that Madison had repeatedly but unsuccessfully urged in the Convention. But there were also things — doubtless reminiscent of the charges Jefferson leveled at the British King in the Declaration of Independence — that Jefferson did not embrace. Principally, these include the omission of a bill of rights and, secondly, the abandonment of the principle of rotation in office, particularly in the case of the president (Koch 1950, 40-41).

cated with them, however interesting, being obliged to lie over till I finish my dispatches for the packet, which dispatches must go from hence the day after to-morrow. I have much to thank you for; first and most for the ciphered paragraph respecting myself. These little informations are very material towards forming my own decisions. I would be glad even to know, when any individual member thinks I have gone wrong in any instance, If I know myself, it would not excite ill blood in me, while it would assist to guide my conduct, perhaps to justify it, and to keep me to my duty, alert. I must thank you, too, for the information in Thomas Burke's case; though you will have found by a subsequent letter, that I have asked of you a further investigation of that matter. It is to gratify the lady who is at the head of the convent wherein my daughters are, and who, by her attachment and attention to them, lays me under great obligations. I shall hope, therefore, still to receive from you the result of all the further inquiries my second letter had asked. The parcel of rice which you informed me had miscarried, accompanied my letter to the Delegates of South Carolina. Mr. Bourgoin was to be the bearer of both, and both were delivered together into the hands of his relation here, who introduced him to me, and who, at a subsequent moment, undertook to convey them to Mr. Bourgoin. This person was 'an engraver, particularly recommended to Dr. Franklin and Mr. Hopkinson. Perhaps he may have mislaid the little parcel of rice among his baggage. I am much pleased that the sale of western lands is so successful. I hope they will absorb all the certificates of our domestic debt speedily, in the first place, and that then, offered for cash, they will do the same by our foreign ones.

The season admitting only of operations in the cabinet, and these being in a great measure secret, I have little to fill a letter. I will, therefore, make up the deficiency, by adding a few words on the Constitution proposed by our convention.

I like much the general idea of framing a government, which should go on of itself, peaceably, without needing continual recurrence to the State legislatures. I like the organization of the government into legislative, judiciary, and executive. I like the power given the legislature to levy taxes, and for that reason solely, I approve of the greater House being chosen by the people directly. For though I think a House so chosen, will be very far inferior to the present Congress, will be very illy qualified to legislate for the Union, for foreign nations, etc., yet this evil does not weigh against the good, of preserving inviolate the fundamental principle, that the people are not to be taxed but by representatives chosen immediately by themselves. I am captivated by the compromise of the opposite claims of the great and little States, of the latter to equal, and the former to proportional influence. I am much pleased, too, with the substitution of the method of voting by person, instead of that of voting by States; and I like the negative given to the Executive, conjointly with a third of either House; though I should have liked it better, had the judiciary been associated for that purpose, or invested separately with a similar power. There are other good things of less moment. I will now tell you what I do not like. First, the omission of a bill of rights, providing clearly, and without the aid of sophism, for freedom of religion, freedom of the press, protection against standing armies, restriction of monopolies, the eternal and unremitting force of the habeas corpus laws, and trials by jury in all matters of fact triable by the laws of the land, and not by the laws of nations. To say, as Mr. Wilson does, that a bill of rights was not necessary, because all is reserved in the case of the general government which is not given, while in the particular ones, all is given which is not reserved, might do for the audience to which it was addressed; but it is surely a gratis dictum, the reverse of which might just as well be said; and it is opposed by strong inferences from the body of the instrument, as well as from the omission of the cause of our present Confederation, which had made the reservation in express terms. It was hard to conclude, because there has been a want of uniformity among the States as to the cases triable by jury, because some have been so incautious as to dispense with this mode of trial in certain cases, therefore, the more prudent States shall be reduced to the same level of calamity. It would have been much more just and wise to have concluded the other way, that as most of the States had preserved with jealousy this sacred palladium of liberty, those who had wandered, should be brought back to it; and to have established general right rather than general wrong. For I consider all the ill as established, which may be established. I have a right to nothing, which another has a right to take away; and Congress will have a right to take away trials by jury in all civil cases. Let me add, that a bill of rights is what the people are entitled to against every government on earth, general or particular; and what no just government should refuse, or rest on inference.

The second feature I dislike, and strongly dislike, is the abandonment, in every instance, of the principle of rotation in office, and most particularly in the case of the President. Reason and experience tell us, that the first magistrate will always be reelected if he may be reelected. He is then an officer for life. This once observed, it becomes of so much consequence to certain nations, to have a friend or a foe at the head of our affairs, that they will interfere with money and with arms. A Galloman, or an Angloman, will be supported by the nation he befriends. If once elected, and at a second or third election outvoted by one or two votes, he will pretend false votes, foul play, hold possession of the reins of government, be supported by the States voting for him, especially if they be the central ones, lying in a compact body themselves, and separating their opponents; and they will be aided by one nation in Europe, while the majority are aided by another. The election of a President of America, some years hence, will be much more interesting to certain nations of Europe, than ever the election of a King of Poland was. Reflect on all the instances in history, ancient and modern, of elective monarchies, and say if they do not give foundation for my fears; the Roman 'Emperors, the Popes while they were of any importance, the German Emperors till they became hereditary in practice, the Kings of Poland, the Deys of the Ottoman dependencies. It may be said, that if elections are to be attended with these disorders, the less frequently they are repeated the better. But experience says, that to free them from disorder, they must be rendered less interesting by a necessity of change. No foreign power, nor domestic party, will waste their blood and money to elect a person, who must go out at the end of a short period. The power of removing every fourth year by the vote of the people, is a power which they will not exercise, and if they were disposed to exercise it, they would not be permitted. The King of Poland is removable every day by the diet. But they never remove him. Nor would Russia, the Emperor, etc., permit them to do it. Smaller objections are, the appeals on matters of fact as well as laws, and the binding all persons, legislative, executive, and judiciary by oath, to maintain that constitution. I do not pretend to decide, what would be the best method of procuring the establishment of the manifold good things in this constitution, and of getting rid of the bad. Whether by adopting it, in hopes of future amendment; or after it shall have been duly weighed and canvassed by the people, after seeing the parts they generally dislike, and those they generally approve, to say to them, "We see now what you wish. You are willing to give to your federal government such and such powers; but you wish, at the same time, to have such and such fundamental rights secured to you, and certain sources of convulsion taken away. Be it so. Send together deputies again. Let them establish your fundamental rights by a sacrosanct declaration, and let them pass the parts of the Constitution you have approved. These will give powers to your federal government sufficient for your happiness."

This is what might be said, and would probably produce a speedy, more perfect and more permanent form of government. At all events, I hope you will not be discouraged from making other trials, if the present one should fail. We are never permitted to despair of the commonwealth. I have thus told you freely what I like, and what I dislike, merely as a matter of curiosity; for I know it is not in my power to offer matter of information to your judgment, which has been formed after hearing and weighing everything which the wisdom of man could offer on these subjects. I own, I am not a friend to a very energetic government. It is always oppressive. It places the governors indeed more at their ease, at the expense of the people. The late rebellion in Massachusetts has given more alarm, than I think it should have done. Calculate that one rebellion in thirteen States in the course of eleven years, is but one for each State in a century and a half. No country should be so long without one. Nor will any degree of power in the hands of government, prevent insurrections. In England, where the hand of power is heavier than with us, there are seldom half a dozen years without an insurrection. In France, where it is still heavier, but less despotic, as Montesquieu supposes, than in some other countries, and where there are always two or three hundred thousand men ready to crush insurrections, there have been three in the course of the three years I have been here, in every one of which greater numbers were engaged than in Massachusetts, and a great deal more blood was spilt. In Turkey, where the sole nod of the despot is death, insurrections are the events of every day. Compare again the ferocious depredations of their insurgents, with the order, the moderation and .the almost self-extinguishment of ours. And say, finally, whether peace is best preserved by giving energy to the government, or information to the people. This last is the most certain, and the most legitimate engine of government. Educate and inform the whole mass of the people. Enable them to see that it is their interest 'to preserve peace and order, and they will preserve them. And it requires no very high degree of education to convince them of this. They are the only sure reliance for the preservation of our liberty. After all, it is my principle that the will of the majority should prevail. If they approve the proposed constitution in all its parts, I shall concur in it cheerfully, in hopes they will amend it, whenever they shall find it works wrong. This reliance cannot deceive us, as long as we remain virtuous; and I think we shall be so, as long as agriculture is our principal object, which will be the case, while there remains vacant lands in any part of America. When we get piled upon one another in large cities, as in Europe, we shall become corrupt as in Europe, and go to eating one another as they do there. I have tired you by this time with disquisitions which you have already heard repeated by others a thousand and a thousand times; and therefore, shall only add assurances of the esteem and attachment with which I have the honor to be, dear Sir, your affectionate friend and servant.

P. S. The instability of our laws is really an immense evil. I think it would be well to provide in our constitutions, that there shall always be a twelve-month between the engrossing a bill and passing it; that it should then be offered to its passage without changing a word; and that if circumstances should be thought to require a speedier passage, it should take two-thirds of both Houses, instead of a bare majority.

ALEXANDER DONALD, 1788, 6:425 - *THOUGH PEACE IS RATHER PROBABLE, WAR IS VERY POSSIBLE.*

To Mr. A. Donald[1]

Paris, February 7, 1788.

Dear Sir, I received duly your friendly letter of November the 12th. By this time, you will have seen published by Congress the new regulations obtained from this court, in favor of our commerce. You will observe, that the arrangement relative to tobacco is a continuation of the order of Berni for five years, only leaving the price to be settled between the buyer and seller. You will see, too, that all contracts for tobacco are forbidden, till it arrives in France. Of course, your proposition for a contract is precluded. I fear the prices here will be low, especially if the market be crowded. You should be particularly attentive to the article, which requires that the tobacco should come in French or American bottoms, as this article will, in no instance, be departed from.

---

1 Alexander Donald was a Richmond tobacco merchant and close friend of Jefferson (Risjord 1978, 299).

I wish with all my soul, that the nine first conventions may accept the new constitution, because this will secure to us the good it contains, which I think great and important. But I equally wish that the four latest conventions, whichever they be, may refuse to accede to it, till a declaration of rights be annexed. This would probably command the offer of such a declaration, and thus give to the whole fabric, perhaps, as much perfection as any one of that kind ever had. By a declaration of rights, I mean one which shall stipulate freedom of religion, freedom of the press, freedom of commerce against monopolies, trial by juries in all cases, no suspensions of the habeas corpus, no standing armies. These are fetters against doing evil, which no honest government should decline. There is another strong feature in the new Constitution, which I as strongly dislike. That is, the perpetual re-eligibility of the President. Of this, I expect no amendment at present, because I do not see that anybody has objected to it on your side the water. But it will be productive of cruel distress to our country, even in your day and mine. The importance to France and England, to have our government in the hands of a friend or a foe, will occasion their interference by money, and even by arms. Our President will be of much more consequence to them than a King of Poland. We must take care, however, that neither this, nor any other objection to the new form, produces a schism in our Union. That would be an incurable evil, because near friends falling out, never re-unite cordially; whereas, all of us going together, we shall be sure to cure the evils of our new Constitution, before they do great harm. The box of books I had taken the liberty to address to you, is but just gone from Havre for New York. I do not see, at present, any symptoms strongly indicating war. It is true, that the distrust existing between the two courts of Versailles and London is so great, that they can scarcely do business together. However, the difficulty and doubt of obtaining money make both afraid to enter into war. The little preparations for war, which we see, are the effect of distrust, rather than of a design to commence hostilities. And in such a state of mind, you know, small things may produce a rupture; so that though peace is rather probable, war is very possible.

Your letter has kindled all the fond recollections of ancient times; recollections much dearer to me than anything I have known since. There are minds which can be pleased by honors and preferments; but I see nothing in them but envy and enmity. It is only necessary to possess them, to know how little they contribute to happiness, or rather how hostile they are to it. No attachments soothe the mind so much as those contracted in early life; nor do I recollect any societies which have given me more pleasure, than those of which you have partaken with me. I had rather be shut up in a very modest cottage, with my books, my family and a few old friends, dining on simple bacon, and letting the world roll on as it liked, than to occupy the most splendid post, which any human power can give. I shall be glad to hear from you often. Give me the small news as well as the great. Tell Dr. Currie, that I believe I am indebted to him a letter, but that like the mass of our countrymen, I am not, at this moment, able to pay all my debts; the post being to depart in an hour, and the last stroke of a pen I am able to send by it, being that which assures you of the sentiments of esteem and attachment, with which I am, dear Sir, your affectionate friend and servant.

JOHN JAY, 1788, 7:2 ~ *THIS COUNTRY STILL PURSUES ITS LINE OF PEACE.*

To John Jay
Paris, May 4, 1788

Sir, I had the honor of addressing you in two letters of the 13th and 16th of March, from Amsterdam, and have since received Mr. Ramson's of February the 20th. I staid at Amsterdam about ten or twelve days after the departure of Mr. Adams, in hopes of seeing the million of the last year filled up. This, however, could not be accomplished on the spot. But the prospect was so good as to have dissipated all fears; and since my return here, I learn (not officially from our bankers but) through a good channel, that they have received near four hundred thousand *florins*, since the date of the statement I sent you, in my letter of March the 16th; and I presume we need not fear the completion of that loan, which will provide for all our purposes of the year 1788, as stated in that paper. I hope, therefore, to receive from the treasury orders in conformity thereto, that I may be able to proceed to the redemption of our captives. A provision for the purposes of the years, 1789 and 1790, as stated in the same paper, will depend on the ratification by Congress of Mr. Adams' bonds of this year, for another million of *florins*. But there arises a new call from this government, for its interest at least. Their silence, hitherto, has made it be believed in general, that they consented to the non-payment of our interest to them, in order to accommodate us. You will perceive in the seventy-fifth and seventy-sixth pages of the *compte rendu*, which I have the honor to send you, that they call for this interest, and will publish whether it be paid or not; and by No. 25, page eighty-one, that they count on its regular receipt, for the purposes of the year. These calls, for the first days of January, 1789 and 1790, will amount to about a million and a half of *florins* more; and if to be raised by loan, it must be for two millions, as well to cover the expenses of the loan, as that loans are not opened for fractions of millions. This publication seems to render a provision for this interest as necessary, as for that of Amsterdam.

I had taken measures to have it believed at Algiers, that our government withdrew its attention from our captives there. This was to prepare their captors for the ransoming them at a reasonable price. I find, however, that Captain O'Bryan is apprized that I have received some authority on this subject. He writes me a cruel letter, supposing me the obstacle to their redemption. Their own interest requires that I should leave them to think thus hardly of me. Were the views of government communicated to them, they could not keep their own secret, and such a price would be demanded for them, as Congress, probably, would think ought not to be given, lest it should be the cause of involving thousands of others of their citizens in the same condition. The moment I have money, the business shall be set in motion.

By a letter from Joseph Chiappe, our agent at Mogadore, I am notified of a declaration of the Emperor of Morocco, that if the States General of the United Netherlands do not, before the month of May, send him an ambassador, to let him know whether it is war or peace between them, he will send one to them with five frigates; and that if their dispositions be unfavorable, their frigates shall proceed to America to make prizes on the Dutch, and to sell them there. It seems to depend on the Dutch, therefore, whether the Barbary powers shall learn the way to our coasts, and whether we shall have to decide the question of the legality of selling in our ports, vessels taken from them. I informed you, in a former letter, of the declaration made by the court of Spain to that of London, relative to its naval armament, and also of the declaration of the Count de Montmorin to the Russian minister here, on the same subject. I have good information, that the court of Spain has itself made a similar and formal declaration to the minister of Russia, at Madrid. So that Russia is satisfied, she is not the object. I doubt whether the English are equally satisfied as to themselves. The season has hitherto prevented any remarkable operation between the Turks and the two empires. The war, however, will probably go on, and the season now admits of more important events. The Empress has engaged Commodore Paul Jones in her service. He is to have the rank of rear admiral, with a separate command, and it is understood that he is in no case to be commanded. He will probably be opposed to the Captain Pacha on the Black Sea. He received this invitation at Copenhagen, and as the season for commencing the campaign was too near to admit time for him to ask and await the permission of Congress, he accepted the offer, only stipulating, that he should be always free to return to the orders of Congress whenever called for, and that he should not be expected to bear arms against France. He conceived that the experience he should gain, would enable him to be more useful to the United States, should they ever have occasion for him. It has been understood, that Congress had had it in contemplation to give him the grade of rear admiral, from the date of the action of the *Serapis*, and it is supposed, that such a mark of their approbation, would have a favorable influence on his fortune in the north. Copies of the letters which passed between him and the Danish Minister are herewith transmitted. I shall immediately represent to Count Bernstorff, that the demand for our prizes can have no connection with a treaty of commerce; that there is no reason why the claims of our seamen should await so distant and uncertain an event; and press the settlement of this claim.

This country still pursues its line of peace. The ministry seem now all united in it; some from a belief of their inability to carry on a war; others from a desire to arrange their internal affairs, and improve their constitution. The differences between the King and parliaments, threaten a serious issue. Many symptoms indicate that the government has in contemplation some 'act of high-handed authority. An extra number of printers have, for several days, been employed, the apartment wherein they are at work being surrounded by a body of guards, who permit nobody either to come out or go in. The commanders of the provinces, civil and military, have been ordered to be at their stations on a certain day of the ensuing week. They are accordingly gone; so that the will of the King is probably to be announced through the whole kingdom, on the same day. The parliament of Paris, apprehending that some innovation is to be attempted, which may take from them the opportunity of deciding on it after it shall be made known, came last night to the resolution, of which I have the honor to enclose you a manuscript copy. This you will perceive to be, in effect, a declaration of rights. I am obliged to close here the present letter, lest I should miss the opportunity of conveying it by a passenger who is to call for it. Should the delay of the packet admit any continuation of these details, they shall be the subject of another letter, to be forwarded by post. The gazettes of Leyden and France accompany this. I have the honor to be, with sentiments of the most perfect esteem and respect, Sir, your most obedient, and most humble servant.

BOARD OF TREASURY, 1788, 7:9 - *IT WOULD BE CRUELTY TO THE CAPTIVES TO LET THEM KNOW WE ARE PROCEEDING TO THEIR REDEMPTION.*

To the Honorable Board of the Treasury
Paris, May 16, 1788

Gentlemen, In a letter of March 29th, which I had the honor of addressing you from Amsterdam, I stated to you what had passed till that date relative to our money affairs in England, and I enclosed you an estimate of these, which looks forward to the end of the year 1790. I mentioned to you also, that the prospect of filling up the loan of the last million was at that moment good, so that I thought you might be at ease as to the payment of the June interest. I have now the pleasure to enclose you a letter from our bankers of the 8th instant, wherein they inform me they have sold bonds enough to pay the June interest and have a surplus sufficient to replace the moneys lent from the Virginia fund, and by Mr. Grand. These advances were but momentary accommodations, made under the mistaken idea that the money was in Amsterdam ready to replace them, and it was not in idea to inscribe them on the roll of the debts of the United States, to take their turn of payment. You will therefore, I hope, think me justifiable in having them replaced immediately, as these is money enough now for that purpose, over and above the June interest. The balance due to Gateau is for one of the medals I had your orders to have made, and has been due upwards of a twelvemonth. Mr. Short's salary I suppose included under your general order that the diplomatic calls shall be regularly paid by our bankers. So far then, I shall venture to draw immediately, perhaps also for the little balance due to Ast, whose distresses call loudly for assistance.[1] He has been obliged to carry his clothes to the pawnbrokers

---

1 William Short was Jefferson's protégé and private secretary; William Ast, secretary to the consulate, was acting as American consul at Lorient (Kimball 1950; 11, 308).

to raise money for his subsistence. All the other articles of the estimate will await your orders, which you will therefore be pleased to give as you think proper. The foreign officers had proposed a meeting, the object of which was, as I heard, to address Congress in terms which would have been very disagreeable, and at the same time to present a petition to the King, claiming his interposition. This would have made a great deal of noise, and produced very disagreeable effects. This was a few days before I went to Amsterdam. I saw Colonel Gouvion the day before I set out, and desired him to quiet them till my return, explaining to him that one of the objects of my journey would be to enable you to pay them. I have since my return, informed them of the prospect of payment, and that your orders for that purpose may be hoped by the month of June. A letter from O'Brian, at Algiers, shows me that he has had an intimation of my being authorized to redeem them, and imputes the delay to me. I have endeavored, on the contrary, to have it believed at Algiers, that the public will not interest itself in their redemption, having been assured by the General of the religious order who is to act for us, that if the *Dey* has the least expectations that the public will interfere, he will hold them at such prices as this order has never given, and cannot consent to give, because of the precedent, and that in this case we shall lose the benefit of their agency. Under these circumstances it would be cruelty to the captives to let them know we are proceeding to their redemption. They could not keep their own secret, and the indiscretion of any one of them might forever blast the prospect of their redemption. For I suppose it to be uncontrovertible that a regard to the safety and liberty of our seamen and citizens in general forbids us to give such prices for those in captivity as will draw on our vessels peculiarly the pursuit of those sea-dogs. It is for the good of the captives themselves, therefore, that we submit to be thought hardly of by them; but no time should be lost unnecessarily in proceeding to their redemption; nor shall a moment be lost after I shall be authorized by your order to receive the money. You perceive that by the extract from the letter of the bankers which I have the honor to enclose you, they expect to place speedily the rest of the bonds. I think I may venture to assure you they can do it at any moment if they are pushed. You know the misunderstandings which exist between these two houses. These are the cause of their not always saying as much as they might venture to say with truth. There is an error in the estimate I sent you, which must be explained. I omitted, when I set out from Paris, to ask Mr. Short for a state of the balance due him, and had always been ignorant of it, as the account remained between him and Mr. Grand. When making the estimate at Amsterdam, therefore, I was obliged to conjecture what that balance was, which I did from a very slight and mistaken circumstance as I now find. The balance due him, instead of being about 5,000 *livres*, as I had guessed, is 13,146 *livres*, as you will see by his account now enclosed.

I have the honor to be, with sentiments of the most perfect esteem and respect, Gentlemen, your most obedient, and most humble servant.

JOHN JAY, 1788, 7:15 ~ *BREAKING MEN TO MILITARY DISCIPLINE IS BREAKING THEIR SPIRITS TO PRINCIPLES OF PASSIVE OBEDIENCE.*

To John Jay[1]

Paris, May 23, 1788

Sir, When I wrote my letter of the 4th instant, I had no reason to doubt that a packet would have sailed on the 10th, according to the established order. The passengers had all, except one, gone down to Havre in this expectation. However, none have sailed, and perhaps none will sail, as I think the suppression of the packets is one of the economies in contemplation. An American merchant, concerned in the commerce of the whale oil, proposed to government to dispatch his ships from Havre and Boston at stated periods, and to take on board the French courier and mail, and the proposition has been well enough received. I avail myself of a merchant vessel going from Havre, to write the present.

In my letter of the 4th, I stated to you the symptoms which indicated that government had some great stroke of authority in contemplation. That night, they sent guards to seize Monsieur d'Epremenil and Monsieur Goisland, two members of parliament, in their houses. They escaped, and took sanctuary in the *Palais* (or parliament house). The parliament assembled itself extraordinarily, summoned the Dukes and Peers specially, and came to the resolution of the 5th, which they sent to Versailles by deputies, determined not to leave the palace till they received an answer. In the course of that night, a battalion of guards surrounded the house. The two members were taken by the officers from among their fellows, and sent off to prison, the one to Lyons, the other (d'Epremenil), the most obnoxious, to an island in the Mediterranean. The parliament then separated. On the 8th, a bed of justice was held at Versailles, wherein were enregistered the six ordinances which had been passed in Council, on the 1st of May, and which I now send you. They were in like manner enregistered in beds of justice, on the same day, in nearly all the parliaments of the kingdom. By these ordinances, 1. the criminal law is reformed, by abolishing examination on the *sellette*, which, like our holding up the hand at the bar, remained a stigma on the party, though innocent; by substituting an oath, instead of torture, on the *question prealable*, which is used after con-

---

1 As Ellis notes, so much history happened in prerevolutionary France during the last two years of Jefferson's ministry that it is not easy to summarize his shifting political positions, except perhaps to say that he presumed that France would emerge from the ferment as some kind of constitutional monarchy. Despite his earlier characterizations of the French king as a drunken sot who was completely out of touch with the needs and frustrations of the French people, by the summer of 1788 Jefferson had come to regard Louis as an enlightened ruler who was anxious to play a crucial role in forging political alliances between the nobility and the members of the Third Estate. This said, Jefferson's hopes for the recovery of political stability in France remained with the group of moderate and enlightened aristocrats, led by his good friend Lafayette, called the Patriots or the Patriot Party. Although he was prepared to acknowledge that the situations were fundamentally different, Jefferson seemed to regard the Patriots in France as counterparts to the Federalists in America; they were, he thought sensible of the abusive government under which they lived, longed for occasions of reforming it, and were dedicated to the establishment of a constitution which might assure their liberty (Ellis 1998, 128).

demnation, to make the prisoner discover his accomplices; (the torture abolished in 1789 [sic], was on the *question preparatoire*, previous to judgment, in order to make the prisoner accuse himself;) by allowing counsel to the prisoner for his defense; obliging the judges to specify in their judgments the offence for which he is condemned; and respiting execution a month, except in the case of sedition. This reformation is unquestionably good, and within the ordinary legislative powers of the crown. That it should remain to be made at this day proves that the monarch is the last person in his kingdom, who yields to the progress of philanthropy and civilization. 2. The organization of the whole judiciary department is changed, by the institution of subordinate jurisdictions, the taking from the parliaments the cognizance of all causes of less value than twenty thousand *livres* , reducing their numbers to about a fourth, and suppressing a number of special courts. Even this would be a great improvement, if it did not imply that the King is the only person in this nation who has any rights or any power. 3. The right of registering the laws is taken from the parliaments, and transferred to a Plenary court, created by the King. This last is the measure most obnoxious to all persons. Though the members are to be for life, yet a great proportion of them are from descriptions of men always candidates for the royal favor in other lines. As yet, the general consternation has not sufficiently passed over, to say whether the matter will end here. I send you some papers, which indicate symptoms of resistance. These are the resolution of the Noblesse of Brittany, the declaration of the Advocate General of Provence, which is said to express the spirit of that province; and the *Arret* of the Chatelet, which is the hustings court of the city of Paris. Their refusal to act under the new character assigned them, and the suspension of their principal functions, are very embarrassing. The clamors this will excite, and the disorders it may admit,' will be loud, and near to the royal ear and person. The parliamentary fragments permitted to remain, have already, some of them, refused, and probably all will refuse, to act under that form. The Assembly of the clergy, which happens to be sitting, have addressed the King to call the States General immediately. Of the Dukes and Peers (thirty-eight in number), nearly half are either minors or superannuated; two-thirds of the acting part seem disposed to avoid taking a part; the rest, about eight or nine; have refused, by letters to the King, to act in the new courts. A proposition excited among the Dukes and Peers, to assemble and address the King for a modification of the Plenary court, seems to show that the government would be willing to compromise on that head. It has been prevented by the Dukes and Peers in opposition, because they suppose that no modification to be made by the government will give to that body the form they desire, which is that of a representative of the nation. They foresee that if the government is forced to this, they will call them, as nearly as they can, in the ancient forms; in which case, less good will be expected from them. But they hope they may be got to concur in a declaration of rights, at least, so that the nation may be acknowledged to have some fundamental rights, not alterable by their ordinary legislature, and that this may form groundwork for future improvements. These seem to be the views of the most enlightened and disinterested characters of the opposition. But they may be frustrated by the nation's making no cry at all, or by a hasty and premature appeal to arms. There is neither head nor body in the nation to promise a successful opposition to two hundred thousand regular troops. Some think the army could not be depended on by the government; but the breaking men to military discipline, is breaking their spirits to principles of passive obedience. A firm, but quiet opposition will be the most likely to succeed. Whatever turn this crisis takes, a revolution in their constitution seems inevitable, unless foreign war supervene, to suspend the present contest. And a foreign war they will avoid, if possible, from an inability to get money. The loan of one hundred and twenty millions, of the present year, is filled up by such subscriptions as may be relied on. But that of eighty millions, proposed for the next year, cannot be filled up in the actual situation of things.

The Austrians have been successful in an attack upon Schabatz, intended as a preliminary to that of Belgrade. In that on Dubitza, another town in the neighborhood of Belgrade, they have been repulsed, and, as is suspected, with considerable loss. It is still supposed the Russian fleet will go into the Mediterranean, though it will be much retarded by the refusal of the English government, to permit its sailors to engage in the voyage. Sweden and Denmark are arming from eight to twelve ships of the line each. The English and Dutch treaties you will find in the Leyden gazettes of May the 9th and 13th. That between England and Prussia is supposed to be stationary. Monsieur de St. Priest, the ambassador from this court to the Hague, has either gone, or is on the point of going. The Emperor of Morocco has declared war against England. I enclose you his orders in our favor on that occasion. England sends a squadron to the Mediterranean for the protection of her commerce, and she is reinforcing her possessions in the two Indies. France is expecting the arrival of an embassy from Tippoo Saib, is sending some regiments to the West Indies, and a fleet of evolution into the Atlantic. Seven ships of the line and several frigates sailed from Cadiz on the 22d of April, destined to perform evolutions off the western islands, as the Spaniards say, but really to their American possessions, as is suspected. Thus, the several powers are, by little and little, taking the position of war, without an immediate intention of waging it. But that the present ill humor will finally end in war is doubted by nobody.

In my letter of February 5th, I had the honor of informing you of the discontent produced by our *Arret* of December the 20th, among the merchants of this country, and of the deputations from the chambers of commerce to the minister on that subject. The articles attacked were the privileges on the sale of our ships, and the *entrepot* for codfish. The former I knew to be valuable; the latter I supposed not so; because during the whole of the time we have had our free ports in this kingdom, we have never used them for the smuggling of fish. I concluded, therefore, the ports of *entrepot* would not be used for that purpose. I saw that the ministers would sacrifice something to quiet the merchants, and was glad to save the valuable article relative to our ships, by abandoning the useless one for our codfish. It was settled, therefore, in our conferences, that an *Arret* should be passed, abridging the former one only as to the *entrepot* of codfish. I was in Holland when the *Arret* came out; and did not get a copy of it till yesterday. Surprised to find that fish oil was thereby also excluded from the *entrepot*, I have been to-day to make some inquiry into the cause; and from what I can learn, I conclude it must have been a mere error in the clerk who formed the *Arret*, and it escaped attention on its passage. The *entrepot* of whale oil was not objected to by a single deputy at the conferences, and the excluding it is contrary to the spirit of encouragement the ministers have shown a disposition to give. I trust, therefore, I may get it altered on the first occasion which occurs, and I believe one will soon occur. In the meantime, we do not store a single drop for reexportation, as all which comes here is needed for the consumption of this country which will alone, according to appearances, become so considerable as to require all we can produce.

By a letter of the 8th instant, from our bankers, I learn that they had disposed of bonds enough to pay our June interest, and to replace the temporary advances made by Mr. Grand, and from a fund placed here by the State of Virginia. I have desired them, accordingly, to replace these moneys, which had been lent for the moment only, and in confidence of immediate repayment. They add that the payment of the June interest and the news from America, will, as they trust, enable them to place the remaining bonds of the last year's million. I suppose, indeed, that there is no doubt of it, and that none would have been expressed, if those two houses could draw better together than they do. In the meantime, I hope the treasury board will send an order for so much as may be necessary for executing the purposes of Congress, as to our captives at Algiers.

I send you herewith a Memoire of Monsieur Caseaux, whose name is familiar on the journals of Congress. He prepared it to be delivered to the King, but I believe he will think better, and not deliver it. The gazettes of France and Leyden accompany this. I have the honor to be, Sir, your most obedient, and most humble servant.

P. S. May 27, 1788. I have kept my letter open to the moment of Mr. Warville's departure, (he being the bearer of it,) that I might add any new incidents that should occur. The refusal of the Chatelet and Grande Chambre of Paris to act in the new character assigned them, continues. Many of the *grandes bailliages* accept, some conditionally, some fully. This will facilitate greatly the measures of government, and may possibly give them a favorable issue. The parliament of Thoulouse, considering the edicts as nullities, went on with their business. They have been exiled in consequence. Monsieur de St. Priest left Paris for the Hague, on the 23d. I mention this fact, because it denotes the acquiescence of this government in the late revolution there. A second division of a Spanish fleet will put to sea soon. Its destination not declared. Sweden is arming to a greater extent than was at first supposed. From twelve to sixteen sail of the line are spoken of, on good grounds. Denmark, for her own security, must arm in proportion to this.

JAMES MADISON, 1788, 7:93 - *DISCIPLINE WELL THE MILITIA AND GUARD THE MAGAZINES WITH THEM.*

To James Madison[1]
Paris, July 31, 1788

Dear Sir, My last letters to you were of the 3d and the 25th of May. Yours from Orange, of April the 22d, came to hand on the 10th instant.

My letter to Mr. Jay, containing all the public news that is well authenticated, I will not repeat it here, but add some details in the smaller way, which you may be glad to know. The disgrace of the Marquis de Lafayette, which at any other period of their history would have had the worst consequences for him, will, on the contrary, mark him favorably to the nation, at present. During the present administration, he can expect nothing; but perhaps it may serve him with their successors, whenever a change shall take place. No change of the Principal will probably take place before the meeting of the States General; though a change & to be' wished, for his operations do not answer the expectations formed of him. These had been calculated on his brilliancy in society. He is very feebly aided, too. Montmorin is weak, though a most worthy character. He is indolent and inattentive, too, in the extreme. Luzerne is considerably inferior in abilities to his brother, whom you know. He is a good man, too, but so much out of his element, that he has the air of one *huskanoyed.* The *Garde des sceaux* is considered as the Principal's bull dog, braving danger like the animal. His talents do not pass mediocrity. The Archbishop's brother, and the new minister Villedeuil, and Lambert, have no will of their own. They cannot raise money for the peace establishment the next year, without the States General; much less if there be war; and their administration will probably end with the States General.

Littlepage, who was here as a secret agent for the King of Poland, rather overreached himself. He wanted more money. The King furnished it, more than once. Still he wanted more, and thought to obtain a high bid by saying he was called for in America, and asking leave to go there. Contrary to his expectation, he received leave; but he went to Warsaw instead of America, and from thence to join the [NOTE: Several paragraphs of this letter are in cipher and a few words here could not be deciphered.] I do not know these facts certainly, but recollect them, by putting several things together. The

---

1 Brodie suggests that, for Jefferson, Paris in 1788 emerged as an increasingly exciting political experience. The growing threat of revolution delighted him, and he eagerly became a quiet, even secret, participant, consulting with Lafayette on several papers pertinent to the ever deepening crisis between the King and the Estates-General, which was to be convened in May 1789, the first time since 1614. While the stream of his letters back to the United States in 1788, particularly to Madison, reflect what would seem to be an almost total absorption in the beginnings of the potentially momentous social experiment, they also show that he expected it to move with a good deal more rationality and less upheaval than it did (Brodie 1975, 237).

King then sent an ancient secretary here, in whom he had much confidence, to look out for a correspondent, a mere letter writer for him. A happy hazard threw Mazzei in his way. He recommended him, and he is appointed. He has no diplomatic character whatever, but is to receive eight thousand *livres* a year, as an intelligencer. I hope this employment may have some permanence. The danger is, that he will overact his part.

The Marquis de la Luzerne had been for many years married to his brother's wife's sister, secretly. She was ugly and deformed, but sensible, amiable, and rather rich. When he was ambassador to London, with ten thousand guineas a year, the marriage was avowed, and he relinquished his cross of Malta, from which he derived a handsome revenue for life, and which was very open to advancement. Not long ago, she died. His real affection for her, which was great and unfeigned, and perhaps the loss of his order for so short-lived a satisfaction, has thrown him almost into a state of despondency. He is now here.

I send you a book of DuPont's, on the subject of the commercial treaty with England. Though its general matter may not be interesting, yet you will pick up in various parts of it, such excellent principles and observations, as will richly repay the trouble of reading it. I send you also, two little pamphlets of the Marquis de Condorcet, wherein is the most judicious statement I have seen, of the great questions which agitate this nation at present. The new regulations present a preponderance of good over their evil; but they suppose that the King can model the constitution at will, or, in other words, that his government is a pure despotism. The question then arising is, whether a pure despotism in a single head, or one which is divided among a king, nobles, priesthood, and numerous magistracy, is the least bad. I should be puzzled to decide; but I hope they will have neither, and that they are advancing to a limited, moderate government, in which the people will have a good share.

I sincerely rejoice at the acceptance of our new constitution by nine States. It is a good canvass, on which some strokes only want retouching. What these are, I think are sufficiently manifested by the general voice from north to south, which calls for a bill of rights. It seems pretty generally understood, that this should go to juries, habeas corpus, standing armies, printing, religion and monopolies. I conceive there may be difficulty in finding general modifications of these, suited to the habits of all the States. But if such cannot be found, then it is better to establish trials by jury, the right of habeas corpus, freedom of the press and freedom of religion, in all cases, and to abolish standing armies in time of peace, and monopolies in all cases, than not to do it in any. The few cases wherein these things may do evil, cannot be weighed against the multitude wherein the want of them will do evil. In disputes between a foreigner and a native, a trial by jury may be improper. But if this exception cannot be agreed to, the remedy will be to model the jury, by giving the *mediatas lingua*, in civil as well as criminal cases. Why suspend the habeas corpus in insurrections and rebellions? The parties who may be arrested may be charged instantly with a well defined crime; of course, the judge will remand them. If the public safety requires that the government should have a man imprisoned on less probable testimony, in those than in other emergencies, let him be taken and tried, retaken and retried, while the necessity continues, only giving him redress against the government, for damages. Examine the history of England. See how few of the cases of the suspension of the habeas corpus law, have been worthy of that suspension. They have been either real treason, wherein the parties might as well have been charged at once, or sham plots, where it was shameful they should ever have been suspected. Yet for the few cases wherein the suspension of the habeas corpus has done real good, that operation is now become habitual, and the minds of the nation almost prepared to live under its constant suspension. A declaration, that the federal government will never restrain the presses from printing anything they please, will not take away the liability of the printers for false facts printed. The declaration, that religious faith shall be unpunished, does not give impunity to criminal acts, dictated by religious error. The saying there shall be no monopolies, lessens the incitements to ingenuity, which is spurred on by the hope of a monopoly for a limited time, as of fourteen years; but the benefit of even limited monopolies is too doubtful, to be opposed to that of their general suppression. If no check can be found to keep the number of standing troops within safe bounds, while they are tolerated as far as necessary, abandon them altogether, discipline well the militia, and guard the magazines with them. More than magazine guards will be useless, if few, and dangerous, if many. No European nation can ever send against us such a regular army as we need fear, and it is hard, if our militia are not equal to those of Canada or Florida. My idea then, is, that though proper exceptions to these general rules are desirable, and probably practicable, yet if the exceptions cannot be agreed on, the establishment of the rules, in all cases, will do ill in very few. I hope, therefore, a bill of rights will be formed, to guard the people against the federal government, as they are already guarded against their State governments, in most instances. The abandoning the principle of necessary rotation in the Senate, has, I see, been disapproved by many; in the case of the President, by none. I readily, therefore, suppose my opinion wrong, when opposed by the majority, as in the former instance, and the totality, as in the latter. In this, however, I should have done it with more complete satisfaction, had we all judged from the same position.

Solicitations, which cannot be directly refused, oblige me to trouble you often, with letters recommending and introducing to you, persons who go from hence to America. I will beg the favor of you, to distinguish the letters wherein I appeal to recommendations from other persons, from those which I write on my own knowledge. In the former, it is never my intention to compromit myself or you. In both instances, I must beg you to ascribe the trouble I give you, to circumstances which do not leave me at liberty to decline it. I am, with very sincere esteem, dear Sir, your affectionate friend and servant.

HECTOR ST. JOHN DE CREVECOEUR, 1788, 7:113 – *WAR, HOWEVER,*
IS NOT THE MOST FAVORABLE MOMENT FOR DIVESTING THE MONARCHY
OF POWER.

To Monsieur de Creve-Coeur[1]

Paris, August 9, 1788

Dear Sir, While our second revolution is just brought to a happy end with you, yours here is but cleverly under way. For some days, I was really melancholy with the apprehension, that arms would be appealed to, and the opposition crushed in its first efforts. But things seem now to wear a better aspect. While the opposition keeps at its highest wholesome point, government, unwilling to draw the sword, is not forced to do it. The contest here is exactly what it was in Holland; a contest between the monarchical and aristocratical parts of the government, for a monopoly of despotism over the people. The aristocracy in Holland, seeing that their common prey was likely to escape out of their clutches, chose rather to retain its former portion, and therefore coalesced with the single head. The people remained victims. Here, I think, it will take a happier turn. The parliamentary part of the aristocracy is alone firmly united. The Noblesse and Clergy, but especially the former, are divided partly between the parliamentary and the despotic party, and partly united with the real patriots, who are endeavoring to gain for the nation what they can, both from the parliamentary and the single despotism. I think I am not mistaken in believing that the King and some of his ministers are well affected to this band; and surely, that they will make great cessions to the people, rather than small ones to the parliament. They are, accordingly, yielding daily to the national reclamations, and will probably end, in according a well-tempered constitution. They promise the States General for the next year, and I have good information that an *Arret* will appear the day after to-morrow, announcing them for May, 1789. How they will be composed, and what they will do, cannot be foreseen. Their convocation, however, will tranquillize the public mind, in a great degree, till their meeting. There are, however, two intervening difficulties: 1. Justice cannot till then continue

---

1 Michel-Guillaume-Jean de Crèvecoeur was born into petty nobility in Caen, Normandy, in 1735. His father was a country gentleman who spent most of the year on the family estate that Michel-Guillaume would be expected to inherit; but around the age of eighteen, Michel was sent to England, perhaps after falling out with his father, and he did not return to France for twenty-five years. From England, he sailed to Canada in 1755, where he enlisted in the French colonial militia. He served as a surveyor and cartographer during the French and Indian War and was wounded in the battle of Quebec in 1759. He then sold his commission and took the very unusual step of emigrating to New York State. There he adopted the name James Hector St. John, married an American, and traveled extensively in the wilderness of northern New York and Vermont as a surveyor and Indian trader. He became a naturalized citizen in 1765 and spent much of the remainder of his life traveling between the United States and France, serving in various diplomatic positions, establishing friendships with the likes of Jefferson, Madison, and Franklin, and helping to strengthen political, cultural, and intellectual ties between France and the United States. In 1789, he was elected to membership in the American Philosophical Society, and played a large part in promoting and reporting the triumphant tour of the Marquis de Lafayette through the United States in 1784. He returned to Europe in 1790 and died in France in 1813 (Downes 2002, 60).

completely suspended, as it now is. The parliament will not resume their functions, but in their entire body. The baillages are afraid to accept of them. What will be done? 2. There are well-founded fears of a bankruptcy before the month of May. In the meantime, the war is spreading from nation to nation. Sweden has commenced hostilities against Russia; Denmark is showing its teeth against Sweden; Prussia against Denmark; and England too deeply engaged in playing the back game, to avoid coming forward, and dragging this country and Spain in with her. But even war will not prevent the assembly of the States General, because it cannot be carried on without them. War, however, is not the most favorable moment for divesting the monarchy of power. On the contrary, it is the moment when the energy of a single hand shows itself in the most seducing form.

A very considerable portion of this country has been desolated by a hail. I considered the newspaper accounts, of hailstones of ten pounds weight, as exaggerations. But in a conversation with the Duke de La Rochefoucault, the other day, he assured me, that though he could not say he had seen such himself, yet he considered the fact as perfectly established. Great contributions, public and private, are making for the sufferers. But they will be like the drop of water from the finger of Lazarus. There is no remedy for the present evil, nor way to prevent future ones, but to bring the people to such a state of ease, as not to be ruined by the loss of a single crop. This hail may be considered as the coup de grace to an expiring victim. In the arts, there is nothing new discovered since you left us, which is worth communicating. Mr. Payne's iron bridge was exhibited here, with great approbation. An idea has been encouraged, of executing it in three arches, at the King's garden. But it will probably not be done.

I am, with sentiments of perfect esteem and attachment, dear Sir, your most obedient, and most humble servant.

GEORGE WASHINGTON, 1788, ME 7:223 ~ *THE POWER OF MAKING WAR OFTEN PREVENTS IT.*

To General Washington[1]
Paris, December 4, 1788

Sir, Your favor of August the 31st came to hand yesterday; and a confidential conveyance offering, by the way of London, I avail myself of it, to acknowledge the receipt.

---

1 In this letter to Washington, then president of the Continental Constitutional Convention (he would not be elected the first president of the United States until 1789) Jefferson succinctly delineates his thoughts on trade, taxes, and war: "The produce of the United States will soon exceed the European demand; what is to be done with the surplus, when there shall be one? It will be employed, without question, to open, by force, a market for itself, with those placed on the same continent with us, and who wish nothing better. Other causes, too, are obvious, which may involve us in war; and war requires every resource of taxation and credit. The power of making war often prevents it, and in our case would give efficacy to our desire of peace. If the new government wears the front which I hope it will, I see no impossibility in the availing ourselves of the wars of others, to open the other parts of America to our commerce, as the price of our neutrality."

I have seen, with infinite pleasure, our new Constitution accepted by eleven States, not rejected by the twelfth; and that the thirteenth happens to be a State of the least importance. It is true, that the minorities in most of the accepting States have been very respectable; so much so as to render it prudent, were it not otherwise reasonable, to make some sacrifice to them. I am in hopes, that the annexation of a bill of rights to the Constitution will alone draw over so great a proportion of the minorities as to leave little danger in the opposition of the residue; and that this annexation may be made by Congress and the Assemblies, without calling a convention, which might endanger the most valuable parts of the system. Calculation has convinced me that circumstances may arise, and probably will arise, wherein all the resources of taxation will be necessary for the safety of the State, For though I am decidedly of opinion we should take no part in European quarrels, but cultivate peace and commerce with all, yet who can avoid seeing the source of war, in the tyranny of those nations, who deprive us of the natural right of trading with our neighbors? The produce of the United States will soon exceed the European demand; what is to be done with the surplus, when there shall be one? It will be employed, without question, to open, by force, a market for itself, with those placed on the same continent with us, and who wish nothing better. Other causes, too, are obvious, which may involve us in war; and war requires every resource of taxation and credit. The power of making war often prevents it, and in our case would give efficacy to our desire of peace. If the new government wears the front which I hope it will, I see no impossibility in the availing ourselves of the wars of others, to open the other parts of America to our commerce, as the price of our neutrality.

The campaign between the Turks and the two empires has been clearly in favor of the former. The Emperor is secretly trying to bring about a peace. The alliance between England, Prussia, and Holland (and some suspect Sweden also), renders their mediation decisive wherever it is proposed. They seemed to interpose it so magisterially between Denmark and Sweden, that the former submitted to its dictates, and there was all reason to believe that the war in the north-western parts of Europe would be quieted. All of a sudden, a new flame bursts out in Poland. The King and his party are devoted to Russia. The opposition rely on the protection of Prussia. They have lately become the majority in the confederated diet, and have passed a vote for subjecting their army to a commission independent of the King, and propose a perpetual diet, in which case he will be a perpetual cipher. Russia declares against such a change in their constitution, and Prussia has put an army into readiness for marching, at a moment's warning, on the frontiers of Poland. These events are too recent to see, as yet, what turn they will take, or what effect they will have on the peace of Europe. So is that also of the lunacy of the King of England, which is a decided fact, notwithstanding all the stuff the English papers publish about his fevers, his deliriums, etc. The truth is that the lunacy declared itself almost at once, and with as few concomitant complaints as usually attend the first development of that disorder. I suppose regency will be established, and if it consists of a plurality of members, it will probably be peaceable. In this event, it will much favor the present wishes of this country, which are so decidedly for peace, that they refused to enter into the mediation between Sweden and Russia, lest it should commit them. As soon as the convocation of the States General was announced, a tranquility took place through the whole kingdom; happily, no open rupture has taken place in any part of it. The parliaments were reinstated in their functions at the same time. This was all they desired; and they had called for the States General only through fear that the crown could not otherwise be forced to reinstate them. Their end obtained, they began to foresee danger to themselves in the States General. They began to lay the foundation for caviling at the legality of that body, if its measures should be hostile to them. The court, to clear itself of the dispute, convened the Notables, who had acted with general approbation on the former occasion, and referred to them the forms of calling and organizing the States General. These Notables consist principally of Nobility and Clergy; the few of the *Tiers Etat* among them being either parliament men, or other privileged persons. The court wished that, in the future States General, the members of the *Tiers Etat* should equal those of both the other orders, and that they should form but one House, all together, and vote by persons, not by orders. But the Notables, in the true spirit of Priests and Nobles, combining together against the people, have voted, by five *bureaux* out of six, that the people, or *Tiers Etat*, shall have no greater number of deputies than each of the other orders separately, and that they shall vote, by orders; so that two orders concurring in a vote, the third will be overruled; for it is not here as in England, where each of the three branches has a negative on the other two. If this project of theirs succeeds, a combination between the two Houses of Clergy and Nobles, will render the representation of the *Tiers Etat* merely nugatory. The *bureaux* are to assemble together, to consolidate their separate votes; but I see no reasonable hope of their changing this. Perhaps the King, knowing that he may count on the support of the nation, and attach it more closely to him, may take on himself to disregard the opinion of the Notables in this instance, and may call an equal representation of the people, in which, precedents will support him. In every event, I think the present disquiet will end well. The nation has been awaked by our Revolution, they feel their strength, they are enlightened, their lights are spreading, and they will not retrograde. The first States General may establish three important points, without opposition from the court: 1. their own periodical convocation; 2. their exclusive right of taxation (which has been confessed by the King); 3. the right of registering laws, and of previously proposing amendments to them, as the parliaments have, by usurpation, been in the habit of doing. The court will consent to this, from its hatred to the parliaments, and from the desire of having to do with one, rather than many legislatures. If the States are prudent, they will not aim at more than this at first, lest they should shock the dispositions of the court, and even alarm the public mind, which must be left to open itself by degrees to successive improvements. These will follow, from the nature of things; how far they can proceed, in the end, towards a thorough reformation of abuse, cannot be foreseen. In my opinion, a kind of influence which none of their plans of reform take into account, will elude them all; I mean the influence of women, in the government. The manners of the nation allow them to visit, alone, all persons in office, to solicit the affairs of the husband, family, or friends, and their solicitations bid defiance to laws and regulations. This obstacle may seem less to those who, like our countrymen, are in the precious habit of considering right, as a barrier against all solicitation. Nor can such an one, without the evidence of his own eyes, believe in the desperate state to which things are reduced in this country from the omnipotence of an influence which, fortunately for the happiness of the sex itself, does not endeavor to extend itself in our country beyond the domestic line.

Your communications to the Count de Moustier, whatever they may have been, cannot have done injury to my endeavors here, to open the West Indies to us. On this head, the ministers are invincibly mute, though I have often tried to draw them into the subject. I have, therefore, found it necessary to let it lie, till war, or other circumstances, may force it on. Whenever they are in war with England, they must open the islands to us, and perhaps, during that war, they may see some price which might make them agree to keep them always open. In the meantime, I have laid my shoulder to the opening the markets of this country to our produce, and rendering its transportation a nursery for our seamen. A maritime force is the only one, by which we can act on Europe. Our navigation law (if it be wise to have any) should be the reverse of that of England. Instead of confining importations to home-bottoms, or those of the producing nation, I think we should confine exportations to home-bottoms, or to those of nations having treaties with us. Our exportations are heavy, and would nourish a great force of our own, or be a tempting price to the nation to whom we should offer a participation of it, in exchange for free access to all their possessions. This is an object to which our government alone is adequate, in the gross; but I have ventured to pursue it here, so far as the consumption of our productions by this country extends. Thus, in our arrangements relative to tobacco, none can be received here, but in French or American bottoms. This is employment for near two thousand seamen, and puts nearly that number of British out of employ. By the *Arret* of December, 1787, it was provided, that our whale oils should not be received here, but in French or American bottoms; and by later regulations, all oils, but those of France and America, are excluded. This will put one hundred English whale vessels immediately out of employ, and one hundred and fifty ere long; and call so many of French and American into service. We have had six thousand seamen formerly in this business, the whole of whom we have been likely to lose. The consumption of rice is growing fast in this country, and that of Carolina gaining ground on every other kind. I am of opinion, the whole of the Carolina rice can be consumed here. Its transportation employs two thousand five hundred sailors, almost all of them English at present; the rice being deposited at Cowes, and brought from thence here. It would be dangerous to confine this transportation to French and American bottoms, the ensuing year, because they will be much engrossed by the transportation of wheat and flour hither, and the crop of rice might lie on hand for want of vessels; but I see no objections to the extensions of our principle to this article also, beginning with the year 1790. However, before there is a necessity of deciding on this, I hope to be able to consult our new government in person, as I have asked of Congress a leave of absence for six months, that is to say, from April to November next. It is necessary for me to pay a short visit to my native country, first, to reconduct my family thither, and place them in the hands of their friends, and secondly, to place my private affairs under certain arrangements. When I left my own house, I expected to be absent but five months, and I have been led by events to an absence of five years. I shall hope, therefore, for the pleasure of personal conferences with your Excellency, on the subject of this letter, and others interesting to our country; of getting my own ideas set to rights by a communication of yours, and of taking again the tone of sentiment of my own country, which we lose, in some degree, after a certain absence. You know, doubtless, of the death of the Marquis de Chastellux. The Marquis de Lafayette is out of favor with the court, but high in favor with the nation. I once feared for his personal liberty, but I hope he is on safe ground at present.

On the subject of the whale fishery, I enclose you some observations I drew up for the ministry here, in order to obtain a correction of their *Arret* of September last, whereby they had involved our oils with the English, in a general exclusion from their ports. They will accordingly correct this, so that our oils will participate with theirs, in the monopoly of their markets. There are several things incidentally introduced, which do not seem pertinent to the general question; they were rendered necessary by particular circumstances, the explanation of which, would add to a letter already too long. I will trespass no further, than to assure you- of the sentiments of sincere attachment and respect with which I have the honor to be, your Excellency's most obedient humble servant.

P. S. The observations enclosed, though printed, have been put into confidential hands only.

DAVID HUMPHREYS, 1789, 7:319 - *THERE ARE RIGHTS WHICH IT IS USELESS TO SURRENDER TO THE GOVERNMENT.*

To Colonel Humphreys[1]
Paris, March 18, 1789

---

1 Born in Connecticut in 1752, David Humphreys served in the continental army aide-de-camp to Generals Putnam, Greene, and Washington. After the war he was with Jefferson, for a time, at Paris on the commission for treaties with foreign powers, and also served as diplomat at Lisbon and Madrid where he was considered a favorite in numerous foreign circles of society. After he had returned to America, he was invited to visit at Mount Vernon, and Washington offered him aid in pursuing a literary plan to write a history of the Revolution But Humphreys declined the offer, although he did go on to publish numerous nonfiction pieces and poetry until his death in 1818 (Marble 1907, 174-175).

Dear Sir, Your favor of November the 29th, 1788, came to hand the last month. How it happened that mine of August, 1787, was fourteen months on its way, is inconceivable. I do not recollect by what conveyance I sent it. I had concluded, however, either that it had miscarried or that you had become in-dolent, as most of our countrymen are, in matters of correspondence.

The change in this country since you left it, is such as you can form no idea of. The frivolities of conversation have given way entirely to politics. Men, women and children talk nothing else; and all, you know, talk a great deal. The press groans with daily productions, which, in point of boldness, makes an Englishman stare, who hitherto has thought himself the boldest of men. A complete revolution in this government has, within the space of two years, (for it began with the Notables of 1787,) been effected merely by the force of public opinion, aided, indeed, by the want of money, which the dissipations of the court had brought on. And this revolution has not cost a single life, unless we charge to it a little riot lately in Bretagne, which began about the price of bread, became afterwards political, and ended in the loss of four or five lives. The assembly of the States General begins the 27th of April. The representation of the people will be perfect. But they will be al-loyed by an equal number of nobility and clergy. The first great question they will have to decide will be, whether they shall vote by orders or persons. And I have hopes that the majority of the Nobles are already disposed to join the *Tiers Etat*, in deciding that the vote shall be by persons. This is the opinion *a la mode* at present, and mode has acted a wonderful part in the present instance. All the handsome young women, for example, are for the *Tiers Etat*, and this is an army more powerful in France, than the two hundred thousand men of the King. Add to this, that the court itself is for the *Tiers Etat*, as the only agent which can relieve their wants; not by giving money themselves, (they are squeezed to the last drop,) but by pressing it from the non-contributing orders. The King stands engaged to pretend no more to the power of laying, continuing or appropriating taxes; to call the States General periodically; to submit *lettres de cachet* to legal restrictions; to consent to freedom of the press; and that all this shall be tied by a fundamental constitution, which shall bind his successors. He has not offered a participation in the legislature, but it will surely be insisted on. The public mind is so ripened on all these subjects, that there seems to be now but one opinion. The clergy, indeed, think separately, and the old men among the Nobles; but their voice is sup-pressed by the general one of the nation. The writings published on this oc-casion are, some of them, very valuable; because, unfettered by the prejudices under which the English labor, they give a full scope to reason, and strike out truths, as yet unperceived and unacknowledged on the other side the chan-nel. An Englishman, dosing under a kind of half reformation, is not excited to think by such gross absurdities as stare a Frenchman in the face, wherever he looks, whether it be towards the throne or the altar. In fine, I believe this nation will, in the course of the present year, have as full a portion of liberty dealt out to them, as the nation can bear at present, considering how uninformed the mass of their people is. This circumstance will prevent the immediate establishment of the trial by jury. The palsied state of the executive in England is a fortunate circumstance for France, as it will give her time to arrange her affairs internally. The consolidation and funding their debts, will give government a credit which will enable them to do what they please. For the present year, the war will be confined to the two empires and Denmark, against Turkey and Sweden. It is not yet evident whether Prussia will be engaged. If the disturbances of Poland break out into overt acts, it will be a power divided in itself, and so of no weight. Perhaps, by the next year, England and France may be ready to take the field. It will depend on the former principally; for the latter, though she may be then able, must wish a little time to see her new arrangements well under way. The English papers and English ministry say the King is well. He is better but not well; no malady requires a longer time to insure against its return, than insanity. Time alone can distinguish accidental insanity from habitual lunacy.

The operations which have taken place in America lately fill me with pleasure. In the first place, they realize the confidence I had, that whenever our affairs go obviously wrong, the good sense of the people will interpose, and set them to rights. The example of changing a constitution, by assembling the wise men of the State, instead of assembling armies, will be worth as much to the world as the former examples we had given them. The Constitution, too, which was the result of our deliberations, is unquestionably the wisest ever yet presented to men, and some of the accommodations of interest which it has adopted, are greatly pleasing to me, who have before had occasions of seeing how difficult those interests were to accommodate. A general concurrence of opinion seems to authorize us to say, it has some defects. I am one of those who think it a defect that the important rights, not placed in security by the frame of the Constitution itself, were not explicitly secured by a supplementary declaration. There are rights which it is useless to surrender to the government, and which governments have yet always been found to invade. These are the rights of thinking, and publishing our thoughts by speaking or writing; the right of free commerce; the right of personal freedom. There are instruments for administering the government, so peculiarly trust-worthy, that we should never leave the legislature at liberty to change them. The new Constitution has secured these in the executive and legislative department; but not in the judiciary. It should have established trials by the people themselves, that is to say, by jury. There are instruments so dangerous to the rights of the nation, and which place them so totally at the mercy of their governors, that those governors, whether legislative or executive, should be restrained from keeping such instruments on foot, but in well defined cases. Such an instrument is a standing army. We are now allowed to say, such a declaration of rights, as a supplement to the Constitution where that is silent, is wanting, to secure us in these points. The general voice has legitimated this objection. It has not, however, authorized me to consider as a real defect, what I thought and still think one, the perpetual re-eligibility of the President. But three States out of eleven, having declared against this, we must suppose we are wrong, according to the fundamental law of every society, the *lex majoris partis*, to which we are bound to submit. And should the majority change their opinion, and become sensible that this trait in their Constitution is wrong, I would wish it to remain uncorrected, as long as we can avail ourselves of the services of our great leader, whose talents and whose weight of character, I consider as peculiarly necessary to get the government so under way, as that it may afterwards be carried on by subordinate characters.

I must give you sincere thanks, for the details of small news contained in your letter. You know how precious that kind of information is to a person absent from his country, and how difficult it is to be procured. I hope to receive soon permission to visit America this summer, and to possess myself anew, by conversation with my countrymen, of their spirit and their ideas. I know only the Americans of the year 1784. They tell me this is to be much a stranger to those of 1789. This renewal of acquaintance is no indifferent matter to one, acting at such a distance, as that instructions cannot be received hot and hot. One of my pleasures, too, will be that of talking over the old and new with you. In the meantime, and at all times, I have the honor to be, with great and sincere esteem, dear Sir, your friend and servant.

WILLIAM CARMICHAEL, 1789, 7:432 - *THE MILITARY AS A CIVIL WEAPON.*

To Mr. William Carmichael [1]
Paris, August 9, 1789

Dear Sir, Since your last of March the 27th, I have only written that of May the 8th. The cause of this long silence, on both parts, has been the expectation I communicated to you of embarking for America. In fact, I have expected permission for this, every hour since the month of March, and, therefore, always thought that by putting off writing to you a few days, my letter, while it should communicate the occurrences of the day, might be a letter of adieu. Should my permission now arrive, I should put off my departure till after the equinox. They write me that my not receiving it, has proceeded from the ceasing of the old government in October last, and the organization of the higher departments in the new, which had not yet taken place when my last letters came away. Bills had been brought in for establishing departments of Foreign Affairs, Finance, and War. The last would certainly be given to General Knox. Mr. Jay would probably have his choice

---

1 William Carmichael was born in Queen Anne's County, Md., near Chestertown, Md., birth date unknown; studied law; was admitted to the bar and practiced in Centreville, Md.; was in London, England, at the beginning of the Revolution; assistant to Silas Deane, secret agent of Congress at Paris, 1776; went to Berlin in American interests in 1776; named secretary to the American commissioners in France in 1777, but did not serve, returning to the United States in May 1778; Member of the Continental Congress, 1778-1779; went to Spain in September 1779 and served as secretary of the legation. He was appointed Chargé d'Affaires at Madrid, Spain, April 20, 1782-May 1794, and died in Madrid on February 9, 1795 (United States Congress 2008).

of the first and second; and it is supposed Hamilton would have that which Mr. Jay declined. Some thought Mr. Jay would prefer and obtain the head of the law department, for which Wilson would be a competitor. In such a case, some have supposed C. Thompson would ask the Foreign Affairs. The Senate and Representatives differed about the title of the President. The former wanted to style him "His Highness, George Washington, President of the United States, and Protector of their liberties." The latter insisted and prevailed, to give no title but that of office, to wit, "George Washington, President of the United States." I hope the terms of Excellency, Honor, Worship, Esquire, forever disappear from among us, from that moment: I wish that of Mr. would follow them. In the impost bill, the Representatives had, by almost a unanimous concurrence, made a difference between nations in treaty with us, and those not in treaty. The Senate had struck out this difference and lowered all the duties. *Quaere,* whether the Representatives would yield? Congress were to proceed about the 1st of June to propose amendments to the new Constitution. The principal would be, the annexing a declaration of rights to satisfy the mind of all, on the subject of their liberties. They waited the arrival of Brown, delegate from Kentucky, to take up the receiving that district as a fourteenth State. The only objections apprehended, were from the partisans of Vermont, who might insist on both coming in together. This would produce a delay, though probably not a long one.

To detail to you the events of this country, would require a volume. It would be useless, too; because those given in the Leyden gazette, though not universally true, have so few and such unimportant errors mixed with them, that you may have a general faith in them. I will rather give you, therefore, what that paper cannot give, the views of the prevailing power, as far as they can be collected from conversation and writings. They will distribute the powers of government into three parts, legislative, judiciary, and executive. The legislative will certainly have no hereditary branch, and probably not even a select one (like our Senate). If they divide it into two chambers at all, it will be by breaking the representative body into two equal halves by lot. But very many are for a single House, and particularly the Turgotists. The imperfection of their legislative body, I think, will be, that not a member of it will be chosen by the people directly. Their representation will be an equal one, in which every man will elect and be elected as a citizen, not as of a distinct order. *Quaere,* whether they will elect placemen and pensioners? Their legislature will meet periodically, and sit at their own will, with a power in the executive to call them extraordinarily, in case of emergencies. There is a considerable division of sentiment whether the executive shall have a negative on the laws. I think they will determine to give such a negative, either absolute or qualified. In the judiciary, the parliaments will be suppressed, less numerous judiciary bodies instituted, and trial by jury established in criminal, if not in civil cases. The executive power will be left entire in the hands of the King. They will establish the responsibility of ministers, gifts and appropriations of money by the National Assembly alone; consequently, a civil list, freedom of the press, freedom of religion, freedom of commerce and industry, freedom of person against arbitrary arrests, and modifications, if not a total prohibition of military agency in civil cases. I do not see how they can prohibit altogether the aid of the 'military in cases of riot, and yet I doubt whether they can descend from the sublimity of ancient military pride, to let a *Marechal* of France with his troops, be commanded by a Magistrate. They cannot conceive that General Washington, at the head of his army, during the late war, could have been commanded by a common Constable to go as his *posse comitatus,* to suppress a mob, and that Count Rochambeau, when he was arrested at the head of his army by a sheriff, must have gone to jail if he had not given bail to appear in court. Though they have gone astonishing lengths, they are not yet thus far. It is probable, therefore, that not knowing how to use the military as a civil weapon, they will do too much or too little with it.

I have said that things will be so and so. Understand by this, that these are only my conjectures, the plan of the constitution not being proposed yet, much less agreed to. Tranquility is pretty well established in the capital; though the appearance of any of the refugees here would endanger it. The Baron de Besenval is kept away; so is M. de la Vauguyon. The latter was so short a time a member of the obnoxious administration, that probably he might not be touched were he here. Seven Princes of the house of Bourbon, and seven ministers, fled into foreign countries, is a wonderful event, indeed.

I have the honor to be, with great respect and attachment, dear Sir, your most obedient, and most humble servant.

JAMES MADISON, 1789, 7:444 - SOLDIERS NOT NATIVES OF THE UNITED STATES SHALL BE INCAPABLE OF SERVING IN THEIR ARMIES BY LAND EXCEPT DURING A FOREIGN WAR.

To James Madison[1]
Paris, August 28, 1789

Dear Sir, My last to you was of July the 22d. Since that, I have received yours of May the 27th, June 13th and 30th. The tranquility of the city has not been disturbed since my last. Dissensions between the French and Swiss guards occasioned some private combats, in which five or six were killed. These dissensions are made up. The want of bread for some days past, has greatly endangered the peace of the city. Some get a little, some none at all. The poor are the best served, because they besiege perpetually the doors of the bakers. Notwithstanding this distress, and the palpable importance of

---

1 While the Congress was deliberating upon amendments to the constitution, Jefferson, in Paris, had afforded them considerable his attention. In this letter, he alludes to the proposals as a "declaration of rights," and indicates that he liked it "as far as it goes; but I should have been for going further." Jefferson also preferred more precise wording in some of the articles. He still opposed the granting of government monopolies and feared a standing army, particularly one composed of foreign mercenaries. These things he would guard against and was confident that they eventually would be prohibited by the Constitution (Rutland 1955, 213).

the city administration to furnish bread to the city, it was not till yesterday, that general leave was given to the bakers to go into the country and buy flour for themselves as they can. This will soon relieve us, because the wheat harvest is well advanced. Never was there a country where the practice of governing too much, had taken deeper root and done more mischief. Their declaration of rights is finished. If printed in time, I will enclose a copy with this. It is doubtful whether they will now take up the finance or the constitution first. The distress for money endangers everything. No taxes are paid, and no money can be borrowed. Mr. Neckar was yesterday to give in a memoir to the Assembly, on this subject. I think they will give him leave to put into execution any plan he pleases, so as to debarrass themselves of this, and take up that of the constitution. No plan is yet reported; but the leading members (with some small difference of opinion) have in contemplation the following: The executive power in a hereditary King, with a .negative on laws, and power to dissolve the legislature; to be considerably restrained in the making of treaties, and limited in his expenses. The legislative is a House of Representatives. They propose a Senate also, chosen on the plan of our federal Senate by the Provincial Assemblies, but to be for life, of a certain age (they talk of forty years), and certain wealth (four or five hundred guineas a year), but to have no other power against the laws but to remonstrate against them to the representatives, who will then determine their fate by a simple majority. This, you will readily perceive, is a mere council of revision, like that of New York, which, in order to be something, must form an alliance with the King, to avail themselves of his veto. The alliance will be useful to both, and to the nation. The representatives to be chosen every two or three years. The judiciary system is less prepared than any other part of the plan; however, they will abolish the parliaments, and establish an order of judges and justices, general and provincial, a good deal like ours, with trial by jury in criminal cases certainly, perhaps also in civil. The provinces will have Assemblies for their provincial government, and the cities a municipal body for municipal government, all founded on the basis of popular election. These subordinate governments, though completely dependent on the general one, will be entrusted with almost the whole of the details which our State governments exercise. They will have their own judiciary, final in all but great cases, the executive business will principally pass through their hands, and a certain local legislature will be allowed them. In short, ours has been professedly their model, in which such changes are made as a difference of circumstances rendered necessary, and some others neither necessary nor advantageous, but into which men will ever run, when versed in theory and new in the practice of government, when acquainted with man only as they see him in their books and not in the world. This plan will undoubtedly undergo changes in the Assembly, and the longer it is delayed, the greater will be the changes; for that Assembly, or rather the patriotic part of it, hooped together heretofore by a common enemy, are less compact since their victory. That enemy (the civil and ecclesiastical aristocracy) begins to raise its head. The lees, too, of the patriotic party, of wicked principles and desperate fortunes, hoping to pillage something in the wreck of their country, are attaching themselves to the faction of the Duke of Orleans; that faction is caballing with the populace, and intriguing at London, the Hague, and Berlin, and have evidently in view the transfer of the crown to the Duke of Orleans. He is a man of moderate understanding, of no principle, absorbed in low vice, and incapable of extracting himself from the filth of that, to direct anything else. His name and his money, therefore, are mere tools in the hands of those who are duping him. *Mirabeau is their chief.* They may produce a temporary confusion, and even a temporary civil war, supported, as they will be, by the money of England; but they cannot have success ultimately. The King, the mass of the substantial people of the whole country, the army, and the influential part of the clergy, form a firm phalanx which must prevail. Should those delays which necessarily attend the deliberations of a body of one thousand two hundred men, give time to this plot to ripen and burst, so as to break up the Assembly before anything definite is done, a constitution, the principles of which are pretty well settled in the minds of the Assembly, will be proposed by the national militia (*that is by their commander*), urged by the individual members of the Assembly, signed by the King, and supported by the nation, to prevail till circumstances shall permit its revision and more regular sanction. This I suppose the *pis aller* of their affairs, while their probable event is a peaceable settlement of them. They fear a war from England, Holland, and Prussia. I think England will give money, but not make war. Holland would soon be a fire, internally, were she to be embroiled in external difficulties. Prussia must know this, and act accordingly.

It is impossible to desire better dispositions towards us, than prevail in this assembly. Our proceedings have been viewed as a model for them on every occasion; and though in the heat of debate men are generally disposed to contradict every authority urged by their opponents, ours has been treated like that of the bible, open to explanation but not to question. I am sorry that in the moment of such a disposition any thing should come from us to check it. The placing them on a mere footing with the English will have this effect. When of two nations, the one has engaged herself in a ruinous war for us, has spent her blood and money to save us, has opened her bosom to us in peace, and receive us almost on the footing of her own citizens, while the other has moved heaven, earth and hell to exterminate us in war, has insulted us in all her councils in peace, shut her doors to us in every part where her interests would admit it, libeled us in foreign nations, endeavored to poison them against the reception of our most precious commodities, to place these two nations on a footing, is to give a great deal more to one than to the other if the maxim be true that to make unequal quantities equal you must add more to the one than the other. To say in excuse that gratitude is never to enter into the motives of national conduct, is to revive a principle which has been buried for centuries with its kindred principles of the lawfulness of assassination, poison, perjury, etc. All of these were legitimate principles in the dark ages which intervened between ancient and modern civilization, but exploded and held in just horror in the 18th century. I know but one code of morality for man whether acting singly or collectively. He who says I will be a rogue when I act in company with a hundred others but an honest man when I act alone will be believed in the former assertion, but not in the latter. I would say with the poet "*hic niger est, hunc tu Romane caveto.*" If the morality of one man produces a just line of conduct in him, acting individually, why should not the morality of 100 men produce a just line of conduct in them acting together? But I indulge myself in these reflections because my own feelings run me into them: with you they were always acknowledged. Let us hope that our new government will take some other occasion to show that they mean to proscribe no virtue from the canons of their conduct with other nations. In every other instance the new government has ushered itself to the world as honest, masculine and dignified. It has shown genuine dignity in my opinion in exploding adulatory titles; they are the offerings of abject baseness, and nourish that degrading vice in the people.

I must now say a word on the declaration of rights you have been so good as to send me. I like it as far as it goes; but I should have been for going further. For instance the following alterations and additions would have pleased me: Article 4. "The people shall not be deprived or abridged of their right to speak to write or *otherwise* to publish any thing but false facts affecting injuriously the life, liberty, property, or reputation of others or affecting the peace of the confederacy with foreign nations. Article 7. All facts put in issue before any judicature shall be tried by jury except 1. in cases of admiralty jurisdiction wherein a foreigner shall be interested, 2. in cases cognizable before a court martial concerning only the regular officers and soldiers of the United States or members of the militia in actual service in time of war or insurrection, and 3. in impeachments allowed by the constitution. Article. 8. No person shall be held in confinement more than _ [blank] days after they shall have demanded and been refused a writ of Hab. corp. by the judge appointed by law nor more than _ [blank] days after such writ shall have been served on the person holding him in confinement and no order given on due examination for his remandment or discharge, nor more than _ [blank] hours in any place at a greater distance than – miles from the usual residence of some judge authorized to issue the writ of Hab. corp. nor shall that writ be suspended for any term exceeding one year nor in any place more than – miles distant from the station or encampment of enemies or of insurgents. Article. 9. Monopolies may be allowed to persons for their own productions in literature and their own inventions in the arts for a term not exceeding – years but for no longer term and no other purpose. Article. 10. All troops of the Unite States shall stand *ipso facto* disbanded at the expiration of the term for which their pay and subsistence shall have been last voted by Congress, and all officers and soldiers not natives of the United States shall be incapable of serving in their armies by land except during a foreign war." These restrictions I think are so guarded as to hinder evil only. However if we do not have them now,

I have so much confidence in my countrymen as to be satisfied that we shall have them as soon as the degeneracy of our government shall render them necessary.

I have no certain news of Paul Jones. I understand only in a general way that some persecution on the part of his officers occasioned his being called to St. Petersburg, and that though protected against them by the empress, he is not yet restored to his station. Silas Deane is coming over to finish his days in America, not having one *sou* to subsist on elsewhere. He is a wretched monument of the consequences of a departure from right. I will before my departure write Colonel Lee fully the measures I pursued to procure success in his business, and which as yet offer little hope, and I shall leave it in the hands of Mr. Short to be pursued if any prospect opens on him. I propose to sail from Havre as soon after the 1st. of October as I can get a vessel; and shall consequently leave this place a week earlier than that. As my daughters will be with me, and their baggage somewhat more than that of mere *voyageures*, I shall endeavor if possible to obtain a passage for Virginia directly. Probably I shall be there by the last of November. If my immediate attendance at New York should be requisite for any purpose, I will leave them with a relation near Richmond and proceed immediately to New York. But as I do not fore-see any pressing purpose for that journey immediately on my arrival, and as it will be a great saving of time to finish at once in Virginia so as to have no occasion to return there after having once gone on to the Northward, I ex-pect to proceed to my own house directly. Staying there two months (which I believe will be necessary) and allowing for the time I am on the road, I may expect to be at New York in February, and to embark from thence, or some eastern port.

You ask me if I would accept any appointment on that side the water? You know the circumstances which led me from retirement, step by step and from one nomination to another, up to the present. My object is a return to the same retirement. Whenever therefore I quit the present, it will not be to engage in any other office, and most especially any one which would require a constant residence from home. The books I have collected for you will go off for Havre in three or four days with my baggage. From that port I shall try to send them by a direct occasion to New York. I am with great and sincere esteem Dr. Sir your affectionate friend and servant.

P.S. I just now learn that Mr. Necker proposed yesterday to the National assembly a loan of eighty millions, on terms more tempting to the lender than the former, and that they approve it, leaving him to arrange the details in order that they might occupy themselves at once about the constitution.

JAMES MADISON, 1789, 7:454 – *NO SOCIETY CAN MAKE A PERPETUAL CONSTITUTION.*

To James Madison[1]

---

1 To preserve the independence of the people and guard the rights of posterity, Jefferson be-lieved that governments should fix the ultimate term for the redemption of public debts

Paris, September 6, 1789

Dear Sir, I sit down to write to you without knowing by what occasion I shall send my letter. I do it, because a subject comes into my head, which I would wish to develop a little more than is practicable in the hurry of the moment of making up general dispatches.

The question, whether one generation of men has a right to bind another, seems never to have been started either on this or our side of the water. Yet it is a question of such consequences as not only to merit decision, but place also among the fundamental principles of every government. The course of reflection in which we are immersed here, on the elementary principles of society, has presented this question to my mind; and that no such obligation can be transmitted, I think very capable of proof. I set out on this ground, which I suppose to be self evident, that the *earth belongs in usufruct to the living*; that the dead have neither powers nor rights over it. The portion occupied by any individual ceases to be his when himself ceases to be, and reverts to the society. If the society has formed no rules for the appropriation of its lands in severalty, it will be taken by the first occupants, and these will generally be the wife and children of the decedent. If they have formed rules of appropriation, those rules may give it to the wife and children, or to some one of them, or to the legatee of the deceased. So they may give it to its creditor. But the child, the legatee or creditor, takes it, not by natural right, but by a law of the society of which he is a member, and to which he is subject. Then, no man can, by *natural right*, oblige the lands he occupied, or the persons who succeed him in that occupation, to the payment of debts contracted by him. For if he could, he might during his own life, eat up the usufruct of the lands for several generations to come; and then the lands would belong to the dead, and not to the living, which is the reverse of our principle.

What is true of every member of the society, individually, is true of them all collectively; since the rights of the whole can be no more than the sum of the rights of the individuals. To keep our ideas clear when applying them to a multitude, let us suppose a whole generation of men to be born on the same day, to attain mature age on the same day, and to die on the same day, leaving a succeeding generation in the moment of attaining their mature age, all together. Let the ripe age be supposed of twenty-one years, and their period

---

within the limits of their rightful powers. The law of nature prescribes the limits of their powers within the period of the life of the majority. This rule would prevent the creation of a perpetual or unjust public debt. The point is so important for Jefferson that he urged the consideration of a fundamental provision in the new French constitution. In writing to Madison, however, Jefferson had more immediate concerns than a declaration of rights in the French constitution. Here, he proposes that Madison should consider the application of this principle to the United States. "It would furnish matter for a fine preamble to our first law for appropriating the public revenue. . . . We have already given, in example, one effectual check to the Dog of war, by transferring the power of letting him loose from the executive to the Legislative body, from those who are to spend to those who are to pay. I should be pleased to see this second obstacle held out by us also in the first instance. No nation can make a declaration against the validity of long-contracted debts so disinterestedly as we, since we do not owe a shilling which may not be paid with ease principal and interest, within the time of our own lives." (Koch 1950, 67)

of life thirty-four years more, that being the average term given by the bills of mortality to persons of twenty-one years of age. Each successive generation would, in this way, come and go off the stage at a fixed moment, as individuals do now. Then I say, the earth belongs to each of these generations during its course, fully and in its own right. The second generation receives it clear of the debts and encumbrances of the first, the third of the second, and so on. For if the first could charge it with a debt, then the earth would belong to the dead and not to the living generation. Then, na generation can contract debts greater than may be paid during the course of its own existence. At twenty-one years of age, they may bind themselves and their lands for thirty-four years to come; at twenty-two, for thirty-three; at twenty-three, for thirty-two; and at fifty-four, for one year only; because these are the terms of life which remain to them at the respective epochs. But a material difference must be noted, between the succession of an individual and that of a whole generation. Individuals are parts only of a society, subject to the laws of a whole. These laws may appropriate the portion of land occupied by a decedent, to his creditor, rather than to any other, or to his child, on condition he satisfies the creditor. But when a whole generation, that is, the whole society, dies, as in the case we have supposed, and another generation or society succeeds, this forms a whole, and there is no superior who can give their territory to a third society, who may have lent money to their predecessors, beyond their faculties of paying.

What is true of generations succeeding one another at fixed epochs, as has been supposed for clearer conception, is true for those renewed daily, as in the actual course of nature. As a majority of the contracting generation will continue in being thirty-four years, and a new majority will then come into possession, the former may extend their engagement to that term, and no longer. The conclusion then, is, that neither the representatives of a nation, nor the whole nation itself assembled, can validly engage debts beyond what they may pay in their own time, that is to say, within thirty-four years of the date of the engagement.

To render this conclusion palpable, suppose that Louis the XIV. and XV. had contracted debts in the name of the French nation, to the amount of ten thousand milliards, and that the whole had been contracted in Holland. The interest of this sum would be five hundred milliards, which is the whole rent-roll or net proceeds of the territory of France. Must the present generation of men have retired from the territory in which nature produces them, and ceded it to the Dutch creditors? No; they have the same rights over the soil on which they were produced, as the preceding generations had. They derive these rights not from them, but from nature. They, then, and their soil are, by nature, clear of the debts of their predecessors. To present this in another point of view, suppose Louis XV. and his contemporary generation, had said to the money lenders of Holland, give us money, that we may eat, drink, and be merry in our day; and on condition you will demand no interest till the end of thirty-four years, you shall then, forever after, receive an annual interest of fifteen per cent. The money is lent on these conditions, is divided among the people, eaten, drunk, and squandered. Would the present generation be obliged to apply the produce of the earth and of their labor, to replace their dissipations? Not at all.

I suppose that the received opinion, that the public debts of one generation devolve on the next, has been suggested by our seeing, habitually, in private life, that he who succeeds to lands is required to pay the debts of his predecessor; without considering that this requisition is municipal only, not moral, flowing from the will of the society, which has found it convenient to appropriate the lands of a decedent on the condition of a payment of his debts; but that between society and society, or generation and generation, there is no municipal obligation, no umpire but the law of nature.

The interest of the national debt of France being, in fact, but a two thousandth part of its rent-roll, the payment of it is practicable enough; and so becomes a question merely of honor or of expediency. But with respect to future debts, would it not be wise and just for that nation to declare in the constitution they are forming, that neither the legislature nor the nation itself, can validly contract more debt than they may pay within their own age, or within the term of thirty-four years? And that all future contracts shall be deemed void, as to what shall remain unpaid at the end of thirty-four years from their date? This would put the lenders, and the borrowers also, on their guard. By reducing, too, the faculty of borrowing within its natural limits, it would bridle the spirit of war, to which too free a course has been procured by the inattention of money lenders to this law of nature, that succeeding generations are not responsible for the preceding.

On similar ground it may be proved, that no society can make a perpetual constitution, or even a perpetual law. The earth belongs always to the living generation; they may manage it, then, and what proceeds from it, as they please, during their usufruct. They are masters, too, of their own persons, and consequently may govern them as they please. But persons and property make the sum of the objects of government. The constitution and the laws of their predecessors are extinguished then, in their natural course, with those whose will gave them being. This could preserve that being, till it ceased to be itself, and no longer. Every constitution, then, and every law, naturally expires at the end of thirty-four years. If it be enforced longer, it is an act of force, and not of right. It may be said, that the succeeding generation exercising, in fact, the power of repeal, this leaves them as free as if the constitution or law had been expressly limited to thirty-four years only. In the first place, this objection admits the right, in proposing an equivalent. But the power of repeal is not an equivalent. It might be, indeed, if every form of government were so perfectly contrived, that the will of the majority could always be obtained, fairly and without impediment. But this is true of no form. The people cannot assemble themselves; their representation is unequal and vicious. Various checks are opposed to every legislative proposition. Factions get possession of the public councils, bribery corrupts them, personal interests lead them astray from the general interests of their constituents; and other impediments arise, so as to prove to every practical man, that a law of limited duration is much more manageable than one which needs a repeal.

This principle, that the earth belongs to the living and not to the dead, is of very extensive application and consequences in every country, and most especially in France. It enters into the resolution of the questions, whether the nation may change the descent of lands holden in tail; whether they may change the appropriation of lands given anciently to the church, to hospitals, colleges, orders of chivalry, and otherwise in perpetuity; whether they may abolish the charges and privileges attached on lands, including the whole catalogue, ecclesiastical and feudal; it goes to hereditary offices, authorities and jurisdictions, to hereditary orders, distinctions and appellations, to perpetual monopolies in commerce, the arts or sciences, with a long train of *et ceteras*; renders the question of reimbursement, a question of generosity and not of right. In all these cases, the legislature of the day could authorize such appropriations and establishments for their own time, but no longer; and the present holders, even where they or their ancestors have purchased, are in the case of bona fide purchasers of what the seller had no right to convey.

Turn this subject in your mind, my dear Sir, and particularly as to the power of contracting debts, and develop it with that cogent logic which is so peculiarly yours. Your station in the councils of our country gives you an opportunity of producing it to public consideration, of forcing it into discussion. At first blush it may be laughed at, as the dream of a theorist; but examination will prove it to be solid and salutary. It would furnish matter for a fine preamble to our first law for appropriating the public revenue; and it will exclude, at the threshold of our new government, the ruinous and contagious errors of this quarter of the globe, which have armed despots with means which nature does not sanction, for binding in chains their fellow-men. We have already given, in example, one effectual check to the dog of war, by transferring the power of declaring war from the executive to the legislative body, from those who are to spend, to those who are to pay. I should be pleased to see this second obstacle held out by us also, in the first instance. No nation can make a declaration against the validity of long-contracted debts, so disinterestedly as we, since we do not owe a shilling which will not be paid, principal and interest, by the measures you have taken, within the time of our own lives. I write you no news, because when an occasion occurs, I shall write a separate letter for that.

I am always, with great and sincere esteem, dear Sir, your affectionate friend and servant.

EDWARD RUTLEDGE, 1790, 8:59 ~ OUR SITUATION IS TOO CHANGING AND TOO IMPROVING TO RENDER AN UNCHANGEABLE TREATY EXPEDIENT FOR US.

To Edward Rutledge, Esq.[1]

New York, July 4, 1790

Dear Sir, Your favor of April 28 came to hand May 11, and found me under a severe indisposition, which kept me from all business more than a month, and still permits me to apply but very sparingly. That of June 20 was delivered me two days ago by young Mr. Middleton, whom I was very glad to see, as I am everybody and everything which comes from you. It will give me great pleasure to be of any use to him, on his father's account as well as yours.

In yours of April 28 you mention Dr. Turnbull's opinion that force alone can do our business with the Algerians. I am glad to have the concurrence of so good an authority on that point. I am clear myself that nothing but a perpetual cruise against them, or at least for eight months of the year, and for several years, can put an end to their piracies; and I believe that a confederacy of the nations not in treaty with them can be effected, so as to make that perpetual cruise, or our share of it, a very light thing, as soon as we shall have money to answer even a light thing; and I am in hopes this may shortly be the case. I participate fully of your indignation at the trammels imposed on our commerce with Great Britain. Some attempts have been made in Congress, and others are still making to meet their restrictions by effectual restriction

---

1 Edward Rutledge was born in Christ Church Parish, S.C., November 23, 1749; completed preparatory studies; studied law at the Middle Temple in London; returned to South Carolina; was admitted to the bar and commenced practice in 1773; Member of the Continental Congress 1774-1776; a signer of the Declaration of Independence; was a delegate to the first provincial congress in 1775 and to the second provincial congress 1775-1776; was appointed a member of the first board of war in June 1776 and member of the general assembly in 1778; was elected a Member of the Continental Congress in 1779 but did not take his seat; captain in the Charleston Battalion of Artillery in the Militia of South Carolina in the Revolution; taken prisoner when the British captured Charleston May 12, 1780, was imprisoned at St. Augustine until July 1781, when he was exchanged; member of the state house of representatives in 1782, 1786, 1788, and 1792; member of the state constitutional convention in 1790 and was author of the act abolishing the law of primogeniture in 1791; was tendered the appointment of Associate Justice of the United States Supreme Court in 1794 by President Washington, but did not accept; elected governor of South Carolina and served from December 6, 1798, until his death in Charleston, S.C., January 23, 1800. (United States Congress, 2008). Dr. Andrew Turnbull was a grantee in the colony New Smyrna, which was located some sixty miles down the coast from St. Augustine, Florida. Established in 1767, the grants reflected Great Britain's intention to promote settlements. Huge tracts of land, involving as many as ten or twenty thousand acres of land each, were offered to responsible individuals as one of the inducements. Turnbull planned to establish a colony of people skilled in the cultivation of the vine and in wine making and also familiar with the manufacture of fine silk goods. Seemingly his marriage to a Greek woman of Smyrna turned his attention to Mediterranean occupations which might be transplanted to the semitropical land of Florida. Turnbull's colony, when finally formed, numbered 1,400 to 1,500 people, many of them from islands of the western Mediterranean. Their arrival in 1767 is believed to be the largest single importation of foreign peoples into this part of the world (Brown 1943, 146).

on our part. It was proposed to double the foreign tonnage for a certain time, and after that to prohibit the exportation of our commodities in the vessels of nations not in treaty with us. This has been rejected. It is now proposed to prohibit any nation from bringing or carrying in their vessels what may not be brought or carried in ours from or to the same ports; also to prohibit those from bringing to us anything not of their own produce, who prohibit us from carrying to them anything but our own produce. It is thought, however, that this cannot be carried. The fear is that it would irritate Great Britain were we to feel any irritation ourselves. You will see by the debates of Congress that there are good men and bold men, and sensible men, who publicly avow these sentiments. Your observations on the expediency of making short treaties are most sound. Our situation is too changing and too improving to render an unchangeable treaty expedient for us. But what are these enquiries on the part of the British minister which leads you to think he means to treat? May they not look to some other object? I suspect they do; and can no otherwise reconcile all circumstances. I would thank you for a communication of any facts on this subject.

Some questions have lately agitated the minds of Congress more than the friends of union on catholic principles would have wished. The general assumption of State debts has been as warmly demanded by some States, as warmly rejected by others. I hope still that this question may be so divested of the injustice imputed to it as to be compromised. The question of residence, you know, was always a heating one. A bill has passed the Senate for fixing this at Philadelphia ten years, and then at Georgetown; and it is rather probable it will pass the lower house. That question then will be put to sleep for ten years; and this and the funding business being once out of the way, I hope nothing else may be able to call up local principles. If the war between Spain and England takes place, I think France will inevitably be involved in it. In that case I hope the new world will fatten on the follies of the old. If we can but establish the armed neutrality for ourselves, we must become the carriers for all parties as far as we can raise vessels.

The President had a hair-breadth escape; but he is now perfectly re-established, and looks much better than before he was sick.[1] I expect daily to see your nephew, Mr. J. Rutledge, arrive here, as he wrote me by the May packet that he would come in that of June. He is a very hopeful young man, sensible, well-informed, prudent and cool. Our southern sun has been accused of sometimes sublimating the temper too highly. I wish all could think as coolly, but as soundly and firmly as you do. Adieu, my dear friend. Yours affectionately.

---

[1] In the spring of 1790, Washington was felled by a severe cold and then by influenza. For several days it was thought that he could not live.

GEORGE GILMER, 1790, 8:63 - *THERE WILL BE WAR ENOUGH TO ENSURE US GREAT PRICES FOR WHEAT FOR YEARS TO COME.*

To Dr. Gilmer[1]

New York, July 25, 1790

Dear Doctor, I wrote you last on the 27th of June. Since that we have had great appearances of an explosion between Spain and England. Circumstances still indicate war. The strongest fact against it is that a British ambassador is actually gone to Madrid. If there be war, France will probably embark in it. I do not think it can disturb her revolution, that is so far advanced as to be out of danger. Be these things as they may, there will be war enough to ensure us great prices for wheat for years to come, and if we are wise we shall become wealthy. McGillivray, and about thirty Creek chiefs, are here. We are in hopes this visit will ensure the continuance of peace with them. The assumption in a proportionate form is likely to pass. The sum to be assumed is twenty-one millions. Of this three and a half millions are allotted to Virginia, being the exact sum it is supposed she will have to contribute of the whole assumption, and sufficient also to cover the whole of her remaining domestic debt. Being therefore to receive exactly what she is to pay, she will neither lose nor gain by the measure. The principal objection now is, that all the debts, general and State, will be to be raised by tax on imposts, which will thus be overburthened; whereas had the States been left to pay the debts themselves, they could I have done it by taxes on land and other property, which would thus have lightened the burthen on commerce. However, the measure was so vehemently called for by the State creditors in some parts of the Union, that it seems to be one of those cases where some sacrifice of opinion is necessary for the sake of peace. Congress will probably rise between the 6th and 13th of August. The President will soon after that go to Mount Vernon, and I shall take advantage of the interregnum to see my neighbors in Albemarle, and to meet my family there. I suppose it will be the 1st of September before I can set out from this place, and shall take that occasion of having my affairs removed hence to Philadelphia, Present me affectionately to Mrs. Gilmer and all my friends. Adieu, dear Doctor, your sincere friend and humble servant.

ATTORNEY GENERAL OF THE DISTRICT OF KENTUCKY, 1791, 8:191 - *NOR CAN A WELL-ORDERED GOVERNMENT TOLERATE SUCH AN ASSUMPTION OF ITS SOVEREIGNTY BY UNAUTHORIZED INDIVIDUALS.*

To the Attorney General of the District of Kentucky

Philadelphia, May 7, 1791

Sir, A certain James O'Fallon is, as we are informed, undertaking to raise, organize and commission an army, of his own authority, and independent of

---

1 A native of Scotland, George Gilmer received his medical training in Edinburg and emigrated to Virginia at an early date; he settled near Charlottesville. He served as a surgeon in the Revolutionary War and was the Jefferson family personal physician, as well as a close personal friend of Thomas Jefferson (Kennedy 1849, 63).

that of the government, the object of which is, to go and possess themselves of lands which have never yet been granted by any authority, which the government admits to be legal, and with an avowed design to hold them by force against any power, foreign or domestic.[1] As this will inevitably commit our whole nation in war with the Indian nations, and perhaps others, it cannot be permitted that all the inhabitants of the United States shall be involved in the calamities of war, and the blood of thousands of them be poured out, merely that a few adventurers may possess themselves of lands; nor can a well ordered government tolerate such an assumption of its sovereignty by unauthorized individuals. I send you herein the Attorney General's opinion of what may legally be done, with a desire that you proceed against the said O'Fallon according to lag. It is not the wish, to extend the prosecution to other individuals, who may have given thoughtlessly into his unlawful proceeding. I enclose you a proclamation to this effect. But they may be assured, that if this undertaking be prosecuted, the whole force of the United States will be displayed to punish the transgression. I enclose you one of O'Fallon's commissions, signed, as is said, by himself. I have the honor to be, with great esteem, Sir, your most obedient humble servant.

THOMAS BARCLAY, 1791, 8:199 - [IT IS] OUR DETERMINATION TO PREFER WAR IN ALL CASES TO TRIBUTE UNDER ANY FORM AND TO ANY PEOPLE WHATEVER.

To Thomas Barclay[2]

---

1 This discontent of the West and the weakness of the ties that bound it to the coastal states had also been shown in proposals by malcontents to England and to Spain. Even George Rogers Clark, the conqueror of the Illinois country in the famous campaign of 1778 and 1779, had desired in 1788 to take service under Spain in return for a liberal land grant. Clark was disgusted with the neglect which Virginia and the United States gave to his claims. His friend and adviser in this period was Dr. James O'Fallon, a Revolutionary soldier, who later married Clark's youngest sister. One of the land companies which purchased from Georgia a part of her western claims was the South Carolina Yazoo Company, of which the active agent was this Dr. O'Fallon. Since the colony was to be located in the region of the present Vicksburg, in territory claimed by Spain, O'Fallon attempted to conciliate that power by assuring Governor Esteban Rodriguez Miro that the colonists had been led to "consent to be the slaves of Spain, under the appearance of a free and independent colony, forming a rampart for the adjoining Spanish territories and establishing with them an eternal reciprocal alliance, offensive and defensive." In this proposed separation from the Union, it was rumored that George Rogers Clark had been selected as chief in command of the battalion which O'Fallon organized (Turner 1898, 652-653).

2 The first formally designated consular officer of the United States actually to serve abroad was Thomas Barclay, of Pennsylvania, who was elected Vice Consul to reside in France on June 26, 1781, and who was commissioned "vice consul in France" on July 10, 1781, with a salary of $1,000 a year. Barclay was an American merchant residing in France who had previously assisted Franklin and Adams in various matters. On October 5, 1781, he was elected and commissioned Consul in France in place of Palfrey. Less than a year after his appointment as Consul, Barclay was being referred to in the Congress as "Consul General." Barclay's duties and services went in fact beyond those of a consul general and included certain special fiscal and diplomatic activities which he performed concurrently with his consular duties. On November 18, 1782, the Congress resolved to appoint a commissioner to settle the public accounts of the United States in Europe, and on the same day it elected Barclay to fill this position. This task, which involved the review and final settlement of all

PHILADELPHIA, MAY 13, 1791

Sir, You are appointed by the President of the United States, to go to the court of Morocco, for the purpose of obtaining from the new Emperor, a recognition of our treaty with his father. As it is thought best that you should go in some definite character, that of consul has been adopted, and you consequently receive a commission as consul for the United States, in the dominions of the Emperor of Morocco, which, having been issued during the recess of the Senate, will, of course, expire at the end of their next session. It has been thought best, however, not to insert this limitation in the commission, as being unnecessary; and it might, perhaps, embarrass. Before the end of the next session of the Senate, it is expected the objects of your mission will be accomplished.

Lisbon being the most convenient port of between us and Morocco, sufficient authority will be given to Colonel Humphreys, resident of the United States at that place, over funds in Amsterdam, for the objects of your mission. On him, therefore, you will draw for the sums herein allowed, or such parts of them as shall be necessary. To that port, too, you had better proceed in the first vessel which shall be going there, as it is expected you will get a ready passage from thence to Morocco.

On your arrival at Morocco, sound your ground, and know how things stand at present. Your former voyage there, having put you in possession of the characters through whom this may be done, who may best be used for approaching the Emperor and effecting your purpose, you are left to use your own knowledge to the best advantage. The object being merely to obtain an acknowledgment of the treaty, we rely that you will be able to do this, giving very moderate presents. As the amount of these will be drawn into precedent, on future similar repetitions of them, it becomes important. Our distance, our seclusion from the ancient world, its politics and usages, our agricultural occupations and habits, our poverty, and lastly, our determination to prefer war in all cases, to tribute under any form, and to any people whatever, will furnish you with topics for opposing and refusing high or dishonoring pretensions; to which may be added, the advantages their people will derive from our commerce, and their sovereign, from the duties laid on whatever we extract from that country.

Keep us regularly informed of your proceedings and progress, by writing by every possible occasion, detailing to us particularly your conferences,

---

financial transactions of American agents in Europe, occupied him for more than two years. Subsequently, under dates of October 5 and 11, 1785, he was commissioned by John Adams and Jefferson, Ministers Plenipotentiary then in Europe, to negotiate a treaty of amity and commerce with Morocco. He carried out this mission successfully, concluding a treaty in the summer of 1786 and submitting it to Adams and Jefferson, who signed a certified translation of it in January 1787. Barclay retained his consular position throughout the remainder of the Continental Congress period. Under date of March 31, 1791, President Washington issued an interim commission to him as Consul for Morocco — forwarded by Jefferson in the above correspondence — but no record has been found of his subsequent nomination to the Senate. Barclay died at Lisbon on January 19, 1793 (Barnes 1961, 28-30).

either private or public, and the persons with whom they are held. We think that Francisco Chiappe has merited well of the United States, by his care of their peace and interests.[1] He has sent an account of disbursements for us, amounting to three hundred and ninety-four dollars. Do not recognize the account, because we are unwilling, by doing that, to give him a color for presenting larger ones hereafter, for expenses which it is impossible for us to scrutinize or control. Let him understand, that our laws oppose the application of public money so informally; but in your presents, treat him handsomely, so as not only to cover this demand, but go beyond it with a liberality which may fix him deeply in our interests. The place he holds near the Emperor renders his friendship peculiarly important. Let us have nothing further to do with his brothers, or any other person. The money which would make one good friend, divided among several, will produce no attachment. The Emperor has intimated that he expects an ambassador from us. Let him understand, that this may be a custom of the old world, but it is not ours; that we never sent an ambassador to any nation. You are to be allowed, from the day of your departure till your return, one hundred and sixty-six dollars and sixty-six cents and two-thirds, a month, for your time and expenses, adding thereto your passage money and sea stores going and coming.

Remain in your post till the 1st of April next, and as much longer as shall be necessary to accomplish the objects of your mission, unless you should receive instructions from hence to the contrary.

With your commission, you will receive a letter to the Emperor of Morocco, a cipher, and a letter to Colonel Humphreys[2,3] I have the honor to be, with great esteem, Sir, your most obedient, and most humble servant.

1 Don Francisco Chiappe was an Italian merchant who served as a confidential American agent in Morocco (*State Papers* 1819, 257).

2 Barclay also received a private instruction on May 13, 1791. He was instructed to commit it to memory: "We rely that you will obtain the friendship of the new Emperor, and his assurances that the treaty shall be faithfully observed, with as little expense as possible. But the sum of ten thousand dollars is fixed as the limit which all your donations together are not to exceed."

3 *The letter to the Emperor of Morocco:*

Great and Magnanimous Friend. Separated by an immense ocean from the more ancient nations of the earth, and little connected with their politics or proceedings, we are late in learning the events which take place among them, and later in conveying to them our sentiments thereon.

The death of the late Emperor, your father and our friend, of glorious memory, is one of those events which, though distant, attracts our notice and concern. Receive, great and good friend, my sincere sympathy with you on that loss; and permit me, at the same time, to express the satisfaction with which I learn the accession of so worthy a successor to the imperial throne of Morocco, and to offer you the homage of my sincere congratulations. May the days of your Majesty's life be many and glorious, and may they ever mark the era during which a great people shall have been most prosperous and happy, under the best and happiest of sovereigns!

The late Emperor, very soon after the establishment of our infant nation, manifested his royal regard and amity to us by many friendly and generous acts, and, particularly, by the protection of our citizens in their commerce with his subjects. And as a further instance of his desire to promote our prosperity and intercourse with his realms, he entered into a

JAMES MADISON, 1793, 9:33 ~ CONGRESS [MUST] BE CALLED [IF THERE] IS A JUSTIFIABLE CAUSE OF WAR.

To James Madison[1]

March, 1793

The idea seems to gain credit that the naval powers combining against France, will prohibit supplies, even of provisions, to that country. Should this be formally notified, I should suppose Congress would be called, because it is a justifiable cause of war, and as the Executive cannot decide the question of war on the affirmative side, neither ought it to do so on the negative side, by preventing the competent body from deliberating on the question. But I should hope that war would not be their choice. I think it will furnish us a happy opportunity of setting another precious example to the world, by showing that nations may be brought to do justice by appeals to their interests as well as by appeals to arms. I should hope that Congress, instead of a denunciation of war, would instantly exclude from our ports all the manufactures, produce, vessels and subjects of the nations committing this aggression, during the continuance of the aggression, and till full satisfaction made for it. This would work well in many ways, safely in all,

---

treaty of amity and commerce with us, for himself and his successors, to continue fifty years. The justice and magnanimity of your Majesty, leave us full confidence that the treaty will meet your royal patronage also; and it will give me great satisfaction to be assured, that the citizens of the United States of America may expect from your imperial Majesty, the same protection and kindness, which the example of your illustrious father has taught them to expect from those who occupy, the throne of Morocco, and to have your royal word, that they may count on a due observance of the treaty which cements the two nations in friendship.

This will be delivered to your Majesty, by our faithful citizen, Thomas Barclay, whom I name consul for these United States in the dominions of your Majesty, and who, to the integrity and knowledge qualifying him for that office, unites the peculiar advantage of having been the agent, through whom our treaty with the late Emperor was received. I pray your Majesty to protect him in the exercise of his functions for the patronage of the commerce between our two countries, and of those who carry it on.

May that God, whom we both adore, bless your imperial Majesty with long life, health and success, and have you always, great and magnanimous friend, under his holy keeping. Written at Philadelphia, the thirty-first day of March, in the fifteenth year of our sovereignty and independence, from your good and faithful friend.

1 On March 16, 1793, came news that the French National Convention had found Louis XVI guilty of treasonable conspiracy against the people, and by a vote of 361 to 360 had sent him to the guillotine. Jefferson believed the execution of the king to be a useful warning to all monarchs and aristocrats; but Washington was silent. Then, as speculation mounted on the probability of open war between France and England, Secretary of State Jefferson advanced the idea that the British would doubtless emerge as aggressors, as he anticipated that England, confident as ever in her control of the sea lanes, would soon decree against American shipment of foodstuffs to France, and probably would begin to impress American sailors into His Majesty's navy. Such outrages, Jefferson felt, would demand retaliation, and the President would have to summon Congress back into special session. "As the Executive cannot decide the question of war on the affirmative side," he wrote to Madison, "neither ought [he] to do so on the negative side by preventing the competent body from deliberating on the question." Jefferson would not urge actual hostilities with England, but he did hope that Congress would "instantly exclude" from the ports of the United States "all the manufactures, produce, vessels and subjects" of all nations at war with the Republic of France (Borden 1971, 14).

---

and introduce between nations another umpire than arms. It would relieve us, too, from the risks and the horrors of cutting throats. The death of the King of France has not produced as open condemnations from the monocrats as I expected. I dined the other day in a company where the subject was discussed. I will name the company in the order in which they manifested their partialities; beginning with the warmest Jacobinism, and proceeding by shades, to the most heartfelt aristocracy: Smith, (N.Y.), Coxe, Stewart, T. Shippen, Bingham, Peters, Breck, Meredith, Wolcott. It is certain that the ladies of this city, of the first circle, are open-mouthed against the murderers of a sovereign, and they generally speak those sentiments which the more cautious husband smothers. Ternant has at length openly hoisted the flag of monarchy by going into deep mourning for his prince. I suspect he thinks a cessation of his visits to me a necessary accompaniment to this pious duty. A connection between him and Hamilton seems to be springing up. On observing that Duer was Secretary to the old Board of Treasury, I suspect him to have been the person who suggested to Hamilton the letter of mine to that board, which he so tortured in his Catullus. Dunlop has refused to print the piece which we had heard of before your departure, and it has been several days in Bache's hands, without any notice of it. The President will leave this about the 27th instant, and return about the 20th of April. Adieu.

C. W. F. DUMAS, 1793, 9:56 ~ PEACE WITH ALL NATIONS, AND THE RIGHT WHICH THAT GIVES US WITH RESPECT TO ALL NATIONS, ARE OUR OBJECT.

To C.W.F. Dumas[1]
Philadelphia, March 24, 1793
Dear Sir,

I have to acknowledge the receipt of your favors of September 20, March 13, and Jan. 9. I shall hope your continuance to send us the Leyden Gazette as usual, but all the other gazettes which you have hitherto usually sent, may be discontinued. The scene in Europe is becoming very interesting. Amidst the confusion of a general war which seems to be threatening that quarter

1 Charles William Frederick Dumas was a native of Switzerland who lived in the Netherlands and served as an American secret agent in that country. A friend and correspondent of Benjamin Franklin's, Dumas was qualified for the post by his familiarity with several languages, his knowledge of international law, and his devotion to the American cause. Franklin asked Dumas to ascertain the disposition of the various courts represented at The Hague with respect to "assistance or alliance, if we should apply for the one or propose for the other." To this end he suggested that Dumas "confer directly with some great ministers, and show them this letter as your credential." Enclosed with the letter was a bill for £100 to reimburse Dumas "for the present" for his time and expenses. Dumas accepted the assignment and carried it out with vigor and enthusiasm, and secretly conversed with the French Minister at The Hague and with various other notables. Dumas carried on a voluminous correspondence with Franklin, with the Committee of Secret Correspondence, and with other American agents in Europe. He acted not only as an observer for the Congress in the Netherlands, but conducted a campaign of liberal propaganda there in favor of America. While his service continued through the Revolution and the period of the Confederation, the recognition and remuneration that he received from the Congress for it were pitifully meager (Barnes 1961, 11-12; Franklin 2006, 47).

of the globe, we hope to be permitted to preserve the line of neutrality. We wish not to meddle with the internal affairs of any country, nor with the general affairs of Europe. Peace with all nations, and the right which that gives us with respect to all nations, are our object. It will be necessary for all our public agents to exert themselves with vigilance for securing to our vessels all the rights of neutrality, and from preventing the vessels of other nations from usurping our flag. This usurpation tends to commit us with the belligerent power, to draw on those vessels truly ours, vigorous visita-tions to distinguish them from the counterfeits, and to take business from us. I recommend these objects to you. I have done the same to Mr. Greenleaf, lately appointed our Consul at Amsterdam. Be so good as to remember to send your account immediately after the 30th of June. I forward for you to Mr. Pinckney a copy of the laws of the late session of Congress; and am, with sincere esteem, dear Sir, your most obedient humble servant.

GEORGE HAMMOND, 1793, 9:89 ~ OUR DESIRE [IS] TO PURSUE OURSELVES THE PATH OF PEACE AS THE ONLY ONE LEADING SURELY TO PROSPERITY.

To George Hammond[1],[2]
Philadelphia, May 15, 1793

Sir, Your several memorials of the 8th instant have been laid before the President, as had been that of the 2d, as soon as received. They have been considered with all the attention and the impartiality which a firm deter-mination to do what is equal and right between all the belligerent powers, could inspire.

---

1 George Hammond was the first British Minister to America. He was born in 1763 in Yorkshire and educated at Merton College, Oxford. In 1783 he went to Paris as secretary to David Hartley, the younger, who was conducting the peace negotiations with France and America. Hammond established the legation at Philadelphia, which was then the capital, and in 1793 married Margaret Allen, of Philadelphia. The Hammonds were obliged to leave America because of the unpopularity of the Jay Treaty, which had been signed in 1794. He served in the Foreign Office in several capacities until his death in London in 1853 (National Archives 2008)

2 At this time — as France had declared war on Britain on February 1, 1793 — Jefferson found himself facing the problem of neutrality, and what constituted "true neutrality" became an immediate problem. When Jefferson benevolently watched the wild scenes of rejoicing which greeted the arrival of the French-captured English ship, the *Grange*, in Philadelphia, he had not realized that this would become the first test of American policy, albeit a com-paratively simple test. The *Grange*, according to Hammond, had been seized by the French frigate *Embuscade*, in American territorial waters. Jefferson assured him that if this were so, adequate steps would be taken to detain both ship and cargo and to prevent further viola-tions of American sovereignty. The second test was almost equally simple. Another British vessel had been sent to Charleston as a French prize and been condemned and offered for sale by the French consul. Again Hammond protested and Jefferson agreed that if the stated facts were true, the entire proceeding had been illegal and the French consul guilty of "an act of disrespect towards the United States." Thus far, Jefferson was acting with rigorous impartiality. The *Grange*, after inquiry, had established the correctness of Hammond's con-tention and was restored to the British; and the overzealous French consul in Charleston had been duly called to account. Jefferson, it seemed, had successfully walked the tightrope of neutrality under provocations from both warring powers, and with little in the way of precedents to guide him (Schachner 1957, 490-491).

In one of these, you communicate, on the information of the British consul at Charleston, that the consul of France at the same place had condemned as legal prize, a British vessel, captured by a French frigate, and you justly add that this judicial act is not warranted by the usage of nations, nor by the stipulations existing between the United States and France. I observe further, that it is not warranted by any law of the land. It is consequently a mere nullity; as such it can be respected in no court, can make no part in the title to the vessel, nor give to the purchaser any other security than what he would have had without it. In short, it is so absolutely nothing as to give no foundation of just concern to any person interested in the fate of the vessel; and in this point of view, Sir, I am in hopes you will see it. The proceeding, indeed, if the British consul has been rightly informed, and we have no other information of it, has been an act of disrespect towards the United States, to which its government cannot be inattentive; a just sense of our own rights and duties, and the obviousness of the principle, are a security that no inconveniences will be permitted to arise from repetitions of it.

The purchase of arms and military accoutrements by an agent of the French government, in this country, with an intent to export them t-o France, is the subject of another of the memorials. Of this fact we are equally uninformed as of the former. Our citizens have been always free to make, vend and export arms. It is the constant occupation and livelihood of some of them. To suppress their callings, the only means perhaps of their subsistence, because a war exists in foreign and distant countries, in which we have no concern, would scarcely be expected. It would be hard in principle, and impossible in practice. The law of nations, therefore, respecting the rights of those at peace, does not require from them such an internal derangement in their occupations. It is satisfied with the external penalty pronounced in the President's proclamation that of confiscation of such portion of these arms as shall fall into the hands of any of the belligerent powers on their way to the ports of their enemies. To this penalty our citizens are warned that they will be abandoned; and that even private contraventions may work no inequality between the parties at war, the benefits of them will be left equally free and open to all.

The capture of the British ship, *Grange*, by the French frigate, *Embuscade*, has on inquiry been found to have taken place within the bay of Delaware and jurisdiction of the United States, as stated in your memorial of the 2d instant. The Government is, therefore, taking measures for the liberation of the crew and restitution of the ship and cargo.

It condemns in the highest degree the conduct of any of our citizens who may personally engage in committing hostilities at sea against any of the nations, parties to the present war, and will exert all the means with which the laws and Constitution have armed them to discover such as offend herein, and bring them to condign punishment. Of these dispositions I am authorized to give assurances to all the parties, without reserve. Our real friendship for them all, our desire to pursue ourselves the path of peace, as the only one leading surely to prosperity, and our wish to preserve the morals of our citizens from being vitiated by courses of lawless plunder and murder, may assure you that our proceedings in this respect, will be with good faith, fervor and vigilance. Instructions are consequently given to the proper law officer, to institute such proceedings as the laws will justify, for apprehending and punishing certain individuals of our citizens, suggested to have been concerned in enterprises of this kind, as mentioned in one of your memorials of the 8th instant.

The practice of commissioning, equipping and manning vessels in our ports, to cruise on any of the belligerent parties, is equally and entirely disapproved; and the Government will take effectual measures to prevent a repetition of it. The remaining point in the same memorial is reserved for further consideration.

I trust, Sir, that in the readiness with which the United States have attended to the redress of such wrongs as are committed by their citizens, or within their jurisdiction, you will see proofs of their justice and impartiality to all parties; and that it will insure to their citizens pursuing their lawful business by sea or by land, in all parts of the world, a like efficacious interposition of governing powers to protect them from injury, and redress it, where it has taken place. With such dispositions on both sides, vigilantly and faithfully carried into effect, we may hope that the blessings of peace on the one part, will be as little impaired, and the evils of war on the other, as little aggravated, as the nature of things will permit; and that this should be so, is, we trust, the prayer of all.

I have the honor to be, with sentiments of respect, Sir, your most obedient, and most humble servant.

OPINION ON THE CAPTURE OF A BRITISH VESSEL, 1793, 3:247 -
MAKING REPRISAL ON A NATION IS A VERY SERIOUS THING.
Opinion Relative to Case of a British Vessel Captured by a French Vessel, Purchased by French Citizens,
and Fitted Out as a Privateer in One of Our Ports.[1]
May 16, 1793

The facts suggested, or to be taken for granted, because the contrary is not known, in the case now to be considered, are, that a vessel was purchased at Charleston, and fitted out as a privateer by French citizens, manned with foreigners chiefly, but partly with citizens of the United States. The command given to a French citizen by a regular commission from his government; that she has made prize of an English vessel in the open sea, and sent her into Philadelphia. The British minister demands restitution, and the question is, whether the Executive of the United States shall undertake to make it?

This transaction may be considered, 1st, as an offence against the United States; 2d, as an injury to Great Britain.

---

1 This opinion provides insight into Jefferson's thought processes with respect to the captured vessels and American pursuit of neutrality.

In the first view it is not now to be taken up. The opinion being, that it has been an act of disrespect to the jurisdiction of the United States, of which proper notice is to be taken at a proper time.

Under the second point of view, it appears to me wrong on the part of the United States (where not constrained by treaties) to permit one party in the present war to do what cannot be permitted to the other. We cannot permit the enemies of France to fit out privateers in our ports, by the 22d article of our treaty. We ought not, therefore, to permit France to do it; the treaty leaving us free to refuse, and the refusal being necessary to preserve a fair neutrality. Yet considering that the present is the first case which has arisen; that it has been in the first moment of the war, in one of the most distant ports of the United States, and before measures could be taken by the government to meet all the cases which may flow from the infant state of our government, and novelty of our position, it ought to be placed by Great Britain among the accidents of loss to which a nation is exposed in a state of war, and by no means as a premeditated wrong on the part of the government. In the last light it cannot be taken, because the act from which it results placed the United States with the offended, and not the offending party. Her minister has seen himself that there could have been on our part neither permission nor connivance. A very moderate apology then from the United States ought to satisfy Great Britain.

The one we have made already is ample, to wit, a pointed disapprobation of the transaction, a promise to prosecute and punish according to law such of our citizens as have been concerned in it, and to take effectual measures against a repetition. To demand more would be a wrong in Great Britain; for to demand satisfaction *beyond* what is adequate, is wrong. But it is proposed further to take the prize from the captors and restore her to the English. This is a very serious proposition.

The dilemma proposed in our conferences, appears to me unanswerable. Either the commission to the commander of the privateer was good, or not good. If not good, then the tribunals of the country will take cognizance of the transaction, receive the demand of the former owner, and make restitution of the capture; and there being, on this supposition, regular remedy at law, it would be irregular for the government to interpose. If the commission be good, then the capture having been made on the high seas, under a valid commission from a power at war with Great Britain, the British owner has lost all his right, and the prize would be deemed good, even in his own courts, were the question to be brought before his own courts. He has now no more claim on the vessel than any stranger would have who never owned her, his whole right being transferred by the laws of war to the captor.

The legal right then being in the captors, on what ground can we take it from him? Not on that of right, for the right has been transferred to him. It can only be by an act of force, that is to say, of reprisal for the offence committed against us in the port of Charleston. But the making reprisal on a nation is a very serious thing. Remonstrance and refusal of satisfaction ought to precede; and when reprisal follows, it is considered as an act of war, and never yet failed to produce it in the case of a nation able to make war; besides, if the case were important enough to require reprisal, and ripe for that step, Congress must be called on to take it; the right of reprisal being expressly lodged with them by the Constitution, and not with the Executive.

I therefore think that the satisfaction already made to the *government* of Great Britain is quite equal to what ought to be desired in the present case; that the property of the British *owner* is transferred by the laws of war to the *captor*; that for us to take it from the captor would be an act of force or reprisal, which the circumstances of the case do not justify, and to which the powers of the Executive are not competent by the Constitution.

JAMES MADISON, 1793, 9:138 ~ A DECLARATION OF NEUTRALITY WAS A DECLARATION THERE SHOULD BE NO WAR.

To James Madison[1]
Philadelphia, June 23, 1793

Dear Sir, My last was of the 17th, if I may reckon a single line anything. Yours of the 13th came to hand yesterday. The proclamation as first proposed was to have been a declaration of neutrality. It was opposed on these grounds: 1. That a declaration of neutrality was a declaration there should be no war, to which the Executive was not competent. 2. That it would be better to hold back the declaration of neutrality, as a thing worth something to the powers at war, that they would bid for it, and we might reasonably ask a price, the *broadest privileges* of neutral nations. The first objection was so far respected as to avoid inserting the term *neutrality*, and the drawing the instrument was left to E. R. That there should be a proclamation was passed unanimously with the approbation or the acquiescence of all parties. Indeed, it was not expedient to oppose it altogether, lest it should prejudice what was the next question, the boldest and greatest that ever was hazarded, and which would have called for extremities had it prevailed. Spain is unquestionably picking a quarrel with us. A series of letters from her commissioners here prove it. We are sending a courier to Madrid. The inevitableness of war with the Creeks, and the probability, I might say the certainty of it with Spain, (for there is not one of us who doubts it,) will certainly occasion your convocation, at what time I cannot exactly say, but you should be prepared for this important change in the state of things. The President has got pretty

---

1 In the spring of 1793, after the Second Congress had adjourned, news had reached Philadelphia that the revolutionary French government had declared war against Great Britain. On April 22, President Washington issued a neutrality proclamation. While the President's Cabinet had unanimously approved a declaration along these lines; but Jefferson had expressed serious misgivings, some of which were of a constitutional nature. The principal objection to the Washington's proclamation, as Jefferson explained in this is letter to Madison, was that since only Congress could declare war, only Congress could commit us to peace. In response to Jefferson's concerns, however, the word "neutrality" — which was understood to respect the future — was omitted from the proclamation and Congress remained free to perform its own duties as it saw fit: it could declare war or not, as it chose (Currie 1997, 174-175).

---

well again; he sets off this day to Mount Vernon, and will be absent a fortnight. The death of his manager, hourly expected, of a consumption is the call; he will consequently be absent on the 4th of July. He travels in a phaeton and pair. Doctor Logan sends you the enclosed pamphlet. Adieu. Yours affectionately.

JAMES MONROE, 1793. 9:161 ~ *NO CITIZEN SHOULD BE FREE TO COMMIT HIS COUNTRY TO WAR.*

To Colonel James Monroe[1]
Philadelphia, July 14, 1793

Dear Sir, Your favor of June 27th, has been duly received. You have most perfectly seized the original idea of the proclamation. When first proposed as a declaration of neutrality, it was opposed, first, because the Executive had no power to declare neutrality. Second, as such a declaration would be premature, and would lose us the benefit for which it might be bartered. It was urged that there was a strong impression in the minds of many that they were free to join in the hostilities on the side of France, others were unapprised of the danger they would be exposed to in carrying contraband goods, etc. It was therefore agreed that a proclamation should issue, declaring that we were in a state of peace, admonishing the people to do nothing contravening it, and putting them on their guard as to contraband. On this ground it was accepted or acquiesced in by all, and E. R., who drew it, brought it to me, the draught, to let me see there was no such word as *neutrality* in it. Circumstances forbid other verbal criticisms. The public, however, soon took it up as a declaration of neutrality, and it came to be considered at length as such. The arming privateers in Charleston, with our means entirely, and partly our citizens, was complained of in a memorial from Mr. Hammond. In our consultation, it was agreed we were by treaty *bound to* prohibit the enemies of France from arming in our ports, and were free to prohibit France also, and that by the laws of neutrality we are bound to permit or forbid the same things to both, as far as our treaties would permit. All, therefore, were forbidden to arm within our ports, and the vessels armed before the prohibition were on the advice of a majority ordered to leave our ports. With respect to our citizens who had joined in hostilities against a nation with whom we are at peace, the subject was thus viewed. Treaties are law. By

---

1 As background to the continuing dialogue regarding American neutrality, it is helpful to note that when France declared war on England in February 1793, the Federalist administration in Philadelphia was thrown into the power struggles of Europe and Americans found themselves all but forced to take sides between England and France. While it was the intention of Washington to remain as neutral as circumstances would permit, to most Virginians Washington's April 1793 Proclamation of Neutrality was proof that the Federalists sought to undermine the republican government of France. Virginians condemned the Proclamation for its apparent failure to reiterate the attachment of the United States to the French revolutionary cause and for what they believed to be its tendency to make the United States further dependent upon Great Britain. In particular, they charged that the members of the mercantile community had sacrificed the political independence of the United States for the sake of their own pocketbooks (Beeman 172, 120-121).

the treaty with England we are in a state of peace with her. He who breaks that peace, if within our jurisdiction, breaks the laws, and is punishable by them. And if he is punishable he ought to be punished, because no citizen should be free to commit his country to war. Some vessels were taken within our bays. There, foreigners as well as natives are liable to punishment. Some were committed in the high seas. There, as the sea is a common jurisdiction to all nations, and divided *by persons*, each having a right to the jurisdiction over their own citizens only, our citizens only were punishable by us. But they were so, because within our jurisdiction. Had they gone into a foreign land and committed a hostility, they would have been clearly out of our jurisdiction and unpunishable by the existing laws. As the armament in Charleston had taken place before our citizens might have reflected on the case, only two were prosecuted, merely to satisfy the complaint made, and to serve as a warning to others. But others having attempted to arm another vessel in New York after this was known, all the persons concerned in the latter case, foreign as well as native, were directed to be prosecuted. The Attorney General gave an official opinion that the act was against law, and coincided with all our private opinions; and the lawyers of this State, New York and Maryland, who were applied to, were unanimously of the same opinion. Lately Mr. Rawle, Attorney of the United States in this district, on a conference with the District Judge, Peters, supposed the law more doubtful. New acts, therefore, of the same kind, are left unprosecuted till the question is determined by the proper court, which will be during the present week. If they declare the act no offence against the laws, the Executive will have acquitted itself towards the nation attacked by their citizens, by having submitted them to the sentence of the laws of their country, and towards those laws by an appeal to them in a case which interested the country, and which was at least doubtful. I confess I think myself that the case is punishable, and that, if found otherwise, Congress ought to make it so, or we shall be made parties in every maritime war in which the piratical spirit of the banditti in our ports can engage. I will write you what the judicial determination is. Our prospects with Spain appear to me, from circumstances taking place on this side the Atlantic, absolutely desperate. Measures are taken to know if they are equally so on the other side, and before the close of the year that question will be closed, and your next meeting must probably prepare for the new order of things. I fear the disgust of France is inevitable. We shall be to blame in past. But the new minister much more so. His conduct is indefensible by the most furious Jacobin. I only wish our countrymen may distinguish between him and his nation, and if the case should ever be laid before them, may not suffer their affection to the nation to be diminished. H., sensible of the advantage they have got, is urging a full appeal by the Government to the people. Such an explosion would manifestly endanger a dissolution of the friendship between the two nations, and ought therefore to be deprecated by every friend to our liberty; and none but an enemy to it would wish to avail himself of the indiscretions of an individual to compromit two nations esteeming each other ardently. It will prove that the agents of the two people are either great bunglers or great rascals, when they cannot preserve that peace which is the universal wish of both. The situation of the St. Domingo fugitives (aristocrats as they are) calls aloud for pity and charity. Never was so deep a tragedy presented to the feelings of man. I deny the power of the General Government to apply money to such a purpose, but I deny it with a bleeding heart. It belongs to the State governments. Pray urge ours to be liberal. The Executive should hazard themselves here on such an occasion, and the Legislature when it meets ought to approve and extend it. It will have a great effect in doing away the impression of other disobligations towards France. I become daily more convinced that all the West India islands will remain in the hands of the people of color, and a total expulsion of the whites sooner or later take place. It is high time we should pursue the bloody scenes which our children certainly, and possibly ourselves, (south of Potomac,) have to wade through, and try to avert them. We have no news from the continent of Europe later than the 1st of May. My love to Mrs. Monroe. Tell her they are paving the street before your new house. Adieu. Yours affectionately.

WILLIAM CARMICHAEL AND WILLIAM SHORT, 1793, 9:148 ~ WE ABHOR THE FOLLIES OF WAR, AND ARE NOT UNTRIED IN ITS DISTRESSES AND CALAMITIES.

To Messrs. Carmichael and Short[1]
Philadelphia, June 30, 1793

Gentlemen, I have received from Messrs. Viar and Jaudenes, the representatives of Spain at this place, a letter, which, whether considered in itself, or as the sequel of several others, conveys to us very disagreeable prospects of the temper and views of their court towards us. If this letter is a faithful expression of that temper, we presume it to be the effect of egregious misrepresentations by their agents in America. Revising our own dispositions and proceedings towards that power, we can find in them nothing but those

---

1 At this time the situation over the Indians, Creeks, Cherokees, Chickasaws and Choctaws, sandwiched between the United States and Spanish American possessions, was becoming more serious. The United States blamed Spanish agents for incitement of the Indians and for supplying them with arms. The Spanish blamed the United States for supplying the Chickasaws with corn and a piece of artillery to make war on the Creeks. The Spanish also sent Jefferson a list of charges against the United States couched in language he considered most offensive, and containing, as Jefferson thought, a threat of war in case of action against the Creeks by the United States. Jefferson notified the Spanish Commissioners that their style was offensive and the question of Indian troubles would be handled at their Court. For this purpose he asked them to furnish the proper passports for a courier to convey these dispatches. The young man selected for this task was James Blake, who was instructed to proceed to Cadiz, thence to Madrid, and place his dispatches — including this June 30, 1793 letter — in the hands of the American Commissioners William Carmichael and William Short. Unfortunately, the arrival of Blake with this arguably belligerent note came at a most inopportune time since Spain had now joined England in war against France. Yet, this seeming lack of consideration on Jefferson's part can be excused as, when Blake left America, Jefferson had not yet received any letters from Carmichael and Short, although they estimated that four of their letters should have reached him (Coe 1928, 93-94).

of peace and friendship for them; and conscious that this will be apparent from a true statement of facts, I shall proceed to give you such a one, to be communicated to the court of Madrid. If they find it very different from that conveyed to them by others, they may think it prudent to doubt, and to take and to give time for mutual inquiry and explanation. I shall proceed to give you this statement, beginning it from an early period.

At the commencement of the late war, the United States laid it down as a rule of their conduct, to engage the Indian tribes within their neighborhood to remain strictly neutral. They accordingly strongly pressed it on them, urg-ing that it was a family quarrel with which they had nothing to do, and in which we wished them to take no part; and we strengthened these recom-mendations by doing them every act of friendship and good neighborhood, which circumstances left in our power. With some, these solicitations pre-vailed; but the greater part of them suffered themselves to be drawn into the war against us. They waged it in their usual cruel manner, murdering and scalping men, women and children, indiscriminately, burning their houses, and desolating the country. They put us to vast expense, as well by the con-stant force we were obliged to keep up in that quarter, as by the expeditions of considerable magnitude which we were under the necessity of sending into their country from time to time.

Peace being at length concluded with England, we had it also to con-clude with them. They had made war on us without the least provocation or pretence of injury. They had added greatly to the cost of that war. They had insulted our feelings by their savage cruelties. They were by our arms com-pletely subdued and humbled. Under all these circumstances, we had a right to demand substantial satisfaction and indemnification. We used that right, however, with real moderation. Their limits with us under the former gov-ernment were generally ill defined, questionable, and the frequent cause of war. Sincerely desirous of living in their peace, of cultivating it by every act of justice and friendship, and of rendering them better neighbors by introduc-ing among them some of the most useful arts, it was necessary to begin by a precise definition of boundary. Accordingly, at the treaties held with them, our mutual boundaries were settled; and notwithstanding our just right to concessions adequate to the circumstances of the case, we required such only as were inconsiderable; and for even these, in order that we might place them in a state of perfect conciliation, we paid them a valuable consideration, and granted them annuities in money which have been regularly paid, and were equal to the prices for which they have usually sold their lands.

Sensible, as they were, of the wrong they had done, they expected to make some indemnification, and were, for the most part, satisfied with the mode and measure of it. In one or two instances, where dissatisfaction was observed to remain as to the boundaries agreed on, or doubts entertained of the authority of those with whom they were agreed, the United States invit-ed the parties to new treaties, and rectified what appeared to be susceptible of it. This was particularly the case with the Creeks. They complained of an

inconvenient cession of lands on their part, and by persons not duly representing their nation. They were, therefore, desired to appoint a proper deputation to revise their treaty; and that there might be no danger of any unfair
practices, they were invited to come to the seat of the General Government,
and to treat with that directly. They accordingly came. A considerable proportion of what had been ceded, was, on the revision, yielded back to them,
and nothing required in lieu of it; and though they would have been better
satisfied to have had the whole restored, yet they had obtained enough to
satisfy them well. Their nation, too, would have been satisfied, for they were
conscious of their aggression, and of the moderation of the indemnity with
which we had been contented. But at that time came among them an adventurer of the name of Bowles, who, acting from an impulse with which we
are unacquainted, flattered them with the hope of some foreign interference,
which should undo what had been done, and force us to consider the naked
grant of their peace as a sufficient satisfaction for their having made war on
us. Of this adventurer the Spanish government rid us; but not of his principles, his practices, and his excitements against us. These were more than
continued by the officers commanding at New Orleans and Pensacola, and
by agents employed by them, and bearing their commission. Their proceedings have been the subject of former letters to you, and proofs of these proceedings have been sent to you. Those, with others now sent, establish the
facts, that they called assemblies of the southern Indians, openly persuaded
them to disavow their treaties, and the limits therein established, promised
to support them with all the powers which depended on them, assured them
of the protection of their sovereign, gave them arms in great quantities for
the avowed purpose of committing hostilities on us, and promised them future supplies to their utmost need. The Chickasaws, the most steady and
faithful friends of these States, have remained unshaken by these practices.
So also have the Chocktaws, for the most part. The Cherokees have been
teased into some expressions of discontent, delivered only to the Spanish
Governors, or their agents; while to us they have continued to speak the language of peace and friendship. One part of the nation only, settled at Cucka-
mogga and mixed with banditti and outcasts from the Shawanese and other
tribes, acknowledging control from none, and never in a state of peace, have
readily engaged in the hostilities against us to which they were encouraged.
But what was much more important, great numbers of the Creeks, chiefly
their young men, have yielded to these incitements, and have now, for more
than a twelvemonth, been committing murders and desolations on our frontiers. Really desirous of living in peace with them, we have redoubled our
efforts to produce the same disposition in them. We have borne with their
aggressions, forbidden all returns of hostility against them, tied up the hands
of our people, insomuch that few instances of retaliation have occurred even
from our suffering citizens; we have multiplied our gratifications to them,
fed them when starving, from the produce of our own fields and labor. No
longer ago than the last winter, when they had no other resource against

famine, and must have perished in great numbers, we carried into their country and distributed among them, gratuitously, ten thousand bushels of corn; and that, too, at the same time, when their young men were daily committing murders on helpless women and children on our frontiers. And though these depredations now involve more considerable parts of the nation, we are still demanding punishment of the guilty individuals, and shall be contented with it. These acts of neighborly kindness and support on our part have not been confined to the Creeks, though extended to them in much the greatest degree. Like wants among the Chickasaws had induced us to send to them also, at first, five hundred bushels of corn, and afterwards, fifteen hundred more. Our language to all the tribes of Indians has constantly been, to live in peace with one another, and in a most especial manner, we have used our endeavors with those in the neighborhood of the Spanish colonies, to be peaceable towards those colonies. I sent you on a former occasion the copy of a letter from the Secretary of War to Mr. Seagrove, one of our agents with the Indians in that quarter, merely to convey to you the general tenor of the conduct marked out for those agents; and I desired you, in placing before the eyes of the Spanish ministry the very contrary conduct observed by their agents here, to invite them to a reciprocity of good offices with our Indian neighbors, each for the other, and to make our common peace the common object of both nations. I can protest that such have hitherto been the candid and zealous endeavors of this government, and that if its agents have in any instance acted in another way, it has been equally unknown and unauthorized by us, and that were even probable proofs of it produced, there would be no hesitation to mark them with the disapprobation of the government. We expected the same friendly condescension from the court of Spain, in furnishing you with proofs of the practices of the Governor de Carondelet in particular practices avowed by him, and attempted to be justified in his letter.

In this state of things, in such dispositions towards Spain and towards the Indians, in such a course of proceedings with respect to them, and while negotiations were instituted at Madrid for arranging these and all other matters which might affect our friendship and good understanding, we received from Messrs. de Viar and Jaudenes their letter of May the 25th, which was the subject of mine of May the 31st to you; and now again we have received that of the 18th instant, a copy of which is enclosed. This letter charges us, and in the most disrespectful style, with

1. Exciting the Chickasaws to war on the Creeks.
2. Furnishing them with provisions and arms.
3. Aiming at the occupation of a post at the *Ecores amargas*.
4. Giving medals and marks of distinction to several Indians.
5. Meddling with the affairs of such as are allies of Spain.
6. Not using efficacious means to prevent these proceedings.

I shall make short observations on these charges.

1. Were the first true, it would not be unjustifiable. The Creeks have now a second time commenced against us a wanton and unprovoked war, and the present one in the face of a recent treaty, and of the most friendly and charitable offices on our part. There would be nothing out of the common course of proceeding then, for us to engage allies, if we needed any, for their punishment. But we neither need, nor have sought them. The fact itself is utterly false, and we defy the world to produce a single proof of it. The declaration of war by the Chickasaws, as we are informed, was a very sudden thing, produced by the murder of some of their people by a party of Creeks, and produced so instantaneously as to give nobody time to interfere, either to promote or prevent a rupture. We had, on the contrary, most particularly exhorted that nation to preserve peace, because in truth we have a most particular friendship for them. This will be evident from a copy of the message of the President to them, among the papers now enclosed.

2. The gift of provisions was but an act of that friendship to them, when in the same distress, which had induced us to give five times as much to the less friendly nation of the Creeks. But we have given arms to them. We believe it is the practice of every white nation to give arms to the neighboring Indians. The agents of Spain have done it abundantly, and, we suppose, not out of their own pockets, and this for purposes of avowed hostility on us; and they have been liberal in promises of further supplies. We have given a few arms to a very friendly tribe, not to make war on Spain, but to defend themselves from the atrocities of a vastly more numerous and powerful people, and one which, by a series of unprovoked and even unrepelled attacks on us, is obliging us to look towards war as the only means left of curbing their insolence.

3. We are aiming, as is pretended, at an establishment on the Mississippi. at the *Ecores amargas*. Considering the measures of this nature with which Spain is going on, having, since the proposition to treat with us on the subject, established posts at the Walnut hills and other places for two hundred miles upwards, it would not have been wonderful if we had taken countervailing measures. But the truth is, we have not done it. We wished to give a fair chance to the negotiation going on, and thought it but common candor to leave things in *statu quo*, to make no innovation pending the negotiation. In this spirit we forbid, and deterred even by military force, a large association of our citizens, under the name of the Yazoo companies, which had formed to settle themselves at those very Walnut hills, which Spain has since occupied. And so far are we from meditating the particular establishment so boldly charged in this letter, that we know not what place is meant by the *Ecores amargas*. This charge then is false also.

4. Giving medals and marks of distinction to the Indian chiefs. This is but blindly hinted at in this letter, but was more pointedly complained of in the former. This has been an ancient custom from time immemorial. The medals are considered as complimentary things, as marks of friendship to those who come to see us, or who do us good offices, conciliatory of their

good will towards us, and not designed to produce a contrary disposition towards others. They confer no power, and seem to have taken their origin in the European practice, of giving medals or other marks of friendship to the negotiators of treaties and other diplomatic characters, or visitors of distinction. The British government, while it prevailed here, practiced the giving medals, gorgets, and bracelets to the savages, invariably. We have continued it, and we did imagine, without pretending to know, that Spain also did it.

5. We meddle with the affairs of Indians in alliance with Spain. We are perfectly at a loss to know what this means. The Indians on our frontier have treaties both with Spain and us. We have endeavored to cultivate their friendship, to merit it by presents, charities, and exhortations to peace with their neighbors, and particularly with the subjects of Spain. We have carried on some little commerce with them, merely to supply their wants. Spain, too, has made them presents, traded with them, kept agents among them, though their country is within the limits established as ours at the general peace. However, Spain has chosen to have it understood that she has some claim to some parts of that country, and that it must be one of the subjects of our present negotiations. Out of respect for her .then, we have considered her pretensions to the country, though it was impossible to believe them serious, as coloring pretensions to a concern with those Indians on the same ground with our own, and we were willing to let them go on till a treaty should set things to right between us.

6. Another article of complaint is that we have not used efficacious means to suppress these practices. But if the charge is false, or the practice justifiable, no suppression is necessary.

And lastly, these gentlemen say that on a view of these proceedings of the United States with respect to Spain and the Indians, their allies, they foresee that our peace with Spain is very problematical in future. The principal object of the letter being our supposed excitements of the Chickasaws against the Creeks, and their protection of the latter, are we to understand from this, that if we arm to repulse the attacks of the Creeks on ourselves, it will disturb our peace with Spain? That if we will not fold our arms and let them butcher us without resistance, Spain will consider it as a cause of war? This is, indeed, so serious an intimation, that the President has thought it could no longer be treated with subordinate characters, but that his sentiments should be conveyed to the government of Spain itself, through you.

We love and we value peace; we know its blessings from experience. We abhor the follies of war, and are not untried in its distresses and calamities. Unmeddling with the affairs of other nations, we had hoped that our distance and our dispositions would have left us free, in the example and indulgence of peace with all the world. We had, with sincere and particular dispositions, courted and cultivated the friendship of Spain. We have made to it great sacrifices of time and interest, and were disposed to believe she would see her interests also in a perfect coalition and good understanding with us. Cherishing still the same sentiments, we have chosen, in the pres-

ent instance, to ascribe the intimations in this letter to the particular character of the writers, displayed in the peculiarity of the style of their communications, and therefore, we have removed the cause from them to their
sovereign, in whose justice and love of peace we have confidence. If we are
disappointed in this appeal, if we are to be forced into a contrary order of
things, our mind is made up. We shall meet it with firmness. The necessity
of our position will supersede all appeal to calculation now, as it has done
heretofore. We confide in our own strength, without boasting of it; we respect that of others, without fearing it. If we cannot otherwise prevail on the
Creeks to discontinue their depredations, we will attack them in force. If
Spain chooses to consider our defense against savage butchery as a cause of
war to her, we must meet her also in war, with regret, but without fear; and
we shall be happier, to the last moment, to repair with her to the tribunal of
peace and reason.

The President charges you to communicate the contents of this letter to
the court of Madrid, with all the temperance and delicacy which the dignity and character of that court render proper; but with all the firmness and
self-respect which befit a nation conscious of its rectitude, and settled in its
purpose.

I have the honor to be, with sentiments of the most perfect esteem and
respect, Gentlemen, your most obedient, and most humble servant.

GOUVERNEUR MORRIS, 1793, 9:180 - A NEUTRAL NATION MUST,
*IN ALL THINGS RELATING TO THE WAR, OBSERVE AN EXACT IMPARTIALITY
TOWARDS THE PARTIES.*

To Gouverneur Morris[1]
Philadelphia, August 16, 1793

Sir, In my letter of January the 13th, I enclosed to you copies of several letters which had passed between Mr. Ternant, Mr. Genet, and myself, on the
occurrences to which the present war had given rise within our ports. The
object of this communication was to enable you to explain the principles on
which our government was conducting itself towards the belligerent parties; principles which might not in all cases be satisfactory to all, but were
meant to be just and impartial to all. Mr. Genet had been then but a little
time with us; and but a little more was necessary to develop in him a char-

---

1 Gouverneur Morris, who represented Pennsylvania at the Convention in Philadelphia in 1787,
  was the author of much of the Constitution and although born into a world of wealth and
  aristocratic values, he came to champion the concept of a free citizenry united in an independent nation. In 1790, he acted as a diplomatic agent for President Washington in
  London to resolve issues left unsettled by the peace treaty, and later he replaced Jefferson as
  ambassador to France, then in the throes of its own revolution. Neither mission proved successful, although he did display great personal courage as the only diplomat who refused
  to flee Paris during the bloody Reign of Terror. Morris returned to New York in 1798 and
  became active in the Federalist party, allying himself with his friend Alexander Hamilton.
  During the last decade of his life Morris became increasingly disenchanted with the policies of President Jefferson and his successors. Although he supported the purchase of the
  Louisiana Territory, he was particularly virulent in his condemnation of the government's
  restrictive economic policies and controls during the War of 1812 (Wright 1987, 112-114).

acter and conduct so unexpected and so extraordinary, as to place us in the most distressing dilemma, between our regard for his nation, which is constant and sincere, and a regard for our laws, the authority of which must be maintained; for the peace of our country, which the executive magistrate is charged to preserve; for its honor, offended in the person of that magistrate; and for its character grossly traduced, in the conversations and letters of this gentleman. In the course of these transactions, it has been a great comfort to us to believe, that none of them were within the intentions or expectations of his employers. These had been too recently expressed in acts which nothing could discolor, in the letters of the Executive Council, in the letter and decrees of the National Assembly, and in the general demeanor of the nation towards us, to ascribe to them things of so contrary a character. Our first duty, therefore, was, to draw a strong line between their intentions and the proceedings of their Minister; our second, to lay those proceedings faithfully before them.

On the declaration of war between France and England, the United States being at peace with both, their situation was so new and inexperienced by themselves, that their citizens were not, in the first instant, sensible of the new duties resulting there from, and of the restraints it would impose even on their dispositions towards the belligerent powers. Some of them imagined (and chiefly their transient sea-faring citizens) that they were free to indulge those dispositions, to take side with either party, and enrich themselves by depredations on the commerce of the other, and were meditating enterprises of this nature, as there was reason to believe. In this state of the public mind, and before it should take an erroneous direction, difficult to be set right and dangerous to themselves and their country, the President thought it expedient, through the channel of a proclamation, to remind our fellow citizens that we were in a state of peace with all the belligerent powers, that in that state it was our duty neither to aid nor injure any, to exhort and warn them against acts which might contravene this duty, and particularly those of positive hostility, for the punishment of which the laws would be appealed to; and to put them on their guard also, as to the risks they would run, if they should attempt to carry articles of contraband to any. This proclamation, ordered on the 19th and signed the 22nd day of April, was sent to you in my letter of the 26th of the same month.

On the day of its publication, we received, through the channel of the newspapers, the first intimation that Mr. Genet had arrived on the 8th of the month at Charleston, in the character of Minister Plenipotentiary from his nation to the United States, and soon after, that he had sent on to Philadelphia the vessel in which he came, and would himself perform the journey by land. His landing at one of the most distant ports of the Union from his points both of departure and destination, was calculated to excite attention; and very soon afterwards, we learned that, he was undertaking to authorize the fitting and arming vessels in that port, enlisting men, foreigners and citizens, and giving them commissions to cruise and commit hostilities on nations at peace with us; that these vessels were taking and bringing prizes into our ports; that the Consuls of France were assuming to hold courts of admiralty on them, to try, condemn, and authorize their sale as legal prize, and all this before Mr. Genet had presented himself or his credentials to the President, before he was received by him, without his consent or consultation, and directly in contravention of the state of peace existing, and declared to exist in the President's proclamation, and incumbent on him to preserve till the constitutional authority should otherwise declare. These proceedings became immediately, as was naturally to be expected, the subject of complaint by the representative here of that power against whom they would chiefly operate. The British minister presented several memorials thereon, to which we gave the answer of May the 15th, heretofore enclosed to you, corresponding in substance with a letter of the same date written to Mr. Ternant, the Minister of France then residing here, a copy of which I send herewith. On the next day Mr. Genet reached this place, about five or six weeks after he had arrived at Charleston, and might have been at Philadelphia, if he had steered for it directly. He was immediately presented to the President, and received by him as the Minister of the Republic; and as the conduct before stated seemed to bespeak a design of forcing us into the war without allowing us the exercise of any free will in the case, nothing could be more assuaging than his assurance to the President at his reception, which he repeated to me afterwards in conversation, and in public to the citizens of Philadelphia in answer to an address from them, that on account of our remote situation and other circumstances, France did not expect that we should become a party to the war, but wished to see us pursue our prosperity and happiness in peace. In a conversation a few days after, Mr. Genet told me that M. de Ternant had delivered him my letter of May the 15th. He spoke something of the case of the *Grange*, and then of the armament at Charleston, explained the circumstances which had led him to it before he had been received by the government and had consulted its will, expressed a hope that the President had not so absolutely decided against the measure but that he would hear what was to be said in support of it, that he would write me a letter on the subject, in which he thought he could justify it under our treaty; but that if the President should finally determine otherwise, he must submit; for that assuredly his instructions were to do what would be agreeable to us. He accordingly wrote the letter of May the 27th. The President took the case again into consideration, and found nothing in that letter which could shake the grounds of his former decision. My letter of June the 5th notifying this to him, his of June the 8th and 14th, mine of the 17th, and his again of the 22nd, will show what further passed on this subject, and that he was far from retaining his disposition to acquiesce in the ultimate will of the President.

It would be tedious to pursue this and our subsequent correspondence through all their details. Referring therefore for these to the letters themselves, which shall accompany this, I will present a summary view only of the points of difference which have arisen, and the grounds on which they rest.

1. Mr. Genet asserts his right of arming in our ports and of enlisting our citizens, and that we have no right to restrain him or punish them. Examining this question under the law of nations, founded on the general sense and usage of mankind, we have produced proofs, from the most enlightened and approved writers on the subject, that a neutral nation must, in all things relating to the war, observe an exact impartiality towards the parties; that favors to one to the prejudice of the other would import a fraudulent neutrality, of which no nation would be the dupe; that no succor should be given to either, unless stipulated by treaty, in men, arms, or any thing else directly serving for war; that the right of raising troops being one of the rights of sovereignty, and consequently appertaining exclusively to the nation itself, no foreign power or person can levy men within its territory without its consent; and he who does, may be rightfully and severely punished; that if the United States have a right to refuse the permission to arm vessels and raise men within their ports and territories, they are bound by the laws of neutrality to exercise that right, and to prohibit such armaments and enlistments. To these principles of the law of nations Mr. Genet answers, by calling them 'diplomatic subtleties,' and 'aphorisms of Vattel and others.' But something more than this is necessary to disprove them; and till they are disproved, we hold it certain that the law of nations and the rules of neutrality forbid our permitting either party to arm in our ports.

But Mr. Genet says, that the twenty-second article of our treaty allows him expressly to arm in our ports. Why has he not quoted the very words of that article expressly allowing it? For that would have put an end to all further question. The words of the article are, 'It shall not be lawful for any foreign privateers not belonging to subjects of the M. C. King, nor citizens of the said United States, who have commissions from any foreign Prince or State in enmity with either nation, to fit their ships in the ports of either the one or the other of the aforesaid parties.' Translate this from the general terms in which it here stands, into the special case produced by the present war. 'Privateers not belonging to France or the United States, and having commissions from the enemies of one of them,' are, in the present state of things,' British, Dutch, and Spanish privateers.' Substituting these then for the equivalent terms, it will stand thus, 'It shall not be lawful for British, Dutch, or Spanish privateers, to fit their ships in the ports of the United States.' Is this an express permission to France to do it? Does the negative to the enemies of France, and silence as to France herself, imply an affirmative to France? Certainly not; it leaves the question as to France open, and free to be decided according to circumstances. And if the parties had meant an affirmative stipulation, they would have provided for it expressly; they would never have left so important a point to be inferred from mere silence or implications. Suppose they had desired to stipulate a refusal to their enemies, but nothing to themselves; what form of expression would they have used? Certainly the one they have used; an express stipulation as to their enemies, and silence as to themselves. And such an intention corresponds not only with the words, but with the circumstances of the times. It was of value to each party to exclude its enemies from arming in the ports of the other, and could in no case embarrass them. They therefore stipulated so far mutually. But each might be embarrassed by permitting the other to arm in its ports. They therefore would not stipulate to permit that. Let us go back to the state of things in France when this treaty was made, and we shall find several cases wherein France could not have permitted us to arm in her ports. Suppose a war between these States and Spain. We know, that by the treaties between France and Spain, the former could not permit the enemies of the latter to arm in her ports. It was honest in her, therefore, not to deceive us by such a stipulation. Suppose a war between these States and Great Britain. By the treaties between France and Great Britain, in force at the signature of ours, we could not have been permitted to arm in the ports of France. She could not then have meant in this article to give us such a right. She has manifested the same sense of it in her subsequent treaty with England, made eight years after the date of ours, stipulating in the sixteenth article of it, as in our twenty-second, that foreign privateers, not being subjects of either crown, should not arm against either in the ports of the other. If this had amounted to an affirmative stipulation that the subjects of the other crown might arm in her ports against us, it would have been in direct contradiction to her twenty-second article with us. So that to give to these negative stipulations an affirmative effect, is to render them inconsistent with each other, and with good faith; to give them only their negative and natural effect, is to reconcile them to one another and to good faith, and is clearly to adopt the sense in which France herself has expounded them. We may justly conclude then, that the article only obliges us to refuse this right, in the present case, to Great Britain and the other enemies of France. It does not go on to give it to France, either expressly or by implication. We may then refuse it. And since we are bound by treaty to refuse it to the one party, and are free to refuse it to the other, we are bound by the laws of neutrality to refuse it to that other. The aiding either party then with vessels, arms, or men, being unlawful by the law of nations, and not rendered lawful by the treaty, it is made a question whether our citizens, joining in these unlawful enterprises, may be punished.

The United States being in a state of peace with most of the belligerent powers by treaty, and with all of them by the laws of nature, murders and robberies committed by our citizens within our territory, or on the high seas, on those with whom we are so at peace, are punishable equally as if committed on our own inhabitants. If I might venture to reason a little formally, without being charged with running into 'subtleties and aphorisms,' I would say, that if one citizen has a right to go to war of his own authority, every citizen has the same. If every citizen has that right, then the nation (which is composed of all its citizens) has a right to go to war, by the authority of its individual citizens. But this is not true either on the general principles of society, or by our constitution, which gives that power to Congress alone, and not to the citizens individually. Then the first position was not true; and no citizen has a right to go to war of his own authority, and for what he does without right, he ought to be punished. Indeed, nothing can be more obviously absurd than to say, that all the citizens may be at war, and yet the nation at peace.

It has been pretended, indeed, that the engagement of a citizen in an enterprise of this nature, was a divestment of the character of citizen, and a transfer of jurisdiction over him to another sovereign. Our citizens are certainly free to divest themselves of that character by emigration and other acts manifesting their intention, and may then become the subjects of another power, and free to do whatever the subjects of that power may do. But the laws do not admit that the bare commission of a crime amounts of itself to a divestment of the character of citizen, and withdraws the criminal from their coercion. They would never prescribe an illegal act among the legal modes by, which a citizen might disfranchise himself; nor render treason, for instance, innocent by giving it the force of dissolution of the obligation of the criminal to his country. Accordingly, in the case of Henfeild, a citizen of these States, charged with having engaged in the port of Charleston, in an enterprise against nations at peace with us, and with having joined in the actual commission of hostilities, the Attorney General of the United States, in an official opinion, declared, that the act with which he was charged was punishable by law. The same thing has been unanimously declared by two of the Circuit Courts of the United States, as you will see in the charges of Chief Justice Jay, delivered at Richmond, and Judge Wilson, delivered at Philadelphia, both of which are herewith sent. Yet Mr. Genet, in the moment he lands at Charleston, is able to tell the Governor, and continues to affirm in his correspondence here, that no law of the United States authorizes their government to restrain either its own citizens or the foreigners inhabiting its territory, from warring against the enemies of France. It is true, indeed, that in the case of Henfeild, the jury which tried, absolved him. But it appeared on the trial, that the crime was not knowingly and willfully committed; that Henfeild was ignorant of the unlawfulness of his undertaking; that in the moment he was apprized of it, he showed real contrition; that he had rendered meritorious services during the late war, and declared he would live and die an American. The jury, therefore, in absolving him, did no more than the constitutional authority might have done, had they found him guilty: the constitution having provided for the pardon of offences in certain cases, and there being no case where it would have been more proper than where no offence was contemplated. Henfeild, therefore, was still an American citizen, and Mr. Genet's reclamation of him was as unauthorized as the first enlistment of him.

2. Another doctrine advanced by Mr. Genet is, that our courts can take no cognizance of questions whether vessels, held by theirs, as prizes, are lawful prizes or not; that this jurisdiction belongs exclusively to their consulates here, which have been lately erected by the National Assembly into

complete courts of admiralty. Let us consider, first, what is the extent of jurisdiction which the consulates of France may rightfully exercise here. Every nation has of natural right, entirely and exclusively, all the jurisdiction which may be rightfully exercised in the territory it occupies. If it cedes any portion of that jurisdiction to judges appointed by another nation, the limits of their power must depend on the instrument of cession. The United States and France have, by their consular convention, given mutually to their Consuls jurisdiction in certain cases especially enumerated. But that convention gives to neither the power of establishing complete courts of admiralty within the territory of the other, nor even of deciding the particular question of prize, or not prize. The consulates of France, then, cannot take judicial cognizance of those questions here. Of this opinion Mr. Genet was, when he wrote his letter of May the 27th, wherein he promises to correct the error of the Consul at Charleston, of whom, in my letter of the 15th instant, I had complained, as arrogating to himself that jurisdiction; though in his subsequent letters he has thought proper to embark in the errors of his Consuls.

But the United States, at the same time, do not pretend any right to try the validity of captures made on the high seas, by France, or any other nation, over its enemies. These questions belong of common usage to the sovereignty of the captor, and whenever it is necessary to determine them, resort must be had to his courts. This is the case provided for in the seventeenth article of the treaty, which says, that such prizes shall not be arrested, nor cognizance taken of the validity thereof; a stipulation much insisted on by Mr. Genet and the Consuls, and which we never thought of infringing or questioning. As the validity of captures then, made on the high seas by France over its enemies, cannot be tried within the United States by their Consuls, so neither can it by our own courts. Nor is this the question between us, though we have been misled into it.

The real question is whether the United States have not a right to protect vessels within their waters and on their coasts? The *Grange* was taken within the Delaware, between the shores of Jersey and of the Delaware State, and several miles above its mouth. The seizing her was a flagrant violation of the jurisdiction of the United States. Mr. Genet, however, instead of apologizing, takes great merit in his letters for giving her up. The William is said to have been taken within two miles of the shores of the United States. When the admiralty declined cognizance of the case, she was delivered to the French Consul according to my letter of June the 25th, to be kept till the executive of the United States should examine into the case; and Mr. Genet was desired by my letter of June the 29th, to have them furnished with the evidence on behalf of the captors, as to the place of capture. Yet to this day it has never been done. The brig Fanny was alleged to be taken within five miles from our shore; the Catharine within two miles and a half. It is an essential attribute of the jurisdiction of every country to preserve peace, to punish acts in breach of it, and to restore property taken by force within its limits. Were the armed vessel of any nation to cut away one of our own from the wharves of Philadelphia, and to choose to call it a prize, would this exclude us from the right of redressing the wrong? Were it the vessel of another nation, are we not equally bound to protect it, while within our limits? Were it seized in any other of our waters, or on the shores of the United States, the right of redressing is still the same: and humble indeed would be our condition, were we obliged to depend for that on the will of a foreign Consul, or on negotiation with diplomatic agents. Accordingly, this right of protection within its waters and to a reasonable distance on its coasts, has been acknowledged by every nation, and denied to none: and if the property seized be yet within their power, it is their right and duty to redress the wrong themselves. France herself has asserted the right in herself and recognized it in us, in the sixth article of our treaty, where we mutually stipulate that we will, by all the means in our power (not by negotiation), protect and defend each other's vessels and effects in our ports or roads, or on the seas near our countries, and recover and restore the same to the right owners. The United Netherlands, Prussia, and Sweden, have recognized it also in treaties with us; and indeed it is a standing formula, inserted in almost all the treaties of all nations, and proving the principle to be acknowledged by all nations.

How, and by what organ of the government, whether judiciary or executive, it shall be redressed, is not yet perfectly settled with us. One of the subordinate courts of admiralty has been of opinion, in the first instance, in the case of the ship *William*, that it does not belong to the judiciary. Another, perhaps, may be of a contrary opinion. The question is still *sub judice*, and an appeal to the court of last resort will decide it finally. If finally the judiciary shall declare that it does not belong to the civil authority, it then results to the executive, charged with the direction of the military force of the Union, and the conduct of its affairs with foreign nations. But this is a mere question of internal arrangement between the different departments of the government, depending on the particular diction of the laws and constitution; and it can in no wise concern a foreign nation to which department these have delegated it.

3. Mr. Genet, in his letter of July the 9th, requires that the ship Jane, which he calls an English privateer, shall be immediately ordered to depart; and to justify this, he appeals to the 22nd article of our treaty, which provides that it shall not be lawful for any foreign privateer to fit their ships in our ports, to sell what they have taken, or purchase victuals, &c. The ship Jane is an English merchant vessel, which has been many years employed in the commerce between Jamaica and these States. She brought here a cargo of produce from that island, and was to take away a cargo of flour. Knowing of the war when she left Jamaica, and that our coast was lined with small French privateers, she armed for her defense, and took one of those commissions usually called letters of marque. She arrived here safely without having had any reencounter of any sort. Can it be necessary to say that a merchant vessel is not a privateer? That though she has arms to defend herself in time of war, in the course of her regular commerce, this no more makes her a privateer, than a

husbandman following his plough in time of war, with a knife or pistol in his pocket, is thereby made a soldier? The occupation of a privateer is attack and plunder, that of a merchant vessel is commerce and self-preservation. The article excludes the former from our ports, and from selling what she has taken, that is what she has acquired by war, to show it did not mean the merchant vessel and what she had acquired by commerce. Were the merchant vessels coming for our produce forbidden to have any arms for their defense, every adventurer who had a boat, or money enough to buy one, would make her a privateer, our coasts would swarm with them, foreign vessels must cease to come, our commerce must be suppressed, our produce remain on our hands, or at least that great portion of it which we have not vessels to carry away, our ploughs must be laid aside, and agriculture suspended. This is a sacrifice no treaty could ever contemplate, and which we are not disposed to make out of mere complaisance to a false definition of the term privateer. Finding that the Jane had purchased new carriages to mount two or three additional guns, which she had brought in her hold, and that she had opened additional port-holes for them, the carriages were ordered to be relanded, the additional port-holes stopped, and her means of defense reduced, to be exactly the same at her departure as at her arrival. This was done on the general principle of allowing no party to arm within our ports.

4. The seventeenth article of our treaty leaves armed vessels free to conduct, whithersoever they please, the ships and goods taken from their enemies without paying any duty, and to depart and be conducted freely to the places expressed in their commissions, which the captain shall be obliged to show. It is evident, that this article does not contemplate a freedom to sell their prizes here; but on the contrary, a departure to some other place, always to be expressed in their commission, where their validity is to be finally adjudged. In such case, it would be as unreasonable to demand duties on the goods they had taken from an enemy, as it would be on the cargo of a merchant vessel touching in our ports for refreshment or advices; and against this the article provides. But the armed vessels of France have been also admitted to land and sell their prize-goods here for a consumption, in which case, it is as reasonable they should pay duties, as the goods of a merchant-man landed and sold for consumption. They have however demanded, and as a matter of right, to sell them free of duty, a right, they say, given by this article of the treaty, though the article does not give the right to sell at all. Where a treaty does not give the principal right of selling, the additional one of selling duty free cannot be given: and the laws, in admitting the principal right of selling, may withhold the additional one of selling duty free. It must be observed, that our revenues are raised almost wholly on imported goods. Suppose prize-goods enough should be brought in to supply our whole consumption. According to their construction we are to lose our whole revenue. I put the extreme case to evince, more extremely, the unreasonableness of the claim. Partial supplies would affect the revenue but partially. They would lessen the evil, but not the error, of the construction: and I believe we

may say, with truth, that neither party had it in contemplation, when penning this article, to abandon any part of its revenue for the encouragement of the sea-robbers of the other.

5. Another source of complaint with Mr. Genet has been that the English take French goods out of American vessels, which he says is against the law of nations, and ought to be prevented by us. On the contrary, we suppose it to have been long an established principle of the law of nations, that the goods of a friend are free in an enemy's vessel, and an enemy's goods lawful prize in the vessel of a friend. The inconvenience of this principle, which subjects merchant vessels to be stopped at sea, searched, ransacked, led out of their course, has induced several nations latterly to stipulate against it by treaty, and to substitute another in its stead, that free bottoms shall make free goods, and enemy bottoms enemy goods; a rule equal to the other in point of loss and gain, but less oppressive to commerce. As far as it has been introduced, it depends on the treaties stipulating it, and forms exceptions, in special cases, to the general operation of the law of nations. We have introduced it into our treaties with France, Holland, and Prussia; and French goods found by the two latter nations in American bottoms are not made prize of. It is our wish to establish it with other nations. But this requires their consent also, is a work of time, and in the mean while, they have a right to act on the general principle, without giving to us or to France cause of complaint. Nor do I see that France can lose by if on the whole. For though she loses her goods when found in our vessels by the nations with whom we have no treaties, yet she gains our goods, when found in the vessels of the same and all other nations: and we believe the latter mass to be greater than the former. It is to be lamented, indeed, that the general principle has operated so cruelly in the dreadful calamity which has lately happened in St. Domingo. The miserable fugitives, who, to save their lives, had taken asylum in our vessels, with such valuable and portable things as could be gathered in the moment out of the ashes of their houses and wrecks of their fortunes, have been plundered of these remains by the licensed sea-rovers of their enemies. This has swelled, on this occasion, the disadvantages of the general principle, that 'an enemy's goods are free prize in the vessels of a friend.' But it is one of those deplorable and unforeseen calamities to which they expose themselves who enter into a state of war, furnishing to us an awful lesson to avoid it by justice and moderation, and not a cause or encouragement to expose our own towns to the same burnings and butcheries, nor of complaint because we do not.

6. In a case like the present, where the missionary of one government construes differently from that to which he is sent, the treaties and laws which are to form a common rule of action for both, it would be unjust in either to claim an exclusive right of construction. Each nation has an equal right to expound the meaning of their common rules; and reason and usage have established, in such cases, a convenient and well understood train of proceeding. It is the right and duty of the foreign missionary to urge his own

constructions, to support them with reasons which may convince, and in terms of decency and respect which may reconcile the government of the country to a concurrence. It is the duty of that government to listen to his reasonings with attention and candor, and to yield to them when just. But if it shall still appear to them that reason and right are on their side, it follows of necessity, that exercising the sovereign powers of the country, they have a right to proceed on their own constructions and conclusions as to whatever is to be done within their limits. The minister then refers the case to his own government, asks new instructions, and, in the mean time, acquiesces in the authority of the country. His government examines his constructions, abandons them if wrong, insists on them if right, and the case then becomes a matter of negotiation between the two nations. Mr. Genet, however, assumes a new and bolder line of conduct. After deciding for himself ultimately, and without respect to the authority of the country, he proceeds to do what even his sovereign could not authorize, to put himself within the country on a line with its government, to act as co-sovereign of the territory; he arms vessels, levies men, gives commissions of war, independently of them, and in direct opposition to their orders and efforts. When the government forbids their citizens to arm and engage in the war, he undertakes to arm and engage them. When they forbid vessels to be fitted in their ports for cruising on nations with whom they are at peace, he commissions them to fit and cruise. When they forbid an unceded jurisdiction to be exercised within their territory by foreign agents, he undertakes to uphold that exercise, and to avow it openly. The privateers *Citoyen Genet* and *Sans Culottes* having been fitted out at Charleston (though without the permission of the government, yet before it was forbidden) the President only required they might leave our ports, and did not interfere with their prizes. Instead, however, of their quitting our ports, the *Sans Culottes* remains still, strengthening and equipping herself, and the *Citoyen Genet* went out only to cruise on our coast, and to brave the authority of the country by returning into port again with her prizes. Though in the letter of June the 5th, the final determination of the President was communicated, that no future armaments in our ports should be permitted, the *Vainqueur de la Bastille* was afterwards equipped and commissioned in Charleston, the *Anti-George* in Savannah, the *Carmagnole* in Delaware, a schooner and a sloop in Boston, and the *Polly* or *Republican* was attempted to be equipped in New York, and was the subject of reclamation by Mr. Genet, in a style which certainly did not look like relinquishing the practice. The *Little Sarah* or *Little Democrat* was armed, equipped, and manned, in the port of Philadelphia, under the very eye of the government, as if meant to insult it. Having fallen down the river, and being evidently on the point of departure for a cruise, Mr. Genet was desired in my letter of July the 12th, on the part of the President, to detain her till some inquiry and determination on the case should be had. Yet within three or four days after, she was sent out by orders from Mr. Genet himself, and is, at this time, cruising on our coasts, as appears by the protest of the master of one of our vessels maltreated by her.

The government thus insulted and set at defiance by Mr. Genet, and committed in its duties and engagements to others, determined still to see in these proceedings but the character of the individual, and not to believe, and it does not believe, that they are by instructions from his employers. They had assured the British Minister here, that the vessels already armed in our ports should be obliged to leave them, and that no more should be armed in them. Yet more had been armed, and those before armed had either not gone away, or gone only to return with new prizes. They now informed him that the order for departure should be enforced, and the prizes made contrary to it should be restored or compensated. The same thing was notified to Mr. Genet in my letter of August the 7th, and that he might not conclude the promise of compensation to be of no concern to him, and go on in his courses, he was reminded that it would be a fair article of account against his nation.

Mr. Genet, not content with using our force, whether we will or not, in the military line against nations with whom we are at peace, undertakes also to direct the civil government; and particularly, for the executive and legislative bodies, to pronounce what powers may or may not be exercised by the one or the other. Thus in his letter of June the 8th, he promises to respect the political opinions of the President, till the Representatives shall have confirmed or rejected them; as if the President had undertaken to decide what belonged to the decision of Congress. In his letter of June the 4th, he says more openly, that the President ought not to have taken on himself to decide on the subject of the letter, but that it was of importance enough to have consulted Congress thereon; and in that of June the 22nd, he tells the President in direct terms, that Congress ought already to have been occupied on certain questions which he had been too hasty in deciding: thus making himself, and not the President, the judge of the powers ascribed by the constitution to the executive, and dictating to him the occasion when he should exercise the power of convening Congress at an earlier day than their own act had prescribed.

On the following expressions, no commentary shall be made.

July 9. "Les principes philosophiques proclamées par le Président."

June 22. "Les opinions privées ou publiques de M. le Président, et cette égide ne paroissant, pas suffisante."

June 22. "Le gouvernement fédéral s'est empressé, poussé par je ne scais quelle influence."

June 22. "Je ne puis attribuer, des démarches de cette nature qu'à des impressions étrangères dont le tems et la vérité triompheront."

June 25. "On poursuit avec acharnement, en vertu des instructions de M. le Président, les armateurs Français."

June 14. "Ce réfus tend à accomplir le système infernal du roi d'Angleterre, et des autres rois ses complices, pour faire pèrir par la famine les Républicains Français avec la liberté."

June 8. "La lache abandon de ses amis."

July 25. "En vain le désir de conserver la paix fait-il sacrifier les intérêts de la France à cet intérêt du moment; en vain le soif des richesses l'emportet-elle sur l'honneur dans la balance politique de l'Amérique. Tout ces ménage-mens, toute cette condescendance, toute cette humilité n'aboutissent à rien; nos ennemis on rient, et les Français trop confiants sont punis pour avoir cru que la nation Américaine, avoit un pavillon, qu'elle avoit quelque égard pour ses loix, quelque conviction de ses forces, et qu'elle tenoit au sentiment de sa dignité. Il ne m'est pas possible de peindre toute ma sensibilité sur ce scandale qui tend à la diminution de votre commerce, à l'oppression du notre, et à l'abaissement, à l'avilissement des républiques. Si nos concitoyens ont été trompés, si vous n'êtes point en état de soutenir la souveraineté de votre peuple, parlez; nous l'avons garantie quand nous étions esclaves, nous saurons la rendre redoutable étant devenus libres."

We draw a veil over the sensations which these expressions excite. No words can render them; but they will not escape the sensibility of a friendly and magnanimous nation, who will do us justice. We see in them neither the portrait of ourselves, nor the pencil of our friends; but an attempt to embroil both; to add still another nation to the enemies of his country, and to draw on both a reproach, which it is hoped will never stain the history of either. The written proofs, of which Mr. Genet was himself the bearer, were too unequivocal to leave a doubt that the French nation are constant in their friendship to us. The resolves of their National Convention, the letters of their Executive Council attest this truth, in terms which render it necessary to seek in some other hypothesis, the solution of Mr. Genet's machinations against our peace and friendship.

Conscious, on our part, of the same friendly and sincere dispositions, we can with truth affirm, both for our nation and government, that we have never omitted a reasonable occasion of manifesting them. For I will not con-sider as of that character, opportunities of sallying forth from our ports to way-lay, rob, and murder defenseless merchants and others, who have done us no injury, and who were coming to trade with us in the confidence of our peace and amity. The violation of all the laws of order and morality which bind mankind together would be an unacceptable offering to a just nation. Recurring then only to recent things, after so afflicting a libel we recollect with satisfaction, that in the course of two years, by unceasing exertions, we paid up seven years' arrearages and installments of our debt to France, which the inefficiency of our first form of government had suffered to be accumu-lating: that pressing on still to the entire fulfillment of our engagements, we have facilitated to Mr. Genet the effect of the installments of the present year, to enable him to send relief to his fellow citizens in France, threatened with famine: that in the first moment of the insurrection which threatened the col-ony of St. Domingo, we stepped forward to their relief with arms and money, taking freely on ourselves the risk of an unauthorized aid, when delay would have been denial: that we have received, according to our best abilities, the wretched fugitives from the catastrophe of the principal town of that colony, who, escaping from the swords and flames of civil war, threw themselves on us naked and houseless, without food or friends, money or other means, their faculties lost and absorbed in the depth of their distresses: that the exclusive admission to sell here the prizes made by France on her enemies, in the present war, though unstipulated in our treaties, and unfounded in her own practice or in that of other nations, as we believe; the spirit manifested by the late grand jury in their proceedings against those who had aided the enemies of France with arms and implements of war; the expressions of attachment to his nation, with which Mr. Genet was welcomed on his arrival and journey from south to north, and our long forbearance under his gross usurpations and outrages of the laws and authority of our country, do not bespeak the partialities intimated in his letters. And for these things he rewards us by endeavors to excite discord and distrust between our citizens and those whom they have entrusted with their government, between the different branches of our government, between our nation and his. But none of these things, we hope, will be found in his power. That friendship which dictates to us to bear with his conduct yet a while, lest the interests of his nation here should suffer injury, will hasten them to replace an agent, whose dispositions are such a misrepresentation of theirs, and whose continuance here is inconsistent with order, peace, respect, and that friendly correspondence which we hope will ever subsist between the two nations. His government will see too that the case is pressing. That it is impossible for two sovereign and independent authorities to be going on within our territory at the same time, without collision. They will foresee that if Mr. Genet perseveres in his proceedings, the consequences would be so hazardous to us, the example so humiliating and pernicious, that we may be forced even to suspend his functions before a successor can arrive to continue them. If our citizens have not already been shedding each other's blood, it is not owing to the moderation of Mr. Genet, but to the forbearance of the government. It is well known that if the authority of the laws had been resorted to, to stop the Little Democrat, its officers and agents were to have been resisted by the crew of the vessel, consisting partly of American citizens. Such events are too serious, too possible, to be left to hazard, or to what is more than hazard, the will of an agent whose designs are so mysterious.

Lay the case then immediately before his government. Accompany it with assurances, which cannot be stronger than true, that our friendship for the nation is constant and unabating; that faithful to our treaties, we have fulfilled them in every point to the best of our understanding; that if in any thing, however, we have construed them amiss, we are ready to enter into candid explanations, and to do whatever we can be convinced is right; that in opposing the extravagances of an agent, whose character they seem not sufficiently to, have known, we have been urged by motives of duty to ourselves and justice to others, which cannot but be approved by those who are just themselves; and finally, that after independence and self-government, there is nothing we more sincerely wish than perpetual friendship with them.

I have the honor to be, with great respect and esteem, Dear Sir, your most obedient and most humble servant.[1]

THOMAS PINCKNEY, 1793, 9:220 ~ LOSS WHICH WOULD RESULT FROM AN ARBITRARY RESTRAINT OF OUR MARKETS, IS A TAX TOO SERIOUS FOR US TO ACQUIESCE IN.

To Thomas Pinckney, U.S. Minister to Great Britain[2],[3]
Philadelphia, September 7, 1793

Sir, We have received, through a channel which cannot be considered as authentic, the copy of a paper, styled "Additional Instructions to the Commanders of his Majesty's Ships of War and Privateers," etc., dated at St. James's, June 8, 1793. If this paper be authentic, I have little doubt but that you will have taken measures to forward it to me. But as your communication of it may miscarry, and time in the mean will be lost, it has been thought better that it should be supposed authentic; that on that supposition I should notice to you its very exceptionable nature, and the necessity of obtaining explanations on the subject from the British government; desiring at the same time, that you will consider this letter as provisionally written

---

1 A copy of the preceding letter was sent, enclosed by the Secretary of State, to Edmond Genet. Edmond Charles Genet, 1763–1834, was a French diplomat, known as Citizen Genet. He had served as a French representative in Berlin, Vienna, and St. Petersburg before the French Revolution, and he continued in Russia until 1792, when he was expelled because of his revolutionary ardor. Sent as minister to the United States in 1793, he was met with wild acclaim by the numerous supporters of France, but President Washington, anxious to preserve U.S. neutrality in the French Revolutionary Wars, was cold to the demonstrations. Genet's efforts to raise troops to strike at Spanish Florida and to commission privateers to prey on British commerce were not approved by Washington. The President, backed by pro-British Alexander Hamilton, forbade the French privateers to use U.S. ports as bases, despite the warm public approval and the provisions of a 1778 treaty with France. Genet challenged Washington's authority by threatening to appeal to the American people, and the U.S. government demanded (1793) his recall. Before he could go back to France, his party, the Girondists, had fallen, and his return would have meant the guillotine. Washington therefore refused to allow his extradition. Genet remained in the United States and married the daughter of Gov. George Clinton of New York (Columbia 2007, 18737).

2 The first British minister to the United States, twenty-seven-year-old George Hammond, arrived in October, 1791, bringing with him instructions to combat anti-British legislation, and to keep a sharp eye "for renewing former Alliances or forming new Connexions" between the United States and France, but otherwise limited severely in his powers. This, seven years after independence, was a step motivated by British self-interest. President Washington reciprocated by sending to London as American minister Thomas Pinckney of South Carolina, a man satisfying to the British government, and one described by Hammond as belonging to the party of the British interest (DeConde 1958, 79).

3 With respect to trade and embargo Jefferson stressed the principle that friendly goods in the vessel of an enemy are free, while enemy goods in the vessel of a friend are prize. Exceptions to this rule did occur, it was true, and it was the effort of the United States to convert the exception into the rule and establish the principle that free ships make free goods. Against this backdrop, in this letter to Pinckney, Jefferson particularly objected to the British naval orders of June 8, 1793, designed to cut off American grain from enemy countries. He insisted that grain was not contraband and that for America to submit would be an unneutral act, tantamount to war upon France. "[Great Britain] may, indeed, feel the desire of starving an enemy nation; but she can have no right of doing it at our loss, nor of making us the instrument of it" (Sears 1927, 44-45).

only, and as if never written, in the event that the paper which is the occasion of it be not genuine.

The first article of it permits all vessels, laden wholly or in part with corn,
flour or meal, bound to any port in France, to be stopped and sent into any
British port, to be purchased by that government, or to be released only on
the condition of security given by the master, that he will proceed to dispose
of his cargo in the ports of some country in *amity with his Majesty.*

This article is so manifestly contrary to the law of nations, that nothing
more would seem necessary than to observe that it is so. Reason and usage
have .established that when two nations go to war, those who choose to live
in peace retain their natural right to pursue their agriculture, manufactures,
and other ordinary vocations, to carry the produce of their industry for exchange to all nations, belligerent or neutral, as usual, to go and come freely
without injury or molestation, and in short, that the war among others shall
be, for them, as if it did not exist. One restriction on their natural rights has
been submitted to by nations at peace, that is to say, that of not furnishing
to either party implements merely of war for the annoyance of the other, nor
anything whatever to a place blockaded by its enemy. What these implements of war are, has been so often agreed and is so well understood as to
leave little question about them at this day. There does not exist, perhaps, a
nation in our common hemisphere, which has not made a particular enumeration of them in some or all of their treaties, under the name of contraband. It
suffices for the present occasion, to say, that corn, flour and meal, are not of
the class of contraband, and consequently remain articles of free commerce.
A culture which, like that of the soil, gives employment to such a proportion
of mankind, could never be suspended by the whole earth, or interrupted
for them, whenever any two nations should think proper to go to war. The
state of war then existing between Great Britain and France, furnishes no
legitimate right either to interrupt the agriculture of the United States, or
the peaceable exchange of its produce with all nations; and consequently,
the assumption of it will be as lawful hereafter as now, in peace as in war.
No ground, acknowledged by the common reason of mankind, authorizes
this act now, and unacknowledged ground may be taken at any time, and at
all times. We see then a practice begun, to which no time, no circumstances
prescribe any limits, and which strikes at the root of our agriculture, that
branch of industry which gives food, clothing and comfort to the great mass
of the inhabitants of these States. If any nation whatever has a right to shut
up to our produce all the ports of the earth except her own and those of her
friends, she may shut up these also, and so confine us within our own limits.
No nation can subscribe to such pretensions; 'no nation can agree, at the
mere will or interest of another, to have its peaceable industry suspended,
and its citizens reduced to idleness and want. The loss of our produce destined for foreign markets, or that loss which would result from an arbitrary
restraint of our markets, is a tax too serious for us to acquiesce in. It is not
enough for a nation to say, we and our friends will buy your produce. We

have a right to answer, that it suits us better to sell to their enemies as well as their friends. Our ships do not go to France to return empty. They go to exchange the surplus of one produce which we can spare, for surpluses of other kinds which they can spare and we want; which they can furnish on better terms, and more to our mind, than Great Britain or her friends. We have a right to judge for ourselves what market best suits us, and they have none to forbid to us the enjoyment of the necessaries and comforts which we may obtain from any other independent country.

This act, too, tends directly to draw us from that state of peace in which we are wishing to remain. It is an essential character of neutrality to furnish no aids (not stipulated by treaty) to one party, which we are not equally ready to furnish to the other. If we permit corn to be sent to Great Britain and her friends, we are equally bound to permit it to France. To restrain it would be a partiality which might lead to war with France; and between re-straining it ourselves, and permitting her enemies to restrain it unrightfully, is no difference. She would consider this as a mere pretext, of which she would not be the dupe; and on what honorable ground could we otherwise explain it? Thus we should see ourselves plunged by this unauthorized act of Great Britain into a war with which we meddle not, and which we wish to avoid if justice to all parties and from all parties will enable us to avoid it. In the case where we found ourselves obliged by treaty to withhold from the enemies of France the right of arming in our ports, we thought ourselves in justice bound to withhold the same right from France also, and we did it. Were we to withhold from her supplies of provisions, we should in like manner be bound to withhold them from her enemies also; and thus shut to ourselves all the ports of Europe where corn is in demand, or make our-selves parties in the war. This is a dilemma which Great Britain has no right to force upon us, and for which no pretext can be found in any part of our conduct. She may, indeed, feel the desire of starving an enemy nation; but she can have no right of doing it at our loss nor of making us the instruments of it.

The President therefore desires that you will immediately enter into ex-planations on this subject with the British government. Lay before them in friendly and temperate terms all the demonstrations of the injury done us by this act, and endeavor to obtain a revocation of it, and full indemnification to any citizens of these States who may have suffered by it in the meantime. Accompany your representations by every assurance of our earnest desire to live on terms of the best friendship and harmony with them, and to found our expectations of justice on their part, on a strict observance of it on ours.

It is with concern, however, I am obliged to observe, that so marked has been the inattention of the British court to every application which has been made to them on any subject, by this government, (not a single answer I be-lieve having ever been given to one of them, except in the act of exchanging a minister) that it may become unavoidable, in certain cases, where an answer of some sort is necessary, to consider their silence as an answer. Perhaps this is their intention. Still, however, desirous of furnishing no color of offence, we do not wish you to name to them any term for giving an answer. Urge one as much as you can without commitment, and on the first day of December be so good as to give us information of the state in which this matter is, that it may be received during the session of Congress.

The second article of the same instruction allows the armed vessels of Great Britain to seize for condemnation all vessels, on their first attempt to enter a blockaded port, except those of Denmark and Sweden, which are to be prevented only, but not seized, on their first attempt, Of the nations inhabiting the shores of the Atlantic ocean, and practicing its navigation, Denmark, Sweden and the United States alone are neutral. To declare then all neutral vessels (for as to the vessels of the *belligerent* powers no order was necessary) to be legal prize, which shall attempt to enter a blockaded port, except those of *Denmark and Sweden,* is exactly to declare *that the vessels of the United States* shall be lawful prize, and those of Denmark and Sweden shall not. It is of little consequence that the article has avoided naming the United States, since it has used a description applicable to them, and to them alone, while it exempts the others from its operation by name. You will be pleased to ask an explanation of this distinction; and you will be able to say, in discussing its justice, that in every circumstance, we treat Great Britain on the footing of the most favored nation where our treaties do not preclude us, and that even these are just as favorable to her, as hers are to us. Possibly she may be bound by treaty to admit this exception in favor of Denmark and Sweden. But she cannot be bound by treaty to withhold it from us. And if it be withheld merely because not established with us by treaty, what might not we, on the same ground, have withheld from Great Britain during the short course of the present war, as well as the peace which preceded it?

Whether these explanations with the British government shall be verbal or in writing, is left to yourself. Verbal communications are very insecure; for it is only to deny them or to change their terms, in order to do away their effect at any time. Those in writing have as many and obvious advantages, and ought to be preferred, unless there be obstacles of which we are not apprized.

I have the honor to be, with great and sincere esteem, dear Sir, your most obedient humble servant.

Enoch Edwards, 1793, 9:276 - No nation has strove more than we have done to merit the peace of all by the most rigorous impartiality to all

To Dr. Edwards[1]

---

1 Enoch Edwards was a member of the Provincial Conference held in Carpenter's Hall, June 18, 1776. He served as a surgeon during the Revolutionary War and was attending physician to General Washington. He was a delegate to the Pennsylvania Convention on the adopting of the Constitution. Governor Mifflin appointed him in 1791 one of the associated or lay justices of the Court of Common Pleas, which office he held until his death in 1802 (Brooklyn Museum 1917, 125.

Philadelphia, December 30, 1793

Dear Sir, I have to acknowledge the receipt of your two favors of July 30th and August 16th, and thank you for the information they contained. We have now assembled a new Congress, being a fuller and more equal representation of the people, and likely, I think, to approach nearer to the sentiments of the people in the demonstration of their own. They have the advantage of a very full communication from the Executive of the ground on which we stand with foreign nations. Some very unpleasant transactions have taken place here with Mr. Genet, of which the world will judge, as the correspondence is now in the press; as is also that with Mr. Hammond on our points of difference with his nation. Of these you will doubtless receive copies. Had they been out yet, I should have had the pleasure of sending them to you; but to-morrow I resign my office, and two days after set out for Virginia, where I hope to spend the remainder of my days in occupations infinitely more pleasing than those to which I have sacrificed eighteen years of the prime of my life; I might rather say twenty-four of them. Our campaign with the Indians has been lost by an unsuccessful effort to effect peace by treaty, which they protracted till the season for action was over. The attack brought on us from the Algerians is a ray from the same centre. I believe we shall endeavor to do ourselves justice in a peaceable and rightful way. We wish to have nothing to do in the present war; but if it is to be forced upon us, I am happy to see in the countenances of all but our paper men a mind ready made up to meet it, unwillingly, indeed, but perfectly without fear. No nation has strove more than we have done to merit the peace of all by the most rigorous impartiality to all. Sir John Sinclair's queries shall be answered from my retirement. I am, with great esteem, dear Sir, your most obedient servant.

TENCH COXE, 1794, 9:285 ~ WE ARE ALARMED...WITH THE APPREHENSIONS OF WAR, AND SINCERELY ANXIOUS THAT IT MAY BE AVOIDED; BUT NOT AT THE EXPENSE EITHER OF OUR FAITH OR HONOR.

To Tench Coxe[1]

Monticello, May 1, 1794

Dear Sir, Your several favors of February the 22d, 27th, and March the 16th, which had been accumulating in Richmond during the prevalence of the smallpox in that place, were lately brought to me, on the permission given the post to resume his communication. I am particularly to thank you for your favor in forwarding the Bee. Your letters give a comfortable view of French affairs, and later events seem to confirm it. Over the foreign powers I am convinced they will triumph completely, and I cannot but hope that that

---

1 Both before and after the Revolution, Tench Coxe preached and promoted the establishment and development of American industries. However, Coxe was a moderate industrialist who fully recognized the importance of agriculture in the economy. He was an exponent of a mixed and well-balanced economic system. Both economically and politically, Coxe stood midway between Hamilton and Jefferson. In the fight over adoption of the Constitution and the public economic policies of the national government, Coxe was a Federalist with some reservations. Subsequently, he became a Republican and was closely associated with Jefferson and Madison for many years (Wilhite 1958, 210-211).

triumph, and the consequent disgrace of the invading tyrants, is destined, Correspondence 285 in order of events, to kindle the wrath of the people of Europe against those who have dared to embroil them in such wickedness, and to bring at length, kings, nobles and priests to the scaffolds which they have been so long deluging with human blood. I am still warm whenever I think of these scoundrels, though I do it as seldom as I can, preferring infinitely to contemplate the tranquil growth of my lucerne and potatoes. I have so completely withdrawn myself from these spectacles of usurpation and misrule, that I do not take a single newspaper, nor read one a month; and I feel myself infinitely the happier for it.

We are alarmed here with the apprehensions of war; and sincerely anxious that it may be avoided; but not at the expense either of our faith or honor. It seems much the general opinion here, the latter has been too much wounded not to require reparation, and to seek it even in war, if that be necessary. As to myself, I love peace, and I am anxious that we should give the world still another useful lesson, by showing to them other modes of punishing injuries than by war, which is as much a punishment to the punisher as to the sufferer. I love, therefore, Mr. Clarke's proposition of cutting off all communication with the nation which has conducted itself so atrociously. This, you will say, may bring on war. If it does, we will meet it like men; but it may not bring on war, and then the experiment will have been a happy one. I believe this war would be vastly more unanimously approved than any one we ever were engaged in; because the aggressions have been so wanton and bare-faced, and so unquestionably against our desire. I am sorry Mr. Cooper and Priestly did not take a more general survey of our country before they fixed themselves. I think they might have promoted their own advantage by it, and have aided the introduction of improvement where it is more wanting. The prospect of wheat for the ensuing year is a bad one. This is all the sort of news you can expect from me. From you I shall be glad to hear all sort of news, and particularly any improvements in the arts applicable to husbandry or household manufacture.

I am, with very sincere affection, dear Sir, your friend and servant.

GEORGE WASHINGTON, 1794, 9:287 - *IT MAY EXTRICATE US FROM THE EVENT OF A WAR, IF THIS CAN BE DONE SAVING OUR FAITH AND OUR RIGHTS.*

To George Washington[1]

---

1 A vital element of Jefferson's approach to international law was his work on behalf of neutrals. His ideas concerning freedom of the seas and contraband succumbed before a great European war. The only rights of neutrals were those maintained by force. But force might be active or passive. The former was war, and a neutral at war ceased to be neutral. But there is a power in passive resistance which many tyrants have learned to respect. And Jefferson determined to turn that power to account in shaping American foreign policy in the difficult years from 1805 to 1809. His solution was the embargo. In 1794, after Jefferson had withdrawn from the cabinet, he again pronounced in favor of commercial retaliation as an efficient substitute for war. The misfortune of war was that it injured the punisher quite as much as the punished. The objection that this might bring on war anyway, he countered

Monticello, May 14, 1794

Dear Sir, I am honored with your favor of April the 24th, and received, at the same time, Mr. Bertrand's agricultural prospectus. Though he mentions my having seen him at a particular place, yet I remember nothing of it, and observing that he intimates an application for lands in America, I conceive his letter meant for me as Secretary of State, and therefore I now send it to the Secretary of State. He has given only the heads of his demonstrations, so that nothing can be conjectured of their details. Lord Kaims once proposed an essence of dung, one pint of which should manure an acre. If he or Mr. Bertrand could have rendered it so portable, I should have been one of those who would have been greatly obliged to them. I find on a more minute examination of my lands than the short visits heretofore made to them permitted, that a ten years' abandonment of them to the ravages of overseers, has brought on them a degree of degradation far beyond what I had expected. As this obliges me to adopt a milder course of cropping, so I find that they have enabled me to do it, by having opened a great deal of lands during my absence. I have therefore determined on a division of my farm into six fields, to be put under this rotation: first year, wheat; second, corn, potatoes, peas; third, rye or wheat, according to circumstances; fourth and fifth, clover where the fields will bring it, and buckwheat dressings where they will not; sixth, folding, and buckwheat dressings. But it will take me from three to six years to get this plan under way. I am not yet satisfied that my acquisition of overseers from the head of Elk has been a happy one, or that much will be done this year towards rescuing my plantations from their wretched condition. Time, patience and perseverance must be the remedy; and the maxim of your letter, "slow and sure," is not less a good one in agriculture than in politics. I sincerely wish it may extricate us from the event of a war, if this can be done saving our faith and our rights. My opinion of the British government is, that nothing will force them to do justice but the loud voice of their people, and that this can never be excited but by distressing their commerce. But I cherish tranquility too much, to suffer political things to enter my mind at all. I do not forget that I owe you a letter for Mr. Young; but I am waiting to get full information. With every wish for your health and happiness, and my most friendly respects for Mrs. Washington, I have the honor to be, dear Sir, your most obedient and most humble servant.

Thomas Pinckney, 1797, 9:389 ~ War is not the best engine for us to resort to; nature has given us one in our commerce.

To Thomas Pinckney[1]

---

by saying that, if it came, we should meet it; if it did not come, the experiment would have paid. A certain reasonableness would at least mark its attempt, inasmuch as the best hope of obtaining justice from the British government lay in bringing pressure upon it from the British people, and, as he writes to Washington, "this can never be excited but by distressing their commerce" (Sears 1927, 47-48).

1 Now serving as John Adams' vice president, Jefferson was particularly alarmed over the cession of Louisiana by Spain to France, thereby placing the latter, in case of war, on America's

Philadelphia, May 29, 1797

Dear Sir, I received from you, before you left England, a letter enclosing one from the Prince of Parma. As I learnt soon after that you were shortly to return to America, I concluded to join my acknowledgments of it with my congratulations on your arrival; and both have been delayed by a blamable spirit of procrastination, forever suggesting to our indolence that we need not do to-day what may be done tomorrow. Accept these now, in all the sincerity of my heart. It is but lately I have answered the Prince's letter. It required some time to establish arrangements which might effect his purpose, and I wished also to forward a particular article or two of curiosity. You have found on your return a higher style of political difference than you had left here. I fear this is inseparable from the different constitutions of the human mind, and that degree of freedom which permits unrestrained expression. Political dissension is doubtless a less evil than the lethargy of despotism, but still it is a great evil, and it would be as worthy the efforts of the patriot as of the philosopher, to exclude its influence, if possibly, from social life. The good are rare enough at best. There is no reason to subdivide them by artificial lines. But whether we shall ever be able so far to perfect the principles of society, as that political opinions shall, in its intercourse, be as inoffensive as those of philosophy, mechanics, or any other, may be well doubted. Foreign influence is the present and just object of public hue and cry, and, as often happens, the most guilty are foremost and loudest in the cry. If those who are truly independent, can so trim our vessel as to beat through the waves now agitating us, they will merit a glory the greater as it seems less possible. When I con template the spirit which is driving us on here, and that beyond the water which will view us as but a mouthful the more, I have little hope of peace. I anticipate the burning of our sea ports, havoc of our frontiers, household insurgency, with a long train of *et ceteras*, which is enough for a man to have met once in his life. The exchange, which is to give us new neighbors in Louisiana (probably the present French armies when disbanded) has opened us to a combination of enemies on that side where we are most vulnerable. War is not the best engine for us to resort to, nature has given us one in our commerce, which, if properly managed, will be a better instrument for obliging the interested nations of Europe to treat us with justice. If the commercial regulations had been adopted which our Legislature were at one time proposing, we should at this moment have been standing on such an eminence of safety and respect as ages can never recover. But having wandered from that, our object should now be to get

most vulnerable flank. "War," he herein declared firmly, reverting to his pet thesis, "is not the best engine for us to resort to, nature has given us one *in our commerce*, which, if properly managed, will be a better instrument for obliging the interested nations of Europe to treat us with justice." If only that potent weapon had been employed at an earlier stage (against England), "we should at this moment have been standing on such an eminence of safety and respect as ages can never recover." In thus harking back to his old idea of an embargo against England, he failed to note the inconsistency of his passionate objection to an embargo against *France*, the current despoiler of American commerce (Schachner 1957, 594-595).

back, with as little loss as possible, and, when peace shall be restored to the world, endeavor so to form our commercial regulations as that justice from other nations shall be their mechanical result. I am happy to assure you that the conduct of Gen. Pinckney has met universal approbation. It is marked with that coolness, dignity, and good sense which we expected from him. I am told that the French government had taken up an unhappy idea that Monroe was recalled for the candor of his conduct in what related to the British treaty, and Gen. Pinckney was sent as having other dispositions towards them. I learn further, that some of their well-informed citizens here are setting them right as to Gen. Pinckney's dispositions, so well known to have been just towards them; and I sincerely hope, not only that he may be employed as Envoy Extraordinary to them, but that their minds will be better prepared to receive him. I candidly acknowledge, however, that I do not think the speech and addresses of Congress as conciliatory as the preceding irritations on both sides would have rendered wise. I shall be happy to hear from you at all times, to make myself useful to you whenever opportunity offers, and to give every proof of the sincerity of the sentiments of esteem and respect with which I am, dear Sir, your most obedient, and most humble servant.

JAMES MADISON, 1798, 10:10 – A MAJORITY'S TAKING MEASURES AS WILL BE SURE TO PRODUCE WAR.

To James Madison[1]
Philadelphia, March 21, 1798

Dear Sir, I wrote you last on the 15th; since that, yours of the 12th has been received. Since that, too, a great change has taken place in the appearance of our political atmosphere. The merchants, as before, continue a respectable part of them, to wish to avoid arming. The French decree operated on them as a sedative, producing more alarm than resentment; on the Representatives, differently. It excited indignation highly in the war party, though I do not know that it had added any new friends to that side of the question. We still hoped a majority of about four; but the insane message which you will see in the public papers has had great effect. Exultation on the one side, and

---

1 The more strained Franco-American relations appeared to be, the more Adams inclined to show the cutting edge of his temper. Madison, out of patience, characterized Adams as headstrong, quick to insult public opinion, ready to gamble on his private beliefs at the cost of plunging the country into war. Jefferson, in turn, herein terms a message that President Adams had delivered to both houses of Congress on March 19 "insane." In the message, Adams announced the failure of the peace mission to France, reviewed the series of American mistakes and mishaps in dealing with France as a "liberal and Pacific policy," and concluded that since it had failed, he would exhort Congress to "adopt, with promptitude, decision and unanimity, such measures as the ample resources of the country afford, for the protection of our seafaring and commercial citizens, for the defence of any exposed portion of our territory, for replenishing our arsenals, establishing founderies and military manufactories, and to provide... revenue... to defray extraordinary expenses." This was so close to being a declaration of war on France that Jefferson later noted that the question of war and peace depended on a toss of "cross and pile" (an English coin toss game similar to heads or tails (Koch 1950, 176-177).

a certainty of victory; while the other is petrified with astonishment. Our Evans, though his soul is wrapt up in the sentiments of this message, yet afraid to give a vote openly for it, is going off to-morrow, as is said. Those who count, say there are still two members of the other side who will come over to that of peace. If so, the members will be for war measures, fifty-two, against them fifty-three; if all are present except Evans. The question is what is to be attempted, supposing we have a majority? I suggest two things: 1. As the President declares he has withdrawn the executive prohibition to arm, that Congress should pass a legislative one. If that should fail in the Senate, it would heap coals of fire on their heads. 2. As, to do nothing and to gain time is everything with us, I propose that they shall come to a resolution of adjournment, "in order to go home and consult their constituents on the great crisis of American affairs now existing." Besides gaining time enough by this, to allow the descent on England to have its effect here as well as there, it will be a means of exciting the whole body of the people from the state of inattention in which they are; it will require every member to call for the sense of his district by petition or instruction; it will show the people with which side of the House their safety as well as their rights rest, by showing them which is for war and which for peace; and their Representatives will return here invigorated by the avowed support of the American people. I do not know, however, whether this will be approved, as there has been little consultation on the subject. We see a new instance of the inefficiency of constitutional guards. We had relied with great security on that provision, which requires two-thirds of the Legislature to declare war. But this is completely eluded by a majority' staking such measures as will be sure to produce war. I wrote you in my last, that an attempt was to be made on that day in Senate, to declare the in expediency of renewing our treaties, but the measure is put off under the hope of its being attempted under better auspices. To return to the subject of war, it is quite impossible, when we consider all the existing circumstances, to find any reason in its favor resulting from views either of interest or honor, and plausible enough to impose even on the weakest mind; and especially, when it would be undertaken by a majority of one or two only. Whatever then be our stock of charity or liberality, we must resort to other views. And those so well known to have been entertained at Annapolis, and afterwards at the grand convention, by a particular set of men, present themselves as those alone which can account for so extraordinary a degree of impetuosity. Perhaps, instead of what was then in contemplation, a separation of the Union, which has been so much the topic to the eastward of late, may be the thing aimed at. I have written so far, two days before the departure of the post. Should anything more occur today or tomorrow, it shall be added. Adieu affectionately.

JAMES LEWIS, JR., 1798, 10:37 ~ *IT IS OUR DUTY STILL TO ENDEAVOR TO AVOID WAR; BUT IF IT SHALL ACTUALLY TAKE PLACE, NO MATTER BY WHOM BROUGHT ON, WE MUST DEFEND OURSELVES.*

To James Lewis, Junior[1]

Philadelphia, May 9, 1798

Dear Sir, I am much obliged by your friendly letter of the 4th instant. As soon as I saw the first of Mr. Martin's letters, I turned to the newspapers of the day, and found Logan's speech, as translated by a common Indian interpreter. The version I had used, had been made by General Gibson. Finding from Mr. Martin's style, that his object was not merely truth, but to gratify pasty passions, I never read another of his letters. I determined to do my duty by searching into the truth, and publishing it to the world, whatever it should be. This I shall do at a proper season. I am much indebted to many persons, who, without any acquaintance with me, have voluntarily sent me information on the subject. Party passions are indeed high. Nobody has more reason to know it than myself. I receive daily bitter proofs of it from people who never saw me, nor know anything of me but through Porcupine and Fenno. At this moment all the passions are boiling over, and one who keeps himself cool and clear of the contagion, is so far below the point of ordinary conversation, that he finds himself insulated in every society. However, the fever will not last. War, land tax and stamp tax, are sedatives which must cool its ardor. They will bring on reflection, and that, with information, is all which our countrymen need, to bring themselves and their affairs to rights. They are essentially republicans. They retain unadulterated the principles of '75, and those who are conscious of no change in themselves have nothing to fear in the long run. It is our duty still to endeavor to avoid war; but if it shall actually take place, no matter by whom brought on, we must defend ourselves. If our house be on fire, without inquiring whether it was fired from within or without, we must try to extinguish it. In that, I have no doubt, we shall act as one man. But if we can ward off actual war till the crisis of England is over, I shall hope we may escape it altogether.

I am, with much esteem, dear Sir, your most obedient humble servant.

---

1 This letter is drawn from the casual slaughter of Indians, which had become commonplace on the Ohio frontier. In April, 1774, a group of whites led by Thomas and Michael Cresap murdered a group of inoffensive Indians, including several women. The murdered Indians consisted of the entire family of a chief, Logan, long known as a friend of the white man. Logan took revenge by having his Shawnees kill a number white settlers, including women and children. Virginia's governor, Lord Dunmore, led a group of militia into the area and defeated the Indians in the Battle of Point Pleasant. The captured chief delivered in his own defense a remarkable speech that was widely reported in the Virginia press in 1775. Jefferson was so enamored by this speech that he copied it and later reproduced it in his *Notes on the State of Virginia* (1781) as an example of Indian eloquence, thus refuting the French naturalist Georges de Buffon's insistence that the American Indian was genetically degenerate (Brodie 1974, 93). A son-in-law of Cresap, Luther Martin, was a leading Federalist politician who for years had defended his father-in-law's reputation, seemingly with an eye to discrediting Jefferson's scientific and research conclusions as Jefferson was perhaps the leading Federalist critic of the time (Bernstein 2003, 120).

ELBRIDGE GERRY, 1799, 10:74 ~ *IT IS THEIR SWEAT WHICH IS TO EARN ALL THE EXPENSES OF THE WAR, AND THEIR BLOOD WHICH IS TO FLOW IN EXPIATION OF THE CAUSES OF IT.*

To Elbridge Gerry[1]

Philadelphia, January 26, 1799

My Dear Sir, Your favor of November the 12th was safely delivered to me by Mr. Binney; but not till December the 28th, as I arrived here only three days before that date. It was received with great satisfaction. Our very long intimacy as fellow-laborers in the same cause, the recent expressions of mutual confidence which had preceded your mission, the interesting course which that had taken, and particularly and personally as it regarded yourself, made me anxious to hear from you on your return. I was the more so too, as I had myself, during the whole of your absence, as well as since your return, been a constant butt for every shaft of calumny which malice and falsehood could form, and the presses, public speakers, or private letters disseminate. One of these, too, was of a nature to touch yourself; as if, wanting confidence in your efforts, I had been capable of usurping powers committed to you, and authorizing negotiations private and collateral to yours. The real truth is, that though Doctor Logan, the pretended missionary, about four or five days before he sailed for Hamburg, told me he was going there, and thence to

---

1 Although largely forgotten, Elbridge Gerry had a distinguished career: a signer of the Declaration of Independence, governor of Massachusetts, special ambassador to France, and fifth vice president of the United States under James Madison (Gerry 1927, viii). The XYZ Affair was a diplomatic incident between French and United States diplomats that resulted in a limited, undeclared war known as the Quasi-War. U.S. and French negotiators restored peace with the Convention of 1800, also known as the Treaty of Mortefontaine. In the late 1700s, the final French Revolutionary government, the Directory, was experiencing problems financing its European wars. Many leaders were also angry that the United States had concluded the Jay Treaty with Great Britain in 1794. Consequently, in 1796 French leaders decided to issue an order allowing for the seizure of American merchant ships, carefully timed to catch as many as possible by surprise. President John Adams dispatched three U.S. envoys to restore harmony between the United States and France—Elbridge Gerry, Charles Cotesworth Pinckney, and John Marshall. These commissioners, like others of the Adams administration, viewed France as a center of decadence and deception, and the rampant intrigue and disparate factions of the Directory made it difficult for the Americans to accomplish their mission. Upon arriving in France, Gerry, Pinkney and Marshall found that they were unable to formally meet with the Foreign Minister, the Marquis de Talleyrand. The U.S. envoys were instead approached by several intermediaries, Nicholas Hubbard (later W,) Jean Hottinguer (X), Pierre Bellamy (Y), and Lucien Hauteval (Z.) Also involved with these negotiations was the playwright Pierre Beaumarchais, who had been involved in funneling French aid to the United States during the American Revolution. These French intermediaries stated that Talleyrand would be willing to meet with the Americans and come to an agreement if several conditions were satisfied. The French demanded that the United States provide France with a low-interest loan, assume and pay American merchant claims against the French, and lastly pay a substantial bribe to Talleyrand. The U.S. envoys were shocked and also skeptical that any concessions would bring about substantial changes in French policy. Talleyrand's strategy was mainly one of delay. He intended to end attacks on U.S. merchant shipping, but wanted first to increase his personal wealth, strengthen his political position within the Directory government, and ensure that he would deal only with Elbridge Gerry, the American commissioner who seemed most friendly to French interests (United States Department of State 2008).

Paris, and asked and received from me a certificate of his citizenship, character, and circumstances of life, merely as a protection, should he be molested on his journey, in the present turbulent and suspicious state of Europe, yet I had been led to consider his object as relative to his private affairs; and though, from an intimacy of some standing, he knew well my wishes for peace1 and my political sentiments in general, he nevertheless received then no particular declaration of them, no authority to communicate them to any mortal, nor to speak to any one in my name, or in anybody's name, on that, or on any other subject whatever; nor did I write by him a scrip of a pen to any person whatever. This he has himself honestly and publicly declared since his return; and from his well-known character and every other circumstance, every candid man must perceive that his enterprise was dictated by his own enthusiasm, without consultation or communication with any one; that he acted in Paris on his own ground, and made his own way. Yet to give some color to his proceedings, which might implicate the republicans in general, and myself particularly, they have not been ashamed to bring forward a suppositious paper, drawn by one of their own party in the name of Logan, and falsely pretended to have been presented by him to the government of France; counting that the bare mention of my name therein, would connect that in the eye of the public with this transaction. In confutation of these and all future calumnies, by way of anticipation, I shall make to you a profession of my political faith; in confidence that you will consider every future imputation on me of a contrary complexion, as bearing on its front the mark of falsehood and calumny.

I do then, with sincere zeal, wish an inviolable preservation of our present federal Constitution, according to the true sense in which it was adopted by the States, that in which it was advocated by its friends, and not that which its enemies apprehended, who therefore became its enemies; and I am opposed to the monarchising its features by the forms of its administration, with a view to conciliate a first transition to a President and Senate for life, and from that to an hereditary tenure of these offices, and thus to worm out the elective principle. I am for preserving to the States the powers not yielded by them to the Union, and to the legislature of the Union its constitutional share in the division of powers; and I am not for transferring all the powers of the States to the General Government, and all those of that government to the executive branch. I am for a government rigorously frugal and simple, applying all the possible savings of the public revenue to the discharge of the national debt; and not for a multiplication of officers and salaries merely to make partisans, and for increasing, by every device, the public debt, on the principle of its being a public blessing. I am for relying, for internal defense, on our militia solely, till actual invasion, and for such a naval force only as may protect our coasts and harbors from such depredations as we have experienced; and not for a standing army in time of peace, which may overawe the public sentiment; nor for a navy, which, by its own expenses and the eternal wars in which it will implicate us, will grind us with public burthens, and sink us under them. I am for free commerce with all nations; political connection with none; and little or no diplomatic establishment. And I am not for linking ourselves by new treaties with the quarrels of Europe; entering that field of slaughter to preserve their balance, or joining in the confederacy of kings to war against the principles of liberty. I am for freedom of religion, and against all maneuvers to bring about a legal ascendancy of one sect over another: for freedom of the press, and against all violations of the Constitution to silence by force and not by reason the complaints or criticisms, just or unjust, of our citizens against the conduct of their agents. And I am for encouraging the progress of science in all its branches; and not for raising a hue and cry against the sacred name of philosophy; for awing the human mind by stories of raw-head and bloody bones to a distrust of its own vision, and to repose implicitly on that of others; to go backwards instead of forwards to look for improvement; to believe that government, religion, morality, and every other science were in the highest perfection in ages of the darkest ignorance, and that nothing can ever be devised more perfect than what was established by our forefathers. To these I will add, that I was a sincere well-wisher to the success of the French revolution, and still wish it may end in the establishment of a free and well-ordered republic; but I have not been insensible under the atrocious depredations they have committed on our commerce. The first object of my heart is my own country. In that is embarked my family, my fortune, and my own existence. I have not one farthing of interest, nor one fibre of attachment out of it, nor a single motive of preference of any one nation to another, but in proportion as they are more or less friendly to us. But though deeply feeling the injuries of France, I did not think war the surest means of redressing them. I did believe, that a mission sincerely disposed to preserve peace, would obtain for us a peaceable and honorable settlement and retribution; and I appeal to you to say, whether this might not have been obtained, if either of your colleagues had been of the same sentiment with yourself.

These, my friend, are my principles; they are unquestionably the principles of the great body of our fellow-citizens, and I know there is not one of them which is not yours also. In truth, we never differed but on one ground, the funding system; and as, from the moment of its being adopted by the constituted authorities, I became religiously principled in the sacred discharge of it to the uttermost farthing, we are united now even on that single ground of difference.

I now turn to your inquiries. The enclosed paper will answer one of them. But you also ask for such political information as may be possessed by me, and interesting to yourself in regard to your embassy. As a proof of my entire confidence in you, I shall give it fully and candidly. When Pinckney, Marshall, and nana were nominated to settle our differences with France, it was suspected by many, from what was understood of their dispositions, that their mission would not result in a settlement of differences, but would produce circumstances tending to widen the breach, and to provoke our citizens to consent to a war with that nation, and union with England. Dana's resignation and your appointment gave the first gleam of hope of a peaceable issue to the mission. For it was believed that you were sincerely disposed to accommodation; and it was not long after your arrival there, before symptoms were observed of that difference of views which had been suspected to exist. In the meantime, however, the aspect of our government towards the French republic had become so ardent, that the people of America generally took the alarm. To the southward, their apprehensions were early excited. In the Eastern States also, they at length began to break out. Meetings were held in many of your towns, and addresses to the government agreed on in opposition to war. The example was spreading like a wildfire. Other meetings were called in other places, and a general concurrence of sentiment against the apparent inclinations of the government was imminent; when, most critically for the government, the dispatches of October 22d, prepared by your colleague Marshall, with a view to their being made public, dropped into their laps. It was truly a God-send to them, and they made the most of it. Many thousands of copies were printed and dispersed gratis, at the public expense; and the zealots for war co-operated so heartily, that there were instances of single individuals who printed and dispersed ten or twelve thousand copies at their own expense. The odiousness of the corruption supposed in those papers excited a general and high indignation among the people. Inexperienced in such maneuvers, they did not permit themselves even to suspect that the turpitude of private swindlers might mingle itself unobserved, and give its own hue to the communications of the French government, of whose participation there was neither proof nor probability. It served, however, for a time, the purpose intended. The people, in many places, gave a loose to the expressions of their warm indignation, and of their honest preference of war to dishonor. The fever was long and successfully kept up, and in the meantime, war measures as ardently crowded. Still, however, as it was known that your colleagues were coming away, and yourself to stay, though disclaiming a separate power to conclude a treaty, it was hoped by the lovers of peace, that a project of treaty would have been prepared, ad referendum, on principles which would have satisfied our citizens, and overawed any bias of the government towards a different policy. But the expedition of the Sophia, and, as was supposed, the suggestions of the person charged with your dispatches, and his probable misrepresentations of the real wishes of the American people, prevented these hopes. They had then only to look forward to your return for such information, either through the executive, or from yourself, as might present to our view the other side of the medal. The dispatches of October 22nd, 1797, had presented one face. That information, to a certain degree, is now received, and the public will see from your correspondence with Talleyrand, that France, as you testify, "was sincere and anxious to obtain a reconciliation, not wishing us to break the British treaty, but only to give her equivalent stipulations; and in general was disposed to a liberal treaty." And they will judge whether Mr. Pickering's report shows an inflexible determination to believe no declarations the French government can make, nor any opinion which you, judging on the spot and from actual view, can give of their sincerity, and to meet their designs of peace with operations of war. The alien and sedition acts have already operated in the south as powerful sedatives of the X. Y. Z. inflammation. In your quarter, where violations of principle are either less regarded or more concealed, the direct tax is likely to have the same effect, and to excite inquiries into the object of the enormous expenses and taxes we are bringing on. And your information supervening, that we might have a liberal accommodation if we would, there can be little doubt of the reproduction of that general movement which had been changed, for a moment, by the dispatches of October 22d. And though small checks and stops, like Logan's pretended embassy, may be thrown in the way from time to time, and may a little retard its motion, yet the tide is already turned, and will sweep before it all the feeble obstacles of art. The unquestionable republicanism of the American mind will break through the mist under which it has been clouded, and will oblige its agents to reform the principles and practices of their administration.

You suppose that you have been abused by both parties. As far as has come to my knowledge, you are misinformed. I have never seen or heard a sentence of blame uttered against you by the republicans; unless we were so to construe their wishes that you had more boldly co-operated in a project of a treaty, and would more explicitly state, whether there was in your colleagues that flexibility, which persons earnest after peace would have practiced? Whether, on the contrary, their demeanor was not cold, reserved, and distant, at least, if not backward? And whether, if they had yielded to those informal conferences which Talleyrand seems to have courted, the liberal accommodation you suppose might not have been effected, even with their agency? Your fellow-citizens think they have a right to full information, in a case of such great concernment to them. It is their sweat which is to earn all the expenses of the war, and their blood which is to flow in expiation of the causes of it. It may be in your power to save them from these miseries by full communications and unrestrained details, postponing motives of delicacy to those of duty. It rests with you to come forward independently; to make your stand on the high ground of your own character; to disregard calumny, and to be borne above it on the shoulders of your grateful fellow-citizens; or to sink into the humble oblivion, to which the federalists (self-called) have secretly condemned you; and even to be happy if they will indulge you oblivion, while they have beamed on your colleagues meridian splendor. Pardon me, my dear Sir, if my expressions are strong. My feelings are so much more so, that it is with difficulty I reduce them even to the tone I use. If you doubt the dispositions towards you, look into the papers, on both sides, for the toasts which were given throughout the States on the Fourth of July. You will there see whose hearts were with you, and whose were ulcerated against you. Indeed, as soon as it was known that you had consented to stay in Paris, there was no measure observed in the execrations of the war party. They openly wished you might be guillotined, or sent to Cayenne, or anything else. And these expressions were finally stifled from a principle of policy only, and to prevent you from being urged to a justification of yourself. From this principle alone proceed the silence and cold respect they observe towards you. Still, they cannot prevent at times the flames bursting from under the embers, as Mr. Pickering's letters, report, and conversations testify, as well as the indecent expressions respecting you, indulged by some of them in the debate on these dispatches. These sufficiently show that you are never more to be honored or trusted by them, and that they wait to crush you for ever only till they can do it without danger to themselves.

When I sat down to answer your letter, but two courses presented themselves, either to say nothing or everything; for half confidences are not in my character. I could not hesitate which was due to you. I have unbosomed myself fully; and it will certainly be highly gratifying if I receive like confidence from you. For even if we differ in principle more than I believe we do, you and I know too well the texture of the human mind, and the slipperiness of human reason, to consider differences of opinion otherwise than differences of form or feature. Integrity of views more than their soundness, is the basis of esteem. I shall follow your direction in conveying this by a private hand; though I know not as yet when one worthy of confidence will occur. And my trust in you leaves me without a fear that this letter, meant as a confidential communication of my impressions, will ever go out of your own hand, or be suffered in anywise to commit my name. Indeed, besides the accidents which might happen to it even under your care, considering the accident of death to which you are liable, I think it safest to pray you, after reading it as often as you please, to destroy at least the second and third leaves. The first contains principles only, which I fear not to avow; but the second and third contain facts stated for your information, and which, though sacredly conformable to my firm belief, yet would be galling to some, and expose me to illiberal attacks. I therefore repeat my prayer to burn the second and third leaves. And did we ever expect to see the day, when, breathing nothing but sentiment; of love to our country and its freedom and happiness, our correspondence must be as secret as if we were hatching its destruction! Adieu, my friend, and accept my sincere and affectionate salutations. I need not add my signature.

THADDEUS KOSCIUSKO, 1799, 10:115 ~ *IF WE ARE FORCED INTO WAR, WE MUST GIVE UP POLITICAL DIFFERENCES OF OPINION AND UNITE AS ONE MAN TO DEFEND OUR COUNTRY.*

To General Thaddeus Kosciusko[1]
Philadelphia, February 21, 1799

Dear Friend, On politics I must write sparingly, lest it should fall into the hands of persons who do not love either you or me. The wonderful ir-

---

1 An engineer and Polish patriot, Thaddeus Kosciusko espoused the American cause and planned the original fortifications at West Point (Oliver 1956, 98). He was commissioned a colonel of engineers by the Congress in 1776, and was breveted a brigadier general in 1783 (Morris 1995, 364). At this time (1799) Kosciusko was living in Paris.

ritation produced in the minds of our citizens by the X.Y.Z. story, has in a great measure subsided. They begin to suspect and to see it coolly in its true light. Mr. Gerry's communications, with other information, prove to them that France is sincere in her wishes for reconciliation; and a recent proposition from that country, through Mr. Murray, puts the matter out of doubt. What course the government will pursue, I know not. But if we are left in peace, I have no doubt the wonderful turn in the public opinion now manifestly taking place and rapidly increasing, will, in the course of this summer, become so universal and so weighty, that friendship abroad and freedom at home will be firmly established by the influence and constitutional powers of the people at large. If we are forced into war, we must give up political differences of opinion, and unite as one man to defend our country. But whether at the close of such a war, we should be as free as we are now, God knows. In fine, if war takes place, republicanism has everything to fear; if peace, be assured that your forebodings and my alarms will prove vain; and that the spirit of our citizens now rising as rapidly as it was then running crazy, and rising with a strength and majesty which show the loveliness of freedom, will make this government in practice, what it is in principle, a model for the protection of man in a state of freedom and order. May heaven have in store for your country a restoration of these blessings, and you be destined as the instrument it will use for that purpose. But if this be forbidden by fate, I hope we shall be able to preserve here an asylum where your love of liberty and disinterested patriotism will be forever protected and honored, and where you will find, in the hearts of the American people, a good portion of that esteem and affection which glow in the bosom of the friend who writes this; and who, with sincere prayers for your health, happiness and success, and cordial salutations, bids you, for this time, adieu.

SAMUEL ADAMS, 1800, 10:153 ~ *I READ IT AS A LESSON AGAINST THE DANGER OF STANDING ARMIES.*

To Samuel Adams
Philadelphia, February 26, 1800

Dear Sir, Mr. Erving delivered me your favor of January 31st, and I thank you for making me acquainted with him. You will always do me a favor in giving me an opportunity of knowing gentlemen as estimable in their principles and talents as I find Mr. Erving to be. I have not yet seen Mr. Winthrop. A letter from you, my respectable friend, after three and twenty years of separation, has given me a pleasure I cannot express. It recalls to my mind the anxious days we then passed in struggling for the cause of mankind. Your principles have been tested in the crucible of time, and have come out pure. You have proved that it was monarchy, and not merely British monarchy, you opposed. A government by representatives, elected by the people at short periods, was our object; and our maxim at that day was, "where annual election ends, tyranny begins;" nor have our departures from it been sanctioned by the happiness of their effects. A debt of an hundred millions growing by usurious interest, and an artificial paper phalanx overruling the agricultural mass of our country, with other et cetera, have a portentous aspect.

I fear our friends on the other side of the water, laboring in the same cause, have yet a great deal of crime and misery to wade through. My confidence has been placed in the head, not in the heart of Bonaparte. I hoped he would calculate truly the difference between the fame of a Washington and a Cromwell.[1] Whatever his views may be, he has at least transferred the destinies of the republic from the civil to the military arm. Some will use this as a lesson against the practicability of republican government. I read it as a lesson against the danger of standing armies.

Adieu, my ever respected and venerable friend. May that kind overruling providence which has so long spared you to our country, still foster your remaining years with whatever may make them comfortable to yourself and soothing to your friends. Accept the cordial salutations of your affectionate friend.

THOMAS PAINE, 1801, 10:223 - *DETERMINED AS WE ARE TO AVOID, IF POSSIBLE, WASTING THE ENERGIES OF OUR PEOPLE IN WAR AND DESTRUCTION, WE SHALL AVOID IMPLICATING OURSELVES WITH THE POWERS OF EUROPE.*

To Thomas Paine[2]
Washington, March 18, 1801[3]

Dear Sir, Your letters of October the 1st, 4th, 6th, and 16th, came duly to hand, and the papers which they covered were, according to your permission, published in the newspapers and in a pamphlet, and under your own name. These papers contain precisely our principles, and I hope they will be generally recognized here. Determined as we are to avoid, if possible, wasting the energies of our people in war and destruction, we shall avoid impli-

---

1 The news of the dissolution of the French Directory, and the appointment of Napoleon as First Consul, had recently reached America (Wells 1888, 368).

2 Thomas Paine, although born and raised in England, spent much of his life in America and France, where he took an active part, through his publications, in the great revolutions which swept over those countries in the late eighteenth century. It was Paine's strength as a propagandist — and also, some argue, perhaps his weakness as a thinker — that he saw man and society entirely in black and white, with no shades of gray. The revolutions of his day were, for him, struggles between unmitigated good and evil. As a student of the Enlightenment, he viewed the past as an almost unbroken reign of ignorance, superstition, and tyranny, and felt that it was his privilege to live in "a morning of reason" when the native good will and common sense of the average man were beginning to assert themselves and would speedily make all things new. At the time, he was best known for writing *Common Sense* (1776), which advocated American independence, and *The American Crisis* (1776-1783), a pro-revolution series (Strauss 1963, 594).

3 Jefferson had been inaugurated as the third president of the United States on March 4, 1801; while democracy appeared to be passing into a long eclipse in Europe, it appeared likely to bask in a new American light with his election. The American people had repudiated the Adams administration, whose infamous Alien and Sedition Acts had attempted to make political opposition a criminal offense. Further, while the discredited Federalists wrung their hands at the imminence of mob rule under President Jefferson, the Republicans acclaimed the victory as a new Declaration of Independence, while Jefferson himself proclaimed limed it the Revolution of 1800 (Smith 1931, 301).

cating ourselves with the powers of Europe, even in support of principles which we mean to pursue. They have so many other interests different from ours, that we must avoid being entangled in them.[1] We believe we can enforce those principles, as to ourselves, by peaceable means, now that we are likely to have our public councils detached from foreign views. The return of our citizens from the frenzy into which they had been wrought, partly by ill conduct in France, partly by artifices practiced on them, is almost entire, and will, I believe, become quite so. But these details, too minute and long for a letter, will be better developed by Mr. Dawson, the bearer of this, a member of the late Congress, to whom I refer you for them. He goes in the Maryland, a sloop of war, which will wait a few days at Havre to receive his letters, to be written on his arrival at Paris. You expressed a wish to get a passage to this country in a public vessel. Mr. Dawson is charged with orders to the captain of the Maryland to receive and accommodate you with a passage back, if you can be ready to depart at such short warning. Robert R. Livingston is appointed Minister Plenipotentiary to the Republic of France, but will not leave this till we receive the ratification of the convention by Mr. Dawson. I am in hopes you will find us returned generally to sentiments worthy of former times. In these, it will be your glory to have steadily labored, and with as much effect as any man living. That you may long live to continue your useful labors, and to reap their reward in the thankfulness of nations, is my sincere prayer.

Accept assurances of my high esteem and affectionate attachment.

ROBERT LIVINGSTON, 1801, 10:277 ~ *THE WRONG WHICH TWO NATIONS ENDEAVOR TO INFLICT ON EACH OTHER MUST NOT INFRINGE ON THE RIGHTS OR CONVENIENCES OF THOSE REMAINING AT PEACE.*

To Robert Livingston[2]

---

1 This determination to "avoid implicating ourselves with the powers of Europe" and "being entangled" in their interests soon underwent a severe test. Jefferson had no love for the British, but Napoleon, the enemy of liberty and democracy, he hated more. Further, the prospect of Napoleon as a neighbor on the southwest struck terror to his heart and he later declared that the moment Napoleon took possession of Louisiana, America would need to align herself with the British fleet and nation (Thomas 1927, 5).

2 Jefferson is on record of believing that blockade and contraband of war are the only two articles in the rights of neutral nations which war can abridge, and he is further inclined to doubt the ultimate validity of the principle of contraband. Yet his views on the question change sufficiently, however, to render his position confusing. In July 1793, he believes "it cannot be doubted, but that by the general law of nations, the goods of a friend found in the vessel of an enemy are free, and the goods of an enemy found in the vessel of a friend are lawful prize." But by this letter it appears that he is no longer even convinced that natural law dictates the principle that the goods follow the owner, holding in substance that the practice of taking the goods of an enemy from the ship of a friend, though sanctioned by the usage of nations, is not so by the law of nature. He now believes that national morality had never sanctioned the seizure of enemy goods in friendly territory; and the ship of a friend is to be regarded as his territory when on the high seas just as much as though in his harbor. "We ... perceive no distinction between the movable and immovable jurisdiction of a friend, which would authorize the entering the one and not the other, to seize the property of an enemy." He then goes on to justify the doctrine against the objection that "this proves too much, as it proves you cannot enter the ship of a friend to search for contraband of war.

Monticello, September 9, 1801

Dear Sir, You will receive, probably by this post, from the Secretary of State, his final instructions for your mission to France. We have not thought it necessary to say anything in them on the great question of the maritime law of nations, which at present agitates Europe; that is to say, whether free ships shall make free goods; because we do not mean to take any side in it during the war. But, as I had before communicated to you some loose thoughts on that subject, and have since considered it with somewhat more attention, I have thought it might be useful that you should possess my ideas in a more matured form than that in which they were before given. Unforeseen circumstances may perhaps oblige you to hazard an opinion, on some occasion or other, on this subject, and it is better that it should not be at variance with ours. I write this, too, myself, that it may not be considered as official, but merely my individual opinion, unadvised by those official counselors whose opinions I deem my safest guide, and should unquestionably take in form, were circumstances to call for a solemn decision of the question.

When Europe assumed the general form in which it is occupied by the nations now composing it, and turned its attention to maritime commerce, we found among its earliest practices, that of taking the goods of an enemy from the ship of a friend; and that into this practice every maritime State went sooner or later, as it appeared on the theatre of the ocean. If, therefore, we are to consider the practice of nations as the sole and sufficient evidence of the law of nature among nations, we should unquestionably place this principle among those of the natural laws. But its inconveniences, as they affected neutral nations peaceably pursuing their commerce, and its tendency to embroil them with the powers happening to be at war, and thus to extend the flames of war, induced nations to introduce by special compacts, from time to time, a more convenient rule; that "free ships should make free goods"; and this latter principle has by every maritime nation of Europe been established, to a greater or less degree, in its treaties with other nations; insomuch, that all of them have, more or less frequently, assented to it, as a rule of action in particular cases. Indeed, it is now urged, and I think with great appearance of reason, that this is the genuine principle dictated by national morality; and that the first practice arose from accident, and the particular convenience of the States which first figured on the water, rather than from well digested reflections on the relations of friend and enemy, on the rights of territorial jurisdiction, and on the dictates of moral law applied to these.[1] Thus it had never been supposed lawful, in the territory of a friend to seize the goods of an enemy. On an element which nature has not subjected to

---

But this is not proving too much. We believe the practice of seizing what is called the contraband of war, is an abusive practice, not founded in natural right. War between two nations cannot diminish the rights of the rest of the world remaining at peace" (Wiltse 1935, 195-196).

1 "States," in this instance, is a reference to Venice and Genoa.

the jurisdiction of any particular nation, but has made common to all for the purposes to which it is fitted, it would seem that the particular portion of it which happens to be occupied by the vessel of any nation, in the course of its voyage, is for the moment, the exclusive property of that nation, and, with the vessel, is exempt from intrusion by any other, and from its jurisdiction, as much as if it were lying in the harbor of its sovereign. In no country, we believe, is the rule otherwise, as to the subjects of property common to all. Thus the place occupied by an individual in a highway, a church, a theatre, or other public assembly, cannot be intruded on, while its occupant holds it for the purposes of its institution. The persons on board a vessel traversing the ocean, carrying with them the laws of their nation, have among themselves a jurisdiction, a police, not established by their individual will, but by the authority of their nation, of whose territory their vessel still seems to compose a part, so long as it does not enter the exclusive territory of another. No nation ever pretended a right to govern by their laws the ship of another nation navigating the ocean. By what law then can it enter that ship while in peaceable and orderly use of the common element? We recognize no natural precept for submission to such a right; and perceive no distinction between the movable and immovable jurisdiction of a friend, which would authorize the entering the one and not the other, to seize the property of an enemy.

It may be objected that this proves too much, as it proves you cannot enter the ship of a friend to search for contraband of war. But this is not proving too much. We believe the practice of seizing what is called contraband of war, is an abusive practice, not founded in natural right. War between two nations cannot diminish the rights of the rest of the world remaining at peace. The doctrine that the rights of nations remaining quietly in the exercise of moral and social duties, are to give way to the convenience of those who prefer plundering and murdering one another, is a monstrous doctrine; and ought to yield to the more rational law, that "the wrong which two nations endeavor to inflict on each other, must not infringe on the rights or conveniences of those remaining at peace." And what is *contraband*, by the law of nature? Either everything which may aid or comfort an enemy, or nothing. Either all commerce which would accommodate him is unlawful, or none is. The difference between articles of one or another description is a difference in degree only. No line between them can be drawn. Either all intercourse must cease between neutrals and belligerents, or all be permitted. Can the world hesitate to say which shall be the rule? Shall two nations turning tigers, break up in one instant the peaceable relations of the whole world? Reason and nature clearly pronounce that the neutral is to go on in the enjoyment of all its rights, that its commerce remains free, not subject to the jurisdiction of another, nor consequently its vessels to search, or to enquiries whether their contents are the property of an enemy, or are of those which have been called contraband of war.

Nor does this doctrine contravene the right of preventing vessels from entering a blockaded port. This right stands on other ground. When the fleet of any nation actually beleaguers the port of its enemy, no other has a right to enter their line, any more than their line of battle in the open sea, or their lines of circumvallation, or of encampment, or of battle array on land. The space included within their lines in any of those cases, is either the property of their enemy, or it is common property assumed and possessed for the moment, which cannot be intruded on, even by a neutral, without committing the very trespass we are now considering, that of intruding into the lawful possession of a friend.

Although I consider the observance of these principles as of great importance to the interests of peaceable nations, among whom I hope the United States will ever place themselves, yet in the present state of things they are not worth a war. Nor do I believe war the most certain means of enforcing them. Those peaceable coercions which are in the power of every nation, if undertaken in concert and in time of peace, are more likely to produce the desired effect.

The opinions I have here given are those which have generally been sanctioned by our government. In our treaties with France, the United Netherlands, Sweden and Prussia, the principle of free bottom, free goods, was uniformly maintained. In the instructions of 1784, given by Congress to their ministers appointed to treat with the nations of Europe generally, the same principle, and the doing away contraband of war, were enjoined, and were acceded to in the treaty signed with Portugal. In the late treaty with England, indeed, that power perseveringly refused the principle of free bottoms, free goods; and it was avoided in the late treaty with Prussia, at the instance of our then administration, lest it should seem to take side in a question then threatening decision by the sword. At the commencement of the war between France and England, the representative of the French republic then residing in the United States, complaining that the British armed ships captured French property in American bottoms, insisted that the principle of "free bottoms, free goods," was of the acknowledged law of nations; that the violation of that principle by the British was a wrong committed on us, and such an one as we ought to repel by joining in the war against that country. We denied his position, and appealed to the universal practice of Europe, in proof that the principle of "free bottoms, free goods," was not acknowledged as of the natural law of nations, but only of its conventional law. And I believe we may safely affirm, that not a single instance can be produced where any nation of Europe, acting professedly under the law of nations alone, unrestrained by treaty, has, either by its executive or judiciary organs, decided on the principle of "free bottoms, free goods." Judging of the law of nations by what has been practiced among nations, we were authorized to say that the contrary principle was their rule, and this but an exception to it, introduced by special treaties in special cases only; that having no treaty with England substituting this instead of the ordinary rule, we had neither the right nor the disposition to go to war for its establishment. But though we would not then, nor will we now, engage in war to establish this principle, we are nevertheless sincerely friendly to it. We think that the nations of Europe have originally set out in error; that experience has proved the error oppressive to the rights and interests of the peaceable part of mankind; that every nation but one has acknowledged this, by consenting to the change, and that one has consented in particular cases; that nations have a right to correct an erroneous principle, and to establish that which is right as their rule of action; and if they should adopt measures for effecting this in a peaceable way, we shall wish them success, and not stand in their way to it. But should it become, at any time, expedient for us to co-operate in the establishment of this principle, the opinion of the executive, on the advice of its constitutional counselors, must then be given; and that of the legislature, an independent and essential organ in the operation, must also be expressed; in forming which, they will be governed, every man by his own judgment, and may, very possibly, judge differently from the executive. With the same honest views, the most honest men often form different conclusions. As far, however, as we can judge, the principle of "free bottoms, free goods," is that which would carry the wishes of our nation.

Wishing you smooth seas and prosperous gales, with the enjoyment of good health, I tender you the assurances of my constant friendship and high consideration and respect.

WILLIAM SHORT, 1801, 10:284 - *PEACE IS OUR MOST IMPORTANT INTEREST, AND A RECOVERY FROM DEBT.*

To William Short[1]
Washington, October 3, 1801

Dear Sir, I trusted to Mr. Dawson to give you a full explanation, verbally, on a subject which I find he has but slightly mentioned to you. I shall therefore now do it. When I returned from France, after an absence of six or seven years, I was astonished at the change which I found had taken place in the United States in that time. No more like the same Correspondence 085 people; their notions, their habits and manners, the course of their commerce, so totally changed, that I, who stood in those of 1784, found myself not at all qualified to speak their sentiments, or forward their views in 1790. Very soon, therefore, after entering on the office of Secretary of State, I recommended to General Washington to establish as a rule of practice, that no person should be continued on foreign mission beyond an absence of six, seven, or eight years. He approved it. On the only subsequent missions which took place in my time, the persons appointed were notified that they could not be continued beyond that period. All returned within it except Humphreys. His

---

1 Peace and economy reinforced each other in Jefferson's opinion. A tax on stock shares had received his approval before election, and, after it, in this letter, he writes William Short, asserting that "Peace is our most important interest, and a recovery from debt." He believed that sound finances could be readily adjusted to emergencies, and that in peace times loans and internal taxes were a mistake, a conviction which the common people seem to have shared. Moreover, he despised the National Bank on political as well as economic principles, fearing its potential disloyalty in periods of crisis (Sears 1925, 26).

term was not quite out when General Washington went out of office. The succeeding administration had no rule for anything; so he continued. Immediately on my coming to the administration, I wrote to him myself, reminded him of the rule I had communicated to him on his departure; that he had then been absent about eleven years, and consequently must return. On this ground solely he was superseded. Under these circumstances, your appointment was impossible after an absence of seventeen years. Under any others, I should never fail to give to yourself and the world proofs of my friendship for you, and of my confidence in you. Whenever you shall return, you will be sensible in a greater, of what I was in a smaller degree, of the change in this nation from what it was when we both left it in 1784. We return like foreigners, and, like them, require a considerable residence here to become Americanized.

The state of political opinions continues to return steadily towards republicanism. To judge from the opposition papers, a stranger would suppose that a considerable check to it had been produced by certain removals of public officers. But this is not the case. All offices were in the hands of the federalists. The injustice of having totally excluded republicans was acknowledged by every man. To have removed one half, and to have placed republicans in their stead, would have been rigorously just, when it was known that these composed a very great majority of the nation. Yet such was their moderation in most of the States, that they did not desire it. In these, therefore, no removals took place but for malversation. In the Middle States, the contention had been higher, spirits were more sharpened and less accommodating. It was necessary in these to practice a different treatment, and to make a few changes to tranquillize the injured party. A few have been made there, a very few still remain to be made. When this painful operation shall be over, I see nothing else ahead of us which can give uneasiness to any of our citizens, or retard that consolidation of sentiment so essential to our happiness and our strength. The Tory papers will still find fault with everything. But these papers are sinking daily, from their dissonance with the sentiments of their subscribers, and very few will shortly remain to keep up a solitary and ineffectual barking.

There is no point in which an American, long absent from his country, wanders so widely from its sentiments as on the subject of its foreign affairs, We have a perfect horror at everything like connecting ourselves with the politics of Europe. It would indeed be advantageous to us to have neutral rights established on a broad ground; but no dependence can be placed in any European coalition for that. They have so many other bye-interests of greater weight, that some one or other will always be bought off. To be entangled with them would be a much greater evil than a temporary acquiescence in the false principles which have prevailed. Peace is our most important interest, and a recovery from debt. We feel ourselves strong, and daily growing stronger. The census just now concluded, shows we have added to our population a third of what it was ten years ago. This will be a duplication in twenty-three or twenty-four years. If we can delay but for a few years the necessity of vindicating the laws of nature on the ocean, we shall be the more sure of doing it with effect. The day is within my time as well as yours, when we may say by what laws other nations shall treat us on the sea. And we will say it. In the meantime, we wish to let every treaty we have drop off without renewal. We call in our diplomatic missions, barely keeping up those to the most important nations. There is a strong disposition in our countrymen to discontinue even these; and very possibly it may be done. Consuls will be continued as usual. The interest which European nations feel, as well as ourselves, in the mutual patronage of commercial intercourse, is a sufficient stimulus on both sides to insure that patronage. A treaty, contrary to that interest, renders war necessary to get rid of it.

I send this by Chancellor Livingston, named to the Senate the day after I came into office, as our Minister Plenipotentiary to France. I have taken care to impress him with the value of your society. You will find him an amiable and honorable man; unfortunately, so deaf that he will have to transact all his business by writing. You will have known long ago that Mr. Skipworth is reinstated in his consulship, as well as some others who had been set aside. I recollect no domestic news interesting to you. Your letters to your brother have been regularly transmitted, and I lately forwarded one from him, to be carried you by Mr. Livingston. Present my best respects to our amiable and mutual friend, and accept yourself assurances of my sincere and constant affection.

REPLY TO ADDRESS, 1801, 10:249 - *THE LAMENTABLE RESOURCE OF WAR IS NOT AUTHORIZED FOR EVILS OF IMAGINATION.*

To Messrs. Eddy, Russel, Thurber, Wheaton, and Smith Washington
March 27, 1801

Gentlemen, I return my sincere thanks for your kind congratulations on my elevation to the first magistracy of the United States. I see with pleasure every evidence of the attachment of my fellow citizens to elective government, calculated to promote their happiness, peculiarly adapted to their genius, habits, and situation, and the best permanent corrective of the errors or abuses of those interests with power. The Constitution on which our union rests, shall be administered by me according to the safe and honest meaning contemplated by the plain understanding of the people of the United States, at the time of its adoption, - a meaning to be found in the explanations of those who advocated, not those who opposed it, and who opposed it merely lest the constructions should be applied which they denounced as possible. These explanations are preserved in the publications of the time, and are too recent in the memories of most men to admit of question. The energies of the nation, as depends on me, shall be reserved for improvement of the condition of man, not wasted in his distinction. The lamentable resource of war is not authorized for evils of imagination, but for those actual injuries only, which would be more destructive of our well-being than war itself. Peace, justice, and liberal intercourse with all the nations of the world, will, I hope, with all nations, characterize this commonwealth. Accept for yourselves, gentlemen, and the respectable citizens of the town of Providence, assurances of my high consideration and respect.

FIRST ANNUAL MESSAGE, 1801, 3:327 - *THE LEGISLATURE WILL DOUBTLESS CONSIDER WHETHER, BY AUTHORIZING MEASURES OF OFFENCE, ALSO, THEY WILL PLACE OUR FORCE ON AN EQUAL FOOTING WITH THAT OF ITS ADVERSARIES.*

First Annual Message[1]
December 8, 1801

Fellow Citizens of the Senate and House of Representatives: It is a circumstance of sincere gratification to me that on meeting the great council of our nation, I am able to announce to them, on the grounds of reasonable certainty, that the wars and troubles which have for so many years afflicted our sister nations have at length come to an end, and that the communications of peace and commerce are once more opening among them. While we devoutly return thanks to the beneficent Being who has been pleased to breathe into them the spirit of conciliation and forgiveness, we are bound with peculiar gratitude to be thankful to him that our own peace has been pre- served through so perilous a season, and ourselves permitted quietly to cultivate the earth and to practice and improve those arts which tend to increase our comforts. The assurances, indeed, of friendly disposition, received from all the powers with whom we have principal relations, had inspired a confidence that our peace with them would not have been disturbed. But a

---

1 In this, Jefferson's first presidential message — and following classic republican beliefs — he considered the first line of national defense to be the local militia and diminished the importance of a standing army, saying, "Nor is it conceived needful or safe that a standing army should be kept up in a time of peace. Uncertain as we must ever be of the particular point in our circumference where an enemy may choose to invade us, the only force which can be ready at every point and competent to oppose them, is the body of neighboring citizens as formed into a militia." Significant for republican thought is the phrase "needful and safe." If citizen-soldiers are properly trained and equipped, they will be as effectively motivated as a standing army to defend their homes and nation, while maintenance of a large standing army in a peacetime republic has consistently been considered a danger to republican liberties (Hart 2002, 205). There were two considerations of particular importance for domestic policy. One was the paragraphs dealing with revenue and economy. The other was his proposal for new naturalization and immigration laws. Albert Gallatin's — Jefferson's Treasury Secretary — long and intensive studies of the fiscal problem bore fruit at the very outset. Jefferson was able to tell the Congress that easing of international tensions and frugality of administration would permit the repeal of all internal taxes. In order to realize such a hope it would be necessary to bring about a "salutary reduction" of regular expenses. But this would accord with basic Republican thought, since the general government "is charged with the external and mutual relations only of these states." The fact was, as Jefferson saw it, that the public payrolls had been padded with large numbers of unnecessary employees, many of whom had been appointed solely for purposes of consolidating the hold of the Federalists on national power. In practice, of course, the Republicans by no means abolished the system of political appointments; and Jefferson himself ran almost immediately into the problem of meeting the claims of deserving party members. But very substantial savings were in fact made, commitments were reduced, and the internal taxes were gradually dropped (Brown 1954, 80).

cessation of the irregularities which had affected the commerce of neutral nations, and of the irritations and injuries produced by them, cannot but add to this confidence; and strengthens, at the same time, the hope, that wrongs committed on unoffending friends, under a pressure of circumstances, will now be reviewed with candor, and will 328 Jefferson's Works be considered as founding just claims of retribution for the past and new assurance for the future.

Among our Indian neighbors, also, a spirit of peace and friendship generally prevails; and I am happy to inform you that the continued efforts to introduce among them the implements and the practice of husbandry, and of the household arts, have not been without success; that they are becoming more and more sensible of the superiority of this dependence for clothing and subsistence over the precarious resources of hunting and fishing; and already we are able to announce, that instead of that constant diminution of their numbers, produced by their wars and their wants, some of them begin to experience an increase of population.

To this state of general peace with which we have been blessed, one only exception exists. Tripoli, the least considerable of the Barbary States, had come forward with demands unfounded either in right or in compact, and had permitted itself to denounce war, on our failure to comply before a given day. The style of the demand admitted but one answer. I sent a small squadron of frigates into the Mediterranean, with assurances to that power of our sincere desire to remain in peace, but with orders to protect our commerce against the threatened attack. The measure was seasonable and salutary. The *Bey* had already declared war in form. His cruisers were out. Two had arrived at Gibraltar. Our commerce in the Mediterranean was blockaded, and that of the Atlantic in peril. The arrival of our squadron dispelled the danger. One of the Tripolitan cruisers having fallen in with, and engaged the small schooner Enterprise, commanded by Lieutenant Sterret, which had gone as a tender to our larger vessels, was captured, after a heavy slaughter of her men, without the loss of a single one on our part. The bravery exhibited by our citizens on that element, will, I trust, be a testimony to the world that it is not the want of that virtue which makes us seek their peace, but a conscientious desire to direct the energies of our nation to the multiplication of the human race, and not to its destruction. Unauthorized by the constitution, without the sanction of Congress, to go beyond the line of defense, the vessel being disabled from committing further hostilities, was liberated with its crew. The legislature will doubtless consider whether, by authorizing measures of offence, also, they will place our force on an equal footing with that of its adversaries. I communicate all material information on this subject, that in the exercise of the important function confided by the constitution to the legislature exclusively, their judgment may form itself on a knowledge and consideration of every circumstance of weight.

I wish I could say that our situation with all the other Barbary States was entirely satisfactory. Discovering that some delays had taken place in the performance of certain articles stipulated by us, I thought it my duty, by immediate measures for fulfilling them, to vindicate to ourselves the right of considering the effect of departure from stipulation on their side. From the papers which will be laid before you, you will be enabled to judge whether our treaties are regarded by them as fixing at all the measure of their demands, or as guarding from the exercise of force our vessels within their power; and to consider how far it will be safe and expedient to leave our affairs with them in their present posture.

I lay before you the result of the census lately taken of our inhabitants, to a conformity with which we are to reduce the ensuing rates of representation and taxation. You will perceive that the increase of numbers during the last ten years, proceeding in geometrical ratio, promises a duplication in little more than twenty-two years. We contemplate this rapid growth, and the prospect it holds up to us, not with a view to the injuries it may enable us to do to others in some future day, but to the settlement of the extensive country still remaining vacant within our limits to the multiplications of men susceptible of happiness, educated in the love of order, habituated to self-government, and valuing its blessings above all price.

Other circumstances, combined with the increase of numbers, have produced an augmentation of revenue arising from consumption, in a ratio far beyond that of population alone, and though the changes of foreign relations now taking place so desirably for Inaugural Addresses and Messages 331 the world, may for a season affect this branch of revenue, yet, weighing all probabilities of expense, as well as of income, there is reasonable ground of confidence that we may now safely dispense with all the internal taxes, comprehending excises, stamps, auctions, licenses, carriages, and refined sugars, to which the postage on newspapers may be added, to facilitate the progress of information, and that the remaining sources of revenue will be sufficient to provide for the support of government, to pay the interest on the public debts, and to discharge the principals in shorter periods than the laws or the general expectations had contemplated. War, indeed, and untoward events, may change this prospect of things, and call for expenses which the imposts could not meet; but sound principles will not justify our taxing the industry of our fellow citizens to accumulate treasure for wars to happen we know not when, and which might not perhaps happen but from the temptations offered by that treasure.

These views, however, of reducing our burdens, are formed on the expectation that a sensible, and at the same time a salutary reduction, may take place in our habitual expenditures. For this purpose those of the civil government, the army, and navy, will need revisal.

When we consider that this government is charged with the external and mutual relations only of these states; that the states themselves have principal care of our persons, our property, and our reputation, constituting the great field of human concerns, we may well doubt whether our organization is not too complicated, too expensive; whether offices and officers have not been multiplied unnecessarily, and sometimes injuriously to the service they were meant to promote. I will cause to be laid before you an essay toward a statement of those who, under public employment of various kinds, draw money from the treasury or from our citizens. Time has not permitted a perfect enumeration, the ramifications of office being too multiplied and remote to be completely traced in a first trial. Among those who are dependent on executive discretion, I have begun the reduction of what was deemed necessary. The expenses of diplomatic agency have been considerably diminished. The inspectors of internal revenue who were found to obstruct the accountability of the institution, have been discontinued. Several agencies created by executive authority, on salaries fixed by that also, have been suppressed, and should suggest the expediency of regulating that power by law, so as to subject its exercises to legislative inspection and sanction. Other reformations of the same kind will be pursued with that caution which is requisite in removing useless things, not to injure what is retained. But the great mass of public offices is established by law, and, therefore, by law alone can be abolished. Should the legislature think it expedient to pass this roll in review, and try all its parts by the test of public utility, they may be assured of every aid and light which executive information can yield. Considering the general tendency to multiply offices and dependencies, and to increase expense to the ultimate term of burden which the citizen can bear, it behooves us to avail ourselves of every occasion which presents itself for taking off the surcharge; that it never may be seen here that, after leaving to labor the smallest portion of its earnings on which it can subsist, government shall itself consume the residue of what it was instituted to guard.

In our care, too, of the public contributions entrusted to our direction, it would be prudent to multiply barriers against their dissipation, by appropriating specific sums to every specific purpose susceptible of definition; by disallowing all applications of money varying from the appropriation in object, or transcending it in amount; by reducing the undefined field of contingencies, and thereby circumscribing discretionary powers over money; and by bringing back to a single department all accountabilities for money where the examination may be prompt, efficacious, and uniform.

An account of the receipts and expenditures of the last year, as prepared by the secretary of the treasury, will as usual be laid before you. The success which has attended the late sales of the public lands, shows that with attention they may be made an important source of receipt. Among the payments, those made in discharge of the principal and interest of the national debt, will show that the public faith has been exactly maintained. To these will be added an estimate of appropriations necessary for the ensuing year. This last will of course be effected by such modifications of the systems of expense, as you shall think proper to adopt.

A statement has been formed by the secretary of war, on mature consideration, of all the posts and stations where garrisons will be expedient, and of the number of men requisite for each garrison. The whole amount is considerably short of the present military establishment. For the surplus, no particular use can be pointed out. For defense against invasion, their number is as nothing; nor is it conceived needful or safe that a standing army should be kept up in time of peace for that purpose. Uncertain as we must ever be of the particular point in our circumference where an enemy may choose to invade us, the only force which can be ready at every point and competent to oppose them, is the body of neighboring citizens as formed into a militia. On these, collected from the parts most convenient, in numbers proportioned to the invading foe, it is best to rely, not only to meet the first attack, but if it threatens to be permanent, to maintain the defense until regulars may be engaged to relieve them. These considerations render it important that we should at every session continue to amend the defects which from time to time show themselves in the laws for regulating the militia, until they are perfect . Nor should we now or at any time separate, until we can say we have done everything for the militia which we could do were an enemy at our door.

The provisions of military stores on hand will be laid before you, that you may judge of the additions still requisite.

With respect to the extent to which our naval preparations should be carried, some difference of opinion may be expected to appear; but just atten-tion to the circumstances of every part of the Union will doubtless reconcile all. A small force will probably continue to be wanted for actual service in the Mediterranean. Whatever annual sum beyond that you may think proper to appropriate to naval preparations, would perhaps be better employed in providing those articles which may be kept without waste or consumption, and be in readiness when any exigence calls them into use. Progress has been made, as will appear by papers now communicated, in providing materials for seventy-four gun ships as directed by law.

How far the authority given by the legislature for procuring and estab-lishing sites for naval purposes has been perfectly understood and pursued in the execution, admits of some doubt. A statement of the expenses already incurred on that subject, shall be laid before you. I have in certain cases sus-pended or slackened these expenditures, that the legislature might deter-mine whether so many yards are necessary as have been contemplated. The works at this place are among those permitted to go on; and five of the seven frigates directed to be laid up, have been brought and laid up here, where, besides the safety of their position, they are under the eye of the executive administration, as well as of its agents, and where yourselves also will be guided - by your own view in the legislative provisions respecting them which may from time to time be necessary. They are preserved in such con-dition, as well the vessels as whatever belongs to them, as to be at all times ready for sea on a short warning. Two others are yet to be laid up so soon as they shall have received the repairs requisite to put them also into sound condition. As a superintending officer will be necessary at each yard, his du-ties and emoluments, hitherto fixed by the executive, will be a more proper subject for legislation. A communication will also be made of our progress in the execution of the law respecting the vessels directed to be sold.

The fortifications of our harbors, more or less advanced, present considerations of great difficulty. While some of them are on a scale sufficiently proportioned to the advantages of their position, to the efficacy of their protection, and the importance of the points within it, others are so extensive, will cost so much in their first erection, so much in their maintenance, and require such a force to garrison them, as to make it questionable what is best now to be done. A statement of those commenced or projected, of the expenses already incurred, and estimates of their future cost, so far as can be foreseen, shall be laid before you, that you may be enabled to judge whether any attention is necessary in the laws respecting this subject.

Agriculture, manufactures, commerce, and navigation, the four pillars of our prosperity, are the most thriving when left most free to individual enterprise. Protection from casual embarrassments, however, may sometimes be seasonably interposed. If in the course of your observations or inquiries they should appear to need any aid within the limits of our constitutional powers, your sense of their importance is a sufficient assurance they will occupy your attention. We cannot, indeed, but all feel an anxious solicitude for the difficulties under which our carrying trade will soon be placed. How far it can be relieved, otherwise than by time, is a subject, of important consideration.

The judiciary system of the United States, and especially that portion of it recently erected, will of course present itself to the contemplation of Congress; and that they may be able to judge of the proportion which the institution bears to the business it has to perform, I have caused to be procured from the several States, and now lay before Congress, an exact statement of all the causes decided since the first establishment of the courts, and of those which were depending when additional courts and judges were brought in to their aid.

And while on the judiciary organization, it will be worthy your consideration, whether the protection of the inestimable institution of juries has been extended to all the cases involving the security of our persons and property. Their impartial selection also being essential to their value, we ought further to consider whether that is sufficiently secured in those States where they are named by a marshal depending on executive will, or designated by the court or by officers dependent on them.

I cannot omit recommending a revisal of the laws on the subject of naturalization. Considering the ordinary chances of human life, a denial of citizenship under a residence of fourteen years is a denial to a great proportion of those who ask it, and controls a policy pursued from their first settlement by many of these States, and still believed of consequence to their prosperity. And shall we refuse the unhappy fugitives from distress that hospitality which the savages of the wilderness extended to our fathers arriving in this land? Shall oppressed humanity find no asylum on this globe? The constitution, indeed, has wisely provided that, for admission to certain offices of important trust, a residence shall be required sufficient to develop character and design. But might not the general character and capabilities of a citizen be safely communicated to every one manifesting a *bona fide* purpose of embarking his life and fortunes permanently with us? With restrictions, perhaps, to guard against the fraudulent usurpation of our flag; an abuse which brings so much embarrassment and loss on the genuine citizen, and so much danger to the nation of being involved in war, that no endeavor should be spared to detect and suppress it.

These, fellow citizens, are the matters respecting the state of the nation, which I have thought of importance to be submitted to your consideration at this time. Some others of less moment, or not yet ready for communication, will be the subject of separate messages. I am happy in this opportunity of committing the arduous affairs of our government to the collected wisdom of the Union. Nothing shall be wanting on my part to inform, as far as in my power, the legislative judgment, nor to carry that judgment into faithful execution. The prudence and temperance of your discussions will promote, within your own walls, that conciliation which so much befriends rational conclusion; and by its example will encourage among our constituents that progress of opinion which is tending to unite them in object and in will. That all should be satisfied with any one order of things is not to be expected, but I indulge the pleasing persuasion that the great body of our citizens will cordially concur in honest and disinterested efforts, which have for their object to preserve the general and State governments in their constitutional form and equilibrium; to maintain peace abroad, and order and obedience to the laws at home; to establish principles and practices of administration favorable to the security of liberty and property, and to reduce expenses to what is necessary for the useful purposes of government.

ADDRESS TO INDIAN NATIONS, 1802, 16:390 ~ *IN A LONG AND BLOODY WAR, WE LOSE MANY FRIENDS AND GAIN NOTHING.*

Washington January 7, 1802

Brothers and friends of the Miamis, Powtewatamies, and Weeauk [Wea][1]

---

1 In an effort to turn away from conflict, the civilization of the Indians by instructing them in agricultural and household arts received vigorous support from Thomas Jefferson. In his first annual message to Congress, he reported success in the program under the intercourse laws; that the Indians had already come to realize the superiority of these means of obtaining clothing and subsistence over the precarious resources of hunting and fishing; and that instead of decreasing in numbers they were beginning to show an increase. He also expressed his views freely in his talks to the Indians, as in this letter to the Miamis, Potawatomis, and Weas: "We shall with great pleasure see your people become disposed to cultivate the earth, to raise herds of useful animals and to spin and weave, for their food and clothing. These resources are certain, they will never disappoint you, while those of hunting may fail, and expose your women and children to the miseries of hunger and cold. We will with pleasure furnish you with implements for the most necessary arts, and with persons who may instruct how to make and use them." Moreover, Jefferson's views were ardently promoted by Secretary of War Henry Dearborn, who kept up a constant battery of instructions to the agents on the use of implements made available under the intercourse laws. He wrote in the name of the president to the territorial governors of the Northwest Territory, Mississippi Territory, and Indiana Territory to encourage them to promote en-

I receive with great satisfaction the visit you have been so kind as to make us at this place, and I thank the Great Spirit who has conducted you to us in health and safety. It is well that friends should sometimes meet, open their minds mutually, and renew the chain of affection. Made by the same Great Spirit, and living in the same land with our brothers, the red men, we consider ourselves as of the same family; we wish to live with them as one people, and to cherish their interests as our own. The evils which of necessity encompass the life of man are sufficiently numerous. Why should we add to them by voluntarily distressing and destroying one another? Peace, brothers, is better than war. In a long and bloody war, we lose many friends, and gain nothing. Let us then live in peace and friendship together, doing to each other all the good we can. The wise and good on both sides desire this, and we must take care that the foolish and wicked among us shall not prevent it. On our part, we shall endeavor in all things to be just and generous towards you, and to aid you in meeting those difficulties which a change of circumstances is bringing on. We shall, with great pleasure, see your people become disposed to cultivate the earth, to raise herds of the useful animals, and to spin and weave, for their food and clothing. These resources are certain; they will never disappoint you: while those of hunting may fail, and expose your women and children to the miseries of hunger and cold. We will with pleasure furnish you with implements for the most necessary arts, and with persons who may instruct you how to make and use them

I consider it as fortunate that you have made your visit at this time, when our wise men from the sixteen States are collected together in council, who being equally disposed to befriend you, can strengthen our hands in the good we all wish to render you.

The several matters you opened to us in your speech the other day, and those on which you have since conversed with the Secretary of War, have been duly considered by us. He will now deliver answers, and you are to consider what he says, as if said by myself, and that what we promise we shall faithfully perform.

PIERRE SAMUEL DUPONT DE NEMOURS, 1802, 10:316 - *PEACE AND ABSTINENCE FROM EUROPEAN INTERFERENCES ARE OUR OBJECTS, AND SO WILL CONTINUE WHILE THE PRESENT ORDER OF THINGS IN AMERICA REMAIN UNINTERRUPTED.*

To Monsieur Dupont de Nemours[1]

---

ergetically the government's plan for civilizing the Indians, and he authorized the employment of blacksmiths and carpenters, necessary to keep the plows and other implements in working order (Prucha 1984, 142-143).

1 By 1802 the observations of Robert Livingston — then America's minister to France — on French imperial plans persuaded Jefferson to announce not only his knowledge of the 1800 Treaty of San Ildefonso — by which Spain returned Louisiana to France — but also his opposition to it; and, shortly thereafter, he began to hint at a rupture between the two countries that would take place as soon as war was resumed in Europe. To avoid this mutually destructive state of affairs, Jefferson suggested that France provide Americans with favorable commercial concessions on the Mississippi indicating, perhaps, that he decided

Washington, April 25, 1802

Dear Sir, The week being now closed, during which you had given me a hope of seeing you here, I think it safe to enclose you my letters for Paris, lest they should fail of the benefit of so desirable a conveyance. They are addressed to Kosciusko, Madame de Corny, Mrs. Short, and Chancellor Livingston. You will perceive the unlimited confidence I repose in your good faith, and in your cordial dispositions to serve both countries, when you observe that I leave the letters for Chancellor Livingston open for your perusal. The first page respects a cipher, as do the loose sheets folded with the letter. These are interesting to him and myself only, and therefore are not for your perusal. It is the second, third, and fourth pages which I wish you to read to possess yourself of completely, and then seal the letter with wafers stuck under the flying seal, that it may be seen by nobody else if any accident should happen to you, I wish you to be possessed of the subject, because you may be able to impress on the government of France the inevitable consequences of their taking possession of Louisiana; and though, as I here mention the cession of New Orleans and the Floridas to us would be a palliation, yet I believe it would be no more, and that this measure will cost France, and perhaps not very long hence, a war which will annihilate her on the ocean, and place that element under the despotism of two nations, which I am not reconciled to the more because my own would be one of them. Add to this the exclusive appropriation of both continents of America as a consequence. I wish the present order of things to continue, and with a view to this I value highly a state of friendship between France and us. You know too well how sincere I have ever been in these dispositions to doubt them. You know, too, how much I value peace, and how unwillingly I should see any event take place which would render war a necessary resource; and that all our movements should change their character and object. I am thus open with you, because I trust that you will have it in your power to impress on that government considerations, in the scale against which the possession of Louisiana is nothing. In Europe, nothing but Europe is seen, or supposed to have any right in the affairs of nations; but this little event, of France's possessing herself of Louisiana, which is thrown in as nothing, as a mere make-weight in the general settlement of accounts, this speck which now appears as an almost invisible point in the horizon, is the embryo of a tornado which will burst on the countries on both sides of the Atlantic, and involve in its effects their highest destinies. That it may yet be avoided is my sincere prayer; and if you can be the means of informing the wisdom of Bonaparte of all its consequences, you have deserved well of both countries. Peace and abstinence

---

to face the fact of French imperialism without waiting for French troops on American soil to rouse him to action. Pierre Samuel Du Pont de Nemours was a distinguished economist and a Jefferson friend for almost twenty years. Although Du Pont was then a resident of the United States and was departing for France for what he thought would be only a brief stay, Jefferson saw an opportunity to exploit the economist's contacts with the French government by having him publicize the seriousness with which the United States regarded the Louisiana cession (Kaplan 1967, 98-99).

from European interferences are our objects, and so will continue while the present order of things in America remain uninterrupted. There is another service you can render. I am told that Talleyrand is personally hostile to us. This, I suppose, has been occasioned by the X.Y.Z. history. But he should consider, that that was the artifice of a party, willing to sacrifice him to the consolidation of their power. This nation has done him justice by dismissing them; that those in power are precisely those who disbelieved that story, and saw in it nothing but an at-tempt to deceive our country; that we entertain towards him personally the most friendly dispositions; that as to the govern-ment of France, we know too little of the state of things there to understand what it is, and have no inclination to meddle in their settlement. Whatever government they establish, we wish to be well with it. One more request, - that you deliver the letter to Chancellor Livingston with your own hands, and, moreover, that you charge Madame DuPont, if any accident happen to you, that she deliver the letter with her own hands. If it passes only through hers and yours, I shall have perfect confidence in its safety. Present her my most sincere respects, and accept yourself assurances of my constant affec-tion, and my prayers, that a genial sky and propitious gales may place you, after a pleasant voyage, in the midst of your friends.

ROBERT LIVINGSTON, 1802, 10:334 - PEACE [IS] INDEED THE MOST IMPORTANT OF ALL THINGS FOR US, EXCEPT THE PRESERVING AN ERECT AND INDEPENDENT ATTITUDE.

To Robert Livingston[1]
Washington, October 10, 1802

Dear Sir, The departure of Madame Brugnard for France furnishes me a safe conveyance of a letter, which I cannot avoid embracing, although I have nothing particular for the subject of it. It is well, however, to be able to inform you, generally, through a safe channel, that we stand completely corrected of the error, that either the government or the nation of France has any remains of friendship for us. The portion of that country which forms an exception, though respectable in weight, is weak in numbers. On the contrary, it appears evident, that an unfriendly spirit prevails in the most important individuals of the government, towards us. In this state .of things, we shall so take our distance between the two rival nations, as, remaining

---

1 In spite of his frequent menaces, in this letter Jefferson told Livingston that the French oc-cupation of Louisiana was not "important enough to risk a breach of peace." And, within a week after this letter was written, New Orleans was closed to American commerce, and a breach of peace seemed unavoidable. Down to that time the Executive had done nothing to check Napoleon. The President had instructed his agents at Paris and Madrid to obtain, if they could, the cession of New Orleans and West Florida, and had threatened an alliance with England in case this request were refused; but England was at peace with France, and Bonaparte was not likely to provoke another war until he should be able to defend Louisiana. So far as any diplomatic action by the United States government was concerned, Madison and Jefferson might equally well have written nothing; and when news arrived that the Mississippi was closed, alarming as the situation became, no new action was at first suggested. The President was contented to accept the assistance of the Spanish and French representatives at Washington (Adams 1930, 424-425).

disengaged till necessity compels us, we may haul finally to the enemy of that which shall make it necessary. We see all the disadvantageous consequences of taking a side, and shall be forced into it only by a more disagreeable alternative; in which event, we must countervail the disadvantages by measures which will give us splendor and power, but not as much happiness as our present system. We wish, therefore, to remain well with France. But we see that no consequences, however ruinous to them, can secure us with certainty against the extravagance of her present rulers. I think, therefore, that while we do nothing which the first nation on earth would deem crouching, we had better give to all our communications with them a very mild, complaisant, and even friendly complexion, but always independent. Ask no favors, leave small and irritating things to be conducted by the individuals interested in them, interfere ourselves but in the greatest cases, and then not push them to irritation. No matter at present existing between them and us is important enough to risk a breach of peace; peace being indeed the most important of all things for us, except the preserving an erect and independent attitude. Although I know your own judgment leads you to pursue this line identically, yet I thought it just to strengthen it by the concurrence of my own. You will have seen by our newspapers, that with the aid of a lying *renegado* from republicanism, the federalists have opened all their sluices of calumny. They say we lied them out of power, and openly avow they will do the same by us. But it was not lies or arguments on our part which dethroned them, but their own foolish acts, sedition laws, alien laws, taxes, extravagances and heresies. Porcupine, their friend, wrote them down. Callendar, their new recruit, will do the same. Every decent man among them revolts at his filth; and there cannot be a doubt, that were a Presidential election to come on this day, they would certainly have but three New England States, and about half a dozen votes from Maryland and North Carolina, these two States electing by districts. Were all the States to elect by a general ticket, they would have but three out of sixteen States. And these three are coming up slowly. We do, indeed, consider Jersey and Delaware as rather doubtful. Elections which have lately taken place there, but their event not yet known here, will show the present point of their varying condition.

My letters to you being merely private, I leave all details of business to their official channel.

Accept assurances of my constant friendship and high respect.

P. S. We have received your letter announcing the arrival of Mr. DuPont.

STATE GOVERNORS, 1803, 10:365 ~ NONE BUT AN ARMED NATION CAN DISPENSE WITH A STANDING ARMY.

Addressee Unknown (to state governors?) [1]

---

[1] Ultimately, the prospect of French control of the Mississippi disturbed Jefferson. While Spain held only a weak and tenuous grip on the river, France was a much stronger power, and Jefferson feared the establishment of a French colonial empire in North America, blocking U.S. expansion. To Jefferson, the United States appeared to have only two options: diplomacy or war; and, in response to growing concerns from the western states, Jefferson, with

Washington, February 25, 1803

Sir, In compliance with a request of the House of Representatives of the United States, as well as with a sense of what is necessary, I take the liberty of urging on you the importance and indispensable necessity of vigorous exertions, on the part of the State governments, to carry into effect the militia system adopted by the national Legislature, agreeable to the powers reserved to the States respectively, by the Constitution of the United States, and in a manner the best calculated to ensure such a degree of military discipline, and knowledge of tactics, as will under the auspices of a benign providence, render the militia a sure and permanent bulwark of national defense.

None but an armed nation can dispense with a standing army; to keep ours armed and disciplined, is, therefore, at all times important, but especially so at a moment when rights the most essential to our welfare have been violated, and an infraction of treaty committed without color or pretext; and although we are willing to believe that this has been the act of a subordinate agent only, yet is it wise to prepare for the possibility that it may have been the leading measure of a system. While, therefore, we are endeavoring, and with a considerable degree of confidence, to obtain by friendly negotiation a peaceable redress of the injury, and effectual provision against its repetition, let us array the strength of the nation, and be ready to do with promptitude and effect whatever a regard to justice and our future security may require.

In order that I may have a full and correct view of the resources of our country in all its different parts, I must desire you, with as little delay as possible, to have me furnished with a return of the militia, and of the arms and accoutrements of your State, and of the several counties, or other geographical divisions of it. Accept assurances of my high consideration and respect.

WILLIAM DUNBAR, 1803, 19:131 ~ *NOTHING BUT DIRE NECESSITY,
SHOULD FORCE US FROM THE PATH OF PEACE WHICH WOULD BE OUR
WISEST PURSUIT.*

To William Dunbar[1]
Washington, March 3, 1803

Sir, Your favor of the 8th of January has been received and I have to return you thanks for the two vocabularies. The memoir of Mr. Durald has been forwarded to the Philosophical Society. We shall be happy to see your history

---

congressional approval, herein called for state governors to raise a militia of in preparation for a possible war with France (Davis 1998, 289).

1 Inasmuch as France never completed her empire in America, there can be no certainty as to the extent to which Jefferson would have gone to counter the moves of Bonaparte. And, during the troublesome days of 1802, his fears often dented the armor of confidence he had built out of hopes that the troubles of the Old World would in some way prove to be his salvation. On such occasions, he would be convinced that France would force the United States into the arms of Britain, and so he took some measure of pleasure in noting every manifestation of friendship on the part of the British. But, generally, Jefferson's embrace of the British was half-hearted and, in the end, nothing but dire necessity — as he suggested in this note to the respected naturalist and explorer William Dunbar — could force the country out of neutrality and into the orbit of Britain (Kaplan 1967, 102-103).

of the Mississippi completed, as it is becoming one of the most interesting parts of our country. The only one where some of the tropical productions can be maintained among us. [illegible] had only a little mistaken the information I gave him [illegible] was not that you were removing altogether, but that you meant shortly to take a trip to Europe which I had understood from some other person [illegible] yourself.

The late interruption of our commerce at New Orleans by the Spanish Intendant, combined with the change of proprietors which Louisiana certainly, and the Floridas possibly, are immediately to undergo have produced a great sensation here; while some have wished to make it the immediate cause of war which might damage our finances and embarrass the administration of our government, which, in the state of their political passions, would be a countervail for the most serious public extremities, we have pursued what we believe a more certain and more speedy means of restoring permanently the rights and conveniences of our commerce, whether we may succeed in the acquisition of the island of New Orleans and the Floridas peaceably for a price far short of the expense of a war, we cannot say. But that we shall obtain peaceably an immediate and firm re-establishment of all our rights under the Spanish treaty every circumstance known to us leads us to believe. If contrary to expectations war should be necessary to restore our rights, it is surely prudent to take a little time for availing ourselves of the division of Europe to strengthen ourselves for that war. Nothing but the failure of every peaceable mode of redress, nothing but dire necessity, should force us from the path of peace which would be our wisest pursuit, to embark in the broils and contentions of Europe and become a satellite to any power there. Yet this must be the consequence if we fail in all possible means of re-establishing our rights were we to enter into the war alone. The Mississippi would be blockaded at least during the continuance of that war by a superior naval power, and all our Western States be deprived of their commerce unless they would surrender themselves to the blockading power.

Great endeavors have been used from this quarter to inflame the western people to take possession of New Orleans without looking forward to the use they could make of it with a blockaded river, but I trust they will be unable, that a peaceable redress will be quickest and most for their interests. We shall endeavor to procure the Indian right of soil, as soon as they can be prevailed on to part with it, the whole left bank of the Mississippi to a respectable breadth, and encourage a prompt settlement, and thereby plant on the Mississippi itself the means of its own defense and present as strong a frontier as that on our Eastern border. I pray you to accept assurances of my great esteem and respect.

Hugh Williamson, 1803, 10:386 - We have obtained by a peaceable appeal to justice, in four months, what we should not have obtained under seven years of war.

To Dr. Hugh Williamson[1]

Washington, April 30, 1803

Dear Sir, I thank you for the information on the subject of navigation of the Herville contained in yours of the 10th. In running the late line between the Choctaws and us, we found the Amite to be about thirty miles from the Mississippi where that line crossed it, which was but a little northward of our southern boundary. For the present we have a respite on that subject, Spain having without delay restored our infracted right, and assured us it is expressly saved by the instrument of her cession of Louisiana to France. Although I do not count with confidence on obtaining New Orleans from France for money, yet I am confident in the policy of putting off the day of contention for it till we have lessened the embarrassment of debt accumulated instead of being discharged by our predecessors, till we obtain more of that strength which is growing on us so rapidly, and especially till we have planted a population on the Mississippi itself sufficient to do its own work without marching men fifteen hundred miles from the Atlantic shores to perish by fatigue and unfriendly climates. This will soon take place. In the meantime we have obtained by a peaceable appeal to justice, in four months, what we should not have obtained under seven years of war, the loss of one hundred thousand lives, an hundred millions of additional debt, many hundred millions worth of produce and property lost for want of market, or in seeking it, and that demoralization which war superinduces on the human mind. To have seized New Orleans, as our federal maniacs wished, would only have changed the character and extent of the blockade of our western commerce. It would have produced a blockade, by superior naval force, of the navigation of the river as well as of the entrance into New Orleans, instead of a paper blockade from New Orleans alone while the river remained open, and I am persuaded that had not the deposit been so quickly rendered we should have found soon that it would be better now to ascend the river

---

1Jefferson's lack of decisive military action upon hearing that New Orleans would pass from Spanish to French hands turned out to be fortuitous. Before Napoleon could dispatch his troops to the North American port, he faced a number of setbacks: the leader of the French expedition bound for New Orleans became trapped in Holland when his entire fleet was frozen in for the winter; and the French troops in Santo Domingo contracted yellow fever and then encountered guerilla warfare, losing 20,000 men before all was over. Accordingly, Napoleon's plans for a North American colony quite suddenly became impossible. Word then reached him that the U.S. Senate was calling for a military takeover of the port, and he knew he could not defend it if the United States pressed its advantage. Before he could even claim New Orleans, Napoleon found it to be a liability; its cost in money and men was simply too high. Still, some Federalists — Jefferson terms them "federal maniacs" in this letter to Hugh Williamson, a friend and fellow intellectual — would later complain that a military takeover of New Orleans would have cost the United States less funds than the Louisiana Purchase; moreover, the French were in no position to resist if the United States had established control of the port; however, this position is drawn largely from hindsight (Sturgis 2002, 94).

to Natchez, in order to be clear of the embarrassments, plunderings, and irritations at New Orleans, and to fatten by the benefits of the depot a city and citizens of our own, rather than those of a foreign nation. Accept my friendly and respectful salutations.

P. S. Water line of the Herville, Amite, and to Ponchartrain, becoming a boundary between France and Spain, we have a double chance of an acknowledgment of our right to use it on the same ground of national right on which we claim the navigation of the Mobile and other rivers heading in our territory and running through the Floridas.

JOHN SINCLAIR, 1803, 10:397 - WE PREFER TRYING EVER OTHER JUST PRINCIPLES, RIGHT AND SAFETY, BEFORE WE WOULD RECUR TO WAR.

To Sir John Sinclair[1]
Washington, June 30, 1803

Dear Sir, It is so long since I have had the pleasure of writing to you, that it would be vain to look back to dates to connect the old and the new. Yet I ought not to pass over my acknowledgments to you for various publications received from time to time, and with great satisfaction and thankfulness. I send you a small one in return, the work of a very unlettered farmer, yet valuable, as it relates plain facts of importance to farmers. You will discover that Mr. Binns is an enthusiast for the use of gypsum. But there are two facts which prove he has a right to be so: 1. He began poor, and has made himself tolerably rich by his farming alone. 2. The county of Loudon, in which he lives, had been so exhausted and wasted by bad husbandry, that it began to depopulate, the inhabitants going southwardly in quest of better lands. Binns' success has stopped that emigration. It is now becoming one of the most productive counties of the State of Virginia, and the price given for the lands is multiplied manifold.

We are still uninformed here whether you are again at war. Bonaparte has produced such a state of things in Europe as it would seem difficult for him to relinquish in any sensible degree, and equally dangerous for Great Britain to suffer to go on, especially if accompanied by maritime preparations on his part. The events which have taken place in France have lessened in the American mind the motives of interest which it felt in that revolution, and its amity towards that country now rests on its love of peace and commerce. We see, at the same time, with great concern, the position in which Great Britain is placed, and should be sincerely afflicted were any disaster to deprive mankind of the benefit of such a bulwark against the torrent which has for some time been bearing down all before it. But her power and powers

---

1 When Jefferson wrote this letter to British agronomist, Sir John Sinclair — "Peace is our passion..." etc. — he seems to be expressing no mere political slogan, but a new theme in his life. Liberation, once his compelling hunger, has long since given way to his need for tranquility. Further, this personal need would come to influence many aspects of his foreign policy, as well as numerous domestic decisions, all the while continuing to dominate his private life (Brodie 1974, 342).

at sea seem to render everything safe in the end. Peace is our passion, and the wrongs might drive us from it. We prefer trying ever other just principles, right and safety, before we would recur to war.

I hope your agricultural institution goes on with success. I consider you as the author of all the good it shall do. A better idea has never been carried into practice. Our agricultural society has at length formed itself. Like our American Philosophical Society, it is voluntary, and unconnected with the public, and is precisely an execution of the plan I formerly sketched to you. Some State societies have been formed heretofore; the others will do the same. Each State society names two of its members of Congress to be their members in the Central society, which is of course together during the sessions of Congress. They are to select matter from the proceedings of the State societies, and to publish it; so that their publications may be called *l'esprit des societes d'agriculture*, etc. The Central society was formed the last winter only, so that it will be some time before they get under way. Mr. Madison, the Secretary of State, was elected their President.

Recollecting with great satisfaction our friendly intercourse while I was in Europe, I nourish the hope it still preserves a place in your mind; and with my salutations, I pray you to accept assurances of my constant attachment and high respect.

EARL OF BUCHAN, 1803, 10:401 ~ *My hope of preserving peace for our country is not founded in the greater principles of non-resistance under every wrong.*

To the Earl of Buchan[1]
Washington, July 10 1803

My Lord, I received, through the hands of Mr. Lenox, on his return to the United States, the valuable volume you were so good as to send me on the life and writings of Fletcher, of Saltoun. The political principles of that patriot were worthy the purest periods of the British Constitution; they are those which were in vigor at the epoch of the American emigration. Our ancestors brought them here, and they needed little strengthening to make us what we are. But in the weakened condition of English Whigs at this day, it requires more firmness to publish and advocate them than it then did to act on them. This merit is peculiarly your Lordship's; and no one honors it more than myself. While I freely admit the right of a nation to change its political principles and constitution at will, and the impropriety of any but its own citizens censuring that change, I expect your Lordship has been disappointed, as I acknowledge I have been, in the issue of the convulsions on the other side the channel. This has certainly lessened the interest which the philanthropist warmly felt in those struggles. Without befriending human liberty,

---

1 President Jefferson, while avowing a pacific policy, felt that his hopes of peace were founded on his power to affect the interests of the belligerents. Moreover, he was confident that he could control France and England. The Louisiana question was settled, and now the field was clear for the United States to take high ground in behalf of neutral rights (Adams, 1930, 357).

a gigantic force has risen up which seems to threaten the world. But it hangs on the thread of opinion, which may break from one day to another. I feel real anxiety on the conflict to which imperious circumstances seem to call your attention, and bless the Almighty Being, who, in gathering together the waters under the heavens into one place, divided the dry land of your hemisphere from the dry lands of ours, and said, at least be there peace. I hope that peace and amity with all nations will long be the character of our land, and that its prosperity under the Charter will react on the mind of Europe, and profit her by the example. My hope of preserving peace for our country is not founded in the greater principles of non-resistance under every wrong, but in the belief that a just and friendly conduct on our part will procure justice and friendship from others. In the existing contest, each of the combatants will find an interest in our friendship. I cannot say we shall be unconcerned spectators of this combat. We feel for human sufferings, and we wish the good of all. We shall look on, therefore, with the sensations which these dispositions and the events of the war will produce.

I feel a pride in the justice which your Lordship's sentiments render to the character of my illustrious countryman, Washington. The moderation of his desires, and the strength of his judgment, enabled him to calculate correctly, that the road to that glory which never dies is to use power for the support of the laws and liberties of our country, not for their destruction; and his will accordingly survives the wreck of everything now living.

Accept, my lord, the tribute of esteem, from one who renders it with warmth to the disinterested friend of mankind, and assurances of my high consideration and respect.

PIERRE JEAN GEORGES CABANIS, 1803, 10:404 ~ WE DO NOT DESPAIR OF BEING ALWAYS A PEACEABLE NATION.

To Monsieur Cabanis[1]
Washington, July 12, 1803

Dear Sir, I lately received your friendly letter of 28 Vendem. an 11, with the two volumes on the relations between the physical and moral faculties of man. This has ever been a subject of great interest to the inquisitive mind, and it could not have got into better hands for discussion than yours. That thought may be a faculty of our material organization, has been believed in the gross; and though the "modus operandi" of nature, in this, as in most other cases, can never be developed and demonstrated to beings limited as we are, yet I feel confident you will have conducted us as far on the road as

---

1 By 1803, Jefferson was no longer hesitant in confessing his belief that France no longer had any remains of friendship for the United States, and the belief was not necessarily unfounded. Napoleon resented republican democracy, and the fact that Jefferson had been an enthusiastic friend of French liberals and was still currently adored by the philosophers who composed the faculty of the *Institut National*, the leading academy of learning under Napoleon, only exacerbated Napoleon's resentment. Jefferson was, in fact, was more than friendly with any number of French ideologues, in particular Pierre Jean Georges Cabanis, the moral philosopher and anatomist whose *Rapports du physique et du moral de l'homme* Jefferson once described as "the most profound of all human compositions (Koch 1950, 234).

we can go, and have lodged us within reconnoitering distance of the citadel itself. While here, I have time to read nothing. But our annual recess for the months of August and September is now approaching, during which time I shall be at the Montrials, where I anticipate great satisfaction in the presence of these volumes. It is with great satisfaction, too, I recollect the agreeable hours I have passed with yourself and M. de La Roche, at the house of our late excellent friend, Madame Helvetius, and elsewhere; and I am happy to learn you continue your residence there. Antevil always appeared to me a delicious village, and Madame Helvetius's the most delicious spot in it. In those days how sanguine we were! And how soon were the virtuous hopes and confidence of every good man blasted! And how many excellent friends have we lost in your efforts towards self-government, *et cui bono*? But let us draw a veil over the dead, and hope the best for the living. If the hero who has saved you from a combination of enemies, shall also be the means of giving you as great a portion of liberty as the opinions, habits and character of the nation are prepared for, progressive preparation may fit you for progressive portions of that first of blessings, and you may in time attain what we erred in supposing could be hastily seized and maintained, in the present state of political information among your citizens at large. In this way all may end well.

You are again at war, I find. But we, I hope, shall be permitted to run the race of peace. Your government has wisely removed what certainly endangered collision between us. I now see nothing which may be devised of keeping nations in the path of justice towards us, by making justice their interest, and injuries to react on themselves. Our distance enables us to pursue a course which the crowded situation of Europe renders perhaps impracticable there.

Be so good as to accept for yourself Roche, my friendly salutations, and great consideration and respect.

THIRD ANNUAL MESSAGE, 1803, 3:358 - *IT IS OUR INTEREST AND DESIRE, TO CULTIVATE THE FRIENDSHIP OF THE BELLIGERENT NATIONS BY EVERY ACT OF JUSTICE.*

Third Annual Message[1]
October 17, 1803

To the Senate and House of Representatives of the United States, In calling you together, fellow citizens, at an earlier day than was contemplated by the act of the last session of Congress, I have not been insensible to the personal inconveniences necessarily resulting from an unexpected change in

---

1 Neutrality presented the Jefferson administration and courts with an unwieldy series of intricate, diverse, and delicate problems. While the administration inherited the Neutrality Act of 1794, which provided the legal basis for enforcing a neutrality policy, particularly in respect to Europe, the policy appeared to have significantly less utility in dealing with the intrigues against Spain either in South America or the Southwestern portion of the United States. So, with war resuming between Britain and France in 1803, Jefferson's third message to Congress sought to outline the policy which the government intended to pursue (Henderson 1985, 56).

your arrangements. But matters of great public concernment have rendered this call necessary, and the interest you feel in these will supersede in your minds all private considerations.

Congress witnessed, at their last session, the extraordinary agitation produced in the public mind by the suspension of our right of deposit at the port of New Orleans, no assignment of another place having been made according to treaty. They were sensible that the continuance of that privation would be more injurious to our nation than any consequences which could flow from any mode of redress, but reposing just confidence in the good faith of the government whose officer had committed the wrong, friendly and reasonable representations were resorted to, and the right of deposit was restored.

Previous, however, to this period, we had not been unaware of the danger to which our peace would be perpetually exposed while so important a key to the commerce of the western country remained under foreign power. Difficulties, too, were presenting themselves as to the navigation of other streams, which, arising within our territories, pass through those adjacent. Propositions had, therefore, been authorized for obtaining, on fair conditions, the sovereignty of New Orleans, and of other possessions in that quarter interesting to our quiet, to such extent as was deemed practicable; and the provisional appropriation of two millions of dollars, to be applied and accounted for by the president of the United States, intended as part of the price, was considered as conveying the sanction of Congress to the acquisition proposed. The enlightened Government of France saw, with just discernment, the importance to both nations of such liberal arrangements as might best and permanently promote the peace, friendship, and interests of both; and the property and sovereignty of all Louisiana, which had been restored to them, have on certain conditions been transferred to the United States by instruments bearing date the 30th of April last. When these shall have received the constitutional sanction of the senate, they will without delay be communicated to the representatives also, for the exercise of their functions, as to those conditions which are within the powers vested by the constitution in Congress. While the property and sovereignty of the Mississippi and its waters secure an independent outlet for the produce of the western States, and an uncontrolled navigation through their whole course, free from collision with other powers and the dangers to our peace from that source, the fertility of the country, its climate and extent, promise in due season important aids to our treasury, an ample provision for our posterity, and a widespread field for the blessings of freedom and equal laws.

With the wisdom of Congress it will rest to take those ulterior measures which may be necessary for the immediate occupation and temporary government of the country; for its incorporation into our Union; for rendering the change of government a blessing to our newly-adopted brethren; for securing to them the rights of conscience and of property; for confirming to the Indian inhabitants their occupancy and self -government, establishing friendly and commercial relations with them, and for ascertaining the geography of the country acquired. Such materials for your information, relative to its affairs in general, as the short space of time has permitted me to collect, will be laid before you when the subject shall be in a state for your consideration.

Another important acquisition of territory has also been made since the last session of Congress. The friendly tribe of Kaskaskia Indians with which we have never had a difference, reduced by the wars and wants of savage life to a few individuals unable to defend themselves against the neighboring tribes, has transferred its country to the United States, reserving only for its members what is sufficient to maintain them in an agricultural way. The considerations stipulated are, that we shall extend to them our patronage and protection, and give them certain annual aids in money, in implements of agriculture, and other articles of their choice. This country, among the most fertile within our limits, extending along the Mississippi from the mouth of the Illinois to and up the Ohio, though not so necessary as a barrier since the acquisition of the other bank, may yet be well worthy of being laid open to immediate settlement, as its inhabitants may descend with rapidity in support of the lower country should future circumstances expose that to foreign enterprise. As the stipulations in this treaty also involve matters within the competence of both houses only, it will be laid before Congress as soon as the senate shall have advised its ratification.

With many other Indian tribes, improvements in agriculture and household manufacture are advancing, and with all our peace and friendship are established on grounds much firmer than heretofore. The measure adopted of establishing trading houses among them, and of furnishing them necessaries in exchange for their commodities, at such moderated prices as leave no gain, but cover us from loss, has the most conciliatory and useful effect upon them, and is that which will best secure their peace and good will.

The small vessels authorized by Congress with a view to the Mediterranean service, have been sent into that sea, and will be able more effectually to confine the Tripoline cruisers within their harbors, and supersede the necessity of convoy to our commerce in that quarter. They will sensibly lessen the expenses of that service the ensuing year.

A further knowledge of the ground in the northeastern and north-western angles of the United States has evinced that the boundaries established by the treaty of Paris, between the British territories and ours in those parts, were too imperfectly described to be susceptible of execution. It has therefore been thought worthy of attention, for preserving and cherishing the harmony and useful intercourse subsisting between the two nations, to remove by timely arrangements what unfavorable incidents might otherwise render a ground of future misunderstanding. A convention has therefore been entered into, which provides for a practicable demarcation of those limits to the satisfaction of both parties.

An account of the receipts and expenditures of the year ending 30th September last, with the estimates for the service of the ensuing year, will be laid before you by the secretary of the treasury so soon as the receipts of the last quarter shall be returned from the more distant States. It is already ascertained that the amount paid into the treasury for that year has been between eleven and twelve millions of dollars, and that the revenue accrued during the same term exceeds the sum counted on as sufficient for our current expenses, and to extinguish the public debt within the period heretofore proposed.

The amount of debt paid for the same year is about three millions one hundred thousand dollars, exclusive of interest, and making, with the payment of the preceding year, a discharge of more than eight millions and a half of dollars of the principal of that debt, besides the accruing interest; and there remain in the treasury nearly six millions of dollars. Of these, eight hundred and eighty thousand have been reserved for payment of the first installment due under the British convention of January 8th, 1802, and two millions are what have been before mentioned as placed by Congress under the power and accountability of the president, toward the price of New Orleans and other territories acquired, which, remaining untouched, are still applicable to that object, and go in diminution of the sum to be funded for it.

Should the acquisition of Louisiana be constitutionally confirmed and carried into effect, a sum of nearly thirteen millions of dollars will then be added to our public debt, most of which is payable after fifteen years; before which term the present existing debts will all be discharged by the established operation of the sinking fund. When we contemplate the ordinary annual augmentation of imposts from increasing population and wealth, the augmentation of the same revenue by its extension to the new acquisition, and the economies which may still be introduced into our public expenditures, I cannot but hope that Congress in reviewing their resources will find means to meet the intermediate interests of this additional debt without recurring to new taxes, and applying to this object only the ordinary progression of our revenue. Its extraordinary increase in times of foreign war will be the proper and sufficient fund for any measures of safety or precaution which that state of things may render necessary in our neutral position.

Remittances for the installments of our foreign debt having been found practicable without loss, it has not been thought expedient to use the power given by a former act of Congress of continuing them by reloans, and of redeeming instead thereof equal sums of domestic debt, although no difficulty was found in obtaining that accommodation.

The sum of fifty thousand dollars appropriated by Congress for providing gun-boats, remains unexpended. The favorable and peaceful turn of affairs on the Mississippi rendered an immediate execution of that law unnecessary, and time was desirable in order that the institution of that branch of our force might begin on models the most approved by experience. The same issue of events dispensed with a resort to the appropriation of a million and a half of dollars contemplated for purposes which were effected by happier means.

We have seen with sincere concern the flames of war lighted up again in Europe, and nations with which we have the most friendly and useful relations engaged in mutual destruction. While we regret the miseries in which we see others involved, let us bow with gratitude to that kind Providence which, inspiring with wisdom and moderation our late legislative councils while placed under the urgency of the greatest wrongs, guarded us from hastily entering into the sanguinary contest, and left us only to look on and to pity its ravages. These will be heaviest on those immediately engaged. Yet the nations pursuing peace will not be exempt from all evil. In the course of this conflict, let it be our endeavor, as it is our interest and desire, to cultivate the friendship of the belligerent nations by every act of justice and of incessant kindness; to receive their armed vessels with hospitality from the distresses of the sea, but to administer the means of annoyance to none; to establish in our harbors such a police as may maintain law and order; to restrain our citizens from embarking individually in a war in which their country takes no part; to punish severely those persons, citizen or alien, who shall usurp the cover of our flag for vessels not entitled to it, infecting thereby with suspicion those of real Americans, and committing us into controversies for the redress of wrongs not our own; to exact from every nation the observance, toward our vessels and citizens, of those principles and practices which all civilized people acknowledge; to merit the character of a just nation, and maintain that of an independent one, preferring every consequence to insult and habitual wrong. Congress will consider whether the existing laws enable us efficaciously to maintain this course with our citizens in all places, and with others while within the limits of our jurisdiction, and will give them the new modifications necessary for these objects. Some contraventions of right have already taken place, both within our jurisdictional limits and on the high seas. The friendly disposition of the governments from whose agents they have proceeded, as well as their wisdom and. regard for justice, leave us in reasonable expectation that they will be rectified and prevented in future; and that no act will be countenanced by them which threatens to disturb our friendly intercourse. Separated by a wide ocean from the nations of Europe, and from the political interests which entangle them together, with productions and wants which render our commerce and friendship useful to them and theirs to us, it cannot be the interest of any to assail us, nor ours to disturb them. We should be most unwise, indeed, were we to cast away the singular blessings of the position in which nature has placed us, the opportunity she has endowed us with of pursuing, at a distance from foreign contentions, the paths of industry, peace, and happiness; of cultivating general friendship, and of bringing collisions of interest to the umpirage of reason rather than of force. How desirable then must it be, in a government like ours, to see its citizens adopt individually the views, the interests, and the conduct which their country should pursue, divesting themselves of those passions and partialities which tend to lessen useful friendships, and to embarrass and embroil us in the calamitous scenes of Europe. Confident, fellow citizens, that you will duly estimate the importance of neutral dispositions toward the observance of neutral conduct, that you will be sensible how much it is our duty to look on the bloody arena spread before us with commiseration indeed, but with no other wish than to see it closed, I am persuaded you will cordially cherish these dispositions in all discussions among yourselves, and in all communications with your constituents; and I anticipate with satisfaction the measures of wisdom which the great interests now committed to you will give you an opportunity bf providing, and myself that of approving and carrying into execution with the fidelity I owe to my country.

FOURTH ANNUAL MESSAGE, 1804, 3:366 ~ *THAT INDIVIDUALS SHOULD UNDERTAKE TO WAGE PRIVATE WAR, INDEPENDENTLY OF THE AUTHORITY OF THEIR COUNTRY, CANNOT BE PERMITTED IN A WELL-ORDERED SOCIETY.*

Fourth Annual Message[1]
November 8, 1804

To the Senate and House of Representatives of the United States, To a people, fellow citizens, who sincerely desire the happiness and prosperity of other nations; to those who justly calculate that their own well-being is advanced by that of the nations with which they have intercourse, it will be a satisfaction to observe that the war which was lighted up in Europe a little before our last meeting has not yet extended its *flames to* other nations, nor been marked by the calamities which sometimes stain the footsteps of war. The irregularities too on the ocean, which generally harass the commerce of neutral nations, have, in distant parts, disturbed ours less than on former occasions. But in the American seas they have been greater from peculiar causes; and even within our harbors and jurisdiction, infringements on the

---

1 Congress passed the Neutrality Act of 1794 to curb private activities in foreign military adventures and prohibited the exportation of any articles of war. Prohibited articles found on board a vessel would be forfeited, and if articles of war were exported to a foreign country, the vessel could be seized and the captain fined. Congress also prohibited American citizens from accepting a commission to serve "a foreign prince or state in war by land or sea." Nor could persons within the United States provide ships of war to be used by a foreign prince or state "to cruise or commit hostilities upon the subjects, citizens or property of another foreign prince or state with whom the United States are at peace." Furthermore, persons within the territory or jurisdiction of the United States were prohibited from providing assistance to "any military expedition or enterprise to be carried on from thence against the territory or dominions of any foreign prince or state with whom the United States are at peace." Jefferson recognized the danger of allowing private citizens to decide by themselves to deploy armed forces. So, in his Fourth Annual Message, he referred to complaints that persons residing within the United States had armed merchant vessels and forced a commerce in defiance of the laws of other countries: "That individuals should undertake to wage private war, independently of the authority of their country, can not be permitted in a well-ordered society." The tendency, he noted, was "to produce aggression on the laws and rights of other nations and to endanger the peace of our own." (Stern 1994, 16)

authority of the laws have been committed which have called for serious attention. The friendly conduct of the governments from whose officers and subjects these acts have proceeded, in other respects and in places more under their observation and control, gives us confidence that our representations on this subject will have been properly regarded.

While noticing the irregularities committed on the ocean by others, those on our own part should not be omitted nor left unprovided for. Complaints have been received that persons residing within the United States have taken on themselves to arm merchant vessels, and to force a commerce into certain ports and countries in defiance of the laws of those countries. That individuals should undertake to wage private war, independently of the authority of their country, cannot be permitted in a well ordered society. Its tendency to produce aggression on the laws and rights of other nations, and to endanger the peace of our own is so obvious, that I doubt not you will adopt measures for restraining it effectually in future.

Soon after the passage of the act of the last session, authorizing the establishment of a district and port of entry on the waters of the Mobile; we learnt that its object was misunderstood on the part of Spain. Candid explanations were immediately given, and assurances that, reserving our claims in that quarter as a subject of discussion and arrangement with Spain, no act was meditated, in the meantime, inconsistent with the peace and friendship existing between the two nations, and that conformably to these intentions would be the execution of the law. That government had, however, thought proper to suspend the ratification of the convention of 1802. But the explanations which would reach them soon after, and still more, the confirmation of them by the tenor of the instrument establishing the port and district, may reasonably be expected to replace them in the dispositions and views of the whole subject which originally dictated the conviction.

I have the satisfaction to inform you that the objections which had been urged by that government against the validity of our title to the country of Louisiana have been withdrawn, its exact limits, however, remaining still to be settled between us. And to this is to be added that, having prepared and delivered the stock created in execution of the convention of Paris, of April 30, 1803, in consideration of the cession of that country, we have received from the government of France an acknowledgment, in due form, of the fulfillment of that stipulation.

With the nations of Europe, in general, our friendship and intercourse are undisturbed, and from the governments of the belligerent powers especially we continue to receive those friendly manifestations which are justly due to an honest neutrality, and to such good offices consistent with that as we have opportunities of rendering.

The activity and success of the small force employed in the Mediterranean in the early part of the present year, the reinforcement sent into that sea, and the energy of the officers having command in the several vessels, will, I trust, by the sufferings of war, reduce the barbarians of Tripoli to the desire of peace on proper terms. Great injury, however, ensues to ourselves as well as to others interested, from the distance to which prizes must be brought for adjudication, and from the impracticability of bringing hither such as are not seaworthy.

The *Bey* of Tunis having made requisitions unauthorized by our treaty, their rejection has produced from him some expressions of discontent. But to those who expect us to calculate whether a compliance with unjust demands will not cost us less than a war, we must leave as a question of calculation far them, also, whether to retire from unjust demands will not cost them less than a war. We can do to each other very sensible injuries by war, but the mutual advantages of peace make that the best interest of both.

Peace and intercourse with the other powers on the same coast continue on the footing on which they are established by treaty.

In pursuance of the act providing for the temporary government of Louisiana, the necessary officers for the territory of Orleans were appointed in due time, to commence the exercise of their functions on the first day of October. The distance, however, of some of them, and indispensable previous arrangements, may have retarded its commencement in some of its parts; the form of government thus provided having been considered but as temporary, and open to such improvements as further information of the circumstances of our brethren there might suggest, it will of course be subject to your consideration.

In the district of Louisiana, it has been thought best to adopt the division into subordinate districts, which had been established under its former government. These being five in number, a commanding officer has been appointed to each, according to the provision of the law, and so soon as they can be at their station, that district will also be in its due state of organization; in the meantime their places are supplied by the officers before commanding there. The functions of the Governor and Judges of Indiana have commenced; the government, we presume, is proceeding in its new form. The lead mines in that district offer so rich a supply of that metal, as to merit attention. The report now communicated will inform you of their state, and of the necessity of immediate inquiry into their occupation and titles.

With the Indian tribes established within our newly-acquired limits, I have deemed it necessary to open conferences for the purpose of establishing a good understanding and neighborly relations between us. So far as we have yet learned, we have reason to believe that their dispositions are generally favorable and friendly; and with these dispositions on their part, we have in our own hands means which cannot fail us for preserving their peace and friendship. By pursuing a uniform course of justice toward them, by aiding them in all the improvements which may better their condition, and especially by establishing a commerce on terms which shall be advantageous to them and only not losing to us, and so regulated as that no incendiaries of our own or any other nation may be permitted to disturb the natural effects of our just and friendly offices, we may render ourselves so necessary to their comfort and prosperity, that the protection of our citizens from their disorderly members will become their interest and their voluntary care. Instead, therefore, of an augmentation of military force proportioned to our extension of frontier, I proposed a moderate enlargement of the capital employed in that commerce, as a more effectual, economical, and humane instrument for preserving peace and good neighborhood with them.

On this side the Mississippi an important relinquishment of native title has been received from the Delawares. That tribe, desiring to extinguish in their people the spirit of hunting, and to convert superfluous lands into the means of improving what they retain, have ceded to us all the country between the Wabash and the Ohio, south of, and including J the road from the rapids towards Vincennes, for which they are to receive annuities in animals and implements for agriculture, and in other necessaries. This acquisition is important, not only for its extent and fertility, but as fronting three hundred miles on the Ohio, and near half that on the Wabash. The produce of the settled countries descending those rivers, will no longer pass in review of the Indian frontier but in a small portion, and with the cession heretofore made with the Kaskaskias, nearly consolidates our possessions north of the Ohio, in a very respectable breadth, from Lake Erie to the Mississippi. The Piankeshaws having some claim to the country ceded by the Delawares, it has been thought best to quiet that by fair purchase also. So soon as the treaties on this subject shall have received their constitutional sanctions, they shall be laid before both houses.

The act of Congress of February 28th, 1803, for building and employing a number of gun-boats, is now in a course of execution to the extent there provided for. The obstacle to naval enterprise which vessels of this construction offer for our seaport towns; their utility toward supporting within our waters the authority of the laws; the promptness with which they will be manned by the seamen and militia of the place the moment they are wanting; the facility of their assembling from different parts of the coast to any point where they are required in greater force than ordinary; the economy of their maintenance and preservation from decay when not in actual service; and the competence of our finances to this defensive provision, without any new burden, are considerations which will have due weight with Congress in deciding on the expediency of adding to their number from year to year, as experience shall test their utility, until all our important harbors, by these and auxiliary means, shall be insured against insult and opposition to the laws.

No circumstance has arisen since your last session which calls for any augmentation of our regular military force. Should any improvement occur in the militia system, that will be always seasonable. Accounts of the receipts and expenditures of the last year, with estimates for the ensuing one, will as usual be laid before you.

The state of our finances continues to fulfill our expectations. Eleven millions and a half of dollars received in the course of the year ending on the 30th of September last, have enabled us, after meeting all the ordinary expenses of the year, to pay upward of $3,600,000 of the public debt, exclusive of interest. This payment, with those of the two preceding years, has extinguished upward of twelve millions of the principal, and a greater sum of interest, within that period; and by a proportional diminution of interest, renders already sensible the effect of the growing sum yearly applicable to the discharge of the principal.

It is also ascertained that the revenue accrued during the last year, exceeds that of the preceding; and the probable receipts of the ensuing year may safely be relied on as sufficient, with the sum already in the treasury, to meet all the current demands of the year, to discharge upward of three millions and a half of the engagements incurred under the British and French conventions, and to advance in the farther redemption of the funded debts as rapidly as had been contemplated. These, fellow citizens, are the principal matters which I have thought it necessary at this time to communicate for your consideration and attention. Some others will be laid before you in the course of the session, but in the discharge of the great duties confided to you by our country, you will take a broader view of the field of legislation. Whether the great interests of agriculture, manufactures, commerce, or navigation, can, within the pale of your constitutional powers, be aided in any of their relations; whether laws are provided in all cases where they are wanting; whether those provided are exactly what they should be; whether any abuses take place in their administration, or in that of the public revenues; whether the organization of the public agents or of the public force is perfect in all its parts; in fine, whether anything can be done to advance the general good, are questions within the limits of your functions which will necessarily occupy your attention. In these and other matters which you in your wisdom may propose for the good of our country, you may count with assurance on my hearty co-operation and faithful execution.

CHOCTAW NATION, 1805, 19:144 ~ *WE WILL NEVER INJURE YOU NOR PERMIT YOU TO BE INJURED BY ANY WHITE PEOPLE.*

To the Brothers of the Choctaw Nation[1]
Washington, March 13, 1805

---

1 Choctaw indebtedness to Europeans and Americans had become sizable by the late 1700s; but as long as the Choctaws remained a significant force in the balance of power between Spain and the United States, their growing economic weakness could be offset by political strength, because neither the United States nor Spain pressed debt claims or cut off trade as long as they valued the Choctaws as potential allies. Although the Choctaws suffered from poor terms of trade, the consequences were postponed; and the whites took no drastic actions that might alienate the nation. When the growing weakness of the Spanish after 1797 crippled the effectiveness of their play-off policy, the Choctaws lay exposed to the full consequences of their depleted forests and economic dependence. The American tactic, advocated by Jefferson, of encouraging the Indians' indebtedness to expedite land cessions, thrived among the Choctaws, and the Americans used the Choctaw debts to arrange for the cession of a huge swath of land along the southern border in 1805. The money paid for the lands did not go to the Choctaws but rather to the traders to pay the Choctaw debts (White 1983, 95-96).

My Children, I learn with great satisfaction that you have leased to us three stations of one mile square each on the road from Chickesaws to Natchez, and one on the Pearl river; and you desire me to send you a paper under my own hand to show to your warriors that these lands are not sold but lent. I now accordingly declare that the property in those lands remains in your nation, that they are lent to us for a rent of four hundred pounds weight of powder annually, and that your nation has a right to take them back at their pleasure; and this paper now signed by my own hand will be evidence of these things to future generations. We will, according to your desire, settle but one white family on each section, and take care that they conduct themselves peaceably and friendly toward you; or being made known to me that they do otherwise they shall be removed. They will be placed there merely for the accommodation of our paper carriers and travelers.

My children, you have asked whether I did not promise to send you ploughs to enable you to improve in husbandry? I did promise it and immediately sent the ploughs; but by a mistake in forwarding them, they were delayed some time before we knew of it. You must, however, have received them before this time.

You ask if I did not promise to send your deputation ten rifles for yourselves and other deserving warriors? I did not promise it. You said they would be acceptable, but I said nothing in reply. But although I did not promise, yet to show my good will to you, I will send you the rifles.

You ask if we will allow commissions to you according to your rank and medals and commissions to such chiefs as you may appoint to assist in the government of your country? It has not been a custom with us to give commissions to our friends among the red men; and it is a new thing. We will take it into consideration. We wish to do what is agreeable to you, if we find we can do it with prudence.

We shall be willing to give medals to a certain number of distinguished chiefs who aid you in the government of your country, and who manifest dispositions to preserve peace and friendship between your nation and ours. We wish you, therefore, to recommend such to us.

My children, persevere in your friendship to the United States. We will never injure you nor permit you to be injured by any white people, and we trust you will take care that none of our people are injured by yours. Encourage among you the cultivation of the earth, raising of cattle, spinning and weaving, and we will assist you in it. With plenty of food and clothing you will raise many children, multiply, be strong and happy. May the Great Spirit protect and prosper you in all your just pursuits. Farewell.

FIFTH ANNUAL MESSAGE, 1805, 3:387 ~ [CONGRESS SHOULD]
CONSIDER WHETHER IT WOULD NOT BE EXPEDIENT, FOR A STATE OF
PEACE AS WELL AS OF WAR, SO TO ORGANIZE OR CLASS THE MILITIA.

Fifth Annual Message[1]
December 3, 1805

To the Senate and House of Representatives of the United States, At a moment when the nations of Europe are in commotion and arming against each other, and when those with whom we have principal intercourse are engaged in the general contest,, and when the countenance of some of them toward our peaceable country threatens that even that may not be unaffected by what is passing on the general theatre, a meeting of the representatives of the nation in both houses of Congress has become more than usually desirable. Coming from every section of our country, they bring with them the sentiments and the information of the whole, and will be enabled to give a direction to the public affairs which the will and wisdom of the whole will approve and support.

In taking a view of the state of our country, we in the first place notice the late affliction of two of our cities under the fatal fever which in latter times has occasionally visited our shores. Providence in his goodness gave it an early termination on this occasion, and lessened the number of victims which have usually fallen before it. In the course of the several visitations by this disease it has appeared that it is strictly local; incident to the cities and on the tide waters only; incommunicable in the country, either by persons under the disease or by goods carried from diseased places; that its access is with the Inaugural Addresses and Messages 385 autumn, and that it disappears with the early frosts. These restrictions within narrow limits of time and space give security even to our maritime cities during three-fourths of the year, and to the country always. Although from these facts it appears unnecessary, yet to satisfy the fears of foreign nations, and cautions on their part not to be complained of in a danger whose limits are yet unknown to them, I have strictly enjoined on the officers at the head of the customs to certify with exact truth for every vessel sailing for a foreign port, the state of

---

1 Jefferson realized that, in the Louisiana Purchase, France had sold to the United States a portion of Spanish America and then had compelled Spain to acquiesce in this disposal of Spanish property. It seemed to him that this memorandum was an invitation to do the same thing over again as to Florida. He therefore talked of preparations for war, and made preparations for peace. In this, his fifth annual message to Congress, he noted that propositions for adjusting amicably the boundaries of Louisiana had not been acceded to. On the contrary, inroads had been made "into the Territories of Orleans and the Mississippi." The president, it seems, had found it necessary to order troops to the frontier to repel by force of arms any similar aggressions in the future. Some of the injuries which he noted clearly could be met only by force. He therefore recommended such preparations as circumstances called for to protect the seaports, to extend the gunboat service, to organize or class the militia, and to provide a military force which could be called upon in any sudden emergency. He declared that the last census showed the United States to contain upward of three hundred thousand men between the ages of eighteen and twenty-six years, and stated that considerable provision had been made towards the collection of materials for the construction of ships of war of seventy-four guns (Channing 1906, 151-152).

health respecting this fever which prevails at the place from which she sails. Under every motive from character and duty to certify the truth, I have no doubt they have faithfully executed this injunction. Much real injury has, however, been sustained from a propensity to identify with this epidemic, and to call by the same name, fevers of very different kinds, which have been known at all times and in all countries, and never have been placed among those deemed contagious. As we advance in our knowledge of this disease, as facts develop the sources from which individuals receive it, the state authorities charged with the care of the public health, and Congress with that of the general commerce, will become able to regulate with effect their respective functions in these departments. The burden of quarantines is felt at home as well as abroad; their efficacy merits examination. Although the health laws of the States should be found to need no present revisal by Congress, yet commerce claims that their attention be ever awake to them.

Since our last meeting the aspect of our foreign relations has considerably changed. Our coasts have been infested and our harbors watched by private armed vessels, some of them without commissions, some with illegal commissions, others with those of legal form but committing piratical acts beyond the authority of their commissions. They have captured in the very entrance of our harbors, as well as on the high seas, not only the vessels of our friends coming to trade with us, but our own also. They have carried them off under pretence of legal adjudication, but not daring to approach a court of justice, they have plundered and sunk them by the way, or in obscure places where no evidence could arise against them; maltreated the crews, and abandoned them in boats in the open sea or on desert shores without food or covering. These enormities appearing to be unreached by any control of their sovereigns, I found it necessary to equip a force to cruise within our own seas, to arrest all vessels of these descriptions found hovering on our coast within the limits of the Gulf Stream, and to bring the offenders in for trial as pirates.

The same system of hovering on our coasts and harbors under color of seeking enemies, has been also carried on by public armed ships, to the great annoyance and oppression of our commerce. New principles, too, have been interloped into the law of nations, founded neither in justice nor the usage or acknowledgment of nations. According to these, a belligerent takes to himself a commerce with its own enemy which it denies to a neutral, on the ground of its aiding that enemy in the war. But reason revolts at such an inconsistency, and the neutral having equal right with the belligerent to decide the question, the interest of our constituents and the duty of maintaining the authority of reason, the only umpire between just nations, impose on us the obligation of providing an effectual and determined opposition to a doctrine so injurious to the rights of peaceable nations. Indeed, the confidence we ought to have in the justice of others, still countenances the hope that a sounder view of those rights will of itself induce from every belligerent a more correct observance of them.

With Spain our negotiations for a settlement of differences have not had a satisfactory issue. Spoliations during the former war, for which she had formally acknowledged herself responsible, have been refused to be compensated, but on conditions affecting other claims in nowise connected with them. Yet the same practices are renewed in the present war, and are already of great amount. On the Mobile, our commerce passing through that river continues to be obstructed by arbitrary duties and vexatious searches. Propositions for adjusting amicably the boundaries of Louisiana have not been acceded to. While, however, the right is unsettled, we have avoided changing the state of things by taking new posts or strengthening ourselves in the disputed territories, n the hope that the other power would not, by contrary conduct, oblige us to meet their example, and endanger conflicts of authority the issue of which may not be easily controlled. But in this hope we have now reason to lessen our confidence. Inroads have been recently made into the territories of Orleans and the Mississippi, our citizens have been seized, and their property plundered in the very parts of the former which had been actually delivered up by Spain, and this by the regular officers and soldiers of that government. I have therefore found it necessary at length to give orders to our troops on that frontier to be in readiness to protect our citizens, and to repel by arms any similar aggression in future. Other details, necessary for your full information of the state of things between this country and that shall be the subject of another communication.

In reviewing these injuries from some of the belligerent powers, the moderation, the firmness, and the wisdom of the legislature will be all called into action. We ought still to hope that. time and a more correct estimate of interest, as well as of character, will produce the justice we are bound to expect. But should any nation deceive itself by false calculations, and disappoint that expectation, we must join in the unprofitable contest of trying which party can do the other the most harm. Some of Inaugural Addresses and Messages 3% these injuries may perhaps admit a peaceable remedy. Where that is competent it is always the most desirable. But some of them are of a nature to be met by force only, and all of them may lead to it. I cannot, therefore, but recommend such preparations as circumstances call for. The first object is to place our seaport towns out of the danger of insult. Measures have been already taken for furnishing them with heavy cannon for the service of such land batteries as may make a part of their defense against armed vessels approaching them. In aid of these it is desirable that we should have a competent number of gun-boats; and the number, to be competent, must be considerable. If immediately begun, they may be in readiness for service at the opening of the next season. Whether it will be necessary to augment our land forces will be decided by occurrences probably in the course of your session. In the meantime, you will consider whether it would not be expedient, for a state of peace as well as of war, so to organize or class the militia as would enable us, on a sudden emergency, to call for the services of the younger portions, unencumbered with the old and those having families.

Upward of three hundred thousand able-bodied men, between the ages of eighteen and twenty-six years, which the last census shows we may now count within our limits, will furnish a competent number for offence or defense in any point where they may be wanted, and will give time for raising regular forces after the necessity of them shall become certain; and the reducing to the early period of life all its active service cannot but be desirable to our younger citizens, of the present as well as future times, inasmuch as it engages to them in more advanced age a quiet and undisturbed repose in the bosom of their families. I cannot, then, but earnestly recommend to your early consideration the expediency of so modifying our militia system as, by a separation of the more active part from that which is less so, we may draw from it, when necessary, an efficient corps fit for real and active service, and to be called to it in regular rotation.

Considerable provision has been made, under former authorities from Congress, of materials for the construction of ships of war of seventy-four guns. These materials are on hand, subject to the further will of the legislature.

An immediate prohibition of the exportation of arms and ammunition is also submitted to your determination.

Turning from these unpleasant views of violence and wrong, I congratulate you on the liberation of our fellow citizens who were stranded on the coast of Tripoli and made prisoners of war. In a government bottomed on the will of all, the life and liberty of every individual citizen become interesting to all. In the treaty, therefore, which has concluded our warfare with that State, an article for the ransom of our citizens has been agreed to. An operation by land, by a small band of our countrymen, and others engaged for the occasion, in conjunction with the troops of the ex-*bashaw* of that country, gallantly conducted by our late consul Eaton, and their successful enterprise on the city of Derne, contributed, doubtless, to the impression which produced peace; and the conclusion of this prevented opportunities of which the officers and men of our squadron destined for Tripoli would have availed themselves, to emulate the acts of valor exhibited by their brethren in the attack of the last year.[1] Reflecting with high satisfaction on the distinguished bravery displayed whenever occasion permitted in the Mediterranean service, I think it ,would be a useful encouragement,, as well as a just reward, to make an opening for some present promotion by enlarging our peace establishment of captains and lieutenants.

---

1 William Eaton, an American army officer, was sent to Tunis as consul in 1798 and learned much about the Barbary States. When he returned to the United States in 1804, he had a scheme to win the war against Tripoli by supporting the claimant to the rule of Tripoli, Hamet Karamanli. Somewhat reluctantly, Congress appointed him "navy agent to the Barbary States" and allowed him to try his plan. In Egypt, Eaton persuaded the claimant to undertake the venture and gathered a mixed army of 400 men, including Greeks, Italians, Arabs, and others. With this small band he set off on the long march overland to take Tripoli from the rear, took the seaport of Derna, and might have taken Tripoli itself if the Tripolitan War had not ended with a truce before he arrived (Columbia 2007, 15013).

With Tunis some misunderstandings have arisen, not yet sufficiently explained, but friendly discussions with their Ambassador recently arrived, and a mutual disposition to do whatever is just and reasonable, cannot fail of dissipating these; so that we may consider our peace on that coast, generally, to be on as sound a footing as it has been at any preceding time. Still it will not be expedient to withdraw, immediately, the whole of our force from that sea.

The law for providing a naval peace establishment fixes the number of frigates which shall be kept in constant service in time of peace, and prescribes that they shall not. be manned by more than two-thirds of their complement of seamen and ordinary seamen. Whether a frigate may be trusted to two-thirds only of her proper complement of men must depend on the nature of the service on which she is ordered; that may sometimes, for her safety, as well as to insure her object, require her fullest complement. In adverting to this subject, Congress will perhaps consider whether the best limitation on the executive discretion in this case would not be by the number of seamen which may be employed in the whole service, rather than by the number of vessels. Occasions oftener arise for the employment of small than of large. vessels, and it would lessen risk as well as expense to be authorized to employ them of preference. The limitation suggested by the number of seamen would admit a selection of vessels best adapted to the service.

Our Indian neighbors are advancing, many of them with spirit and others beginning to engage, in the pursuits of agriculture and household manufacture. They are becoming sensible that the earth yields subsistence with less labor and more certainty than the forest, and find it their interest, from time to time, to dispose of parts of their surplus and waste lands for the means of improving those they occupy, and of subsisting their families while they are preparing their farms. Since your last session, the northern tribes have sold to us the lands between the Connecticut reserve and the former Indian boundary; and those on the Ohio, from the same boundary to the rapids, and for a considerable depth inland. The Chickasaws and Cherokees have sold us the country between and adjacent to the two districts of Tennessee, and the Creeks, the residue of their lands in the fork of Ocmulgee, up to the Ulcofauhatche. The three former purchases are important, inasmuch as they consolidate disjointed parts of our settled country, and render their intercourse secure; and the second particularly so, as with the small point on the river which we expect is by this time ceded by the Piankeshaws, it completes our possession of the whole of both banks of the Ohio, from its source to near its mouth, and the navigation of that river is thereby rendered forever safe to our citizens settled and settling on its extensive waters. The purchase from the Creeks too has been for some time particularly, interesting to the State of Georgia.

The several treaties which have been mentioned will be submitted to both houses of Congress for the exercise of their respective functions.

Deputations now on their way to the seat of government, from various nations of Indians inhabiting the Missouri and other parts beyond the Mississippi, come charged with the assurances of their satisfaction with the new relations in which they are placed with us, of their disposition to cultivate our peace and friendship, and their desire to enter into commercial intercourse with us. A statement of our progress in exploring the principal rivers of that country, and of the information respecting them hitherto obtained, will be communicated so soon as we shall receive some further relations which we have reason shortly to expect.

The receipts at the treasury during the year ending the 30th day of September last, have exceeded the sum of thirteen millions of dollars, which, with not quite five millions in the treasury at the beginning of the year, have enabled us, after meeting other demands, to pay nearly two millions of the debt contracted under the British treaty and convention, upward of four millions of principal of the public debt, and four millions of interest. These payments, with those which had been made in three years and a half preceding, have extinguished of the funded debt nearly eighteen millions of principal. Congress, by their act of November 10th, 1803, authorized us to borrow one million seven hundred and fifty thousand dollars, toward meeting the claims of our citizens assumed by the convention with France. We have not, however, made use of this authority, because the sum of four millions and a half, which remained in the treasury on the same 30th day of September last, with the receipts which we may calculate on for the ensuing year, besides paying the annual sum of eight millions of dollars appropriated to the funded debts, and meeting all the current demands which may be expected, will enable us to pay the whole sum of three millions seven hundred and fifty thousand dollars assumed by the French convention, and still leaves a surplus of nearly a million of dollars at our free disposal. Should you concur in the provisions of arms and armed vessels recommended by the circumstances of the times, this surplus will furnish the means of doing so.

On this first occasion of addressing Congress, since, by the choice of my constituents, I have entered on a second term of administration, I embrace the opportunity to give this public assurance, that I will exert my best endeavors to administer faithfully the executive department, and will zealously co-operate with you in every measure which may tend to secure the liberty, property, and personal safety of our fellow citizens, and to consolidate the republican forms and principles of our government. In the course of your session, you shall receive all the aid which I can give for the dispatch of the public business, and all the information necessary for your deliberations, of which the interests of our own country and the confidence reposed in us by others will admit a communication.

MESSAGE ON SPANISH SPOILIATIONS, 1805, 3:400 ~ THE
PROTECTION OF OUR CITIZENS, THE SPIRIT AND HONOR OF OUR COUNTRY,
REQUIRE THAT FORCE SHOULD BE INTERPOSED TO A CERTAIN DEGREE.

Confidential Message on Spanish Spoliations[1,2]
December 6, 1805

To the Senate and House of Representatives of the United States, The
depredations which had been committed on the commerce of the United
States during a preceding war, by persons under the authority of Spain, are
sufficiently known to all. These made it a duty to require from that government indemnifications for our injured citizens. A convention was accordingly entered into between the Ministers of the United States at Madrid and
the Minister of that government for foreign affairs, by which it was agreed
that spoliations committed by Spanish subjects and carried into ports of
Spain should be paid for by that nation; and that those committed by French
subjects, and carried into Spanish ports should remain for further discussion. Before this Convention was returned to Spain with our ratification, the
transfer of Louisiana by France to the United States took place, an event
as unexpected as disagreeable to Spain. From that moment she seemed to
change her conduct and dispositions towards us. It was first manifested by
her protest against the right of France to alienate Louisiana to us, which
however was soon retracted, and the right confirmed. Then high offence was
manifested at the act of Congress establishing a collection district on the
Mobile, although by an authentic declaration immediately made, it was expressly confined to our acknowledged limits. And she now refused to ratify
the Convention signed by her own Minister under the eye of his Sovereign,
unless we would relinquish all consent to alterations of its terms which
would have affected our claims against her for the spoliations by the French
subjects carried into Spanish ports.

To obtain justice, as well as to restore friendship, I thought a special mission advisable, and accordingly appointed James Monroe, Minister Extraordinary and Plenipotentiary, to repair to Madrid, and in conjunction with our
Minister resident there, to endeavor to procure a ratification of the former
Convention, and to come to an understanding with Spain as to the boundaries of Louisiana. It appeared at once that her policy was to reserve herself for
events, and in the meantime [to avoid all explanations and engagements] to
keep our differences in an undetermined state. This will be evident from the

---

1 The Louisiana treaty, signed in May, 1803, was followed by two years of diplomatic activity. The necessary secrecy of diplomacy gave to every president the power to involve the
country without its knowledge in dangers which could not be afterward escaped, and
the Republican Party neither invented nor suggested means by which this old evil of ir-
responsible politics could be cured; but of all presidents, none used these arbitrary powers with more freedom and secrecy than Jefferson. His ideas of presidential authority in
foreign affairs were little short of royal. He loved the sense of power and freedom from
oversight which diplomacy gave, and thought with reason that as his knowledge of Europe
was greater than that of other Americans, so he should be left to carry out his policy undisturbed (Adams 1930, 245).

2 NOTE: The words enclosed in brackets were crossed out in the final document.

papers now communicated to you. After [yielding to their delays until their object could no longer be doubted] nearly five months of fruitless endeavor to bring them to some definite [accommodation] and satisfactory result our Ministers ended the conferences, without having been able to obtain indemnity for spoliations of any description, or any satisfaction as to the boundaries of Louisiana, other than a declaration [on their part] that we had no rights Eastward of the Iberville, and that our line to the west was one which would have left us but a string of land on that bank of the river Mississippi. Our injured citizens were thus left without any prospect of retribution from the wrong-doer; and as to the boundary each party was to take its own course. That which they have chosen to pursue will appear from the documents now communicated. They authorize the inference that it is their intention to advance on our possessions until they shall be repressed by an opposing force. Considering that Congress alone is constitutionally invested with the power of changing our condition from peace to war, I have thought it my duty to await their authority for using force in any degree which could be avoided. I have barely instructed the officers stationed in the neighborhood of the aggressions to protect our citizens from violence, to patrol within the borders actually delivered to us, and not to go out of them but when necessary to repel an inroad, or to rescue a citizen or his property. And the Spanish officers remaining at New Orleans are required to depart ' without further delay. It ought to be noted here that since the late change in the state of affairs in Europe, Spain has ordered her cruisers and courts to respect our treaty with her.

The conduct of France, and the part she may take in the misunderstandings between the United States and Spain, are too important to be unconsidered. She was prompt and decided in her declarations that our demands on Spain for French spoliations carried into Spanish ports, were included in the settlement between the United States and France. She took at once the ground that she had acquired no right from Spain and had meant to deliver us none, Eastward of the Iberville: her silence as to the Western boundary leaving us to infer her opinion [in favor of our claims to the Rio Bravo: and we know that her commissary had orders to require possession to that river] might be against Spain in that quarter. Whatever direction she might mean to give to these differences, it does not appear that [is sufficient reason to believe I am satisfied] she has [not] contemplated their proceeding to actual rupture, or that, as the date of our last advices from Paris, her government had any suspicion of a host& attitude Spain had taken here. On the contrary we [are without a doubt] have reason to believe that she was disposed to effect a settlement on a plan analogous to what our ministers had proposed, and so comprehensive as to remove as far as possible the grounds of future [misunderstanding] collision and controversy on the Eastern as well as Western side of the Mississippi.

The present crisis in Europe is favorable for pressing such a settlement: and not a moment should be lost in availing ourselves of it. Should it pass unimproved, our situation would become much more difficult. Formal war is not necessary. It is not probable it will follow. But the protection of our citizens, the spirit and honor of our country, require that force should be interposed to a certain degree. It will probably contribute to advance the object of peace. But the course to be pursued will require the command of means which it belongs to Congress exclusively to yield or to deny. To them I communicate every fact material for their information, and the documents necessary to enable them to judge for themselves. To their wisdom then I look for the course I am to take, and will pursue with sincere zeal that which they shall approve.

JAMES MONROE, 1806, 11:106 ~ *WE ASK FOR PEACE AND JUSTICE FROM ALL NATIONS; AND WE WILL REMAIN UPRIGHTLY NEUTRAL IN FACT.*

To Colonel James Monroe[1]
Washington, May 4, 1806

Dear Sir, I wrote you on the 16th of March by a common vessel, and then expected to have had, on the rising of Congress, an opportunity of peculiar confidence to you. Mr. Beckley then supposed he should take a flying trip to London, on private business. But I believe he does not find it convenient . He could have let you into the *arcana rerum*, which you have interests in knowing. Mr. Pinckney's pursuits having been confined to his peculiar line, he has only that general knowledge of what has passed here which the public possess. He has a just view of things so far as known to him. Our old friend, Mercer, broke off from us some time ago; at first professing to disdain joining the federalists, yet, from the habit of voting together, becoming soon identified with them. Without carrying over with him one single person, he is now in a state of as perfect obscurity as if his name had never been known. Mr. J. Randolph is in the same track, and will end in the same way. His course has excited considerable alarm. Timid men consider it as a proof of the weak-ness of our government, and that it is to be rent into pieces by demagogues, and to end in anarchy. I survey the scene with a different eye, and draw a

---

1 In America, hopes were high in the spring of 1806 and, at the beginning of May, Jefferson looked upon the future of Anglo-American relations with a marked optimism. Monroe was serving as Minister to Great Britain and there was promise that a new treaty — to re-place the Jay Treaty of 1794 — could be negotiated. But what makes this May 4, 1806 letter even more striking is the fact that Jefferson was writing these words of friendship only a few weeks after yet another incident had occurred outside New York to inflame American passions. On April 25, the British ship *Leander*, in attempting to stop the American sloop *Delaware*, fired a shot which killed the American helmsman. The act stirred national outrage. The inhabitants of New York, enraged by the British assault, stopped a boat that the purser of the *Leander* had laden with provisions, placed the supplies in carts, and paraded around the town with the British colors placed on a pole under the American flag. After giving the supplies to the Alms House, they burned the British colors. As Jefferson well realized — and his optimism notwithstanding — such incidents as this were inevitable at a time when the British sea captains, confident after their successes over the French, were empowered by the Admiralty to search American ships directly off the American coast (Horsman 1962, 83-84).

different augury from it. In a House of Representatives of a great mass of good sense, Mr. Randolph's popular eloquence gave him such advantages as to place him unrivalled as the leader of the House; and, although not conciliatory to those whom he led, principles of duty and patriotism induced many of them to swallow humiliations he subjected them to, and to vote as was right, as long as he kept the path of right himself. The sudden defection of such a man could not but produce a momentary astonishment, and even dismay; but for a moment only. The good sense of the House rallied around its principles, and without any leader pursued steadily the business of the session, did it well, and by a strength of vote which has never before been seen. Upon all trying questions, exclusive of the federalists, the minority of republicans voting with him has been from four to six or eight, against from ninety to one hundred; and although he yet treats the federalists with ineffable contempt, yet, having declared eternal opposition to this administration, and consequently associated with them in his votes, he will, like Mercer, end with them. The augury I draw from this is, that there is a steady, good sense in the Legislature, and in the body of the nation, joined with good intentions, which will lead them to discern and to pursue the public good under all circumstances which can arise, and that no *ignis fatuus* will be able to lead them long astray. In the present case, the public sentiment, as far as declarations of it have yet come in, is, without a single exception, in firm adherence to the administration. One popular paper is endeavoring to maintain equivocal ground; approving the administration in all its proceedings, and Mr. Randolph in all those which have heretofore merited approbation, carefully avoiding to mention his late aberration. The ultimate view of this paper is friendly to you; and the editor, with more judgment than him who assumes to be at the head of your friends, sees that the ground of opposition to the administration is not that on which it would be advantageous to you to be planted. The great body of your friends are among the firmest adherents to the administration; and in their support of you, will suffer Mr. Randolph to have no communications with them. My former letter told you the line which both duty and inclination would lead me sacredly to pursue. But it is unfortunate for you to be embarrassed with such a soi-disant friend. You must not commit yourself to him. These views may assist you to understand such details as Mr. Pinckney will give you. If you are here at any time before the fall, it will be in time for any object you may have, and by that time the public sentiment will be more decisively declared. I wish you were here at present, to take your choice of the two governments of Orleans and Louisiana, in either of which I could now place you; and I verily believe it would be to your advantage to be just that much withdrawn from the focus of the ensuing contest, until its event should be known. The one has a salary of five thousand dollars, the other of two thousand dollars; both with excellent hotels for the Governor. The latter at St. Louis, where there is good society, both French and American; a healthy climate, and the finest field in the United States for acquiring property. The former not unhealthy, if you begin a residence there in the month of November. The Mrs. Trists and their connections are established there. As I think you can within four months inform me what you say to this, I will keep things in their present state till the last day of August, for your answer.

The late change in the ministry I consider as insuring us a just settlement of our differences, and we ask no more. In Mr. Fox, personally, I have more confidence than in any man in England, and it is founded in what, through unquestionable channels, I have had opportunities of knowing of his honesty and his good sense. While he shall be in the administration, my reliance on that government will be solid. We had committed ourselves in a line of proceedings adapted to meet Mr. Pitt's policy and hostility, before we heard of his death, which self respect did not permit us to abandon afterwards; and the late unparalleled outrage on us at New York excited such sentiments in the public at large, as did not permit us to do less than has been done. It ought not to be viewed by the ministry as looking towards them at all, but merely as the consequences of the measures of their predecessors, which their nation has called on them to correct. I hope, therefore, they will come to just arrangements. No two countries upon earth have so many points of common interest and friendship; and their rulers must be great bunglers indeed, if, with such dispositions, they break them asunder. The only rivalry that can arise is on the ocean. England may, by petty larceny thwartings, check us on that element a little, but nothing she can do will retard us there one year's growth. We shall be supported there by other nations, and thrown into their scale to make a part of the great counterpoise to her navy. If, on the other hand, she is just to us, conciliatory, and encourages the sentiment of family feelings and conduct, it cannot fail to befriend the security of both. We have the seamen and materials for fifty ships of the line, and half that number of frigates; and were France to give us the money, and England the dispositions to equip them, they would give to England serious proofs of the stock from which they are sprung, and the school in which they have been taught; and added to the efforts of the immensity of seacoast lately united under one power, would leave the state of the ocean no longer problematical. Were, on the other hand, England to give the money, and France the dispositions to place us on the sea in all our force, the whole world, out of the continent of Europe, might be our joint monopoly. We wish for neither of these scenes. We ask for peace and justice from all nations; and we will remain uprightly neutral in fact, though leaning in belief to the opinion that an English ascendancy on the ocean is safer for us than that of France. We begin to broach the idea that we consider the whole Gulf Stream as of our waters, in which hostilities and cruising are to be frowned on for the present, and prohibited so soon as either consent or force will permit us. We shall never permit another privateer to cruise within it, and shall forbid our harbors to national cruisers. This is essential for our tranquility and commerce. Be so good as to have the enclosed letters delivered, to present me to your family, and be assured yourself of my unalterable friendship.

For fear of accidents, I shall not make the unnecessary addition of my name.

WILLIAM DUANE, 1806, 11:94 ~ WE ARE FOR A PEACEABLE ACCOMMODATION WITH ALL... NATIONS IF IT CAN BE EFFECTED HONORABLY.

To William Duane[1]
Washington, March 22, 1806

I thank you, my good Sir, cordially, for your letter of the 12th, which however I did not receive till the 20th. It is a proof of sincerity, which I value above all things; as, between those who practice it, falsehood and malice work their efforts in vain. There is an enemy somewhere endeavoring to sow discord among us. Instead of listening first, then doubting, and lastly believing anile tales handed round without an atom of evidence, if my friends will address themselves to me directly, as you have done, they shall be informed with frankness and thankfulness. There is not a truth on earth which I fear or would disguise. But secret slanders cannot be disarmed, because they are secret. Although you desire no answer, I shall give you one to those articles admitting a short answer, reserving those which require more explanation than the compass of a letter admits, to conversation on your arrival here. And as I write this for your personal satisfaction, I rely that my letter will, under no circumstances, be communicated to any mortal, because you well know how every syllable from me is distorted by the ingenuity of my political enemies.

In the first place, then, I have had less communication, directly or indirectly, with the republicans of the east, this session, than I ever had before. This has proceeded from accidental circumstances, not from design. And if there be any coolness between those of the south and myself, it has not been from me towards them. Certainly there has been no other reserve than to avoid taking part in the divisions among our friends. That Mr. R. has openly attacked the administration is sufficiently known.[2] We were not disposed to join in league with Britain, under any belief that she is fighting for the liberties of mankind, and to enter into war with Spain, and consequently

1 By this time, the British-American pendulum had far to swing between projected alliance and actual warfare. The same observers who, in February, 1806, predicted that America would not fight either Great Britain or Spain, declared in March that war was imminent. But these were not in the confidence of the administration. At the moment when they were scenting war, Jefferson, in this letter, was assuring journalist William Duane — who was also a trusted advisor and confidant — that the government aspired to nothing beyond a rigid neutrality. "We were not disposed to join in league with Britain, under any belief that she is fighting for the liberties of mankind and enter into war with Spain, and consequently France...We are for a peaceable accommodation with all those nations, if it can be effected honorably" (Sears 1927, 307-308).

2 "Mr. R" is a reference to John Randolph, chairman of the powerful House Committee on Ways and Means. Randolph was a leader of a group of dissident Republicans who had grown increasingly unhappy with Jefferson's experiments with federal constitutional power and who began to question Jefferson's use of national governmental authority (Bernstein 2003, 159).

France. The House of Representatives were in the same sentiment, when they rejected Mr. R.'s resolutions for raising a body of regular troops for the western service. We are for a peaceable accommodation with all those nations, if it can be effected honorably. This, perhaps, is not the only ground of his alienation; but which side retains its orthodoxy, the vote of eighty-seven to eleven republicans may satisfy you; but you will better satisfy yourself on coming here, where alone the true state of things can be known, and where you will see republicanism as solidly embodied on all essential points, as you ever saw it on any occasion.

That there is only one minister who is not opposed to me, is totally unfounded. There never was a more harmonious, a more cordial administration, nor ever a moment when it has been otherwise. And while differences of opinion have been always rare among us, I can affirm, that as to present matters, there was not a single paragraph in my message to Congress, or those supplementary to it, in which there was not a unanimity of concurrence in the members of the unanimity of concurrence in the members of the administration. The fact is, that in ordinary affairs every head of a department consults me on those of his department, and where anything arises too difficult or important to be decided between us, the consultation becomes general.

That there is an ostensible Cabinet and a concealed one, a public profession and concealed counteraction, is false.

That I have denounced republicans by the epithet of Jacobins, and declared I would appoint none but those called moderates of both parties, and that I have avowed or entertain any predilection for those called the third party, or Quids, is in every tittle of it false.

That the expedition of Miranda was countenanced by me, is an absolute falsehood, let it have gone from whom it might; and I am satisfied it is equally so as to Mr. Madison. To know as much of it as we could was our duty, but not to encourage it.[1]

Our situation is difficult; and whatever we do is liable to the criticisms of those who wish to represent it awry. If we recommend measures in a public message, it may be said that members are not sent here to obey the mandates of the President, or to register the edicts of 2 sovereign. If we express opinions in conversation, we have then our Charles Jenkinsons, and back-door

---

1 Francisco de Miranda, a native of Venezuela, entered the army of Spain after graduating from school and fought in North Africa and the Caribbean during the 1770s and 1780s. In the military, native Spaniards looked down upon him as a colonial, and he resented their condescension. He left the army in 1785 and spent a great deal of time in the United States, England, and France, where he embraced the notion of Spanish-American independence. In the 1790s, he rose to the rank of general in the French army but then shifted his allegiance to England, where he tried to recruit political and financial support for the independence of Spain's colonies in the New World. In 1805, after putting together a small volunteer army, Miranda attacked Venezuela but fled when he failed to inspire a general uprising or secure British naval support. When Venezuela declared its independence in 1810, Miranda returned home and became a leader in the rebellion. When the revolution faltered, in 1815, Miranda was arrested by royalist officials and died in a Spanish prison in 1816 (Olson 1992, 406-407).

counselors. If we say nothing, "we have no opinions, no plans, no Cabinet." In truth it is the fable of the old man, his son and ass, over again.

These are short facts which may suffice to inspire you with caution, until you can come here and examine for yourself. No other information can give you a true insight into the state of things; but you will have no difficulty in understanding them when on the spot. In the meantime, accept my friendly salutations and cordial good wishes.

BARNABAS BIDWELL, 1806, 11:114 ~ *BONAPARTE WILL CONQUER THE WORLD, IF THEY DO NOT LEARN HIS SECRET OF COMPOSING ARMIES OF YOUNG MEN.*

To Barnabas Bidwell[1]
Washington, July 5, 1806

Sir, Your favor of June the 21st has been duly received. We have not as yet heard from General Skinner on the subject of his office. Three persons are proposed on the most respectable recommendations, and under circumstances of such equality as renders it difficult to decide between them. But it shall be done impartially. I sincerely congratulate you on the triumph of republicanism in Massachusetts. The Hydra of federalism has now lost all its heads but two. Connecticut I think will soon follow Massachusetts. Delaware will probably remain what it ever has been a mere county of England, conquered indeed, and held under by force, but always disposed to counter-revolution. I speak of its majority only.

Our information from London continues to give us hopes of an accommodation there on both the points of "accustomed commerce and impressment." In this there must probably be some mutual concession, because we cannot expect to obtain everything and yield nothing. But I hope it will be such an one as may be accepted. The arrival of the Hornet in France is so recently known, that it will yet be some time before we learn our prospects there. Notwithstanding the efforts made here, and made professedly to assassinate that negotiation in embryo, if the good sense of Bonaparte should prevail over his temper, the present state of things in Europe may induce him to require of Spain that she should do us justice at least. That he should require her to sell us East Florida, we have no right to insist; yet there are not wanting considerations which may induce him to wish a permanent foundation for peace laid between us. In this treaty, whatever it shall be, our old enemies the federalists, and their new friends, will find enough to carp at. This is a thing of course, and I should suspect error where they found no fault The buzzard feeds on carrion only. Their rallying point is "war with France and

---

1 The causes of John Randolph's break with the administration have long interested historians. One explanation, offered originally by Jefferson's private secretary William A. Burwell, was Randolph's desire to be sole government leader in Congress. As early as 1803 he had complained to Jefferson that his position as floor leader was being damaged because Thomas Mann Randolph and John Wayles Eppes, Jefferson's sons-in-law, were introducing administration measures. This sore was reopened in the early spring of 1806, thought Burwell, when the administration began depending more and more on a Massachusetts Republican, Barnabas Bidwell, to carry its measures through Congress (Risjord 1965, 33).

Spain, and alliance with Great Britain:" and everything is wrong with them which checks their new ardor to be fighting for the liberties of mankind; on the sea always excepted. There one nation is to monopolize all the liberties of the others.

I read with extreme regret, the expressions of an inclination on your part to retire from Congress. I will not say that this time, more than all others, calls for the service of every man; but I will say, there never was a time when the services of those who possess talents, integrity, firmness, and sound judgment, were more wanted in Congress. Some one of that description is particularly wanted to take the lead in the House of Representatives, to consider the business of the nation as his own business, to take it up as if he were singly charged with it, and carry it through. I do not mean that any gentleman, relinquishing his own judgment, should implicitly support all the measures of the administration; but that, where he does not disapprove of them, he should not suffer them to go off in sleep, but bring them to the attention of the House, and give them a fair chance. Where he disapproves, he will of course leave them to be brought forward by those who concur in the sentiment. Shall I explain my idea by an example? The classification of the militia was communicated to General Varnum and yourself merely as a proposition, which, if you approved, it was trusted you would support.[1] I knew, indeed, that General Varnum was opposed to anything which might break up the present organization of the militia: but when so modified as to avoid this, I thought he might, perhaps, be reconciled to it. As soon as I found it did not coincide with your sentiments, I could not wish you to support it; but using the same freedom of opinion, I procured it to be brought forward elsewhere. It failed there, also, and for a time, perhaps, may not prevail; but a militia can never be used for distant service on any other plan; and Bonaparte will conquer the world, if they do not learn his secret of composing armies of young men only, whose enthusiasm and health enable them to surmount all obstacles. When a gentleman, through zeal for the public service, undertakes to do the public business, we know that we shall hear the cant of backstairs' councilors. But we never heard this while the declaimer was himself a backstairs' man, as he calls it, but in the confidence and views of the administration, as may more properly and respectfully be said. But if the members are to know nothing but what is important enough to be put into a public message, and indifferent enough to be made known to all the world; if the Executive is to keep all other information to himself, and the House to

---

1 Following Randolph's outright break with the administration in 1806, and the election of Joseph Varnum as Speaker in the Tenth (1807 to 1809) and Eleventh (1809 to 1811) Congresses, House Republicans returned to floor leadership with the same mixed results this arrangement had yielded in the past. From Jefferson's perspective — whose presidency ran from 1801 to 1809 — such floor leaders as George Washington Campbell and Barnabus Bidwell appeared successful, marshaling administration forces on such key issues as the embargo and other high-profile measures aimed at limiting British aggression. However, it is difficult to separate their contributions from the effects of other strategies the executive applied (Davidson 1998, 19).

plunge on in the dark, it becomes a government of chance and not of design. The imputation was one of those artifices used to despoil an adversary of his most effectual arms; and men of mind will place themselves above a gabble of this order. The last session of Congress was indeed an uneasy one for a time; but as soon as the members penetrated into the views of those who were taking a new course, they rallied in as solid a phalanx as I have ever seen act together. Indeed I have never seen a House of better dispositions. Perhaps I am not entitled to speak with so much frankness; but it proceeds from no motive which has not a right to your forgiveness. Opportunities of candid explanation are so seldom afforded me, that I must not lose them when they occur.

The information I receive from your quarter agrees with that from the south; that the late schism has made not the smallest impression on the public, and that the seceders are obliged to give to it other grounds than those which we know to be the true ones. All we have to wish is, that at the ensuing session, every one may take the part openly which he secretly befriends. I recollect nothing new and true, worthy communicating to you. As for what is not true, you will always find abundance in the newspapers. Among other things, are those perpetual alarms as to the Indians, for no one of which has there ever been the slightest ground. They are the suggestions of hostile traders, always wishing to embroil us with the Indians, to perpetuate their own extortionate commerce. I salute you with esteem and respect.

SIXTH ANNUAL MESSAGE, 1806, 3:414 - *IF WAR BE FORCED UPON US IN SPITE OF OUR LONG AND VAIN APPEALS TO THE JUSTICE OF NATIONS, RAPID AND VIGOROUS MOVEMENTS IN ITS OUTSET WILL GO FAR TOWARD SECURING US IN ITS COURSE.*

Sixth Annual Message[1]
December 2, 1806

To the Senate and House of Representatives of the United States in Congress Assembled, It would have given me, fellow citizens, great satisfaction to announce in the moment of your meeting that the difficulties in our foreign relations, existing at the time of your last separation, had been amicably and justly terminated. I lost no time in taking those measures which were most likely to bring them to such a termination, by special missions charged with such powers and instructions as in the event of failure could leave no imputation on either our moderation or forbearance. The delays which have since taken place in our negotiations with the British government appears to have proceeded from causes which do not forbid the expectation that during the course of the session I may be enabled to lay before you their final issue, What will be that of the negotiations for settling ,our differences with Spain, nothing which had taken place at the date of the last dispatches enables us

---

1 Note how Jefferson invokes the expansive, more democratic "will of the people" argument in
   this Sixth Annual Message seemingly in order to justify — or perhaps substantiate — the
   expansion of federal and presidential prerogative (Lim 2002).

to pronounce. On the western side of the Mississippi she advanced in considerable force, and took post at the settlement of Bayou Pierre, on the Red river. This village was originally settled by France, was held by her as long as she held Louisiana, and was delivered to Spain only as a part of Louisiana. Being small, insulated, and distant, it was not observed, at the moment of redelivery to France and the United States, that she continued a guard of half a dozen men which had been stationed there. A proposition, however, having been lately made by our commander-in-chief, to assume the Sabine river as a temporary line of separation between the troops of the two nations until the issue of our negotiation shall be known; this has been referred by the Spanish commandant to his superior, and in the meantime, he has withdrawn his force to the western side of the Sabine river. The correspondence on this subject, now communicated, will exhibit more particularly the present state of things in that quarter.

The nature of that country requires indispensably that an unusual proportion of the force employed there should be cavalry or mounted infantry. In order, therefore, that the commanding officer might be enabled to act with effect, I had authorized him to call on the Governors of Orleans and Mississippi for a corps of five hundred volunteer cavalry. The temporary arrangement he has proposed may perhaps render this unnecessary, But I inform you with great pleasure of the promptitude with which the inhabitants of those territories have tendered their services in defense of their country. It has done honor to themselves, entitled them to the confidence of their fellow-citizens in every part of the Union, and must strengthen the general determination to protect them efficaciously under all circumstances which may occur.

Having received information that in another part of the United States a great number of private individuals were combining together, arming and organizing themselves contrary to law, to carry on military expeditions against the territories of Spain, I thought it necessary, by proclamations as well as by special orders, to take measures for preventing and suppressing this enterprise, for seizing the vessels, arms, and other means provided for it, and for arresting and bringing to justice its authors and abettors. It was due to that good faith which ought ever to be the rule of action in public as well as in private transactions; it was due to good order and regular government, that while the public force was acting strictly on the defensive and merely to protect our citizens from aggression, the criminal attempts of private individuals to decide for their country the question of peace or war, by commencing active and unauthorized hostilities, should be promptly and efficaciously suppressed.

Whether it will be necessary to enlarge our regular force will depend on the result of our negotiation with Spain; but as it is uncertain when that result will be known, the provisional measures requisite for that, and to meet any pressure intervening in that quarter, will be a subject for your early consideration.

The possession of both banks of the Mississippi reducing to a single point the defense of that river, its waters, and the country adjacent, it becomes highly necessary to provide for that point a more adequate security. Some position above its mouth, commanding the passage of the river, should be rendered sufficiently strong to cover the armed vessels which may be stationed there for defense, and in conjunction with them to present an insuperable obstacle to any force attempting to pass. The approaches to the city of New Orleans, from the eastern quarter also, will require to be examined, and more effectually guarded. For the internal support of the country, the encouragement of a strong settlement on the western side of the Mississippi, within reach of New Orleans, will be worthy the consideration of the legislature.

The gun-boats authorized by an act of the last session are so advanced that they will be ready for service in the ensuing spring. Circumstances permitted us to allow the time necessary for their more solid construction. As a much larger number will still be wanting to place our seaport towns and waters in that state of defense to which we are competent and they entitled, a similar appropriation for a further provision for them is recommended for the ensuing year.

A further appropriation will also be necessary for repairing fortifications already established, and the erection of such works as may have real effect in obstructing the approach of an enemy to our seaport towns, or their remaining before them.

In a country whose constitution is derived from the will of the people, directly expressed by their free suffrages; where the principal executive functionaries, and those of the legislature, are renewed by them at short periods; where under the characters of jurors, they exercise in person the greatest portion of the judiciary powers; where the laws are consequently so formed and administered as to bear with equal weight and favor on all, restraining no man in the pursuits of honest industry, and securing to every one the property which that acquires, it would not be supposed that any safeguards could be needed against insurrection or enterprise on the public peace or authority. The laws, however, aware that these should not be trusted to moral restraints only, have wisely provided punishments for these crimes when committed. But would it not be salutary to give also the means of preventing their commission? Where an enterprise is meditated by private individuals against a foreign nation in amity with the United States, powers of prevention to a certain extent are given by the laws; would they not be as reasonable and useful were the enterprise preparing against the United States? While adverting to this branch of the law, it is proper to observe, that in enterprises meditated against foreign nations, the ordinary process of binding to the observance of the peace and good behavior, could it be extended to acts to be done out of the jurisdiction of the United States, would be effectual in some cases where the offender is able to keep out of sight every indication of his purpose which could draw on him the exercise of the powers now given by law.

The states on the coast of Barbary seem generally disposed at present to respect our peace and friendship; with Tunis alone some uncertainty remains. Persuaded that it is our interest to maintain our peace with them on equal terms, or not at all, I propose to send in due time a reinforcement into the Mediterranean, unless previous information shall show it to be unnecessary.

We continue to receive proofs of the growing attachment of our Indian neighbors, and of their disposition to place all their interests under the patronage of the United States. These dispositions are inspired by their confidence in our justice, and in the sincere concern we feel for their welfare; and as long as we discharge these high and honorable functions with the integrity and good faith which alone can entitle us to their continuance, we may expect to reap the just reward in their peace and friendship.

The expedition of Messrs. Lewis and Clarke, for exploring the river Missouri, and the best communication from that to the Pacific ocean, has had all the success which could have been expected. They have traced the Missouri nearly to its source, descended the Columbia to the Pacific ocean, ascertained with accuracy the geography of that interesting communication across our continent, learned the character of the country, of its commerce, and inhabitants; and it is but justice to say that Messrs. Lewis and Clarke, and their brave companions, have by this arduous service deserved well of their country.

The attempt to explore the Red river, under the direction of Mr. Freeman, though conducted with a zeal and prudence meriting entire approbation, has not been equally successful. After proceeding up it about six hundred miles, nearly as far as the French settlements had extended while the country was in their possession, our geographers were obliged to return without completing their work.

Very useful additions have also been made to our knowledge of the Mississippi by Lieutenant Pike, who has ascended to its source, and whose journal and map, giving the details of the journey, will shortly be ready for communication to both houses of Congress. Those of Messrs. Lewis and Clarke, and Freeman, will require further time to be digested and prepared. These important surveys, in addition to those before possessed, furnish materials for commencing an accurate map of the Mississippi, and its western waters. Some principal rivers, however, remain still to be explored, toward which the authorization of Congress, by moderate appropriations, will be requisite.

I congratulate you, fellow citizens, on the approach of the period at which you may interpose your authority constitutionally, to withdraw the citizens of the United States from all further participation in those violations of human rights which have been so long continued on the unoffending inhabitants of Africa, and which the morality, the reputation, and the best interests of our country, have long been eager to proscribe. Although no law you may pass can take prohibitory effect till the first day of the year one thousand eight hundred and eight, yet the intervening period is not too long to prevent, by timely notice, expeditions which cannot be completed before that day.

The receipts at the treasury during the year ending on the 30th of September last, have amounted to near fifteen millions of dollars, which have enabled us, after meeting the current demands, to pay two millions seven hundred thousand dollars of the American claims, in parts of the price of Louisiana; to pay of the funded debt upward of three millions of principal, and nearly four of interest; and in addition, to reimburse, in the course of the present month, near two millions of five and a half per cent stock. These payments and reimbursements of the funded debt, with those which have been made in four years and a half preceding, will, at the close of the present year, have extinguished upward of twenty-three millions of principal.

The duties composing the Mediterranean fund will cease by law at the end of the present season. Considering, however, that they are levied chiefly on luxuries, and that we have an impost on salt, a necessary of life, the free use of which otherwise is so important, I recommend to your consideration the suppression of the duties on salt, and the continuation of the Mediterranean fund, instead thereof, for a short time, after which that also will become unnecessary for any purpose now within contemplation.

When both of these branches of revenue shall in this way be relinquished, there will still ere long be an accumulation of moneys in the treasury beyond the installments of public debt which we are permitted by contract to pay. They cannot, then, without a modification assented to by the public creditors, be applied to the extinguishment of this debt, and the complete liberation of our revenues – the most desirable of all objects; nor, if our peace continues, will they be wanting for any other existing purpose. The question, therefore, now comes forward, to what other objects shall these surpluses be appropriated, and the whole surplus of impost, after the entire discharge of the public debt, and during those intervals when the purposes of war shall not call for them? Shall we suppress the impost and give that advantage to foreign over domestic manufactures? On a few articles of more general and necessary use, the suppression in due season will doubtless be right, but the great mass of the articles on which impost is paid is foreign luxuries, purchased by those only who are rich enough to afford themselves the use of them. Their patriotism would certainly prefer its continuance and application to the great purposes of the public education, roads, rivers, canals, and such other objects of public improvement as it may be thought proper to add to the constitutional enumeration of federal powers. By these operations new channels of communication will be opened between the States; the lines of separation will disappear, their interests will be identified, and their union cemented by new and indissoluble ties. Education is here placed among the articles of public care, not that it would be proposed to take its ordinary branches out of the hands of private enterprise, which manages so much better all the concerns to which it is equal; but a public institution can alone supply those sciences which, though rarely called for, are yet necessary to complete the circle, all the parts of which contribute to the improvement of the country, and some of them to its preservation. The subject is now proposed for the consideration of Congress, because, if approved by the time the State legislatures shall have deliberated on this extension of the federal trusts, and the laws shall be passed, and other arrangements made for their execution, the necessary funds will be on hand and without employment. I suppose an amendment to the Constitution, by consent of the States, necessary, because the objects now recommended are not among those enumerated in the Constitution, and to which it permits the public moneys to be applied.

The present consideration of a national establishment for education, particularly, is rendered proper by this circumstance also, that if Congress, approving the proposition, shall yet think it more eligible to found it on a donation of lands, they have it now in their power to endow it with those which will be among the earliest to produce the necessary income. This foundation would have the advantage of being independent on war, which may suspend other improvements by requiring for its own purposes the resources destined for them.

This, fellow citizens, is the state of the public interest at the present moment, and according to the information now possessed. But such is the situation of the nations of Europe, and such, too, the predicament in which we stand with some of them, that we cannot rely with certainty on the present aspect of our affairs that may change from moment to moment, during the course of your session or after you shall have separated. Our duty is, therefore, to act upon things as they are, and to make a reasonable provision for whatever they may be. Were armies to be raised whenever a speck of war is visible in our horizon, we never should have been without them. Our resources would have been exhausted on dangers which have never happened, instead of being reserved for what is really to take place. A steady, perhaps a quickened pace in preparations for the defense of our seaport towns and waters; an early settlement of the most exposed and vulnerable parts of our country; a militia so organized that its effective portions can be called to any point in the Union, or volunteers instead of them to serve a sufficient time, are means which may always be ready yet never preying on our resources until actually called into use. They will maintain the public interests while a more permanent force shall be in course of preparation. But much will depend on the promptitude with which these means can be brought into activity. If war be forced upon us in spite of our long and vain appeals to the justice of nations, rapid and vigorous movements in its outset will go far toward securing us in its course and issue, and toward throwing its burdens on those who render necessary the resort from reason to force.

The result of our negotiations, or such incidents in their course as may enable us to infer their probable issue; such further movements also on our western frontiers as may show whether war is to be pressed there while negotiation is protracted elsewhere, shall be communicated to you from time to time as they become known to me, other information I possess or may receive, which may aid your deliberations on the interests committed to your charge.

ANDREW JACKSON, 1806, 19:156 ~ WE MUST MEET OUR DUTY AND CONVINCE THE WORLD THAT WE ARE JUST FRIENDS AND BRAVE ENEMIES.

To Andrew Jackson[1]

Washington, December 3, 1806

Sir, I have duly received your letter, proffering the services of a very respectable corps of volunteers, should the injuries offered our country render it necessary. Always a friend to peace and believing it to promote eminently the happiness and prosperity of mankind, I am ever unwilling that it should be disturbed as long as the rights and interests of the nations can be preserved. But whensoever hostile aggressions on these require a resort to war, we must meet our duty and convince the world that we are just friends and brave enemies. Whether our difficulties with Spain will issue in peace or war is still uncertain, and what provisional measures shall be taken for the latter alternative, is now under consideration of the legislature. The offer of service which your patriotism has now made to your country is a pledge that ,it will not be withheld in whatever the national councils may authorize.

Accept my thanks on the public behalf for the readiness with which you have made this honorable tender, with respectful salutations and assurances of great consideration and esteem.

---

1 Andrew Jackson was born in 1767 at Waxhall settlement on the border between North and South Carolina. His attachment to military life began during the Revolutionary War when, in 1781, at age fourteen, along with his brother, he volunteered for militia duty only to be captured by the British at Hanging Rock. the two brothers were taken as prisoners of war to Camden, South Carolina. Subsequently released, he found himself an orphan, educated himself, and ultimately settled in Nashville where, over the next several years, he served as district attorney general, joined the militia, and begin his enterprise in land speculation. As Tennessee moved toward statehood, Jackson served as a delegate to the convention which drafted the new state's first constitution in 1795-1796. With Tennessee admitted to the Union, Jackson became its first and, at that juncture, only member of the U.S. House of Representatives. His brief tenure in the House was followed in 1797 by an almost equally brief tenure in the U.S. Senate, a seat from which he resigned in 1798. At the time of this letter from Jefferson, Jackson was actively involved in the buying and selling of land. He eventually established himself as a slave-holding planter, and he was elected to the rank of major general in the Tennessee militia. This, of course, prompted him to be drawn into the War of 1812, a war which would give him national fame as "Old Hickory," ultimately setting the stage for his subsequent election and inauguration as president March 4, 1829 (Binning 1999, 227-229). For all intents and purposes, Jackson believed that war with Spain should be regarded as all but begun, and he had communicated to Jefferson his willingness to serve the country. Jefferson replied in this December 3rd note to Jackson, who might well have been the first volunteer for the Spanish war. But while Jefferson chose still to philosophize and remain noncommittal, he perhaps should have been more frank and told Jackson that, for the present, all real ideas of war with Spain had been abandoned (McCaleb 1936, 75).

THE MANDAN NATION, 1806, 16:412 - IF [NATIONS] WILL CEASE
TO MAKE WAR ON ONE ANOTHER...[THEIR] MEN WILL NOT BE DESTROYED
IN WAR.

To the Wolf and People of the Mandan Nation
Washington, December 30, 1806

My Children, the Wolf and people of the Mandan nation, I take you by the hand of friendship and give you a hearty welcome to the seat of the government of the United States. The journey which you have taken to visit your fathers on this side of our island is a long one, and your having undertaken it is a proof that you desired to become acquainted with us. I thank the Great Spirit that he has protected you through the journey and brought you safely to the residence of your friends, and I hope He will have you constantly in His safe keeping, and restore you in good health to your nations and families.

My friends and children, we are descended from the old nations which live beyond the great water, but we and our forefathers have been so long here that we seem like you to have grown out of this land. We consider ourselves no longer of the old nations beyond the great water, but as united in one family with our red brethren here. The French, the English, the Spaniards, have now agreed with us to retire from all the country which you and we hold between Canada and Mexico, and never more to return to it. And remember the words I now speak to you, my children, they are never to return again. We are now your fathers; and you shall not lose by the change. As soon as Spain had agreed to withdraw from all the waters of the Missouri and Mississippi, I felt the desire of becoming acquainted with all my red children beyond the Mississippi, and of uniting them with us as we have those on this side of that river, in the bonds of peace and friendship. I wished to learn what we could do to benefit them by furnishing them the necessaries they want in exchange for their furs and peltries. I therefore sent our beloved man, Captain Lewis, one of my own family, to go up the Missouri river to get acquainted with all the Indian nations in its neighborhood, to take them by the hand, deliver my talks to them, and to inform us in what way we could be useful to them. Your nation received him kindly, you have taken him by the hand and been friendly to him. My children, I thank you for the services you rendered him, and for your attention to his words. He will now tell us where we should establish trading houses to be convenient to you all, and what we must send to them.

My friends and children, I have now an important advice to give you. I have already told you that you and all the red men are my children, and I wish you to live in peace and friendship with one another as brethren of the same family ought to do. How much better is it for neighbors to help than to hurt one another; how much happier must it make them. If you will cease to make war on one another, if you will live in friendship with all mankind, you can employ all your time in providing food and clothing for yourselves and your families. Your men will not be destroyed in war, and your women and children will lie down to sleep in their cabins without fear of being surprised by their enemies and killed or carried away. Your numbers will be increased instead of diminishing, and you will live in plenty and in quiet. My children, I have given this advice to all your red brethren on this side of the Mississippi; they are following it, they are increasing in their numbers, are learning to clothe and provide for their families as we do. Remember then my advice, my children, carry it home to your people, and tell them that from the day that they have become all of the same family, from the day that we became father to them all, we wish, as a true father should do, that we may all live together as one household, and that before they strike one another, they should go to their father and let him endeavor to make up the quarrel.

My children, you are come from the other side of our great island, from where the sun sets, to see your new friends at the sun rising. You have now arrived where the waters are constantly rising and falling every day, but you are still distant from the sea. I very much desire that you should not stop here, but go and see your brethren as far as the edge of the great water. I am persuaded you have so far seen that every man by the way has received you as his brothers, and has been ready to do you all the kindness in his power. You will see the same thing quite to the sea shore; and I wish you, therefore, to go and visit our great cities in that quarter, and see how many friends and brothers you have here. You will then have travelled a long line from west to east, and if you had time to go from north to south, from Canada to Florida, you would find it as long in that direction, and all the people as sincerely your friends. I wish you, my children, to see all you can, and to tell your people all you see; because I am sure the more they know of us, the more they will be our hearty friends. I invite you, therefore, to pay a visit to Baltimore, Philadelphia, New York, and the cities still beyond that, if you are willing to go further. We will provide carriages to convey you and a person to go with you to see that you want for nothing. By the time you come back the snows will be melted on the mountains, the ice in the rivers broken up, and you will be wishing to set out on your return home.

My children, I have long desired to see you; I have now opened my heart to you, let my words sink into your hearts and never be forgotten. If ever lying people or bad spirits should raise up clouds between us, call to mind what I have said, and what you have seen yourselves. Be sure there are some lying spirits between us; let us come together as friends and explain to each other what is misrepresented or misunderstood, the clouds will fly away like morning fog, and the sun of friendship appear and shine forever bright and clear between us.

My children, it may happen that while you are here occasion may arise to talk about many things which I do not now particularly mention. The Secretary of War will always be ready to talk with you, and you are to consider whatever he says as said by myself. He will also take care of you and see that you are furnished with all comforts here.

THE OSAGE NATION, 1806, 16:417 ~ A NATION, WHILE IT HOLDS
TOGETHER, IS STRONG AGAINST ITS ENEMIES, BUT, BREAKING INTO PARTS,
IT IS EASILY DESTROYED.

To the Chiefs of the Osage Nation
Washington, December 31, 1806

My Children, Chiefs of the Osage Nation, I well come you sincerely to the seat of the government of the United States. The journey you have taken is long and fatiguing, and proved your desire to become acquainted with your new brothers of this country. I thank the Master of life, who has preserved you by the way and brought you safely here. I hope you have found your-selves, through the whole journey, among brothers and friends, who have used you kindly, and convinced you they wish to live always in peace and harmony with you.

My children, your forefathers have doubtless handed it down to you that in ancient times the French were the fathers of all the red men in the country called Louisiana, that is to say, all the country on the Mississippi and on all its western waters. In the days of your fathers France ceded that country to the Spaniards and they became your fathers; but six years ago they restored it to France and France ceded it to us, and we are now become your fathers and brothers; and be assured you will have no cause to regret the change. It is so long since our forefathers came from beyond the great water, that we have lost the memory of it, and seem to have grown out of this land as you have done. Never more will you have occasion to change your fathers. We are all now of one family, born in the same land, and bound to live as brothers, and to have nothing more to do with the strangers who live beyond the great water. The Great Spirit has given you strength and has given us strength, not that we should hurt one another, but to do each other all the good in our power. Our dwellings indeed are very far apart, but not too far to carry on commerce and useful intercourse. You have furs and peltries which we want, and we have clothes and other useful things which you want. Let us employ ourselves, then, in making exchanges of these articles useful to both. In order to prepare ourselves for this commerce with our new children, we have found it necessary to send some of our trusty men up the different rivers of Louisiana, to see what nations live upon them, what number of peltries they can furnish, what quantities and kinds of merchandise they want, and where are the places most convenient to establish trading houses with them. With this view we sent a party to the head of the Missouri and the great water beyond that, who are just returned. We sent another party up the Red river, and we propose, the ensuing spring, to send one up the Arkansas as far as its head. This party will consist, like the others, of between twenty and thirty persons. I shall instruct them to call and see you at your towns, to talk with my son the Big Track, who, as well as yourselves and your people, will I hope receive them kindly, protect them and give them all the information they can as to the people on the same river above you. When they return they will be able to tell us how we can best establish a trade with you, and how otherwise we can be useful to them.

My children, I was sorry to learn that a difference had arisen among the people of your nation, and that a part of them had separated and removed to a great distance on the Arkansas. This is a family quarrel with which I do not pretend to intermeddle. Both parties are my children, and I wish equally well to both. But it would give me great pleasure if they could again reunite, because a nation, while it holds together, is strong against its enemies, but, breaking into parts, it is easily destroyed. However I hope you will at least make friends again, and cherish peace and brotherly love with one another. If I can be useful in restoring friendship between you, I shall do it with great pleasure. It is my wish that all my red children live together as one family, that when differences arise among them, their old men should meet together and settle them with justice and in peace. In this way your women and children will live in safety, your nation will increase and be strong.

As you have taken so long a journey to see your fathers, we wish you not to return till you have visited our country and towns towards the sea coast. This will be new and satisfactory to you, and it will give you the same knowledge of the country on this side of the Mississippi, which we are endeavoring to acquire of that on the other side, by sending trusty persons to explore them. We propose to do in your country only what we are desirous you should do in ours. We will provide accommodations for your journey, for your comfort while engaged in it, and for your return in safety to your own country, carrying with you those proofs of esteem with which we distinguish our friends, and shall particularly distinguish you. On your return, tell your chief, the Big Track, and all your people, that I take them by the hand, that I become their father hereafter, that they shall know our nation only as friends and benefactors, that we have no views upon them but to carry on a commerce useful to them and us, to keep them in peace with their neighbors, that their children may multiply, may grow up and live to a good old age, and their women no longer fear the tomahawk of any enemy.

My children, these are my words, carry them to your nation, keep them in your memories and our friendship in your hearts, and may the Great Spirit look down upon us and cover us with the mantle of His love.

JOHN SHEE, 1807, 11:140 ~ *I FEEL A PERFECT CONFIDENCE THAT THE ENERGY AND ENTERPRISE DISPLAYED BY MY FELLOW CITIZENS IN THE PURSUITS OF PEACE, WILL BE EQUALLY EMINENT IN THOSE OF WAR.*

To General John Shee[1]

---

1 The Office of Indian Trade was established by Congress in 1806. Before that time, there had been no official in the government whose full duties concerned the Indians; the secretary of war, under the president, looked after what business might arise. The first superintendent appointed by Jefferson was John Shee of Philadelphia, who assumed office on July 8, 1806. He was a shadowy figure who made no appreciable mark on the office, and he was replaced in October 1807 by John Mason, president of the Bank of Columbia in the District of Columbia (Prucha 1984, 120-121).

Washington, January 14, 1807

Sir, Your letter of the 16th ult. was duly received, conveying a tender of the Philadelphia republican militia legion, of their voluntary services, against either foreign or domestic foes . The pressure of business, usual at this sea-son, has prevented its earlier acknowledgment, and the return of my thanks, on the public behalf, for this example of patriotic spirit. Always a friend to peace, and believing it to promote eminently the happiness and prosperity of nations, I am ever unwilling that it should be disturbed, until greater and more important interests call for an appeal to force. Whenever that shall take place, I feel a perfect confidence that the energy and enterprise displayed by my fellow citizens in the pursuits of peace, will be equally eminent in those of war. The Legislature have now under consideration, in what manner, and to what extent, the executive may be permitted to accept the service of vol-unteers: should the public peace be disturbed, either from without or within. In whatever way they shall give that authority, the legion may be assured that no unreasonable use shall be made of the proffer which their laudable zeal has prompted them to make. With my just acknowledgments to them, I pray you to accept personally the assurance of my high consideration and respect.

CHANDLER PRICE, 1807, 11:159 - *THE SPIRIT OF THIS COUNTRY IS TOTALLY ADVERSE TO A LARGE MILITARY FORCE.*

To Chandler Price[1]

Washington, February 28, 1807

Sir, Your favor of the 24th was received this morning. The greatest favor which can be done me is the communication of the opinions of judicious men, of men who do not suffer their judgments to be biased by either interests or passions. Of this character, I know Mr. Morgan to be. I return you the origi-nal of the letter of January 15th, having copied it to a mark in the 4th page, which you will see. I retain, as I understand, with your permission, the cop-ies of those of January 22d and 27th, because they are copies; and the original of December 31st, because it relates wholly to public matters. They shall be sacredly reserved to myself, and for my own information only. The fortifica-tion of New Orleans will be taken up on a sufficient footing; but the other part of Mr. Morgan's wish, an additional regular force, will not prevail. The spirit of this country is totally adverse to a large military force. I have tried for two sessions to prevail on the Legislature to let me plant thirty thousand well chosen volunteers on donation lands on the west side of the Mississippi, as a militia always at hand for the defense of New Orleans; but I have not yet succeeded. The opinion grows, and will perhaps ripen by the next session. A great security for that country is, that there is a moral certainty that nei-ther France nor England would meddle with that country, while the present

---

1 Chandler Price was a Philadelphia merchant long associated with New Orleans trade issues (Ritter 1860, 194).

state of Europe continues, and Spain we fear not. Accept my salutations, and assurances of esteem and respect.

> COMTE DIODATI, 1807, 11:181 ~ *WARS AND CONTENTIONS INDEED*
> *FILL THE PAGES OF HISTORY WITH MORE MATTER. BUT MORE BLEST IS*
> *THAT NATION WHOSE SILENT COURSE OF HAPPINESS FURNISHES NOTHING*
> *FOR HISTORY TO SAY.*

To Monsieur Le Comte Diodati[1]
Washington, March 29, 1807

My Dear and Ancient Friend, Your letter of August the 29th reached me on the 18th of February. It enclosed a duplicate of that written from Brunswick five years before, but which I never received, or had notice of, but by this duplicate. Be assured, my friend, that I was incapable of such negligence towards you, as a failure to answer it would have implied. It would illy have accorded with those sentiments of friendship I entertained for you at Paris, and which neither time nor distance has lessened. I often pass in review the many happy hours I spent with Madame Diodati and yourself on the banks of the Seine, as well as at Paris, and I count them among the most pleasing I enjoyed in France. Those were indeed days of tranquility and happiness. They had begun to cloud a little before I left you; but I had no apprehension that the tempest, of which I saw the beginning, was to spread over such an extent of space and time. I have often thought of you with anxiety, and wished to know how you weathered the storm, and into what port you had retired. The letters now received give me the first information, and I sincerely felicitate you on your safe and quiet retreat. Were I in Europe, *pax et panis* would certainly be my motto. Wars and contentions, indeed, fill the pages of history with more matter. But more blest is that nation whose silent course of happiness furnishes nothing for history to say. This is what I ambition for my own country, and what it has fortunately enjoyed for now upwards of twenty years, while Europe has been in constant volcanic eruption. I again, my friend, repeat my joy that you have escaped the overwhelming torrent of its lava.

At the end of my present term, of which two years are yet to come, I propose to retire from public life, and to close my days on my patrimony of Monticello, in the bosom of my family. I have hitherto enjoyed uniform health; but the weight of public business begins to be too heavy for me, and I long for the enjoyments of rural life, among my books, my farms and my family. Having performed my *quadragena stipendia*, I am entitled to my discharge, and should be sorry, indeed, that others should be sooner sensible than myself when I ought to ask it. I have, therefore, requested my fellow-citizens to think of a successor for me, to whom I shall deliver the public concerns with greater joy than I received them. I have the consolation too of having added nothing to my .private fortune, during my public service, and of retiring with hands as clean as they are empty. Pardon me these egotisms, which, if ever

---

1 Diodati was a fellow intellectual and an associate from Jefferson's days in Paris.

excusable, are so when writing to a friend to whom our concerns are not un-interesting. I shall always be glad to hear of your health and happiness, and having been out of the way of hearing of any of our cotemporaries of the *corps diplomatique* at Paris, any details of their subsequent history which you will favor me with, will be thankfully received. I pray you to make my friendly respects acceptable to Madame la Comtesse Diodati, to assure M. Tronchin of my continued esteem, and to accept yourself my affectionate salutations, and assurances of constant attachment and respect.

JAMES MADISON, 1807, 11:202 ~ *THE CLASSIFICATION OF OUR MILITIA IS NOW THE MOST ESSENTIAL THING THE UNITED STATES HAVE TO DO.*

To James Madison
Monticello, May 5, 1807

I return you the pamphlet of the author of *War in Disguise.*[1] Of its first half, the topics and the treatment of them are very commonplace; but from page 118 to 130 it is most interesting to all nations, and especially to us. Convinced that a militia of all ages promiscuously are entirely useless for distant service, and that we never shall be safe until we have a selected corps for a year's distant service at least, the classification of our militia is now the most es-sential thing the United States have to do. Whether, on Bonaparte's plan of making a class for every year between certain periods, or that recommended in my message, I do not know, but I rather incline to his. The idea is not new, as, you may remember, we adopted it once in Virginia during the revolution, but abandoned it too soon. It is the real secret of Bonaparte's success. Could H. Smith put better matter into his paper than the twelve pages above men-tioned, and will you suggest it to him? No effort should be spared to bring the public mind to this great point. I salute you with sincere affection.

GEORGE CLINTON, 1807, 11:258 ~ *THE POWER OF DECLARING WAR BEING WITH THE LEGISLATURE, THE EXECUTIVE SHOULD DO NOTHING NECESSARILY COMMITTING THEM TO DECIDE FOR WAR IN PREFERENCE OF NON-INTERCOURSE.*

To the Vice President of the United States (George Clinton)[2]

---

1 In October 1805, the famous pamphlet *War in Disguise or, the Frauds of the Neutral Flags*, by James Stephen, was presented to the English public. Stephen was a lawyer who had practiced in the West Indies from 1783 to 1794 and had then worked at the prize appeal court of the Privy Council. The pamphlet offers perhaps the best contemporary account of the philoso-phy which lay behind England's commercial policy towards the United States in the years before the War of 1812. Accepted as an extremely well-reasoned work, Stephen considered in detail the origins and extent of the American carrying trade and contended that from the outbreak of war between France and England in 1793 the United States had taken advan-tage of every British concession to build an extensive commerce (Horsman 1962, 39-40).

2 On 22 June 1807, just outside territorial waters, the U.S. frigate *Chesapeake* was fired on at practically point blank range by the British ship *Leopard*. After sustaining brutal punish-ment for about fifteen minutes, the American ship surrendered, and British officers came on board and took four seamen who were allegedly deserters from the Royal Navy. With three men killed and eight seriously wounded, *Chesapeake* hobbled back to Norfolk (Hagan

Washington, July 6, 1807

Dear Sir, I congratulate you on your safe arrival with Miss Clinton at New York, and especially on your escape from British violence. This aggression is of a character so distinct from that on the *Chesapeake*, and of so aggravated a nature, that I consider it as a very material one to be presented with that to the British Government. I pray you, therefore, to write me a letter, stating the transaction, and in such a form as that it may go to that Government. At the same time, I must request you to instruct Mr. Gelston, from me, to take the affidavits of the Captain of the revenue cutter, and of such other persons as you shall direct, stating the same affair, and to be forwarded, in like manner, to our Minister in London.

You will have seen by the proclamation, the measures adopted. We act on these principles, 1. That the usage of nations requires that we shall give the offender an opportunity of making reparation and avoiding war. 2. That we should give time to our merchants to get in their property and vessels and our seamen now afloat. And 3. That the power of declaring war being with the Legislature, the executive should do nothing, necessarily committing them to decide for war in preference of non-intercourse, which will be preferred by a great many. They will be called in time to receive the answer from Great Britain, unless new occurrences should render it necessary to call them sooner.

I salute you with friendship and respect.

THOMAS COOPER, 1807, 11:265 - *BOTH REASON AND THE USAGE OF NATIONS REQUIRED WE SHOULD GIVE GREAT BRITAIN AN OPPORTUNITY OF DISAVOWING AND REPAIRING THE INSULT OF THEIR OFFICERS.*

To the Honorable Thomas Cooper[1]
Washington, July 9, 1807

Dear Sir, Your favor of June 23d is received. I had not before learned that a life of Dr. Priestley had been published, or I should certainly have procured it; for no man living had a more affectionate respect for him. In religion, in politics, in physics, no man has rendered more service.

I had always expected that when the republicans should have put down all things under their feet, they would schismatize among themselves. I al-

---

1986, 71). Following this naval incident, the American public demanded a swift response from Jefferson. And although he called his Cabinet into session, there was little else he felt he could do, without further powers from Congress, then not in session. His rationale — particularly with respect to declaring war — is succinctly detailed in this letter to Vice President Clinton (Schachner 1957, 840-841).

1 The Republican opposition to the extension of the powers of the central government in 1798 was not exclusively political. Dr. Thomas Cooper, an admirer of the English Radical Joseph Priestley and a friend of Jefferson's, published a pamphlet that explained the Republican stand in economic terms. The dispute with France, Cooper suggested, involved fundamentally not the question of diplomatic representation but foreign trade and rights as neutrals. Further, any attempt to defend this trade by military action was uneconomic because the cost of maintaining a large navy was greater than the profits derived from the trade. Moreover, the preparations for war would inevitably result in heavy taxes on the people for the benefit only of the pro-British merchants in the commercial cities (Risjord 1965, 14).

ways expected, too, that whatever names the parties might bear, the real division would be into moderate and ardent republicanism. In this division there is no great evil, not even if the minority obtain the ascendency by the accession of federal votes to their candidate; because this gives us one shade only, instead of another, of republicanism. It is to be considered as apostasy only when they purchase the votes of federalists, with a participation in honor and power. The gross insult lately received from the English has forced the latter into a momentary coalition with the mass of republicans; but the moment we begin to act in the very line they have joined in approving, all will be wrong, and every act the reverse of what it should have been. Still, it is better to admit their coalescence, and leave to themselves their short-lived existence. Both reason and the usage of nations required we should give Great Britain an opportunity of disavowing and repairing the insult of their officers. It gives us at the same time an opportunity of getting home our vessels, our property, and our seamen, the only means of carrying on the kind of war we should attempt. The only difference, I believe, between your opinion and mine, as to the protection of commerce, is the forcing the nation to take the best road, and the letting them take the worse, if such is their will. I salute you with great esteem and respect.

MARQUIS DE LAFAYETTE, 1807, 11:276 – 'REPARATION FOR THE PAST, AND SECURITY FOR THE FUTURE,' IS OUR MOTTO.

To the Marquis de la Lafayette[1]
Washington, July 14, 1807

My Dear Friend, I received last night your letters of February the 20th and April 29th, and a vessel just sailing from Baltimore enables me hastily to acknowledge them; to assure you of the welcome with which I receive whatever comes from you, and the continuance of my affectionate esteem for yourself and family. I learn with much concern, indeed, the state of Madame de Lafayette's health. I hope I have the pleasure yet to come of learning its entire re-establishment. She is too young not to give great confidence to that hope.

Measuring happiness by the American scale, and sincerely wishing that of yourself and family, we had been anxious to see them established this side of the great water. But I am not certain that any equivalent can be found for the loss of that species of society to which our habits have been formed from infancy. Certainly, had you been, as I wished, at the head of the government of Orleans, Burr would never have given me one moment's uneasiness. His conspiracy has been one of the most flagitious of which history will ever furnish an example. He meant to separate the western States from us, to add Mexico to them, place himself at their head, establish what he would deem an energetic government, and thus provide an example and an instrument for the subversion of our freedom. The man who could expect to effect this,

---

1 At this time, Lafayette was nearing his fiftieth birthday and was spending his time at *La Grange*, his wife's ancestral home near Paris (Unger 202, 337).

with American materials, must be a fit subject for Bedlam. The seriousness of the crime, however, demands more serious punishment. Yet, although there is not a man in the United States who doubts his guilt, such are the jealous provisions of our laws in favor of the accused against the accuser, that I question if he is convicted. Out of forty-eight jurors to be summoned, he is to select the twelve who are to try him, and if there be any one who will not concur in finding him guilty, he is discharged of course. I am sorry to tell you that Bollman was Burr's right hand man in all his guilty schemes. On being brought to prison here, he communicated to Mr. Madison and myself the whole of the plans, always, however, apologetically for Burr, as far as they would bear. But his subsequent tergiversations have proved him conspicuously base. I gave him a pardon, however, which covers him from everything but infamy. I was the more astonished at his engaging in this business, from the peculiar motives he should have felt for fidelity. When I came into the government, I sought him out on account of the services he had rendered you, cherished him, offered him two different appointments of value, which, after keeping them long under consideration, he declined for commercial views, and would have given him anything for which he was fit. Be assured he is unworthy of ever occupying again the care of any honest man. Nothing has ever so strongly proved the innate force of our form of government, as this conspiracy. Burr had probably engaged one thousand men to follow his fortunes, without letting them know his projects, otherwise than by assuring them the government approved of them. The moment a proclamation was issued, undeceiving them, he found himself left with about thirty desperadoes only. The people rose in mass wherever he was, or was suspected to be, and by their own energy the thing was crushed in one instant, without its having been necessary to employ a man of the military, but to take care of their respective stations. His first enterprise was to have been to seize New Orleans, which he supposed would powerfully bridle the upper country, and place him at the door of Mexico. It is with pleasure I inform you that not a single native Creole, and but one American of those settled there before we received the place, took any part with him. His partisans were the new emigrants from the United States and elsewhere, fugitives from justice or debt, and adventurers and speculators of all descriptions.

I enclose you a proclamation, which will show you the critical footing on which we stand at present with England. Never, since the battle of Lexington, have I seen this country in such a state of exasperation as at present. And even that did not produce such unanimity. The federalists themselves coalesce with us as to the object, although they will return to their old trade of condemning every step we take towards obtaining it. "Reparation for the past, and security for the future," is our motto. Whether these will be yielded freely, or will require resort to non-intercourse, or to war, is yet to be seen, We have actually near two thousand men in the field, covering the exposed parts of the coast, and cutting off supplies from the British vessels.

I am afraid I have been very unsuccessful in my endeavors to serve Madame de Tess6 in her taste for planting. A box of seeds, etc., which I sent her in the close of 1805, was carried with the vessel into England, and discharged so late that I fear she lost their benefit for that season. Another box, which I prepared in the autumn of 1806, has, I fear, been equally delayed from other accidents. However, I will persevere in my endeavors.

Present me respectfully to her, M. de Tesse, Madam de Lafayette and your family, and accept my affectionate salutations, and assurances of constant esteem and respect.

MADAME STAEL-HOLSTEIN, 1807, 11:282 - IF NATIONS GO TO WAR FOR EVERY DEGREE OF INJURY, THERE WOULD NEVER BE PEACE ON EARTH.

To Madame Stael-Holstein[1]
Washington, July 16, 1807

I have received, Madam, the letter which you have done me the favor to write from Paris on the 24th of April, and M. le Ray de Chaumont informs me that the book you were so kind as to confide to him, not having reached Nantes when he sailed, will come by the first vessel from that port to this country. I shall read with great pleasure whatever comes from your pen, having known its powers when I was in a situation to judge, nearer at hand, the talents which directed it.

Since then, Madam, wonderful are the scenes which have passed ! Whether for the happiness of posterity, must be left to their judgment. Even of their effect on those now living, we, at this distance, undertake not to decide. Unmeddling with the affairs of other nations, we presume not to prescribe or censure their course. Happy, could we be permitted to pursue our own in peace, and to employ all our means in improving the condition of our citizens. Whether this will be permitted, is more doubtful now than at any preceding time. We have borne patiently a great deal of wrong, on the consideration that if nations go to war for every degree of injury, there would never be peace on earth. But when patience has begotten false estimates of its motives, when wrongs are pressed because it is believed they will be borne, resistance becomes morality.

The grandson of Mr. Neckar cannot fail of a hearty welcome in a country which so much respected him. To myself, who loved the virtues and honored the great talents of the grandfather, the attentions I received in his natal house, and particular esteem for yourself, are additional titles to whatever service I can render him. In our cities he will find distant imitations of the cities of Europe. But if he wishes to know the nation, its occupations, manners, and principles, they reside not in the cities; he must travel through the country, accept the hospitalities of the country gentlemen, and visit with

---

1 Anne-Louise-Germaine Necker, Baroness de Stael-Holstein, was a novelist, literary critic, and political thinker. Her father was a financier and minister to Louis XVI (Newman 1987, 1014).

them the school of the people. One year after the present will complete for me the *quadragena stipendia*, and will place me among those to whose hospitality I recommend the attentions of your son. He will find a sincere welcome at Monticello, where I shall then be in the bosom of my family, occupied with my books and my farms, and enjoying, under the government of a successor, the freedom and tranquility I have endeavored to secure for others.

Accept the homage of my respectful salutations, and assurances of great esteem and consideration.

ROBERT FULTON, 1807, 11:327 ~ *I SUPPOSE WE MUST HAVE A CORPS OF NAVAL ENGINEERS.*

To Colonel Robert Fulton[1]

Monticello, August 16, 1807

Sir, Your letter of July 28th, came to hand just as I was about leaving Washington, and it has not been sooner in my power to acknowledge it. I consider your torpedoes as very valuable means of the defense of harbors, and have no doubt that we should adopt them to a considerable degree. Not that I go the whole length (as I believe you do) of considering them as solely to be relied on. Neither a nation nor those entrusted with its affairs, could be justifiable, however sanguine its expectations, in trusting solely to an engine not yet sufficiently tried, under all the circumstances which may occur, and against which we know not as yet what means of parrying may be devised. If, indeed, the mode of attaching them to the cable of a ship be the only one proposed, modes of prevention cannot be difficult. But I have ever looked to the submarine boat as most to be depended on for attaching them, and though I see no mention of it in your letter, or your publications, I am in hopes it is not abandoned as impracticable. I should wish to see a corps of young men trained to this service. It would belong to the engineers if at hand, but being nautical, I suppose we must have a corps of naval engineers, to practice and use them. I do not know whether we have authority to put any part of our existing naval establishment in a course of training, but it shall be the subject of a consultation with the Secretary of the Navy. General Dearborn has informed you of the urgency of our want of you at New Orleans for the locks there.

I salute you with great respect and esteem.

---

1 By the late eighteenth century, the principle of scientific immunity had become an established part of the laws and customs of war, and there was little military objection to this principle in the era of Franklin and Jefferson. Whether they served conservative monarchies or radical republics, the military and naval establishments of the eighteenth and early nineteenth centuries made little effort to apply scientific discoveries to problems of national defense. Napoleon, for example, eliminated observation balloons from the French army, and the Duke of Wellington refused to employ the new Congreve rocket artillery. At sea, the French Republic rejected Robert Fulton's submarine (in part because its method of attack was thought to be contrary to the laws of war) and American naval officers later opposed use of the naval mines Fulton had invented (Carnahan. 1992, 531).

JOHN NICHOLAS, 1807, 11:332 ~ IN NO CASE IS THE LOAN OF ARMS
TO MILITIA, REMAINING AT HOME, PERMITTED OR PRACTICED.

To John Nicholas[1]
Monticello, August 18, 1807

Dear Sir, Your favor of the 2d did not reach me till yesterday. That from General Hall, communicating the patriotic resolutions of the county of Ontario, was received the day before. Considering war as one of the alternatives which Congress may adopt on the failure of proper satisfaction for the outrages committed on us by Great Britain, I have thought it my duty to put into train every preparation for that which the executive powers, and the interval left for their exercise, will admit of. Whenever militia take the field of actual service, the deficiencies of their arms are of course supplied from the public magazines, and the law also permits us to lend arms to volunteers engaged, and training for immediate service. In no case is the loan of arms to militia, remaining at home, permitted or practiced. The establishment of deposits of arms, to be resorted to when occasion presses, is within the executive direction. A distribution of these deposits, wherever there may be occasion, and in proportion to the probable occasion, either defensive or offensive, is one of the branches of preparation which circumstances call on us to make. It will be done in due time; and although nothing specific can now be said, yet I may safely assure you, that, whenever we proceed to settle the general arrangement, the section of country which is the subject of your letter, shall receive a just portion of our attention and provisions.

I learn with particular satisfaction that volunteers will be readily engaged on that part of our frontier. It is a quarter in which they will be particularly useful. I presume that, in consequence of the call on the several States, the Governor will have put the engagement of volunteers into such a course as will avail us of the favorable disposition which prevails towards that service. I salute you with great esteem and respect.

JOHN TAYLOR, 1808, 11:413 ~ THE EMBARGO KEEPING AT HOME
OUR VESSELS, CARGOES AND SEAMEN, SAVES US THE NECESSITY
OF MAKING THEIR CAPTURE THE CAUSE OF IMMEDIATE WAR.

To John Taylor, Esq.[2]
Washington, January 6, 1808

Dear Sir, Your ingenious friend, Mr. Martin, formerly made for me a drill of very fine construction. I am now very desirous of sending one of them to the Agricultural Society of Paris, with whom I am in correspondence, and who

---

1 John Nicholas was a member of Virginia's House of Representatives delegation (Ferling 2004, 189).

2 John Taylor was a Virginia publicist who studied law but then turned his attention to agricultural experiment and reform. As a young man, he saw service in the Revolution in the vicinity of New York and Philadelphia and rose to the rank of major. Near the close of the war, he returned to Virginia, where he served as lieutenant colonel in the state militia. Much of his life was spent in retirement on a country estate on the banks of the Rappahannock, Virginia (Mudge 1939, 1).

are sending me a plough supposed to be of the best construction ever known. On trial with their best ploughs, by a dynamometer, it is drawn by from one-half to two-thirds of the force requisite to their best former ploughs. Will you be so good as to get Mr. Martin to make me one of his best drills, sparing no pains to make the workmanship worthy of the object, to pack it in a box, and contrive it for me to Fredericksburg. The cost shall be remitted him as soon as known. I see by the agricultural transactions of the Paris Society, they are cultivating the Jerusalem artichoke for feeding their animals. They make 10,000 lb. to the acre, which they say is three times as much as they generally make of the potato. The African Negroes brought over to Georgia a seed which they called *beni*, and the botanists *sesamum*. I lately received a bottle of the oil, which was eaten with salad by various companies. All agree it is equal to the olive oil. A bushel of seed yields three gallons of oil. I propose to cultivate it for my own use at least. The embargo keeping at home our vessels, cargoes and seamen, saves us the necessity of making their capture the cause of immediate war; for, if going to England, France had determined to take them, if to any other place, England was to take them. Till they return to some sense of moral duty, therefore, we keep within ourselves. This gives time. Time may produce peace in Europe; peace in Europe removes all causes of difference, till another European war; and by that time our debt may be paid, our revenues clear, and our strength increased. I salute you with great friendship and respect.

NEW YORK TAMMANY SOCIETY, 1808, 16:301 ~ [IT IS A] SACRED PRINCIPLE, THAT IN OPPOSING FOREIGN WRONG THERE MUST BE BUT ONE MIND.

To the Society of Tammany, or Columbian Order, No.1, of the City of New York[1]
Washington, February 29, 1808

I have received your address, fellow citizens, and, thankful for the expressions so personally gratifying to myself, I contemplate with high satisfaction the ardent spirit it breathes of love to our country, and of devotion to its liberty and independence. The crisis in which it is placed, cannot but be unwelcome to those who love peace, yet spurn at a tame submission to wrong. So fortunately remote from the theatre of European contests, and carefully avoiding to implicate ourselves in them, we had a right to hope for an exemption from the calamities which have afflicted the contending nations, and to be permitted unoffendingly to pursue paths of industry and peace.

But the ocean, which, like the air, is the common birthright of mankind, is arbitrarily wrested from us, and maxims consecrated by time, by usage, and by an universal sense of right, are trampled on by superior force. To give time for this demoralizing tempest to pass over, one measure only remained

---

1 The Tammany Society of New York City was originally a social and benevolent fraternity. However, during the 1790s, Republicans gradually gained control of the organization, drove out the Federalists, and turned it into a Republican organization (Foner 1976, 7).

which might cover our beloved country from its overwhelming fury: an appeal to the deliberate understanding of our fellow citizens in a cessation of all intercourse with the belligerent nations, until it can be resumed under the protection of a returning sense of the moral obligations which constitute a law for nations as well as individuals. There can be no question, in a mind truly American, whether it is best to send our citizens and property into certain captivity, and then wage war for their recovery, or to keep them at home, and to turn seriously to that policy which plants the manufacturer and the husbandman side by side, and establishes at the door of every one that exchange of mutual labors and comforts, which we have hitherto sought in distant regions, and under perpetual risk of broils with them. Between these alternatives your address has soundly decided, and I doubt not your aid, and that of every real and faithful citizen, towards carrying into effect the measures of your country, and enforcing the sacred principle, that in opposing foreign wrong there must be but one mind.

I receive with sensibility our kind prayers for my future happiness, and I supplicate a protecting Providence to watch over your own and our country's freedom and welfare.

SPECIAL MESSAGE, 1808, 3:472 - WE FIND NO CONDUCT ON OUR PART, HOWEVER IMPARTIAL AND FRIENDLY, HAS BEEN SUFFICIENT TO INSURE FROM EITHER BELLIGERENT A JUST RESPECT FOR OUR RIGHTS.

Special Message to the Senate and Home of Representatives of the United States[1]
March 22, 1808

To the Senate and Home of Representatives of the United States, At the opening of the present session I informed the legislature that the measures which had been taken with the government of Great Britain for the settlement of our neutral and national rights, and of the conditions of commercial intercourse with that nation, had resulted in articles of a treaty which could not be acceded to on our part; that instruction had consequently been sent to our Ministers there to resume the negotiations, and to endeavor to obtain certain alterations; and that this was interrupted by the transaction which took place between the frigates *Leopard* and *Chesapeake*. The call on that government for reparation of this wrong produced, as Congress have already been informed, the mission of a special Minister to this country, and the occasion is now arrived when the public interest permits and requires that the whole of these proceedings should be made known to you.

---

1 It would not be until April 14 — in the debate on a resolution granting the president the power to suspend the Embargo, during the absence of Congress — did any administration supporter present in full the arguments in favor of the Embargo. George W. Campbell of Tennessee, long close to both Jefferson and Madison, examined the arguments of the critics of the Embargo and decided that that it was a wise measure. Campbell denied that the Embargo was dictated by France, a charge based upon an extremely loose interpretation of a phrase from Jean Champagny, Minister of Foreign Affairs to General John Armstrong, United States Minister to France. Ultimately, Campbell's analysis confronted the nation with three choices, submission, war, or embargo (Varg 1963, 197).

I therefore now communicate the instructions given to our Minister resident at London, and his communications to that government on the subject of the *Chesapeake*, with the correspondence which has taken place here between the Secretary of State and Mr. Rose, the special Minister charged with the adjustment of that difference; the instructions to our Ministers for the formation of a treaty; their correspondence with the British commissioners and with their own government on that subject; the treaty itself, and written declaration of the British commissioners accompanying it, and the instructions given by us for resuming the negotiations, with the proceedings and correspondence subsequent thereto. To these I have added a letter lately addressed to the Secretary of State from one of our late Ministers, which, though not strictly written in an official character, I think it my duty to communicate, in order that his views of the proposed treaty and its several articles may be fairly presented and understood.

Although I have heretofore and from time to time made such communications to Congress as to keep them possessed of a general and just view of the proceedings and dispositions of the government of France toward this country, yet, in our present critical situation, when we find no conduct on our part, however impartial and friendly, has been sufficient to insure from either belligerent a just respect for our rights, I am desirous that nothing shall be omitted on my part which may add to your information on this subject, or contribute to the correctness of the views which should be formed. The papers which for these reasons I now lay before you embrace all the communications, official or verbal, from the French government, respecting the general relations between the two countries which have been transmitted through our Minister there, or through any other accredited channel, since the last session of Congress, to which time all information of the same kind had from time to time been given them. Some of these papers have already been submitted to Congress; but it is thought better to offer them again, in order that the chain of communications, of which they make a part, may be presented unbroken.

When, on the 26th of February, I communicated to both houses the letter of General Armstrong to M. Champagny, I desired it might not be published, because of the tendency of that practice to restrain injuriously the freedom of our foreign correspondence. But perceiving that this caution, proceeding purely from a regard for the public good, has furnished occasion for disseminating unfounded suspicions and insinuations, I am induced to believe that the good which will now result from its publication, by confirming the confidence and union of our fellow citizens, will more than countervail the ordinary objection to such publications. It is my wish, therefore, that it may be now published.

BENJAMIN SMITH, 1808, 12:61 ~ *How LONG THE CONTINUANCE OF THE EMBARGO MAY BE PREFERABLE TO WAR, IS A QUESTION WE SHALL HAVE TO MEET.*

To General Benjamin Smith[1]
Monticello, May 20, 1808

Sir, I return you my thanks for the communication by your letter of April 19th, of the resolutions of the Grand Jury of Brunswick, approving of the embargo. Could the alternative of war or the embargo have been presented to the whole nation, as it occurred to their representatives, there could have been but the one opinion that it was better to take the chance of one year by the embargo, within which the orders and decrees producing it may be repealed, or peace take place in Europe, which may secure peace to us. How long the continuance of the embargo may be preferable to war, is a question we shall have to meet, if the decrees and orders and war continue. I am sorry that in some places, chiefly on our northern frontier, a disposition even to oppose the law by force has been manifested. In no country on earth is this so impracticable as in one where every man feels a vital interest in maintaining the authority of the laws, and instantly engages in it as in his own personal cause. Accordingly, we have experienced this spontaneous aid of our good citizens in the neighborhoods where there has been occasion, as I am persuaded we ever shall on such occasions. Through the body of our country generally our citizens appear heartily to approve and support the embargo. I am also to thank you for the communication of the Wilmington proceedings, and I add my salutations and assurances of great respect.

PHILADELPHIA DEMOCRATIC REPUBLICANS, 1808, 16:303 ~ *THE OCEAN HAVING BECOME A FIELD OF LAWLESS VIOLENCE, A SUSPENSION OF OUR NAVIGATION FOR A TIME WAS EQUALLY NECESSARY TO AVOID CONTEST, OR ENTER IT WITH ADVANTAGE.*

To the Delegates of the Democratic Republicans of the City of Philadelphia in General Ward Committee Assembled[2]
Washington, May 25, 1808

The epoch, fellow citizens, into which our lot has fallen, has indeed been fruitful of events, which require vigilance, and embarrass deliberation. That during such a period of difficulty, and amidst the perils surrounding us, the public measures which have been pursued should meet your approbation, is a source of great satisfaction. It was not expected in this age, that nations so

---

1 Benjamin Smith was born in Brunswick County, North Carolina. He served in the Continental Army as a colonel, as well as serving as General Washington's aide-de-camp in 1776. He a member of the Continental Congress, and served as a delegate to the 1788 and 1789 state constitutional conventions. A brigadier general in the state militia, he was elected governor of North Carolina in 1810 (National Governors Association, 2008).

2 With the embargo in the balance, the support of the Democratic Republicans of the City of Philadelphia must have been rewarding. And, if nothing else, whatever the temptation to oppose the embargo, congressmen, at least from Philadelphia, were not allowed to forget the favor it enjoyed among the people back home (Sears 1927; 66, 220).

honorably distinguished by their advances in science and civilization would suddenly cast away the esteem they had merited from the world, and, revolting from the empire of morality, assume a character in history, which all the tears of their posterity will never wash from its pages. But during this delirium of the warring powers, the ocean having become a field of lawless violence, a suspension of our navigation for a time was equally necessary to avoid contest, or enter it with advantage. This measure will, indeed, produce some temporary inconvenience; but promises lasting good by promoting among ourselves the establishment of manufactures hitherto sought abroad, at the risk of collisions no longer regulated by the laws of reason or morality.

It is to be lamented that any of our citizens, not thinking with the mass of the nation as to the principles of our government, or of its administration, and seeing all its proceedings with a prejudiced eye, should so misconceive and misrepresent our situation as to encourage aggressions from foreign nations. Our expectation is, that their distempered views will be understood by others as they are by ourselves; but should wars be the consequence of these delusions, and the errors of our dissatisfied citizens find atonement only in the blood of their sounder brethren, we must meet it as an evil necessarily flowing from that liberty of speaking and writing which guards our other liberties; and I have entire confidence in the assurances that your ardor will be animated, in the conflicts brought on, ,by considerations of the necessity, honor, and justice of our cause.

I sincerely thank you, fellow citizens, for the concern you so kindly express for my future happiness. It is a high and abundant reward for endeavors to be useful; and I supplicate the care of Providence over the well-being of yourselves and our beloved country.

THOMAS LEIPER, 1808, 12:65 ~ *GIVE US PEACE TILL OUR REVENUES ARE LIBERATED FROM DEBT, AND THEN, IF WAR BE NECESSARY, IT CAN BE CARRIED ON WITHOUT A NEW TAX.*

To Mr. Leiper[1]
Monticello, May 25, 1808

Dear Sir, I received your favor of April 22d a little before I was to leave Washington, much engaged with dispatching the business rendered necessary by the acts of Congress just risen, and preparatory to a short visit to this place. Here again I have been engrossed with some attentions to my own affairs, after a long absence, added to the public business which presses on me here as at Washington. I mention these things to apologize for the long delay of an answer to the address of the Democratic republicans of Philadelphia, enclosed in your letter, and which has remained longer unanswered than I wished. I have been happy in my journey through the country to this place, to find the people unanimous in their preference of the embargo to

---

1 Thomas Leiper was an influential merchant and friend of Jefferson's from Philadelphia (Sears 1927, 211).

war, and the great sacrifice they make, rendered a cheerful one from a sense of its necessity.

Whether the pressure on the throne from the suffering people of England, and of their Islands, the conviction of the dishonorable as well as dishonest character of their orders of council, the strength of their parliamentary opposition, and remarkable weakness of the defense of their ministry, will produce a repeal of these orders and cessation of our embargo, is yet to be seen. To nobody will a repeal be so welcome as to myself. Give us peace till our revenues are liberated from debt, and then, if war be necessary, it can be carried on without a new tax or loan, and during peace we may chequer our whole country with canals, roads, etc. This is the object to which all our endeavors should be directed. I salute you with great friendship and respect.

JAMES BOWDOIN, 1808, 12:68 ~ *OUR SITUATION WILL BE THE MORE SINGULAR, AS WE MAY HAVE TO CHOOSE BETWEEN TWO ENEMIES, WHO HAVE BOTH FURNISHED CAUSE OF WAR.*

To James Bowdoin[1]
Monticello, May 29, 1808

Dear Sir, I received the favor of your letter, written soon after your arrival, a little before I left Washington, and during a press of business preparatory to my departure on a short visit to this place; this has prevented my earlier congratulations to you on your safe return to your own country. There, judging from my own experience, you will enjoy much more of the tranquil happiness of life, than is to be found in the noisy scenes of the great cities of Europe. I am also aware that you had at Paris additional causes of disquietude; these seem inseparable from public life, and, indeed, are the greatest discouragements to entering into or continuing in it. Perhaps, however, they sweeten the hour of retirement, and secure us from all dangers of regret. On the subject of that disquietude, it is proper for me only to say that, however unfortunate the incident, I found in it no cause of dissatisfaction with yourself, nor of lessening the esteem I entertain for your virtues and talents; and, had it not been disagreeable to yourself, I should have been well pleased that you could have proceeded on your original destination.

While I thank you for the several letters received from you during your absence, I have to regret the miscarriage of some of those I wrote you.. Not having my papers here, I cannot cite their dates by memory; but they shall be the subject of another letter on my return to Washington.

You find us on your return in a crisis of great difficulty. An embargo had, by the course of events, become the only peaceable card we had to play. Should neither peace, nor a revocation of the decrees and orders in Europe take place, the day cannot be distant when that will cease to be preferable to open hostility. Nothing just or temperate has been omitted on our part,

---

1 James Bowdoin III was involved in Massachusetts politics from 1786 to 1796 and was Jefferson's Minister Plenipotentiary to the Court of Spain and Co-commissioner to France from 1805 to 1808, living in Paris (Bowdoin College 2008).

to retard or to avoid this unprofitable alternative. Our situation will be the more singular, as we may have to choose between two enemies, who have both furnished cause of war. With one of them we could never come into contact; with the other great injuries may be mutually inflicted and received. Let us still hope to avoid, while we prepare to meet them.

Hoping you will find our cloudless skies and benign climate more favorable to your health than those of Europe, I pray you to accept my friendly salutations, and assurances of great esteem and consideration.

ROBERT R. LIVINGSTON, 1808, 12:170 ~ *THE FRENCH EMPEROR...*
*DOES NOT WISH US TO GO TO WAR WITH ENGLAND, KNOWING WE HAVE
NO SHIPS TO CARRY ON THAT WAR.*

To Robert R. Livingston[1]
Washington, October 15, 1808

Sir, Your letter of September the 22d waited here for my return, and it is not till now that I have been able to acknowledge it. The explanation of his principles given you by the French Emperor, in conversation, is correct as far as it goes. He does not wish us to go to war with England, knowing we have no ships to carry on that war. To submit to pay to England the tribute on our commerce which she demands by her orders of council, would be to aid her in the war against him, and would give him just ground to declare war with us. He concludes, therefore, as every rational man must, that the embargo, the only remaining alternative, was a wise measure. These are acknowledged principles, and should circumstances arise which may offer advantage to our country in making them public, we shall avail ourselves of them. But as it is not usual nor agreeable to governments to bring their conversations before the public, I think it would be well to consider this on your part as confidential, leaving to the government to retain or make it public, as the general good may require. Had the Emperor gone further, and said that he condemned our vessels going voluntarily into his ports in breach of his municipal laws, we might have admitted it rigorously legal, though not friendly. But his condemnation of vessels taken on the high seas, by his privateers, and carried involuntarily into his ports, is justifiable by no law, is piracy, and this is the wrong we complain of against him.

Supposing that you may be still at Clermont, from whence your letter is dated, I avail myself of this circumstance to request your presenting my friendly respects to Chancellor Livingston. I salute you with esteem and respect.

W. C. C. CLAIBORNE, 1808, 12:186 ~ *WE WISH TO AVOID THE
NECESSITY OF GOING TO WAR TILL OUR REVENUE SHALL BE ENTIRELY
LIBERATED FROM DEBT.*

To Governor W. C. C. Claiborne[2]

---

1 Livingston was living in New York at this time, having mostly retired from public life.
2 W. C. C. Claiborne was Governor of the Orleans Territory from 1803 to 1812, and then chosen by the Assembly to be Governor of the State of Louisiana, from 1812 to 1816. As Claiborne's

Washington, October 29, 1808

Sir, I send the enclosed letter under the benefit of your cover, and open, because I wish you to know its contents. I thought the person to whom it is addressed a very good man when here, he is certainly ,a very learned and able one. I thought him peculiarly qualified to be useful with you. But in the present state of my information, I can say no more than I have to him. When you shall have read the letter, be so good as to stick a wafer in it, and not let it be delivered till it is dry, that he may not know that any one but himself sees it. The Spanish paper you enclosed me is an atrocious one. I see it has been republished in the Havana. The truth is that the patriots of Spain have no warmer friends than the administration of the United States, but it is our duty to say nothing and to do nothing for or against either. If they succeed, we shall be well satisfied to see Cuba and Mexico remain in their present dependence; but very unwilling to see them in that of either France or England, politically or commercially. We consider their interests and ours as the same, and that the object of both must be to exclude all European influence from this hemisphere. We wish to avoid the necessity of going to war, till our revenue shall be entirely liberated from debt. Then it will suffice for war, without creating new debt or taxes. These are sentiments which I would wish you to express to any proper characters of either of these two countries, and particularly that we have nothing more at heart than their friendship. I salute you with great esteem and respect.

EIGHTH ANNUAL MESSAGE, 1808, 3:475 - *FOR A PEOPLE WHO ARE FREE AND WHO MEAN TO REMAIN SO, A WELL-ORGANIZED AND ARMED MILITIA IS THEIR BEST SECURITY.*

Eighth Annual Message[1]
November 8, 1808

To the Senate and House of Representatives of the United States, It would have been a source, fellow citizens, of much gratification, if our last communications from Europe had enabled me to inform you that the belligerent nations, whose disregard of neutral rights has been so destructive to our commerce, had become awakened to the duty and true policy of revoking their unrighteous edicts. That no means might be omitted to produce this salutary effect, I lost no time in availing myself of the act authorizing a

---

term of office drew to a close it was clear he had welded the bonds of statehood and went on to serve Louisiana in the Fifteenth Congress in 1817 (Howard 1971, 27).

1 It was with a readiness to avoid final responsibility that Jefferson drafted this, his last Annual Message to Congress. He regretted, he said, that he could not tell them that the Embargo had been suspended — as he had been given power to do — because the belligerent Powers had revoked their "unrighteous edicts." Therefore the Embargo had continued. Nor had the *Chesapeake* affair been settled. Some 103 gunboats, he continued, had been built during the year, which he thought were sufficient for defense. But he did hope that a "well organized and armed militia" would be instituted. Not a word of the deplorable economic state of the country, of the armed resistance to the Embargo, of the threat of certain Federalists to break up the Union, of the fact that if there were surpluses in the Treasury, they might shortly have to be put to more ominous and destructive uses than the praiseworthy projects he envisaged (Schachner 1957, 881-882).

suspension, in whole or in part, of the several embargo laws. Our ministers at London and Paris were instructed to explain to the respective governments there, our disposition to exercise the authority in such manner as would withdraw the pretext on which the aggressions were originally founded, and open the way for a renewal of that commercial intercourse which it was alleged on all sides had been reluctantly obstructed. As each of those governments had pledged its readiness to concur in renouncing a measure which reached its adversary through the incontestable rights of neutrals only, and as the measure had been assumed by each as a retaliation for an asserted acquiescence in the aggressions of the other, it was reasonably expected that the occasion would have been seized by both for evincing the sincerity of their profession, and for restoring to the commerce of the United States its legitimate freedom. The instructions to our ministers with respect to the different belligerents were necessarily modified with reference to their different circumstances, and to the condition annexed by law to the executive power of suspension, requiring a degree of security to our commerce which would not result from a repeal of the decrees of France. Instead of a pledge, therefore, of a suspension of the embargo as to her in case of such a repeal, it was presumed that a sufficient inducement might be found in other considerations, and particularly in the change produced by a compliance with our just demands by one belligerent, and a refusal by the other, in the relations between the other and the United States. To Great Britain, whose power on the ocean is so ascendant, it was deemed not inconsistent with that condition to state explicitly, that on her rescinding her orders in relation to the United States their trade would be opened with her, and remain shut to her enemy, in case of his failure to rescind his decrees also. From France 1 no answer has been received, nor any indication that the requisite change in her decrees is contemplated. The favorable reception of the proposition to Great Britain was the less to be doubted, as her orders of council had not only been referred for their vindication to an acquiescence on the part of the United States no longer to be pretended, but as the arrangement proposed, while it resisted the illegal decrees of France, involved, moreover, substantially, the precise advantages professedly aimed at by the British orders. The arrangement has nevertheless been rejected.

This candid and liberal experiment having thus failed, and no other event having occurred on which a suspension of the embargo by the executive was authorized, it necessarily remains in the extent originally given to it. We have the satisfaction, however, to reflect, that in return for the privations by the measure, and which our fellow citizens in general have borne with patriotism, it has had the important effects of saving our mariners and our vast mercantile property, as well as of affording time for prosecuting the defensive and provisional measures called for by the occasion. It has demonstrated to foreign nations the moderation and firmness which govern our councils, and to our citizens the necessity of uniting in support of the laws and the rights of their country, and has thus long frustrated those usurpations and spoliations which, if resisted, involve war; if submitted to, sacrificed a vital principle of our national independence.

Under a continuance of the belligerent measures which, in defiance of laws which consecrate the rights of neutrals, overspread the ocean with danger, it will rest with the wisdom of Congress to decide on the course best adapted to such a state of things; and bringing with them, as they do, from every part of the Union, the sentiments of our constituents, my confidence is strengthened, that in forming this decision they will, with an unerring regard to the essential rights and interests of the nation, weigh and compare the painful alternatives out of which a choice is to be made. Nor should I do justice to the virtues which on other occasions have marked the character of our fellow citizens, if I did not cherish an equal confidence that the alternative chosen, whatever it may be, will be maintained with all the fortitude and patriotism which the crisis ought to inspire.

The documents containing the correspondences on the subject of the foreign edicts against our commerce, with the instructions given to our ministers at London and Paris, are now laid before you.

The communications made to Congress at their last session explained the posture in which the close of the discussion relating to the attack by a British ship of war on the frigate *Chesapeake* left a subject on which the nation had manifested so honorable a sensibility. Every view of what had passed authorized a belief that immediate steps would be taken by the British government for redressing a wrong, which, the more it was investigated, appeared the more clearly to require what had not been provided for in the special mission. It is found that no steps have been taken for the purpose. On the contrary, it will be seen, in the documents laid before you, that the inadmissible preliminary which obstructed the adjustment is still adhered to; and, moreover, that it is now brought into connection with the distinct and irrelative case of the orders in council. The instructions which had been given to our ministers at London with a view to facilitate, if necessary, the reparation claimed by the United States, are included in the documents communicated.

Our relations with the other powers of Europe have undergone no material changes since your last session. The important negotiations with Spain, which had been alternately suspended and resumed, necessarily experience a pause under the extraordinary and interesting crisis which distinguished her internal situation.

With the Barbary powers we continue in harmony, with the exception of an unjustifiable proceeding of the *Dey* of Algiers toward our consul to that regency. Its character and circumstances are now laid before you, and will enable you to decide how far it may, either now or hereafter, call for any measures not within the limits of the executive authority.

With our Indian neighbors the public peace has been steadily maintained. Some instances of individual wrong have, as at other times, taken place, but in nowise implicating the will of the nation. Beyond the Mississippi, the Iowas, the Sacs, and the Alabamas, have delivered up for trial and punishment individuals from among themselves accused of murdering citizens of the United States. On this side of the Mississippi, the Creeks are exerting themselves to arrest offenders of the same kind; and the Choctaws have manifested their readiness and desire for amicable and just arrangements respecting depredations committed by disorderly persons of their tribe. And, generally, from a conviction that we consider them as part of ourselves, and cherish with sincerity their rights and interests, the attachment of the Indian tribes is gaining strength daily, is extending from the nearer to the more remote, and will amply requite us for the justice and friendship practiced towards them. Husbandry and household manufacture are advancing among them, more rapidly with the southern than the northern tribes, from circumstances of soil and climate; and one of the two great divisions of the Cherokee nation have now under consideration to solicit the citizenship of the United States, and to be identified with us in laws and government, in such progressive manner as we shall think best.

In consequence of the appropriations of the last session of Congress for the security of our seaport towns and harbors, such works of defense have been erected as seemed to be called for by the situation of the several places, their relative importance, and the scale of expense indicated by the amount of the appropriation. These works will chiefly be finished in the course of the present season, except at New York and New Orleans, where most was to be done; and although a great proportion of the last appropriation has been expended on the former place, yet some further views will be submitted to Congress for rendering its security entirely adequate against naval enterprise. A view of what has been done at the several places, and of what is proposed to be done, shall be communicated as soon as the several reports are received.

Of the gun-boats authorized by the act of December last, it has been thought necessary to build only one hundred and three in the present year. These, with those before possessed, are sufficient for the harbors and waters exposed, and the residue will require little time for their construction when it is deemed necessary.

Under the act of the last session for raising an additional military force, so many officers were immediately appointed as were necessary for carrying on the business of recruiting, and in proportion as it advanced, others have been added. We have reason to believe their success has been satisfactory, although such returns have not yet been received as enable me to present to you a statement of the numbers engaged.

I have not thought it necessary in the course of the last season to call for any general detachments of militia or volunteers under the law passed for that purpose. For the ensuing season, however, they will require to be in readiness should their services be wanted. Some small and special detachments have been necessary to maintain the laws of embargo on that portion of our northern frontier which offered peculiar facilities for evasion, but these were replaced as soon as it could be done by bodies of new recruits. By the aid of these, and of the armed vessels called into actual service in other quarters, the spirit of disobedience and abuse which manifested itself early, and with sensible effect while we were unprepared to meet it, has been considerably repressed.

Considering the extraordinary character of the times in which we live, our attention should unremittingly be fixed on the safety of our country. For a people who are free, and who mean to remain so, a well-organized and armed militia is their best security. It is, therefore, incumbent on us, at every meeting, to revise the condition of the militia, and to ask ourselves if it is prepared to repel a powerful enemy at every point of our territories exposed to invasion. Some of the States have paid a laudable attention to this object; but every degree of neglect is to be found among others. Congress alone have power to produce a uniform state of preparation in this great organ of defense; the interests which they so deeply feel in their own and their country's security will present this as among the most important objects of their deliberation.

Under the acts of March 11th and April 23d, respecting arms, the difficulty of procuring them from abroad, during the present situation and dispositions of Europe, induced us to direct our whole efforts to the means of internal supply. The public factories have, therefore, been enlarged, additional machineries erected, and in proportion as artificers can be found or formed, their effect, already more than with doubled, may be increased so as to keep pace the yearly increase of the militia. The annual sums appropriated by the latter act, have been directed to the encouragement of private factories of arms, and contracts have been entered into with individual undertakers to nearly the amount of the first year's appropriation.

The suspension of our foreign commerce, produced by the injustice of the belligerent powers, and the consequent losses and sacrifices of our citizens, are subjects of just concern. The situation into which we have thus been forced, has impelled us to apply a portion of our industry and capital to internal manufactures and improvements. The extent of this conversion is daily increasing, and little doubt remains that the establishments formed and forming will-under the auspices of cheaper materials and subsistence, the freedom of labor from taxation with us, and of protecting duties and prohibitions become permanent. The commerce with the Indians, too, within our own boundaries, is likely to receive abundant aliment from the same internal source, and will secure to them peace and the progress of civilization, undisturbed by practices hostile to both.

The accounts of the receipts and expenditures during the year ending on the 30th day of September last, being not yet made up, a correct statement will hereafter be transmitted from the Treasury. In the meantime, it is ascertained that the receipts have amounted to near eighteen millions of dollars, which, with the eight millions and a half in the treasury at the beginning of the year, have enabled us, after meeting the current demands and interest incurred, to pay two millions three hundred thousand dollars of the principal of our funded debt, and left us in the treasury, on that day, near fourteen millions of dollars. Of these, five millions three hundred and fifty thousand dollars will be necessary to pay what will be due on the first day of January next, which will complete the reimbursement of the eight per cent stock. These payments, with those made in the six years and a half preceding, will have extinguished thirty-three millions five hundred and eighty thousand dollars of the principal of the funded debt, being the whole which could be paid or purchased within the limits of the law and our contracts; and the amount of principal thus discharged will have liberated the revenue from about two millions of dollars of interest, and added that sum annually to the disposable surplus. The probable accumulation of the surpluses of revenue beyond what can be applied to the payment of the public debt, whenever the freedom and safety of our commerce shall be restored, merits the consideration of Congress. Shall it lie unproductive in the public vaults? Shall the revenue be reduced? Or shall it rather be appropriated to the improvements of roads, canals, rivers, education, and other great foundations of prosperity and union, under the powers which Congress may already possess, or such amendment of the constitution as may be approved by the States? While uncertain of the course of things, the time may be advantageously employed in obtaining the powers necessary for a system of improvement, should that be thought best.

Availing myself of this the last occasion which will occur of addressing the two houses of the legislature at their meeting, I cannot omit the expression of my sincere gratitude for the repeated proofs of confidence manifested to me by themselves and their predecessors since my call to the administration, and the many indulgences experienced at their hands. The same grateful acknowledgments are due to my fellow citizens generally, whose support has been my great encouragement under all embarrassments. In the transaction of their business I cannot have escaped error. It is incident to our imperfect nature. But I may say with truth, my errors have been of the understanding, not of intention; and that the advancement of their rights and interests has been the constant motive for every measure. On these considerations I solicit their indulgence. Looking forward with anxiety to their future destinies, I trust that, in their steady character unshaken by difficulties, in their love of liberty, obedience to law, and support of the public authorities, I see a sure guaranty of the permanence of our republic; and retiring from the charge of their affairs, I carry with me the consolation of a firm persuasion that Heaven has in store for our beloved country long ages to come of prosperity and happiness.

YOUNG REPUBLICANS OF PITTSBURGH, 1808, 16:323 ~ *THE EVILS OF WAR ARE GREAT IN THEIR ENDURANCE, AND HAVE A LONG RECKONING FOR AGES TO COME.*

To the Young Republicans of Pittsburg and its Vicinities

Washington, December 2, 1808

The sentiments which you express in your address of October 27th, of attachment to the rights of your country, of your determination to support them with your lives and fortunes, and of disregard of the inconveniences which must be encountered in resisting insult and aggression, are honorable to yourselves, and encouraging to your country. They are particularly solacing to those who, having labored faithfully in establishing the right of self-government, see in the rising generation, into whose hands it is passing, that purity of principle, and energy of character, which will protect and preserve it through their day, and deliver it over to their sons as they receive it from their fathers. The measure of a temporary suspension of commerce was adopted to cover us from greater evils. It has rescued from capture an important capital, and our seamen from the jails of Europe. It has given time to prepare for defense, and has shown to the aggressors of Europe that evil, as well as good actions, recoil on the doers. If these evils have involved our inoffending neighbors also, towards whom we have not a sentiment but of friendship and useful intercourse, it results from that state of violence by which the interests of the American hemisphere are directed to the objects of Europe. Endowed by nature with a system of interests and connections of its own, it is drawn from these by the unnatural bonds which enchain its different parts to the conflicting interests and fortunes of another world, and render its inhabitants strangers and enemies, to their neighbors and mutual friends.

Believing that the happiness of mankind is best promoted by the useful pursuits of peace, that on these alone a stable prosperity can be founded, that the evils of war are great in their endurance, and have a long reckoning for ages to come, I have used my best endeavors to keep our country uncommitted in the troubles which afflict Europe, and which assail us on every side. Whether this can be done longer, is to be doubted. I am happy that so far my conduct meets the approbation of my fellow citizens. It is the highest reward I can receive for my endeavors to serve them; and I am particularly thankful to yourselves for the kind expressions of esteem and confidence, and tender my best wishes for your personal happiness and prosperity.

NIAGARA COUNTY REPUBLICANS, 1809, 16:343 - *THE UNITED STATES ARE LEFT SINGLE-HANDED TO MAINTAIN THE RIGHTS OF NEUTRALS, AND THE PRINCIPLES OF PUBLIC RIGHT AGAINST A WARRING WORLD.*

The Republicans of the County of Niagara Convened at Clarence on the 26th of January, 1809
Washington, February 24, 1809

The eventful crisis in our national affairs so truly portrayed in your very friendly address, has justly excited your serious attention. The nations of the earth prostrated at the foot of power, the ocean submitted to the despotism of a single nation, the laws of nature and the usages which have hitherto regulated the intercourse of nations and interposed some restraint between power and right, now totally disregarded. Such is the state of things when the United States are left single-handed to maintain the rights of neutrals, and the principles of public right against a warring world. Under these circumstances, it is a great consolation to receive the assurances of our faithful citizens that they will unite their destiny with their government, will rally under the banners of their country, and with their lives and fortunes, defend and support their civil and religious rights. This declaration, too, is the more honorable from those whose frontier residence will expose them particularly to the inroads of a foe.

I receive with great pleasure your approbation of the impartial neutrality we have so invariably pursued, and of the trying measure of embargo rendered necessary by the belligerent edicts, which has saved our seamen and our property, has given us time to prepare for vindicating our honor and preserving our national independence, and has excited the spirit of manufacturing for ourselves those things which, though we raised the raw material, we have hitherto sought from other countries at the risk of war and rapine.

I thank you for your kind wishes for my future happiness in retiring from public life to the bosom of my family. Nothing will contribute more to it than the assurance that my fellow citizens approve of my endeavors to serve them, and the hope that we shall be continued in the blessings we have enjoyed under the favor of Heaven.

NEW LONDON REPUBLICANS, 1809, 16:339 - *WHILE PRUDENCE WILL ENDEAVOR TO AVOID THIS ISSUE [OF WAR], BRAVERY WILL PREPARE TO MEET IT.*

To the Republican Young Men of New London, Benjamin Hempstead, Chairman

Washington, February 24, 1809

The approbation which you are pleased to express of my past administration, is highly gratifying to me. That in a free government there should be differences of opinion as to public measures and the conduct of those who direct them, is to be expected. It is much, however, to be lamented, that these differences should be indulged at a crisis which calls for the undivided councils and energies of our country, and in a form calculated to encourage our enemies in the refusal of justice, and to force their country into war as the only resource for obtaining it.

You do justice to the government in believing that their utmost endeavors have been used to steer us clear of wars with other nations, and honor to yourselves in declaring that if these endeavors prove ineffectual, and your country is called upon to defend its rights and injured honor by an appeal to arms, you will be ready for the contest, and will meet our enemies at the threshold of our country. While prudence will endeavor to avoid this issue, bravery will prepare to meet it.

I thank you, fellow citizens, for your kind expressions of regard for myself, and prayers for my future happiness, and I join in supplications to that Almighty Being who has heretofore guarded our councils, still to continue His gracious benedictions towards our country, and that yourselves may be under the protection of His divine favor.

DANIEL D. TOMPKINS, 1809, 16:341 - *THE TIMES DO CERTAINLY RENDER IT INCUMBENT...[TO] RALLY AROUND THE STANDARD OF THEIR COUNTRY IN OPPOSITION TO THE OUTRAGES OF FOREIGN NATIONS.*

To His Excellency Governor Daniel D. Tompkins[1]
Washington, February 24, 1809

Sir, I received, a few days ago, your Excellency's favor of the 9th inst., covering the patriotic resolutions of the legislature of New York, of the 3d. The times do certainly render it incumbent on all good citizens, attached to the rights and honor of their country, to bury in oblivion all internal differences, and rally around the standard of their country in opposition to the outrages of foreign nations. All attempts to enfeeble and destroy the exertions of the General Government, in vindication of our national rights, or to loosen the bands of union by alienating the affections of the people, or opposing the authority of the laws at so eventful a period, merit the discountenance of all.

The confidence which the legislature expresses in the national administration is highly consolatory, and their determination to support the just rights of their country with their lives and fortunes, are worthy of the high character of the State of New York.

By all, I trust, the Union of these States will ever be considered as the Palladium of their safety, their prosperity and glory, and all attempts to sever it will be frowned on with reprobation and abhorrence. And I have equal confidence, that all moved by the sacred principles of liberty and patriotism will prepare themselves for any crisis we may be able to meet, and will be ready to co-operate with each other, and with the constituted authorities, in resisting and repelling the aggressions of foreign nations.

The legislature may be assured that every exertion will be used to put the United States in the best condition of defense, that we may be fully prepared to meet the dangers which menace the peace of our country. I avail myself with pleasure of every occasion to tender to your Excellency the assurances of my high respect and consideration.

GEORGETOWN REPUBLICANS, 1809, 16:349 - *FROM THE MOMENT WHICH SEALED OUR PEACE AND INDEPENDENCE, OUR NATION HAS WISELY PURSUED THE PATHS OF PEACE AND JUSTICE.*

To the Republicans of Georgetown
Washington, March 8, 1809

The affectionate address of the republicans of Georgetown on my retirement from public duty, is received with sincere pleasure. In the review of my

---

1 Tompkins was then governor of New York.

political life, which they so indulgently take, if it be found that I have done my duty as other faithful citizens have done, it is all the merit I claim. Our lot has been cast on an awful period of human history. The contest which began with us, which ushered in the dawn of our national existence and led us through various and trying scenes, was for everything dear to free-born man. The principles on which we engaged, of which the charter of our independence is the record, were sanctioned by the laws of our being, and we but obeyed them in pursuing undeviatingly the course they called for. It issued finally in that inestimable state of freedom which alone can ensure to man the enjoyment of his equal rights. From the moment which sealed our peace and independence, our nation has wisely pursued the paths of peace and justice. During the period in which I have been charged with its concerns, no effort has been spared to exempt us from the wrongs and the rapacity of foreign nations, and with you I feel assured that no American will hesitate to rally round the standard of his insulted country, in defense of that freedom and independence achieved by the wisdom of sages, and consecrated by the blood of heroes.

The favorable testimony of those among whom I have lived, and lived happily as a fellow citizen, as a neighbor, and in the various relations of social life, will enliven the days of my retirement, and be felt and cherished with affection and gratitude.

I thank you, fellow citizens, for your kind prayers for my future happiness. I shall ever retain a lively sense of your friendly attentions, and continue to pray for your prosperity and well being.

ALLEGHANY COUNTY CITIZENS, 1809, 16:357 ~ *THE MEASURES RESPECTING OUR INTERCOURSE WITH FOREIGN NATIONS WERE THE RESULT, AS YOU SUPPOSE, OF A CHOICE BETWEEN TWO EVILS.*

To the Citizens of Alleghany County, in Maryland
Monticello, March 31, 1809

The sentiments of attachment, respect, and esteem, expressed in your address of the 20th ult., have been read with pleasure, and would sooner have received my thanks, but for the mass of business engrossing the last moments of a session of Congress. I am gratified by your approbation of our efforts for the general good, and our endeavors to promote the best interests of our country, and to place them on a basis firm and lasting. The measures respecting our intercourse with foreign nations were the result, as you suppose, of a choice between two evils, either to call and keep at home our seamen and property, or suffer them to be taken under the edicts of the belligerent powers. How a difference of opinion could arise between these alternatives is still difficult to explain on any acknowledged ground; and I am persuaded, with you, that when the storm and agitation characterizing the present moment shall have subsided, when passion and prejudice shall have yielded to reason its usurped place, and especially when posterity shall pass its sentence on the present times, justice will be rendered to the course which has been pursued. To the advantages derived from the choice which was made will be added the improvements and discovers made and making in the arts, and the establishments in domestic manufacture, the effects whereof will be permanent and diffused through our wide-extended continent. That we may live to behold the storm which seems to threaten us, pass like a summer's cloud away, and that yourselves may continue to enjoy all the blessings of peace and prosperity, is my fervent prayer.

QUEEN ANNE'S COUNTY REPUBLICANS, 1809, 16:362 – WAR
HAS BEEN AVOIDED FROM A DUE SENSE OF THE MISERIES.

To the Republicans of Queen Anne's County
Monticello, April 13, 1809

I have received, fellow citizens, your farewell address, with those sentiments of respect and satisfaction which its very friendly terms are calculated to inspire. With the consciousness of having endeavored to serve my fellow citizens according to their best interests, these testimonies of their good will are the sole and highest remuneration my heart has ever desired; I am sensible of the indulgence with which you review the measures which have been pursued; and approving our sincere endeavors to observe a strict neutrality with respect to foreign powers. It is with reason you observe that, if hostilities must succeed, we shall have the consolation that justice will be on our side. War has been avoided from a due sense of the miseries, and the demoralization it produces, and of the superior blessings of a state of peace and friendship with all mankind. But peace on our part, and war from others, would neither be for our happiness or honor; and should the lawless violences of the belligerent powers render it necessary to return their hostilities, no nation has less to fear from a foreign enemy.

I thank you, fellow citizens, for your very kind wishes for my happiness, and pray you to accept the assurances of my cordial esteem, and grateful sense of your favor.

ABRAHAM BLOODGOOD AND JUDAH HAMMOND, 1809, 12:316 –
OUR NATURAL AND PROGRESSIVE GROWTH SHOULD LEAVE US NOTHING TO FEAR FROM FOREIGN ENTERPRISE.

To Messrs. Bloodgood and Hammond[1]
Monticello, September 30, 1809

Gentlemen, The very friendly sentiments which my republican fellow citizens of the city and county of New York have been pleased to express through yourselves as their organ, are highly grateful to me, and command my sincere thanks; and their approbation of the measures pursued, while I was entrusted with the administration of their affairs, strengthens my hope that they were favorable to the public prosperity. For any errors which may have been committed, the indulgent will find some apology in the difficul-

---

1 Abraham Bloodgood, Chairman, and Judah Hammond, Secretary, were officers in the General Republican Committee of the City and County of New York (Republican Party 1809, 8).

ties resulting from the extraordinary state of human affairs, and the astonishing spectacles these have presented. A world in arms and trampling on
all those moral principles which have heretofore been deemed sacred in the
intercourse between nations, could not suffer us to remain insensible of all
agitation. During such a course of lawless violence, it was certainly wise
to withdraw ourselves from all intercourse with the belligerent nations, to
avoid the desolating calamities inseparable from war, its pernicious effects
on manners and morals, and the dangers it threatens to free governments;
and to cultivate our own resources until our natural and progressive growth
should leave us nothing to fear from foreign enterprise. That the benefits
derived from these measures were lessened by an opposition of the most
ominous character, and that a continuance of injury was encouraged by the
appearance of domestic weakness which that presented, will doubtless be a
subject of deep and durable regret to such of our well-intentioned citizens
as participated in it, under mistaken confidence in men who had other views
than the good of their own country. Should foreign nations, however, deceived by this appearance of division and weakness, render it necessary to
vindicate by arms the injuries to our country, I believe, with you, that the
spirit of the revolution is unextinguished, and that the cultivators of peace
will again, as on that occasion, be transformed at once into a nation of warriors who will leave us nothing to fear for the natural and national rights of
our country.

Your approbation of the reasons which induced me to retire from the
honorable station in which my fellow citizens had placed me, is a proof of
your devotion to the true principles of our Constitution. These are wisely
opposed to all perpetuations of power, and to every practice which may
lead to hereditary establishments; and certain I am that any services which I
could have rendered will be more than supplied by the wisdom and virtues
of my successor.

I am very thankful for the kind wishes you express for my personal happiness. It will always be intimately connected with the prosperity of our
country, of which I sincerely pray that my fellow-citizens of the city and
county of New York may have their full participation.

VALENTINE DE FORONDA, 1809, 12:319 - *OUR HOSTILITY SHOULD
NEVER BE EXERCISED BY... PETTY MEANS.*

To Don Valentine de Foronda[1]
Monticello, October 4, 1809

Dear Sir, Your favor of August the 26th came to hand in the succeeding
month, and I have now to thank you for the pamphlet it contained. I have
read it with pleasure, and find the constitution proposed would probably be
as free as is consistent with hereditary institutions. It has one feature which
I like much: that which provides that when the three co-ordinate branches

---

1 Don Valentine de Foronda was the Spanish Minister to the United States (Jameson 1898,
676).

differ in their construction of the constitution, the opinion of two branches shall overrule the third. Our Constitution has not sufficiently solved this difficulty.[1]

Among the multitude of characters with which public office leads us to official intercourse, we cannot fail to observe many, whose personal worth marks them as objects of particular esteem, whom we would wish to select for our society in private life. I avail myself gladly of the present occasion of assuring you that I was peculiarly impressed with your merit and talents, and that I have ever entertained for them a particular respect. To those whose views are single and direct, it is a great comfort to have to do business with frank and honorable minds. And here give me leave to make an avowal, for which, in my present retirement, there can be no motive but a regard for truth. Your predecessor, soured on a question of etiquette against the administration of this country, wished to impute wrong to them in all their actions, even where he did not believe it himself. In this spirit, he wished it to be believed that we were in unjustifiable co-operation in Miranda's expedition. I solemnly, and on my personal truth and honor, declare to you that this was entirely without foundation, and that there was neither cooperation, nor connivance on our part. He informed us he was about to attempt the liberation of his native country from bondage, and intimated a hope of our aid, or connivance at least. He was at once informed, that although we had great cause of complaint against Spain, and even of war, yet whenever we should think proper to act as her enemy, it should be openly and above board, and that our hostility should never be exercised by such petty means. We had no suspicion that he expected to engage men here, but merely to purchase military stores. Against this there was no law, nor consequently any authority for us to interpose obstacles. On the other hand, we deemed it improper to betray his voluntary communication to the agents of Spain. Although his measures were many days in preparation at New York, we never had the least intimation or suspicion of his engaging men in his enterprise, until he was gone'; and I presume the secrecy of his proceeding kept them equally unknown to the Marquis Yrujo at Philadelphia, and the Spanish consul at New York, since neither of them gave us any information of the enlistment of men, until it was too late for any measures taken at Washington to prevent their departure. The officer in the Customs, who participated in this transaction with Miranda, we immediately removed, and should have had him and others further punished, had it not been for the protection given them by

---

1 A note of interest: Since Jefferson never fully develops his views on the Constitution in any single passage, it is difficult to determine with certainty what attitude he took toward certain constitutional problems. He seems to have held that each of the three branches of the government should have final authority to interpret a document insofar as it relates to them. However, in this letter to Valentine de Foronda, Jefferson suggests that he had been impressed by the principle laid down in a proposed Spanish constitution: that "when the three coordinate branches differ in their construction of the constitution, the opinion of two branches shall overrule the third." He then adds the comment "our constitution has not sufficiently solved this difficulty" (Wiltse 1935, 97).

private citizens at New York, in opposition to the government, who, by their impudent falsehoods and calumnies, were able to overbear the minds of the jurors. Be assured, Sir, that no motive could induce me, at this time, to make this declaration so gratuitously, were it 'not founded in sacred truth; and I will add further, that I never did, or countenanced, in public life, a single act inconsistent with the strictest good faith; having never believed there was one code of morality for a public, and another for a private man.

I receive, with great pleasure, the testimonies of personal esteem which breathes through your letter; and I pray you to accept those equally sincere with which I now salute you.

CAESAR RODNEY, 1810, 12:357 ~ *IN TIMES OF PEACE THE PEOPLE LOOK MOST TO THEIR REPRESENTATIVES; BUT IN WAR, TO THE EXECUTIVE SOLELY.*

To Caesar A. Rodney[1]
Monticello, February 10, 1810

My Dear Sir, I have to thank you for your favor of the 31st ultimo, which is just now received. It has been peculiarly unfortunate for us, personally, that the portion in the history of mankind, at which we were called to take a share in the direction of their affairs, was such an one as history has never before presented. At any other period, the even-handed justice we have observed towards all nations, the efforts we have made to merit their esteem by every act which candor or liberality could exercise, would have preserved our peace, and secured the unqualified confidence of all other nations in our faith and probity. But the hurricane which is now blasting the world, physical and moral, has prostrated all the mounds of reason as well as right. All those calculations which, at any other period, would have been deemed honorable, of the existence of a moral sense in man, individually or associated, of the connection which the laws of nature have established between his duties and his interests, of a regard for honest fame and the esteem of our fellow men, have been a matter of. reproach on us, as evidences of imbecility. As if it could be a folly for an honest man to suppose that others could be honest also, when it is their interest to be so. And when is this state of things to end? The death of Bonaparte , would, to be sure, remove the first and chiefest apostle of the desolation of men and morals, and might withdraw the scourge of the land. But what is to restore order and safety on the ocean? The death of George III? Not at all. He is only stupid; and his ministers, however weak and profligate in morals, are ephemeral. But his nation is permanent, and it is that which is the tyrant of the ocean. The principle that force is right, is become the principle of the nation itself. They would not permit an honest minister, were accident to bring such an one into power, to relax their

---

1 Caesar Augustus Rodney, of Delaware, served as Attorney General of the United States in the Cabinets of Presidents Thomas Jefferson and James Madison (United States Congress 2008).

system of lawless piracy. These were the difficulties when I was with you. I know they are not lessened, and I pity you.

It is a blessing, however, that our people are reasonable; that they are kept so well informed of the state of things as to judge for themselves, to see the true sources of their difficulties, and to maintain their confidence undiminished in the wisdom and integrity of their functionaries. *Macte virtute* therefore. Continue to go straight forward, pursuing always that which is right, as the only clue which can lead us out of the labyrinth. Let nothing be spared of either reason or passion, to preserve the public confidence entire, as the only rock of our safety. In times of peace, the people look most to their representatives; but in war, to the executive solely. It is visible that their confidence is, even now veering in that direction; that they are looking to the executive to give the proper direction to their affairs, with a confidence as auspicious as it is well founded.

I avail myself of this, the first occasion of writing to you, to express all the depth of my affection for you; the sense I entertain of your faithful co-operation in my late labors, and the debt I owe for the valuable aid I received from you. Though separated from my fellow laborers in place and pursuit, my affections are with you all, and I offer daily prayers that ye love one another, as I love you. God bless you.

WILLIAM A. BURWELL, 1810, 12:363 ~ OUR COASTING TRADE IS THE FIRST AND MOST IMPORTANT BRANCH, NEVER TO BE YIELDED BUT WITH OUR EXISTENCE.

To William A. Burwell[1]
Monticello, February 25, 1810

Dear Sir, Yours of the 16th, has given me real uneasiness. I was certainly very unfortunate in the choice of my expression, when I hit upon one which could excite any doubt of my unceasing affections for you. In observing that you might use the information as you should find proper, I meant merely that you might communicate it to the President, the Secretaries of State or War, or to young Mr. Lee, as should be judged by yourself most proper. I meant particularly, to permit its communication to Mr. Lee, to enlighten his enquiries, for I do not know that his father received the medal. I could only conduct the information to the completion of the die and striking off a proof. With such assurances as I have of your affection, be assured that nothing but the most direct and unequivocal proofs can ever make me suspect, its abatement, and conscious of as warm feelings towards yourself, I hope you will ever be as unready to doubt them. Let us put this, then, under our feet.

I like your convoy bill, because although it does not assume the maintenance of all our maritime rights, it assumes as much as it is our interest to maintain. Next to that is the carriage of our own productions in our own vessels, and bringing back the returns for our own consumption; so far I would

---

1 William Armisted Burwell, served in the Congress from Virginia. He also served as Jefferson's private secretary (United States Congress 2008).

protect it, and force every part of the Union to join in the protection at the point of the bayonet. But though we have a right to the remaining branch of carrying for other nations, its advantages do not compensate its risks. Your bill first rallies us to the ground the Constitution ought to have taken, and to which we ought to return without delay; the moment is the most favorable possible, because the Eastern States, by declaring they will not protect that cabotage by war, and forcing us to abandon it, have released us from every future claim for its protection on that part. Your bill is excellent in another view: it presents still one other ground to which we can retire before we resort to war; it says to the belligerents, rather than go to war, we will retire from the brokerage of other nations, and confine ourselves to the carriage and exchange of our own productions; but we will vindicate that in all its rights — a if you touch it, it is war.

The present delightful weather has drawn us all into our farms and gardens; we have had the most devastating rain which has ever fallen within my knowledge. Three inches of water fell in the space of about an hour. Every hollow of every hill presented a torrent which swept everything before it. I have never seen the fields so much injured. Mr. Randolph's farm is the only one which has not suffered; his horizontal furrows arrested the water at every step till it was absorbed, or at least had deposited the soil it had taken up. Everybody in this neighborhood is adopting his method of ploughing, except tenants who have no interest in the preservation of the soil.

Present me respectfully to Mrs. Burwell, and be assured of my constant affection.

THADDEUS KOSCIUSKO, 1810, 12:365 ~ *FROM THE MOMENT THAT THE AFFAIR OF THE CHESAPEAKE RENDERED THE PROSPECT OF WAR IMMINENT, EVERY FACULTY WAS EXERTED TO BE PREPARED FOR IT.*

To General Thaddeus Kosciusko
Monticello, February 26, 1810

My Dear General and Friend, I have rarely written to you; never but by safe, conveyances; and avoiding everything political, lest coming from one in the station I then held, it might be imputed injuriously to our country, or perhaps even excite jealousy of you. Hence my letters were necessarily dry. Retired now from public concerns, totally unconnected with them, and avoiding all curiosity about what is done or intended, what I say is from myself only, the workings of my own mind, imputable to nobody else.

The anxieties which I know you have felt, on seeing exposed to the jostlings of a warring world, a country to which, in early life, you devoted your sword and services when oppressed by foreign dominion, were worthy of your philanthropy and disinterested attachment to the freedom and happiness of man. Although we have not made all the provisions which might be necessary for a war in the field of Europe, yet we have not been inattentive to such as would be necessary here. From the moment that the affair of the *Chesapeake* rendered the prospect of war imminent, every faculty was exerted to be prepared for it, and I think I may venture to solace you with the assurance, that we are, in a good degree, prepared. Military stores for many campaigns are on hand, all the necessary articles (sulfur excepted), and the art of preparing them among ourselves, abundantly; arms in our magazines for more men than will ever be required in the field, and forty thousand new stand yearly added, of our own fabrication, superior to any we have ever seen from Europe; heavy artillery much beyond our need; an increasing stock of field pieces, several foundries casting one every other day each; a military school of about fifty students, which has been in operation a dozen years; and the manufacture of men constantly going on, and adding forty thousand young soldiers to our force every year that the war is deferred; at all our seaport towns of the least consequence we have erected works of defense, and assigned them gunboats, carrying one or two heavy pieces, either eighteen, twenty-four, or thirty-two pounders, sufficient in the smaller harbors to repel the predatory attacks of privateers or single armed ships, and proportioned in the larger harbors to such more serious attacks as they may probably be exposed to. All these were nearly completed, and their gunboats in readiness, when I retired from the government. The works of New York and New Orleans alone, being on a much larger scale, are not yet completed. The former will be finished this summer, mounting four hundred and thirty-eight guns, and, with the aid of from fifty to one hundred gunboats, will be adequate to the resistance of any fleet which will ever be trusted across the Atlantic. The works for New Orleans are less advanced. These are our preparations. They are very different from what you will be told by newspapers, and travelers, even Americans. But it is not to them the government communicates the public condition. Ask one of them if he knows the exact state of any particular harbor, and you will find probably that he does not know even that of the one he comes from. You will ask, perhaps, where are the proofs of these preparations for one who cannot go and see them. I answer, in the acts of Congress, authorizing such preparations, and in your knowledge of me, that, if authorized, they would be executed.

Two measures have not been adopted, which I pressed on Congress repeatedly at their meetings. The one, to settle the whole ungranted territory of Orleans, by donations of land to able-bodied young men, to be engaged and carried there at the public expense, who would constitute a force always ready on the spot to defend New Orleans. The other was, to class the militia according to the years of their birth, and make all those from twenty to twenty-five liable to be trained and called into service at a moment's warning. This would have given us a force of three hundred thousand young men, prepared by proper training, for service in any part of the United States; while those who had passed through that period would remain at home, liable to be used in their own or adjacent States. These two measures would have completed what I deemed necessary for the entire security of our country. They would have given me, on my retirement from the government of the nation, the consolatory reflection, that having found, when I was called to it, not a single seaport town in a condition to repel a levy of contribution by a single privateer or pirate, I had left every harbor so prepared by works and gunboats, as to be in a reasonable state of security against any probable attack; the territory of Orleans acquired, and planted with an internal force sufficient for its protection; and the whole territory of the United States organized by such a classification of its male force, as would give it the benefit of all its young population for active service, and that of a middle and advanced age for stationary defense. But these measures will, I hope, be completed by my successor, who, to the purest principles of republican patriotism, adds a wisdom and foresight second to no man on earth.

So much as to my country. Now a word as to myself. I am retired to Monticello, where, in the bosom of my family, and surrounded by my books, I enjoy a repose to which I have been long a stranger. My mornings are devoted to correspondence. From breakfast to dinner, I am in my shops, my garden, or on horseback among my farms; from dinner to dark, I give to society and recreation with my neighbors and friends; and from candle light to early bed-time, I read. My health is perfect; and my strength considerably reinforced by the activity of the course I pursue; perhaps it is as great as usually falls to the lot of near sixty-seven years of age. I talk of ploughs and harrows, of seeding and harvesting, with my neighbors, and of politics too, if they choose, with as little reserve as the rest of my fellow citizens, and feel, at length, the blessing of being free to say and do what I please, without being responsible for it to any mortal. A part of my occupation, and by no means the least pleasing, is the direction of the studies of such young men as ask it. They place themselves in the neighboring village, and have the use of my library and counsel, and make a part of my society. In advising the course of their reading, I endeavor to .keep their attention fixed on the main objects of all science, the freedom and happiness of man. So that coming to bear a share in the councils and government of their country, they will keep ever in view the sole objects of all legitimate government.

Instead of the unalloyed happiness of retiring unembarrassed and independent, to the enjoyment of my estate, which is ample for my limited views, I have to pass such a length of time in a thraldom of mind never before known to me. Except for this, my happiness would have been perfect. That yours may never know disturbance, and that you may enjoy as many years of life, as health and ease to yourself shall wish, is the sincere prayer of your constant and affectionate friend

THOMAS LAW, 1811, 12:437 - NOTHING BUT MINDS PLACING
THEMSELVES ABOVE THE PASSIONS...COULD HAVE PRESERVED US FROM
THE WAR TO WHICH... PROVOCATIONS HAVE BEEN CONSTANTLY URGING
US.

To Thomas Law[1]
Monticello, January 15, 1811

---

1 Thomas Law was a real estate dealer of English origins (Greene 1984, 423).

Dear Sir, An absence from home of some length has prevented my sooner acknowledging the receipt of your letter, covering the printed pamphlet, which the same absence has as yet prevented me from taking up, but which I know I shall read with great pleasure. Your favor of December the 22d, is also received.

Mr. Wagner's malignity, like that of the rest of his tribe of brother printers, who deal out calumnies for federal readers, gives me no pain. When a printer cooks up a falsehood, it is as easy to put it into the mouth of a Mr. Fox, as of a smaller man, and safer into that of a dead than a living one. Your sincere attachment to this country, as well as to your native one, was never doubted by me; and in that persuasion, I felt myself free to express to you my genuine sentiments with respect to England. No man was more sensible than myself of the just value of the friendship of that country. There are between us so many of those circumstances which naturally produce and cement kind dispositions, that if they could have forgiven our resistance to their usurpations, our connections might have been durable, and have insured duration to both our governments. I wished, therefore, a cordial friendship with them, and I spared no occasion of manifesting this in our correspondence and intercourse with them; not disguising, however, my desire of friendship with their enemy also. During the administration of Mr. Addington, I thought I discovered some friendly symptoms on the part of that government; at least, we received some marks of respect from the administration, and some of regret at the wrongs we were suffering from their country. So, also, during the short interval of Mr. Fox's power. But every other administration since our Revolution has been equally wanton in their injuries and insults, and have manifested equal hatred and aversion. Instead, too, of cultivating the government itself, whose principles are those of the great mass of the nation, they have adopted the miserable policy of teasing and embarrassing it, by allying themselves with a faction here, not a tenth of the people, noisy and unprincipled, and which never can come into power while republicanism is the spirit of the nation, and that must continue to be so, until such a condensation of population shall have taken place as will require centuries. Whereas, the good will of the government itself would give them, and immediately, every benefit which reason or justice would permit it to give. With respect to myself, I saw great reason to believe their ministers were weak enough to credit the newspaper trash about a supposed personal enmity in myself towards England. This wretched party imputation was beneath the notice of wise men. England never did me a personal injury, other than in open war; and for numerous individuals there, I have great esteem and friendship. And I must have had a mind far below the duties of my station, to have felt either national partialities or antipathies in conducting the affairs confided to me. My affections were first for my own country, and then, generally, for all mankind; and nothing but minds placing themselves above the passions, in the functionaries of this country, could have preserved us from the war to which their provocations have been constantly urging us.

The war interests in England include a numerous and wealthy part of their population; and their influence is deemed worth courting by ministers wishing to keep their places. Continually endangered by a powerful opposition, they find it convenient to humor the popular passions at the expense of the public good. The shipping interest, commercial interest, and their janizaries of the navy, all fattening on war, will not be neglected by ministers of ordinary minds. Their tenure of office is so infirm that they dare not follow the dictates of wisdom, justice, and the well-calculated interests of their country. This vice in the English constitution, renders a dependence on that government very unsafe. The feelings of their King, too, fundamentally adverse to us, have added another motive for unfriendliness in his ministers. This obstacle to friendship, however, seems likely to be soon removed; and I verily believe the successor will come in with fairer and wiser dispositions towards us; perhaps on that event their conduct may be changed. But what England is to become on the crush of her internal structure, now seeming to be begun, I cannot foresee. Her monied interest, created by her paper system, and now constituting a baseless mass of wealth equal to that of the owners of the soil, must disappear with that system, and the medium for paying great taxes thus failing, her navy must be without support. That it shall be supported by permitting her to claim dominion of the ocean, and to levy tribute on every flag traversing that, as lately attempted and not yet relinquished, every nation must contest, even *ad internecionem*. And yet, that retiring from this enormity, she should continue able to take a fair share in the necessary equilibrium of power on that element, would be the desire of every nation.

I feel happy in withdrawing my mind from these anxieties, and resigning myself, for the remnant of life, to the care and guardianship of others. Good wishes are all an old man has to offer to his country or friends. Mine attend yourself, with sincere assurances of esteem and respect, which, however, I should be better pleased to tender you in person, should your rambles ever lead you into the vicinage of Monticello.

THADDEUS KOSCIUSKO, 1811, 13:41 ~ PEACE...HAS BEEN OUR PRINCIPLE, PEACE IS OUR INTEREST, AND PEACE HAS SAVED TO THE WORLD THIS ONLY PLANT OF FREE AND RATIONAL GOVERNMENT NOW EXISTING IN IT.

To General Thaddeus Kosciusko
Monticello, April 13, 1811

My Dear General and Friend, My last letter to you was of the 26th of February of the last year. Knowing of no particular conveyance, I confided it to the Department of State, to be put under the cover of their public dispatches to General Armstrong or Mr. Warden. Not having been able to learn whether it ever got to hand, I now enclose a duplicate.

Knowing your affections to this country, and the interest you take in whatever concerns it, I therein gave you a tableau of its state when I retired from the administration. The difficulties and embarrassments still continued in our way by the two great belligerent powers, you are acquainted with. In other times, when there was some profession of regard for right, some respect to reason, when a gross violation of these marked a deliberate design of pointed injury, these would have been causes of war. But when we see two antagonists contending *ad internecionem*, so eager for mutual destruction as to disregard all means, to deal their blows in every direction regardless on whom they may fall, prudent bystanders, whom some of them may wound, instead of thinking it cause to join in the maniac contest, get out of the way as well as they can, and leave the cannibals to mutual ravin. It would have been perfect Quixotism in us to have encountered these Bedlamites, to have undertaken the redress of all wrongs against a world avowedly rejecting all regard to right. We have, therefore, remained in peace, suffering frequent injuries, but, on the whole, multiplying, improving, prospering beyond all example. It is evident to all, that in spite of great losses much greater gains have ensued. When these gladiators shall have worried each other into ruin or reason, instead of lying among the dead on the bloody arena, we shall have acquired a growth and strength which will place us *hors d'insulte*. Peace then has been our principle, peace is our interest, and peace has saved to the world this only plant of free and rational government now existing in it. If it can still be preserved, we shall soon see the final extinction of our national debt, and liberation of our revenues for the defense and improvement of our country. These revenues will be levied entirely on the rich, the business of household manufacture being now so established that the farmer and labor-er clothe themselves entirely. The rich alone use imported articles, and on these alone the whole taxes of the General Government are levied. The poor man who uses nothing but what is made in his own farm or family, or within his own country, pays not a farthing of tax to the general government, but on his salt; and should we go into that manufacture also, as is probable, he will pay nothing. Our revenues liberated by the discharge of the public debt, and its surplus applied to canals, roads, schools, etc., the farmer will see his government supported, his children educated, and the face of his country made a paradise by the contributions of the rich alone, without his being called on to spend a cent from his earnings. However, therefore, we may have been reproached for pursuing our Quaker system, time will affix the stamp of wisdom on it, and the happiness and prosperity of our citizens will attest its merit. And this, I believe, is the only legitimate object of government, and the first duty of governors, and not the slaughter of men and devastation of the countries placed under their care, in pursuit of a fantastic honor, unallied to virtue or happiness: or in gratification of the angry passions, or the pride of administrators, excited by personal incidents, in which their citizens have no concern. Some merit will be ascribed to the converting such times of destruction into times of growth and strength for us. And behold! Another example of man rising in his might and bursting the chains of his oppressor, and in the same hemisphere. Spanish America is all in revolt. The insurgents are triumphant in many of the States, and will be so in all. But there the danger is that the cruel arts of their oppressors have enchained their minds, have kept them in the ignorance of children, and as incapable of self government as children. If the obstacles of bigotry and priest-craft can be surmounted, we may hope that common sense will suffice to do everything else. God send them a safe deliverance. As to the private matter explained in my letter of February 26, the time I shall have occasion for your indulgence will not be longer than there stated, and may be shortened if either your convenience or will should require it. God bless you, and give you many years of health and happiness, and that you may live to see more of the liberty you love than present appearances promise.

P. S. Mr. Barnes is now looking out for bills for your usual annual remittance.

WILLIAM WIRT, 1811, 13:52 - *FOR US TO ATTEMPT BY WAR TO REFORM ALL EUROPE...WOULD SHOW US TO BE ONLY MANIACS OF ANOTHER CHARACTER.*

To William Wirt[1]
Monticello, May 3, 1811

Dear Sir, The interest you were so kind as to take, at my request, in the case of Duane, and the communication to you of my first letter to him, entitles you to a communication of the second, which will probably be the last. I have ventured to quote your letter in it, without giving your name, and even softening some of its expressions respecting him. It is possible Duane may be reclaimed as to Mr. Madison. But as to Mr. Gallatin, I despair of it. That enmity took its rise from a suspicion that Mr. Gallatin interested himself in the election of their governor against the views of Duane and his friends. I do not believe Mr. Gallatin meddled in it. I was in conversation with him nearly every day during the contest, and never heard him express any bias in the case. The ostensible grounds of the attack on Mr. Gallatin are all either false or futile. 1st. They urge his conversations with John Randolph. But who has revealed these conversations? What evidence have we of them? Merely some oracular sentences from J.R., uttered in the heat of declamation, and never stated with all their circumstances. For instance, that a Cabinet member informed him there was no Cabinet. But Duane himself has always denied there could be a legal one. Besides, the fact was true at that moment, to wit: early in the session of Congress. I had been absent from Washington from the middle of July to within three weeks of their meeting. During the separation of the members there could be no consultation, and between our return to Washington and the meeting of Congress, there really had arisen

---

1 William Wirt, an attorney, served as clerk of the Virginia House of Delegates in 1800 and his political involvement led to friendships with several prominent Virginians, including Thomas Jefferson, James Madison, and James Monroe. In 1807, President Jefferson appointed Wirt prosecuting attorney in the treason trial of Aaron Burr. Though Burr was acquitted of all charges, Wirt had entered the national political arena. He continued to practice law, but he was also a Latin scholar and an author. He served as U.S. Attorney General from 1817 to 1829, the longest tenure in history (West's 2008).

nothing requiring general consultation, nothing which could. not be done in the ordinary way by consultation between the President and the head of the department to which the matter belonged, which is the way everything is transacted which is not difficult as well as important. Mr. Gallatin might therefore have said this as innocently as truly, and a malignant perversion of it was perfectly within the character of John Randolph. But the story of the two millions. Mr. Gallatin satisfied us that this affirmation of J. R. was as unauthorized as the fact itself was false. It resolves itself, therefore, into his inexplicit letter to a committee of Congress. As to this, my own surmise was that Mr. Gallatin might have used some hypothetical expression in conversing on that subject, which J. R. made a positive one, and he being a duelist, and Mr. Gallatin with a wife and children depending on him for their daily subsistence, the latter might wish to avoid collision and insult from such a man. But they say he was hostile to me. This is false. I was indebted to nobody for more cordial aid than to Mr. Gallatin, nor could any man more solicitously interest himself in behalf of another than he did of myself. His conversations with Erskine are objected as meddling out of his department. Why, then, do they not object Mr. Smith's with Rose? The whole nearly, of that negotiation, as far as it was transacted verbally, was by Mr. Smith. The business was in this way explained informally, and on understandings thus obtained, Mr. Madison and myself shaped our formal proceedings. In fact, the harmony among us was so perfect, that whatever instrument appeared most likely to effect the object, was always used without jealousy. Mr. Smith happened to catch Mr. Rose's favor and confidence at once. We perceived that Rose would open himself more frankly to him than to Mr. Madison, and we therefore made him the medium of obtaining an understanding of Mr. Rose. Mr. Gallatin's support of the bank has, I believe, been disapproved by many. He was not in Congress when that was established, and therefore had never committed himself, publicly, .on the constitutionality of that institution, nor do I recollect ever to have heard him declare himself on it. I know he derived immense convenience from it, because they gave the effect of ubiquity to his money wherever deposited. Money in New Orleans or Maine was at his command, and by their agency transformed in an instant into money in London, in Paris, Amsterdam or Canton. He was, therefore, cordial to the bank. I often pressed him to divide the public deposits among all the respectable banks, being indignant myself at the open hostility of that institution to a government on whose treasuries they were fattening. But his repugnance to it prevented my persisting. And if he was in favor of the bank, what is the amount of that crime or error in which he had a majority save one in each House of Congress as participators? Yet on these facts, endeavors are made to drive from the administration the ablest man except the President, who ever was in it, and to beat down the President himself, because he is unwilling to part with so able a counselor. I believe Duane to be a very honest man and sincerely republican; but his passions are stronger than his prudence, and his personal as well as general antipathies render him very intolerant. These traits lead him astray, and require his readers, even those who value him for his steady support of the republican cause, to be on their guard against his occasional aberrations. He is eager for war against England, hence his abuse of the two last Congresses. But the people wish for peace. The re-elections of the same men prove it. And indeed, war against Bedlam would be just as rational as against Europe in its present condition of total demoralization. When peace becomes more losing than war, we may prefer the latter on principles of pecuniary calculation. But for us to attempt, by war, to reform all Europe, and bring them back to principles of morality and a respect for the equal rights of nations, would show us to be only maniacs of another character. We should, indeed, have the merit of the good intentions as well as of the folly of the hero of La Mancha. But I am getting beyond the object of my letter, and will therefore here close it with assurances of my great esteem and respect.

WILLIAM DUANE, 1811, 13:65 - *TO THE PRINCIPLES OF UNION I SACRIFICE ALL MINOR DIFFERENCES OF OPINION.*

To Colonel William Duane
Monticello, July 25, 1811

Dear Sir, Your letter of the 5th, with the volume of Montesquieu accompanying it, came to hand in due time; the latter indeed in lucky time, as, enclosing it by the return of post, I was enabled to get it into Mr. Warden's hands before his departure, for a friend abroad to whom it will be a most acceptable offering. Of the residue of the copies I asked, I would wish to receive one well bound for my own library, the others in boards as that before sent. One of these in boards may come to me by post, for use until the others are received, which I would prefer having sent by water, as vessels depart almost daily from Philadelphia for Richmond. Messrs. Gibson & Jefferson of that place will receive and forward the packet to me. Add to it, if you please, a copy of Franklin's works, bound, and send me by post a note of the amount of the whole, and of my newspaper account, which has been suffered to run in arrear by the difficulty of remitting small and fractional sums to a distance, from a canton having only its local money, and little commercial intercourse beyond its own limits.

I learnt with sincere regret that my former letters had given you pain. Nothing could be further from their intention. What I had said and done was from the most friendly dispositions towards yourself, and from a zeal for maintaining the Republican ascendency. Federalism, stripped as it now nearly is, of its landed and laboring support, is monarchism and Anglicism, and whenever our own dissensions shall let these in upon us, the last ray of free government closes on the horizon of the world. I have been lately reading Komarzewski's *coup d'oeil* on the history of Poland. Though without any charms of style or composition, it gives a lesson which all our countrymen should study; the example of a country erased from the map of the world by the dissensions of its own citizens. The papers of every day read them the counter lesson of the impossibility of subduing a people acting with an undivided will. Spain, under all her disadvantages, physical and mental, is an encouraging example of this. She proves, too, another truth not less valuable, that a people having no king to sell them for a mess of pottage for himself, no shackles to restrain their powers of self-defense, find resources within themselves equal to every trial. This we did during the Revolutionary War, and this we can do again, let who will attack us, if we act heartily with one another. This is my creed. To the principles of union I sacrifice all minor differences of opinion. These, like differences of face, are a law of our nature, and should be viewed with the same tolerance. The clouds which have appeared for some time to be gathering around us, have given me anxiety lest an enemy, always on the watch, always prompt and firm, and acting in well-disciplined phalanx, should find an opening to dissipate hopes, with the loss of which I would wish that of life itself. To myself personally the sufferings would be short. The powers of life have declined with me more in the last six months than in as many preceding years. A rheumatic indisposition, under which your letter found me, has caused this delay in acknowledging its receipt, and in the expressions of regret that I had inadvertently said or done anything which had given you uneasiness. I pray you to be assured that no unkind motive directed me, and that my sentiments of friendship and respect continue the same.

JAMES MAURY, 1812, 13:144 - *IF EVER I WAS GRATIFIED WITH THE POSSESSION OF POWER...IT WAS ON THAT OCCASION WHEN I WAS ENABLED TO USE [IT] FOR THE PREVENTION OF WAR.*

To James Maury[1]
Monticello, April 25, 1812

My Dear and Ancient Friend and Classmate, Often has my heart smote me for delaying acknowledgments to you, receiving, as I do, such frequent proofs of your kind recollection in the transmission of papers to me. But instead of acting on the good old maxim of not putting off to tomorrow what we can do today, we are too apt to reverse it, and not to do today what we can put off to tomorrow. But this duty can be no longer put off. Today we are at peace; tomorrow, war. The curtain of separation is drawing between us, and probably will not be withdrawn till one, if not both of us, will be at rest with our fathers. Let me now, then, while I may, renew to you the declarations of my warm attachment, which in no period of life has ever been weakened, and seems to become stronger as the remaining objects of our youthful affections are fewer.

---

1 Both Jefferson and Madison had been students under James Maury's father, and, upon Jefferson's recommendation, in 1790 President Washington commissioned Maury as Consul at Liverpool, the third consular commission issued under the Constitution. Maury's service under that commission continued until the outbreak of the War of 1812. President Madison recommissioned him Consul at Liverpool on March 3, 1815, and he served under that commission until his retirement Sept. 1, 1829 (Barnes 1961, 105).

Our two countries are to be at war, but not you and I. And why should our two countries be at war, when by peace we can be so much more useful to one another? Surely the world will acquit our government from having sought it. Never before has there been an instance of a nation's bearing so much as we have borne. Two items alone in our catalogue of wrongs will forever acquit us of being the aggressors: the impressment of our seamen, and the excluding us from the ocean. The first foundations of the social compact would be broken up, were we definitively to refuse to its members the protection of their persons and property, while in their lawful pursuits. I think the war will not be short, because the object of England, long obvious, is to claim the ocean as her domain, and to exact transit duties from every vessel traversing it. This is the sum of her orders of council, which were only a step in this bold experiment, never meant to be retracted if it could be permanently maintained. And this object must continue her in war with all the world. To this, I see no termination, until her exaggerated efforts, so much beyond her natural strength and resources, shall have exhausted her to bankruptcy. The approach of this crisis is, I think, visible in the departure of her precious metals, and depreciation of her paper medium. We, who have gone through that operation, know its symptoms, its course, and consequences. In England they will be more serious than elsewhere, because half the wealth of her people is now in that medium, the private revenue of her money-holders, or rather of her paper-holders, being, I believe, greater than that of her land-holders. Such a proportion of property, imaginary and baseless as it is, cannot be reduced to vapor but with great explosion. She will rise out of its ruins, however, because her lands, her houses, her arts will remain, and the greater part of her men. And these will give her again that place among nations which is proportioned to her natural means, and which we all wish her to hold. We believe that the just standing of all nations is the health and security of all. We consider the overwhelming power of England on the ocean, and of France on the land, as destructive of the prosperity and happiness of the world, and wish both to be reduced only to the necessity of observing moral duties. We believe no more in Bonaparte's fighting merely for the liberty of the seas, than in Great Britain's fighting for the liberties of mankind. The object of both is the same, to draw to themselves the power, the wealth and the resources of other nations. We resist the enterprises of England first, because they first come vitally home to us. And our feelings repel the logic of bearing the lash of George the III for fear of that of Bonaparte at some future day. When the wrongs of France shall reach us with equal effect, we shall resist them also. But one at a time is enough; and having offered a choice to the champions, England first takes up the gauntlet.

The English newspapers suppose me the personal enemy of their nation. I am not so. I am an enemy to its injuries, as I am to those of France. If I could permit myself to have national partialities, and if the conduct of England would have permitted them to be directed towards her, they would have been so. I thought that in the administration of Mr. Addington, I discovered some dispositions toward justice, and even friendship and respect for us, and began to pave the way for cherishing these dispositions, and improving them into ties of mutual good will. But we had then a federal minister there, whose dispositions to believe himself, and to inspire others with a belief, in our sincerity, his subsequent conduct has brought into doubt; and poor Merry, the English minister here, had Jefferson's Works learned nothing of diplomacy but its suspicions, without head enough to distinguish when they were misplaced. Mr. Addington and Mr. Fox passed away too soon to avail the two countries of their dispositions. Had I been personally hostile to England, and biased in favor of either the character or views of her great antagonist, the affair of the *Chesapeake* put war into my hand. I had only to open it and let havoc loose. But if ever I was gratified with the possession of power, and of the confidence of those who had entrusted me with it, it was on that occasion when I was enabled to use both for the prevention of war, towards which the torrent of passion here was directed almost irresistibly, and when not another person in the United States, less supported by author-ity and favor, could have resisted it. And now that a definitive adherence to her impressments and orders of council renders war no longer avoidable, my earnest prayer is that our government may enter into no compact of com-mon cause with the other belligerent, but keep us free to make a separate peace, whenever England will separately give us peace and future security. But Lord Liverpool is our witness that this can never be but by her removal from our neighborhood.

I have thus, for a moment, taken a range into the field of politics, to pos-sess you with the view we take of things here. But in the scenes which are to ensue, I am to be but a spectator. I have withdrawn myself from all politi-cal intermeddlings, to indulge the evening of my life with what have been the passions of every portion of it, books, science, my farms, my family and friends. To these every hour of the day is now devoted. I retain a good activ-ity of mind, not quite as much of body, but uninterrupted health. Still the hand of age is upon me. All my old friends are nearly gone. Of those in my neighborhood, Mr. Divers and .Mr. Lindsay alone remain. If you could make it a *partie quarree*, it would be a comfort indeed. We would beguile our lin-gering hours with talking over our youthful exploits, our hunts on Peter's mountain, with a long train of *et cetera*, in addition, and feel, by recollection at least, a momentary flash of youth. Reviewing the course of a long and suf-ficiently successful life, I find in no portion of it happier moments than those were. I think the old hulk in which you are, is near her wreck, and that like a prudent rat, you should escape in time. However, here, there, and every-where, in peace or in war, you will have my sincere affections and prayers for your life, health and happiness.

JAMES MADISON, 1812, 13:139 ~ *I THINK A PEOPLE WOULD GO THROUGH A WAR WITH MUCH LESS IMPATIENCE IF THEY COULD DISPOSE OF THEIR PRODUCE.*

To the President of the United States (James Madison)
Monticello, April 17, 1812

Dear Sir, The enclosed papers will explain themselves. Their coming to me is the only thing not sufficiently explained.

Your favor of the 3d came duly to hand. Although something of the kind had been apprehended, the embargo found the farmers and planters only getting their produce to market, and selling as fast as they could get it there. I think it caught them in this part of the State with one-third of their flour or wheat and three-quarters of their tobacco undisposed of. If we may suppose the rest of the middle country in the same situation, and that the upper and lower country may be judged by that as a mean, these will perhaps be the proportions of produce remaining in the hands of the producers. Supposing the objects of the government were merely to keep our vessels and men out of harm's way, and that there is no idea that the want of our flour will starve Great Britain, the sale of the remaining produce will be rather desirable, and what would be desired even in war, and even to our enemies. For I am favorable to the opinion which has been urged by others, sometimes acted on, and now partly so by France and Great Britain, that commerce, under certain restrictions and licenses, may be indulged between enemies mutually advantageous to the individuals, and not to their injury as belligerents. The capitulation of Amelia Island, if confirmed, might favor this object, and at any rate get off our produce now on hand. I think a people would go through a war with much less impatience if they could dispose of their produce, and that unless a vent can be provided for them, they will soon become querulous and clamor for peace. They appear at present to receive the embargo with perfect acquiescence and without a murmur, seeing the necessity of taking care of our vessels and seamen. Yet they would be glad to dispose of their produce in any way not endangering them, as by letting it go from a neutral place in British vessels. In this way we lose the carriage only; but better that than both carriage and cargo. The rising of the price of flour, since the first panic is passed away, indicates some prospects in the merchants of disposing of it. Our wheat had greatly suffered by the winter, but is as remarkably recovered by the favorable weather of the spring. Ever affectionately yours.

ROBERT WRIGHT, 1812, 13:184 ~ *IT SHOULD TAKE MORE TO MAKE PEACE THAN TO PREVENT WAR. THE SWORD ONCE DRAWN, FULL JUSTICE MUST BE DONE.*

To the Honorable Robert Wright[1]

---

1 Robert Wright was born in Maryland in 1752. During the Revolutionary War, he fought in several battles, and earned the rank of captain by the time he was mustered out in 1777. Wright entered politics in 1777, serving as a member of the Maryland House of Delegates. He also served as a member of the Maryland State Senate in 1801, and was a member of the U.S. Senate from 1801 to 1806. Wright was elected governor of Maryland on November

Monticello, August 8, 1812

Dear Sir, I receive and return the congratulations of your letter of July 6 with pleasure, and join the great mass of my fellow citizens in saying, "Well done, good and faithful servants, receive the benedictions which your constituents are ready to give you." The British government seem to be doing late, what done earlier might have prevented war; to wit: repealing the orders in Council. But it should take more to make peace than to prevent war. The sword once drawn, full justice must be done. "Indemnification for the past and security for the future," should be painted on our banners. For 1,000 ships taken, and 6,000 seamen impressed, give us Canada for indemnification, and the only security they can give us against their Henrys, and the savages, and agree that the American flag shall protect the persons of those sailing under it, both parties exchanging engagements that neither will receive the seamen of the other on board their vessels. This done, I should be for peace with England and then war with France. One at a time is enough, and in fighting the one we need the harbors of the other for our prizes. Go on as you have begun, only quickening your pace, and receive the benedictions and prayers of those who are too old to offer anything else.

JAMES RONALDSON, 1813, 13:204 ~ *TO KEEP THE WAR POPULAR, WE MUST KEEP OPEN THE MARKETS. AS LONG AS GOOD PRICES CAN BE HAD, THE PEOPLE WILL SUPPORT THE WAR CHEERFULLY.*

To James Ronaldson[1]
Monticello, January 12, 1813

Dear Sir, Your favor of November 2d arrived a little before I set out on a journey on which I was absent between five and six weeks. I have still therefore to return you my thanks for the seeds accompanying it, which shall be duly taken care of, and a communication made to others of such as shall prove valuable. I have been long endeavoring to procure the Cork tree from Europe, but without success. A plant which I brought with me from Paris died after languishing some time, and of several parcels of acorns received from a correspondent at Marseilles, not one has ever vegetated. I shall continue my endeavors, although disheartened by the nonchalance of our Southern fellow citizens, with whom alone they can thrive. It is now twenty-five years since I sent them two shipments (about 500 plants) of the Olive tree of Aix, the finest Olives in the world. If any of them still exist, it is merely as a curiosity in their gardens; not a single orchard of them has been planted. I sent them also the celebrated species of sainfoin from Malta, which yields good crops without a drop of rain through the season. It was lost. The upland rice which I procured fresh from Africa and sent them, has been preserved and spread in

---

10, 1806. He was reelected to a second term in 1807, and to a third term in 1808 (National Governors Association, 2008).

1 James Ronaldson, a Scottish immigrant, was a type maker who began corresponding with Jefferson in late 1805. Their early letters generally dealt with the promotion of business and manufacturing, perhaps prompting Jefferson, in this letter, to comment, "To keep the war [of 1812] popular, we must keep open the markets" (Creesy 2003, 4).

the upper parts of Georgia, and I believe in Kentucky. But we must acknowledge their services in furnishing us an abundance of cotton, a substitute for silk, flax and hemp. The ease with which it is spun will occasion it to supplant the two last, and its cleanliness the first. Household manufacture is taking deep root with us. I have a carding machine, two spinning machines, and looms with the flying shuttle In full operation for clothing my own family; and I verily believe that by the next winter this State will not need a yard of imported coarse or middling clothing. I think we have already a sheep for every inhabitant, which will suffice for clothing, and one-third more, which a single year will add, will furnish blanketing. With respect to marine hospitals, which are one of the subjects of your letter, I presume you know that such establishments have been made by the general government in the several States, that a portion of seaman's wages is drawn for their support, and the government furnishes what is deficient. Mr. Gallatin is attentive to them, and they will grow with our growth. You doubt whether we ought to permit the exportation of grain to our enemies; but Great Britain, with her own agricultural support, and those she can command by her access into every sea, cannot be starved by withholding our supplies. And if she is to be fed at all events, why may we not have the benefit of it as well as others? I would not, indeed, feed her armies landed on our territory, because the difficulty of inland subsistence is what will prevent their ever penetrating far into the country, and will confine them to the sea coast. But this would be my only exception. And as to feeding her armies in the peninsula, she is fighting our battles there, as Bonaparte is on the Baltic. He is shutting out her manufactures from that sea, and so far assisting us in her reduction to extremity But if she does not keep him out of the peninsular, if he gets full command of that, instead of the greatest and surest of all our markets, as that has uniformly been, we shall be excluded from it, or so much shackled by his tyranny and ignorant caprices, that it will become for us what France now is. Besides, if we could by starving the English armies, oblige hem to withdraw from the peninsular, it would be to send them here; and I think we had better feed them there for pay, than feed and fight them here for nothing. A truth, too, not to be lost sight of is, that no country can pay war taxes if you suppress all their resources. To keep the war popular, we must keep open the markets. As long as good prices can be had, the people will support the war cheerfully. If you should have an opportunity of conveying to Mr. Heriot my thanks for his book, you will oblige me by doing it. Accept the assurance of my great esteem and respect.

WILLIAM SHORT, 1813, ME 13:257 ~ *MY PRINCIPLE HAS EVER BEEN THAT WAR SHOULD NOT SUSPEND EITHER EXPORTS OR IMPORTS.*

To William Short
Monticello, June 18, 1812

Dear Sir, Yours of the 2d is received, and a copy of Higgenbotham's mortgage is now enclosed. The journey to Bedford which I proposed in my last my engagements here have obliged me to postpone till after harvest, which is now approaching; it is the most unpromising one I have seen. We have been some days in expectation of seeing M. Correa. If he is on the road, he has had some days of our very hottest weather. My thermometer has been for two days at 92 and 92 1/2 [degrees], the last being the maximum ever seen here. Although we usually have the hottest day of the year in June; yet it is soon interrupted by cooler weather. In July the heat, though not so great, is more continuous and steady.

On the duration of the war I think there is uncertainty. Ever since the rupture of the treaty of Amiens, the object of Great Britain has visibly been the permanent conquest of the ocean, and levying a tribute on every vessel she permits to sail on it, as the Barbary powers do on the Mediterranean, which they call their sea. She must be conscious she cannot from her own resources maintain the exaggerated fleet she now has, and which is necessary to maintain her conquest; she must, therefore, levy the deficiency of duties of transit on other nations. If she should get another ministry with sense enough to abandon this senseless scheme, the war with us ought to be short, because there is no material cause now existing but impressment; and there our only difference is how to establish a mode of discrimination between our citizens which she does not claim, and hers which it is neither our wish nor interest ever to employ. The seamen which our navigation raises had better be of our own. If this be all she aims at, it may be settled at Saint Petersburg. My principle has ever been that war should not suspend either exports or imports. If the piracies of France and England, however, are to be adopted as the law of nations, or should become their practice, it will oblige us to manufacture at home all the material comforts.

This may furnish a reason to check imports until necessary manufactures are established among us. This offers the advantage, too, of placing the consumer of our produce near the producer, but I should disapprove of the prohibition of exports even to the enemy themselves, except indeed refreshments and water to their cruisers on our coast, in order to oblige them to intermit their cruises to go elsewhere for these supplies. The idea of starving them as to bread, is a very idle one. It is dictated by passion, not by reason. If the war is lengthened, we shall take Canada, which will relieve us from Indians, and Halifax, which will put an end to their occupation of the American seas, because every vessel must then go to England to repair every accident. To retain these would become objects of first importance to us, and of great importance to Europe, as the means of curtailing the British marine. But at present, being merely in posse, they should not be an impediment to peace. We have a great and a just claim of indemnifications against them for the thousand ships they have taken piratically, and six thousand seamen impressed. Whether we can, on this score, successfully insist on curtailing their American possessions, by the meridian of Lake Huron, so as to cut them off from the Indians bordering on us, would be matter for conversation and experiment at the treaty of pacification. I sometimes allow my mind to wander thus into the political field, but rarely, and with reluctance. It is my desire as well as my duty to leave to the vigor of younger minds to settle concerns which are no longer mine, but must long be theirs. Affectionately adieu.

JAMES MONROE, 1813, 13:261 - *IT IS MORE A SUBJECT OF JOY THAT WE HAVE SO FEW OF THE DESPERATE CHARACTERS WHICH COMPOSE MODERN REGULAR ARMIES.*

To Colonel James Monroe[1]
Monticello, June 18, 1813

Dear Sir, Your favors of the 7th and 16th are received, and I now return you the memoir enclosed in the former I am much gratified by its communication, because, as the plan appeared in the newspapers soon after the new Secretary of War came into office, we had given him the credit of it. Every line of it is replete with wisdom; and we might lament that our tardy enlistments prevented its execution, were we not to reflect that these proceeded from the happiness of our people at home. It is more a subject of joy that we have so few of the desperate characters which compose modern regular armies. But it proves more forcibly the necessity of obliging every citizen to be a soldier; this was the case with the Greeks and Romans, and must be that of every free State. Where there is no oppression there will be no pauper hirelings. We must train and classify the whole of our male citizens, and make military instruction a regular part of collegiate education. We can never be safe till this is done.

I have been persuaded, *ab initio*, that what we are to do in Canada must be done quickly; because our enemy, with a little time, can empty pickpockets upon us faster than we can enlist honest men to oppose them. If we fail in this acquisition, Hull is the cause of it. Pike, in his situation, would have swept their posts to Montreal, because his army would have grown as it went along. I fear the reinforcements arrived at Quebec will be at Montreal before General Dearborn, and if so, the game is up. If the marching of the militia into an enemy's country be once ceded as unconstitutional (which I hope it never will be), then will their force, as now strengthened, bid us permanent defiance. Could we acquire that country, we might perhaps insist

---

1 Although Jefferson never quite came to support Hamilton's views concerning a standing army, he did come around to believing in the maintenance of a military establishment based upon universal liability to service. In this 1813 letter to Monroe, commenting on a memoir of the Secretary of War, he wrote: "It is more a subject of joy that we have so few of the desperate characters which compose modern regular armies..." And, in retrospect, it is one of the ironies of history that Hamilton's political opponents Jefferson and Madison did more than Hamilton himself to give effect to his protectionist and nationalist views of economic policy. The Embargo, which Jefferson initiated in December 1807, the Non-Intercourse Act, and the succeeding war with Great Britain (upon which Madison reluctantly embarked) had the practical result of closing virtually all avenues of foreign trade and making the United States dependent upon its own resources for manufacturing the munitions of war. Further, the industries which were born under the stress and necessity of the years 1808 to 1815 were the infants to which the nation gave protection in 1816 and in a succession of tariff acts thereafter (Dupuy 1956, 303).

successfully at St. Petersburg on retaining all westward of the meridian of Lake Huron, or of Ontario, or of Montreal, according to the pulse of the place, as an indemnification for the past and security for the future. To cut them off from the Indians even west of the Huron would be a great future security.

Your kind answer of the 16th, entirely satisfies my doubts as to the employment of a navy, if kept within striking distance of our coast, and shows how erroneous views are apt to be with those who have not all in view. Yet, as I know by experience that profitable suggestions sometimes come from lookers on, they may be usefully tolerated, provided they do not pretend to the right of an answer. They would cost very dear, indeed, were they to occupy the time of a high officer in writing when he should be acting.

PIERRE SAMUEL DUPONT DE NEMOURS, 1813, 19:195 - *I CONSIDER OURSELVES AS NOW POSSESSED OF EVERYTHING FROM FLORIDA POINT TO THE WALLS OF QUEBEC.*

To Dupont de Nemours
Monticello, November 29, 1813

My Very Dear and Estimable Friend, In answering the several very kind letters I have received from you, I owe to yourself and to the most able and estimable author of the Commentaries on Montesquieu to begin by assuring you that I am not the author of that work, and of my own consciousness that it is far beyond my qualifications. In truth I consider it as a most profound and logical work which has been presented to the present generation. On the subject of government particularly there is a purity which renders it precious to our country particularly, where I trust it will become the elementary work for the youth of our academies and colleges. The paradoxes of Montesquieu have been too long uncorrected. I will not fail to send you a copy of the work if possible to get it through the perils of the sea.

I am next to return you thanks for the copy of the works of Turgot now completed by the receipt of the last volume. In him we know not which most to admire, the comprehensiveness of his mind or the benevolence and purity of his heart. In his *Distribution of Riches* and other general works, and in the great principles developed in his smaller work we admire the gigantic stature of his mind, but when we see that mind thwarted, harassed, maligned and forced to exert all its powers in the details of provincial administration we regret to see a Hercules laying his shoulder to the wheel of an ox-cart. The sound principles which he establishes in his particular as well as general works, are a valuable legacy to ill-governed man, and will spread from their provincial limits to the great circle of mankind.

I am indebted to you also for your letter by Mr. Correa, and the benefit it procured me of his acquaintance. He was so kind as to pay me a visit at Monticello, which enabled me to see for myself that he was still beyond all the eulogies with which yourself and other friends had preconized him. Learned beyond any one I had before met with, good, modest and of the simplest manners, the idea of losing him again filled me with regret, and how much did I lament that we could not place him at the head of that great institution which I have so long nourished the hope of seeing established in my country, and towards which you had so kindly contributed your luminous views. But, my friend, that institution is still in embryo as you left it, and from the complexion of our popular legislature and the narrow and niggardly views of ignorance courting the suffrage of ignorance to obtain a seat in it, I see little prospect of such an establishment until the national government shall be authorized to take it up and form it on the comprehensive basis of all the useful sciences.

The inauspicious commencement of our war has damped at first the hopes of fulfilling your injunctions to add the Floridas and Canada to our confederacy. The former indeed might have been added but for our steady adherence to the sound principles of national integrity which forbade us to take what was a neighbor's merely because it suited us and especially from a neighbor under circumstances of peculiar affliction. But seeing now that his afflictions do not prevent him from making those provinces a focus of hostile and savage combinations of the massacre of our women and children by the tomahawk and scalping knife of the Indian, these scruples must yield to the necessities of self-defense. And I trust that the ensuing session of Congress will authorize the incorporation of it with ourselves. Their inhabitants universally wish it, and they are in truth the only legitimate proprietors of the soil and government.

Canada might have been ours in the preceding year but for the treachery of our general, who unfortunately commanded on its border. There could have been no serious resistance to the progress of the force he commanded in its march through Upper Canada, but he sold and delivered his army, fortified and furnished as it was, to an enemy one-fourth his numbers. This was followed by a series of losses flowing from the same source of unqualified commanders; carelessness, cowardice, foolhardiness and sheer imbecility lost us four other successive bodies of men, who, under faithful and capable leaders, would have saved us from the affliction and the English from the crime of the thousands of men, women and children murdered and scalped by the savages under her procurement and direction of British officers, some on capitulation, some in the field and some in their houses and beds. The determined bravery of our men, whether regulars or militia, evidenced in every circumstance when the treachery or imbecility of their commanders permitted, still kept up our confidence and sounder and abler men now placed at their head have given us possession of the whole of Upper Canada and the lakes. At the moment I am writing I am in hourly expectation of learning that General Wilkinson, who, about the 10th instant, was descending upon Montreal has taken possession of it, the force of the enemy there being not such as to give us much apprehension. Between that place and Quebec there is nothing to stop us but the advance of the season.

The achievements of our little navy have claimed and obtained the admiration of all, in spite of the endeavors of the English by lying misrepresentations of the force of their vessels on both sides to conceal the truth, the loss indeed of one-half a dozen frigates and sloops of war is no sensible diminution of numbers to them, but the loss of the general opinion that they were invincible at sea, the lesson taught to the world that they can be beaten by an equal force, has by its moral effect lost them half their physical force. I consider ourselves as now possessed of everything from Florida point to the walls of Quebec. This last place is not worth the blood it would cost. It may be considered as impregnable to an enemy not possessing the water. I hope, therefore, we shall not attempt it, but leave it to be voluntarily evacuated by its inhabitants, cut off from all sources of subsistence by the loss of the upper country. I will ask you no questions, my friend, about your return to the United States at your time of life; it is scarcely perhaps advisable. An exchange of the society, the urbanity and the real comforts to which you have been formed by the habits of a long life would be a great and real sacrifice. Whether, therefore, I shall ever see you again or not, let me live in your esteem as you ever will in mine, most affectionately and devotedly.

P.S. Monticello, Dec. 14. We have been disappointed in the result of the expedition against Montreal. The second in command, who had been detached ashore with a large portion of the army, failing to join the main body according to orders at the entrance of the Lake St. Francis, the enterprise was of necessity abandoned at that point, and the inclemency of the winter being already set in, the army was forced to go into winter quarters near that place. Since the date of my letter I have received yours of September 18 and a printed copy of your plan of national education of which I possessed the MS. If I can get this translated and printed, it will contribute to advance the public mind to undertake the institution; the persuading those of the benefit of science who possess none is a slow operation.

THADDEUS KOSCIUSKO, 1813, 19:200 ~ *WHAT IS ATROCIOUS AS AN EXAMPLE BECOMES A DUTY TO REPRESS BY RETALIATION.*

To Thaddeus Kosciusko
Monticello, November 30, 1813

My Dear Friend, I have to acknowledge the receipt of yours of Dec. 1, '12, and its duplicate of May 30, '13, and am pleased that our arrangement with Mr. Morton proves satisfactory. I believed it would be so, and that a substantial and friendly house there might sometimes be a convenience, when, from the dangers of the sea, difficulty of finding good bills, or other casualties, Mr. Barnes' remittances might incur unavoidable delay. He is at this time making arrangements with Mr. Williams, the correspondent of Mr. Morton, for the usual remittance, having for some time past been unable to get a good bill.

You have heard without doubt of the inauspicious commencement of our war by land. Our old officers of high command were all withdrawn by death or age. Scott closed the list of the dead a few weeks ago, and happy for us would it have been could we have followed your advice in appointing new generals; and could we have been directed in our choice to those only who were good. But this is a lottery in which are few prizes and our first draught fell among the blanks. The first called into action delivered his army and fort up to a quarter of his own numbers of the English. He might have taken possession of all Upper Canada almost without resistance. This was followed by cases of surprise, of cowardice, of foolhardiness and of sheer imbecility, by which bodies of men were successively lost as fast as they could be raised; and thus the first year of the war was lost. General Wilkinson, who you knew in the late war, has at length been called from the Southern Department; General Hampton also; and they are doing what their predecessors ought to have done last year. We have taken all the posts and country on Lakes Erie and Ontario; and General Wilkinson, on the 10th instant, was about entering the Lake St. Francis in his descent to Montreal, and would, in three or four days, reach Montreal, where the British force is such as not to give uneasiness for the result. I trust he is now in possession of it, and there being neither a post nor a man between that and Quebec, we may consider ourselves as commanding the whole country to the walls of that city. The season, however, will probably oblige us to make Montreal our winter quarters.

Kingston, at the east end of Lake Ontario, has been left unmolested, because being of some strength and well garrisoned, it would have required a siege and the advance of the season would have disappointed us as to all below; insulated as it is from succors and subsistence it must capitulate at our leisure. This, my friend, is the present state of things by land; and as I know not yet how or when this letter is to go, I may by a P. S., be able to add what shall have actually taken place at Montreal. It is a duty, however, to add that in every instance our men, militia as well as regulars, have acted with an intrepidity which would have honored veteran legions, and have proved that, had their officers understood their duty as well as those of our little navy, they would have shown themselves equally superior to our enemy who had dared to despise us.

On the ocean we have taught a lesson of value to all mankind, that they can be beaten there with equal force. We have corrected the idea of their invincibility, which by its moral effect annihilates half their physical force. I do not believe the naval history of the world has furnished a more splendid achievement of skill and bravery than that of Perry on Lake Erie. They threaten now to hang our prisoners reclaimed by them, although naturalized with us, and if we retaliate, to burn our cities. We shall certainly retaliate, and if they burn New York, Norfolk, Charleston, we must burn London, Portsmouth, Plymouth, not with our ships but by our money; not with our own hands, but by those of their own incendiaries. They have in their streets thousands of famished wretches, who, for a loaf of bread to keep off death one day longer and more eagerly for a million of dollars, will spread to them the flames which they shall kindle in New York. It is not for those who live in glass houses to set the example of throwing stones, what is atrocious as an example becomes a duty to repress by retaliation.

If we have taken, as I expect, the residue of their troops above Quebec, we have as many of their troops taken by honorable fighting as they have of ours purchased or surprised. I have less fear now for our war than for the peace which is to conclude it. Your idea that our line of future demarcation should be from some point in Lake Champlain is a good one, because that would shut up all their scalp markets, but that of their entire removal from the continent is a better one. While they hold a single spot in it, it will be a station from which they will send forth their Henrys upon us to debauch traitors, nourish conspiracies, smuggle in their manufactures and defeat our commercial laws. Unfortunately our peace commissioners left us while our affairs were still under the depression of Hull's treason and its consequences, and they would as soon learn their revival in the moon as in St. Petersburg. The English newspapers will still fill their ears, as those of all Europe, with lies and induce them to offer terms of peace under these erroneous impressions; and a peace which does not leave us the Canadas will be but a truce. As for the Floridas, they are giving themselves to us. I hope, therefore, no peace will be made which does not yield us this indemnification for the thousand of ships they took during peace, the thousands of our citizens impressed, their machinations for dissevering our Union, the insults they have -heaped upon us, the inhuman war they have waged with the tomahawk and scalping knife of the savage, the suffocation of our prisoners in pestiferous jails and prison ships, and the other atrocities against national and individual morality which have degraded them from the rank of civilized nations. The longer the peace is delayed, the more firm will became the establishment of our manufactures. The growth and extent of these can be conceived by none who does not see them. Of coarse and middling fabrics we never again shall import. The manufacture of the fine cottons is carried also to great extent and perfection. A million of cotton spindles nearly being, I think, now employed in the United States. This single advancement in economy, begun by our embargo law, continued by that of non-importation, and confirmed by the present total cessation of commercial intercourse, was worth alone all the war will cost us.

I have thus, my dear friend, given you the present state of things with us, which I had done with the more minuteness because I know that no native among us takes a livelier interest in them than you do. The tree which you had so zealously assisted in planting you cannot but delight in seeing watered and flourishing. Happy for us would it have been if a valor, fidelity and skill like yours had directed those early efforts which were so unfortunately confided to unworthy hands. We should have been a twelve month ago where we now are, and now where we shall be a twelve month hence. However from one man we can have but one life, and you gave us the most valuable and active part of yours, and we are now enjoying and improving its effects. Every sound American, every sincere votary of freedom, loves and honors you, and it was its enemies only and the votaries of England who saw with cold indifference and even secret displeasure your short-lived return to us. They love none who do not love kings, and kings of England above all others. Cod bless you under every circumstance, whether still reserved for the good of your native country or destined to leave us in the fullness of time with the consciousness of successful efforts for the establishment of freedom in one country and of all which man could have done for its success in another. The lively sense I entertain of all you have done and deserved from both countries, can be extinguished only with the lamp of life, during which I shall ever be, affectionately and devotedly, yours.

P. S. Monticello, Dec. 14. We have been disappointed in the result of the expedition against Montreal, and again by the fault of a general who refused with his large detachment ashore to meet the main body, according to orders, at the entrance of Lake St. Francis. The expedition was of necessity suspended at that point and the army obliged by the severity of the season to go into winter quarters.

WILLIAM SHORT, 1814, 18:280 - *THE DESTRUCTIVE PASSIONS SEEM TO HAVE BEEN IMPLANTED IN MAN, AS ONE OF THE OBSTACLES TO HIS TOO GREAT MULTIPLICATION.*

To William Short
Monticello, August 20, 1814

Dear Sir, Since my short letter by Mr. Rives I have to acknowledge the receipt of your two favors of June 9 and July 30. A few days before the last came to hand I had written to Colonel Monroe, and prayed him to name a day in the autumn (when the fall of the leaves shall have rendered a survey in the woods practicable), and to procure an engagement from Champe Carter to attend and let us have a surveyor and arbitrators on the spot to settle the questioned boundary. I delayed answering your last letter in the hope that he might in the instant of receiving my letter write to me off-hand. Having failed to do this, the time of his answering is too indefinite to postpone further the giving you the present state and prospect of the business which you desire.

The state of the case is this: John Carter, eldest son of the family, sold to Monroe, bounding him "on the South by a run on the Eastern side of Dick's plantation, and running thence to the source of the said run," but no line was actually marked or examined by either party. It is said that John Carter had no right to sell, but that Champe, from family considerations, concluded to acquiesce. I do not know that this fact is true, having it only from neighborhood report. Champe afterwards sold to you, and attended us in surveying and marking the line. Ascending the run far above Dick's plantation, it forked, each run being equally large, and extending nearly to the top of the mountain, but the southern branch something the nearest. We knew nothing of the line specified in Monroe's deed, but Mr. Carter, professing to know it and to lead the surveyor, started from the fork and run a straight line between the two branches to the top of the mountain, thus dividing the interval which the two branches rendered doubtful; but not a word of any doubt was then expressed; I presumed he knew what was right and was doing it. Colonel Monroe, sometime after his return from Europe, mentioned to me in conversation that the line as run between you and him by Mr. Carter, was, as he had been informed, questionable, but he could not then explain to me how; nor did I ever learn how till after the sale to Higgenbotham. Indeed from the continued silence on the subject I believed the claim dropped till I received a line from Higginbotham informing me Mr. Hay had notified him of it, and Colonel Monroe soon afterwards called on me, showed his deed, and explained to me for the first time the nature of his claim. We agreed that Mr. Carter should be desired to attend, that we would take two neighbors as arbitrators, go on the land and settle the question on view. The topics of your right are these: I. If Champe Carter's confirmation of John's sale were necessary to supply the defect of title, then the demarcation of the line which he made in person was a declaration of the precise extent to which he did confirm. II. The run, which was made the boundary to its source, branching by the way, and each branch being equally entitled to be considered as the run whose source was to decide, neither could claim exclusively to be called Dick's run; the compromise made by Mr. Carter by running the line between them was a fair one, and after an acquiescence of 21 years, and that length of actual and adverse possession in you, ought to be considered as satisfactory to the parties, and especially when no effective step had been taken to maintain a contrary claim till after the land had been long notified as for sale, and a sale actually made; the delay of the settlement has entirely rested with the other party. Price, who knows the two branches, thinks there may be about 25 acres between them, one half of which only is within the actual line.

Next, as to the prospect. On closing this letter I shall write to John Carter, who lives in Amherst, for information as to his right and his idea of the boundary, and if his information is of consequence I shall either get his deposition taken by consent of parties, or require his personal attendance as a witness. I must press upon Colonel Monroe the fixing a day when he can attend, and some one to act for him if he does not attend. Champe Carter, I suppose, will readily agree to be bound if he does not attend. I should have been very confident of finishing this at Monroe's next visit, for he is anxious to finish it, but that the call of Congress, the nineteenth of September will render his attendance difficult. If so, I will endeavor to prevail on him to appoint some one here to act for him; for his personal presence cannot be of much importance.

I think the downfall of Bonaparte a great blessing for Europe, which never could have had peace while he was in power. Every national society there also will be restored to their ancient limits, and to the kind of government, good or bad, which they choose. I believe the restoration of the Bourbons is the only point on which France could be rallied, and that their reestablishment is better for that country than civil wars, whether they should be a peaceable nation under a fool or a warring one under a military despot of genius. To us alone this brings misfortune. It rids of all other enemies a tyrannical nation, fully armed, and deeply embittered by the wrongs they have done us. They may greatly distress individuals in their circumstances; but the soil and the men will remain unconquerable by them, and drinking deeper daily a more deadly, unquenchable, and everlasting hatred to them. How much less money would it cost to them and pain to us, to nourish mutual affections and mutual interests and happiness. But the destructive passions seem to have been implanted in man, as one of the obstacles to his too great multiplication. While we are thus gnawed, however, by national hatreds we retire with delight into the bosom of our individual friendships; in the full feeling of which I salute you affectionately.

THOMAS COOPER, 1814, 14:179 ~ *THE GREEKS AND ROMANS HAD NO STANDING ARMIES, YET THEY DEFENDED THEMSELVES. THE GREEKS BY THEIR LAWS, AND THE ROMANS BY THE SPIRIT OF THEIR PEOPLE.*

To Dr. Thomas Cooper[1],[2]
Monticello, September 10, 1814

Dear Sir, I regret much that I was so late in consulting you on the subject of the academy we wish to establish here.[3] The progress of that business has obliged me to prepare an address to the President of the Board of Trustees—a plan for its organization. I send you a copy of it with a broad margin, that, if your answer to mine of August 25th be not on the way, you may be so good as to write your suggestions either in the margin or on a separate paper. We shall still be able to avail ourselves of them by way of amendments.

Your letter of August 17th is received. Mr. Ogilvie left us four days ago, on a tour of health, which is to terminate at New York, from whence he will take his passage to Britain to receive livery and seisin of his new dignities and fortunes. I am in the daily hope of seeing M. Corrica, and the more anxious as I must in two or three weeks commence a journey of long absence from home.

---

1 In his executive capacity, Jefferson came into intimate contact with military discouragements through his nominal command of the militia. He found it a poor tool, yet all his life he remained an advocate of voluntary in preference to professional military service. That the militia of the Revolution was a poor reliance appeared to Jefferson no justification for the curse of standing armies, and no excuse to the citizen for the evasion of his highest duty (Sears 1927, 7). Now, to Cooper, he straightforwardly states: "The Greeks and Romans had no standing armies, yet they defended themselves. The Greeks by their laws, and the Romans by the spirit of their people, took care to put into the hands of their rulers no such engine of oppression as a standing army."

2 Jefferson felt that the corruption and poverty that he observed during his travels through Europe as ambassador to France were the products of the unequal division of property among the people, the dependency this created for laborers upon the landed few, and the consequent impoverishment created by an excess labor force and an inability of workers to bargain for fair incomes. Now, some thirty years later, in this letter to Cooper he (perhaps too) idealistically notes that in the United States "we have no paupers" and that "the old and crippled among us, who possess nothing and have not families to take care of them" are too few to constitute a separate portion of society or to constitute "a separate estimate" (Hart 2002, 194).

3 This is a reference to the University of Virginia (Jefferson 1999, 136).

A comparison of the conditions of Great Britain and the United States, which is the subject of your letter of August 17th, would be an interesting theme indeed. To discuss it minutely and demonstratively would be far beyond the limits of a letter. I will give you, therefore, in brief only, the result of my reflections on the subject. I agree with you in your facts, and in many of your reflections. My conclusion is without doubt, as I am sure yours will be, when the appeal to your sound judgment is seriously made. The population of England is composed of three descriptions of persons (for those of minor note are. too inconsiderable to affect a general estimate). These are, 1. The aristocracy, comprehending the nobility, the wealthy commoners, the high grades of priesthood, and the officers of government. 2. The laboring class. 3. The eleemosynary class, or paupers, who are about one-fifth of the whole. The aristocracy, which have the laws and government in their hands, have so managed them as to reduce the third description below the means of supporting life, even by labor; and to force the second, whether employed in agriculture or the arts, to the maximum of labor which the construction of the human body can endure, and to the minimum of food, and of the meanest kind, which will preserve it in life, and in strength sufficient to perform its functions. To obtain food enough, and clothing, not only their whole strength must be unremittingly exerted, but the utmost dexterity also which they can acquire; and those of great dexterity only can keep their ground, while those of less must sink into the class of paupers. Nor is it manual dexterity alone, but the acutest resources of the mind also which are impressed into this struggle for life; and such as have means a little above the rest, as the master-workmen, for instance, must strengthen themselves by acquiring as much of the philosophy of their trade as will enable them to compete with their rivals, and keep themselves above ground. Hence the industry and manual dexterity of their journeymen and day-laborers, and the science of their master-workmen, keep them in the foremost ranks of competition with those of other nations; and the less dexterous individuals, falling into the eleemosynary ranks, furnish materials for armies and navies to defend their country, exercise piracy on the ocean, and carry conflagration, plunder and devastation, on the shores of all those who endeavor to withstand their aggressions. A society thus constituted possesses certainly the means of defense. But what does it defend? The pauperism of the lowest class, the abject oppression of the laboring, and the luxury, the riot, the domination and the vicious happiness of the aristocracy. In their hands, the paupers are used as tools to maintain their own wretchedness, and to keep down the laboring portion by shooting them whenever the desperation produced by the cravings of their stomachs drives them into riots. Such is the happiness of scientific England; now let us see the American side of the medal.

And, first, we have no paupers, the old and crippled among us, who possess nothing and have no families to take care of them, being too few to merit notice as a separate section of society, or to affect a general estimate. The great mass of our population is of laborers; our rich, who can live without labor, either manual or professional, being few, and of moderate wealth. Most of the laboring class possess property, cultivate their own lands, have families, and from the demand for their labor are enabled to exact from the rich and, the competent such prices as enable them to be fed abundantly, clothed above mere decency, to labor moderately and raise their families. They are not driven to the ultimate resources of dexterity and skill, because their wares will sell although not quite so nice as those of England. The wealthy, on the other hand, and those at their ease, know nothing of what the Europeans call luxury. They have only somewhat more of the comforts and decencies of life than those who furnish them. Can any condition of society be more desirable than this? Nor in the class of laborers do I mean to withhold from the comparison that portion whose color has condemned them, in certain parts of our Union, to a subjection to the will of others. Even these are better fed in these States, warmer clothed, and labor less than the journeymen or day-laborers of England. They have the comfort, too, of numerous families, in the midst of whom they live without want, or fear of it; a solace which few of the laborers of England possess. They are subject, it is true, to bodily coercion; but are not the hundreds of thousands of British soldiers and seamen subject to the same, without seeing, at the end of their career, when age and accident shall have rendered them unequal to labor, the certainty, which the other has, that he will never want? And has not the British seaman, as much as the African, been reduced to this bondage by force, in flagrant violation of his own consent, and of his natural right in his own person? and with the laborers of England generally, does 0 not the moral coercion of want subject their will as despotically to that of their employer, as the physical constraint does the soldier, the seaman, or the slave? But do not mistake me. I am not advocating slavery. I am not justifying the wrongs we have committed on a foreign people, by the example of another nation committing equal wrongs on their own subjects. On the contrary, there is nothing I would not sacrifice to a practicable plan of abolishing every vestige of this moral and political depravity. But I am at present comparing the condition and degree of suffering to which oppression has reduced the man of one color, with the condition and degree of suffering to which oppression has reduced the man of another color; equally condemning both. Now let us compute by numbers the sum of happiness of the two countries. In England, happiness is the lot of the aristocracy only; and-the proportion they bear to the laborers and paupers, you know better than I do. Were I to guess that they are four in every hundred, then the happiness of the nation would be to its misery as one in twenty-five. In the United States it is as eight millions to zero, or as all to none. But it is said they possess the means of defense, and that we do not. How so? Are we not men? Yes; but our men are so happy at home that they will not hire themselves to be shot at for a shilling a day. Hence, we can have no standing armies for defense, because we have no paupers to furnish the materials. The Greeks and Romans had no standing armies, yet they defended themselves. The Greeks by their laws, and the Romans by the spirit of their people, took care to put into the hands of their rulers no such engine of oppression as a standing army. Their system was to make every man a soldier, and oblige him to repair to the standard of his country whenever that was reared. This made them invincible; and the same remedy will make us so. In the beginning of our government we were willing to introduce the least coercion possible on the will of the citizen. Hence a system of military duty was established too indulgent to his indolence. This is the first opportunity we have had of trying it, and it has completely failed; an issue foreseen by many, and for which remedies have been proposed. That of classing the militia according to age, and allotting each age to the particular kind of service to which it was competent, was proposed to Congress in 1805 ,and subsequently; and, on the last trial was lost, I believe, by a single vote only. Had it prevailed, what has now happened would not have happened. Instead of burning our Capitol, we should have possessed theirs in Montreal and Quebec. We must now adopt it, and all will be safe. We had in the United States in 1805, in round numbers of free, able-bodied men,

120,000 of the ages of 18 to 21 inclusive.

200,000 " " 22 " 26 "

200,000 " " 27 " 35 "

200,000 " " 35 " 45 "

In all, 720,000 " " 18 " 45 "

With this force properly classed, organized, trained, armed and subject to tours of a year of military duty, we have no more to fear for the defense of our country than those who have the resources of despotism and pauperism.

But, you will say, we have been devastated in the meantime. True, some of our public buildings have been burnt, and some scores of individuals on the tide-water have lost their movable property and their houses. I pity them, and execrate the barbarians who delight in unavailing mischief. But these individuals have their lands and their hands left. They are not paupers, they have still better means of subsistence than 24/25 of the people of England. Again, the English have burnt our Capitol and President's house by means of their force. We can burn their St. James' and St. Paul's by means of our money, offered to their own incendiaries, of whom there are thousands in London who would do it rather than starve. But it is against the laws of civilized warfare to employ secret incendiaries. Is it not equally so to destroy the works of art by armed incendiaries? Bonaparte, possessed , at times of almost every capital of Europe, with all his despotism and power, injured no monument of art. If a nation, breaking through all the restraints of civilized character, uses its means of destruction (power, for example) without distinction of objects, may we not use our means (our money and their pauperism) to retaliate their barbarous ravages? Are we obliged to use for resistance exactly the weapons chosen by them for aggression? When they destroyed Copenhagen by superior force, against all the laws of God and man, would it have been unjustifiable for the Danes to have destroyed their ships by torpedoes? Clearly not; and they and we should now be justifiable in the conflagration of St. James' and St. Paul's. And if we do not carry it into execution, it is because we think it more moral and more honorable to set a good example, than follow a bad one.

So much for the happiness of the people of England, and the morality of their government, in comparison with the happiness and the morality of America. Let us pass to another subject.

The crisis, then, of the abuses of banking is arrived. The banks have pronounced their own sentence of death. Between two and three hundred millions of dollars of their promissory notes are in the hands of the people, for solid produce and property sold, and they formally declare they will not pay them. This is an act of bankruptcy of course, and will be so pronounced by any court before which it shall be brought. But *cui bono*? The law can only uncover their insolvency, by opening to its suitors their empty vaults. Thus by the dupery of our citizens, and tame acquiescence of our legislators, the nation is plundered of two or three hundred millions of dollars, treble the amount of debt contracted in the Revolutionary war, and which, instead of redeeming our liberty, has been expended on sumptuous houses, carriages, and dinners. A fearful tax! if equalized on all; but overwhelming and convulsive by its partial fall. The crush will be tremendous; very different from that brought on by our paper money. That rose and fell so gradually that it kept all on their guard, and affected severely only early or long-winded contracts. Here the contract of yesterday crushes in an instant the one or the other party. The banks stopping payment suddenly, all their mercantile and city debtors do the same; and all, in short, except those in the country, who, possessing property, will be good in the end. But this resource will not enable them to pay a cent on the dollar. From the establishment of the United States Bank, to this day, I have preached against this system, but have been sensible no cure could be hoped but in the catastrophe now happening. The remedy was to let banks drop gradation at the expiration of their charters, and for the State governments to relinquish the power of establishing others. This would not, as it should not, have given the power of establishing them to Congress. But Congress could then have issued treasury notes payable within a fixed period, and founded on a specific tax, the proceeds of which, as they came in, should be exchangeable for the notes of that particular emission only. This depended, it is true, on the will of the State legislatures, and would have brought on us the phalanx of paper interest. But that interest is now defunct. Their gossamer castles are dissolved, and they can no longer impede and overawe the salutary measures of the government. Their paper was received on a belief that it was cash on demand. Themselves have declared it was nothing, and such scenes are now to take place as will open the eyes of credulity and of insanity itself, to the dangers of a paper medium abandoned to the discretion of avarice and of swindlers. It is impossible not to deplore our past follies, and their present consequences, but let them at least be warnings against like follies in future. The banks have discontinued themselves. We are now without any medium; and necessity, as well as patriotism and confidence, will make us all eager to receive treasury notes, if founded on specific taxes. Congress may now borrow of the public, and without interest, all the money they may want, to the amount of a competent circulation, by merely issuing their own promissory notes, of proper denominations for the larger purposes of circulation, but not for the small. Leave that door open for the entrance of metallic money. And, to give readier credit to their bills, without obliging themselves to give cash for them on demand, let their collectors be instructed to do so, when they have cash; thus, in some measure, performing the functions of a bank, as to their own notes. Providence seems, indeed, by a special dispensation, to have put down for us, without a struggle, that very paper enemy which the interest of our citizens long since required ourselves to put down, at whatever risk. The work is done. The moment is pregnant with futurity, and if not seized at once by Congress, I know not on what shoal our bark is next to be stranded. The State legislatures should be immediately urged to relinquish the right of establishing banks of discount. Most of them will comply, on patriotic principles, under the convictions of the moment; and the non-complying may be crowded into concurrence by legitimate devices. *Vale, et me, ut amaris, ama.*

JAMES MADISON, 1814, 14:202 - *THE WAR, UNDERTAKEN, ON BOTH SIDES...IS DECLARED BY GREAT BRITAIN TO HAVE CHANGED ITS OBJECT, AND TO HAVE BECOME A WAR OF CONQUEST.*

To James Madison[1]
Monticello, October 15, 1814[2]

I thank you for the information of your letter of the 10th. It gives, at length, a fixed character to our prospects. The war, undertaken, on both sides, to settle the questions of impressment, and the orders of council, now that these are done away by events, is declared by Great Britain to have changed its object, and to have become a war of conquest, to be waged until she conquers from us our fisheries, the province of Maine, the lakes, States and territories north of the Ohio, and the navigation of the Mississippi; in other words, till she reduces us to unconditional submission. On our part, then, we ought to propose, as a counterchange of object, the establishment of the meridian of the mouth of the Sorel northwardly, as the western boundary of all her possessions. Two measures will enable us to effect it, and without these, we cannot even defend ourselves. 1. To organize the militia into classes, assigning to each class the duties for which it is fitted, (which, had it been done when proposed, years ago, would have prevented all our misfortunes,) abolishing by a declaratory law the doubts which abstract scruples in some, and cow-

---

1 At this time — and having succeeded Jefferson — Madison was serving as the fourth president of the United States.

2 To put things in perspective, it should be noted that on August 24, 1814 — a scant three weeks prior to the crafting of this letter — the British had arrived in Washington at about 6 o'clock in the evening. That night they burned the Capitol, the President's House, the Treasury, State and Navy Department Buildings, and a number of private houses on Capitol Hill (Caemmerer 1932, 45).

ardice and treachery in others, have conjured up about passing imaginary lines, and limiting, at the same time, their services to the *contiguous* provinces of the enemy. The 2d is the ways and means. You have seen my ideas on this subject, and I shall add nothing but a rectification of what either I have ill expressed, or you have misapprehended. If I have used any expression restraining the emissions of treasury notes to a sufficient medium, as your letter seems to imply, I have done it inadvertently, and under the impression then possessing me, that the war would be very short. A sufficient medium would not, on the principles of any writer, exceed thirty millions of dollars, and on those of some not ten millions. Our experience has proved it may be run up to two or three hundred millions, without more than doubling what would be the prices of things under a sufficient medium, or say a metallic one, which would always keep itself at the sufficient point; and, if they rise to this term, and the descent from it be gradual, it would not produce sensible revolutions in private fortunes. I shall be able to explain my views more definitely by the use of numbers. Suppose we require, to carry on the war, an annual loan of twenty millions, then I propose that, in the first year, you shall lay a tax of two millions, and emit twenty millions of treasury notes, of a size proper for circulation, and bearing no interest, to the redemption of which the proceeds of that tax shall be inviolably pledged and applied, by recalling annually their amount of the identical bills funded on them. The second year lay another tax of two millions, and emit twenty millions more. The third year the same, and so on, until you have reached the maximum of taxes which ought to be imposed. Let me suppose this maximum to be one dollar a head, or ten millions of dollars, merely as an exemplification more familiar than would be the algebraical symbols x or y. You would reach this in five years. The sixth year, then, still emit twenty millions of treasury notes, and continue all the taxes two years longer. The seventh year twenty millions more, and continue the whole taxes another two years; and so on. Observe, that although you emit twenty millions of dollars a year, you call in ten millions, and, consequently, add but ten millions annually to the circulation. It would be in thirty years, then, *prima facie*, that you would reach the present circulation of three hundred millions, or the ultimate term to which we might adventure. But observe, also, that in that time we shall have become thirty millions of people to whom three hundred millions of dollars would be no more than one hundred millions to us now; which sum would probably not have raised prices more than fifty per cent. on what may be deemed the standard, or metallic prices. This increased population and consumption, while it would be increasing the proceeds of the redemption tax, and lessening the balance annually thrown into circulation, would also absorb, without saturation, more of the surplus medium, and enable us to push the same process to a much higher term, to one which we might safely call indefinite, because extending so far beyond the limits, either in time or expense, of any supposable war. All we should have to do would be, when the war should be ended, to leave the gradual extinction of these notes to the operation of the taxes pledged for their redemption; not to suffer a dollar of paper to be emitted either by public or private authority, but let the metallic medium flow back into the channels of circulation, and occupy them until another war should oblige us to recur, for its support, to the same resource, and the same process, on the circulating medium. The citizens of a country like ours will never have unemployed capital. Too many enterprises are open, offering high profits, to permit them to lend their capitals on a regular and moderate interest. They are too enterprising and sanguine themselves not to believe they can do better with it.[1] I never did believe you could have gone beyond a first or a second loan, not from a want of confidence in the public faith, which is perfectly sound, but from a want of disposable funds in individuals. The circulating fund is the only one we can ever command with certainty. It is sufficient for all our wants; and the impossibility of even defending the country without its aid as a borrowing fund, renders it indispensable that the nation should take and keep it in their own hands, as their exclusive resource. I have trespassed on your time so far, for explanation only. I will do it no further than by adding the assurances of my affectionate and respectful attachment.

Years.	Emissions.	Taxes and Redemptions.	Bal. in circulation at end of year.
1815	20 millions	2 millions	18 millions.
1816	20 millions	4 millions	34 millions.
1817	20 millions	6 millions	48 millions.
1818	20 millions	8 millions	60 millions.
1819	20 millions	10 millions	70 millions.
1820	20 millions	10 millions	80 millions.
1821	20 millions	10 millions	90 millions.
	140		

Suppose the war to terminate here, to wit, at the end of seven years, the reduction will proceed as follows:

Years.	Taxes and Redemptions.	Bal. in circulation at end of year.
1822	10 millions	80 millions
1823	10 millions	70 millions

---

1 The financial requirements of the War of 1812 would prompt the United States to seek to change from being a nation whose predominant interests were centered in foreign trade and agriculture to one whose principal energies were devoted to manufacturing. This conflict, even more than the Revolutionary War, stimulated the development of the West and started an era of geographical specialization which carried the nation to new heights of industrialization (Steiner 1942, 1-3).

Years.	Taxes and Redemptions.	Bal. in circulation at end of year.
1824	10 millions	60 millions
1825	10 millions	50 millions
1826	10 millions	40 millions
1827	10 millions	30 millions
1828	10 millions	20 millions
1829	10 millions	10 millions
1830	10 millions	0 millions
	140	

This is a tabular statement of the amount of emissions, taxes, redemptions, and balances left in circulation every year, on the plan above sketched.

JAMES MONROE, 1814, 14:207 - IT IS NONSENSE TO TALK OF REGULARS. THEY ARE NOT TO BE HAD AMONG A PEOPLE SO EASY AND HAPPY AT HOME AS OURS.

To James Monroe[1]

MONTICELLO, OCTOBER 16, 1814

Dear Sir, Your letter of the 10th has been duly received. The objects of our contest being thus entirely changed by England, we must prepare for interminable war. To this end we should put our house in order, by providing men and money to indefinite extent. The former may be done by classing our militia, and assigning each class to the description of duties for which it is fit. It is nonsense to talk of regulars. They are not to be had among a people so easy and happy at home as ours. We might as well rely on calling down an army of angels from heaven. I trust it is now seen that the refusal to class the militia, when proposed years ago, is the real source of all our misfortunes in this war. The other great and indispensable object is to enter on such a system of finance, as can be permanently pursued to any length of time whatever. Let us be allured by no projects of banks, public or private, or ephemeral expedients, which, enabling us to gasp and flounder a little longer, only increase, by protracting the agonies of death.   Perceiving, in a letter from the President,

---

1 With respect to the consideration of a militia. In reality, if nothing more than a skeleton standing army was to be tolerated, then America's main reliance must be upon the militia. But to be effective, the militia would have to be equipped and trained. It would have to be classified by age group, with the main obligation falling upon the younger men. It would also have to be available, in wartime, outside the borders of its particular state and for periods of longer than the usual ninety days. But these steps were never taken, as they entailed a form of conscription, inconvenience, and expense. Still, Jefferson and Madison knew what was needed, and it was quite clear that an efficient militia was in agreement with Republican doctrine. So, essentially, in this letter, Jefferson was informing Monroe — who was then holding joint appointments as both Secretary of War and Secretary of State — of what he already knew when he wrote, "It is nonsense to talk of regulars...." etc. But, too, it is fair to say that Jefferson both exaggerated and oversimplified, for some professional soldiers were obviously required and some were indeed raised (May 1960, 35).

that either I had ill expressed my ideas on a particular part of this subject, in the letters I sent you, or he had misapprehended them, I wrote him yesterday an explanation; and as you have thought the other letters worth a perusal, and a communication to the Secretary of the Treasury, I enclose you a copy of this, lest I should be misunderstood by others also. Only be so good as to return me the whole when done with, as I have no other copies.

Since writing the letter now enclosed, I have seen the report of the committee of finance, proposing taxes to the amount of twenty millions. This is a dashing proposition. But, if Congress pass it, I shall consider it sufficient evidence that their constituents generally can pay the tax. No man has greater confidence than I have, in the spirit of the people, to a rational extent. Whatever they can, they will. But, without either market or medium, I know not how it is to be done. All markets abroad, and all at home, are shut to us; so that we have been feeding our horses on wheat. Before the day of collection, bank-notes will be but as oak leaves; and of specie, there is not within all the United States, one-half of the proposed amount of the taxes. I had thought myself as bold as was safe in contemplating, as possible, an annual taxation of ten millions, as a fund for emissions of treasury notes; and, when further emissions should be necessary, that it would be better to enlarge the time, than the tax for redemption. Our position, with respect to our enemy, and our markets, distinguishes us from all other nations; inasmuch, as a state of war, with us, annihilates in an instant all our surplus produce, that on which we depended for many comforts of life. This renders peculiarly expedient the throwing a part of the burdens of war on times of peace and commerce. Still, however, my hope is that others see resources, which, in my abstraction from the world, are unseen by me; that there will be both market and medium to meet these taxes, and that there are circumstances which render it wiser to levy twenty millions at once on the people, than to obtain the same sum on a tenth of the tax.

I enclose you a letter from Colonel James Lewis, now of Tennessee, who wishes to be appointed Indian agent, and I do it lest he should have relied solely on this channel of communication. You know him better than I do, as he was long your agent. I have always believed him an honest man, and very good-humored and accommodating. Of his other qualifications for the office, you are the best judge. Believe me to be ever affectionately yours.

WILLIAM SHORT, 1814, 14:211 ~ *[IF ANOTHER NATION THROWS]* *DOWN THE GAUNTLET OF WAR OR SUBMISSION AS THE ONLY ALTERNATIVES, WE CANNOT BLAME THE GOVERNMENT FOR CHOOSING THAT OF WAR.*

To William Short
Monticello, November 28, 1814

Dear Sir, Yours of October 28th came to hand on the 15th instant only. The settlement of your boundary with Colonel Monroe, is protracted by circumstances which seem foreign to it. One would hardly have expected that the hostile expedition to Washington could have had any connection with an operation one hundred miles distant. Yet preventing his attendance, nothing could be done. I am satisfied there is no unwillingness on his part, but on the contrary a desire to have it settled; and therefore, if he should think it indispensable to be present at the investigation, as is possible, the very first time he comes here I will press him to give a day to the decision, without regarding Mr. Carter's absence. Such an occasion must certainly offer soon after the fourth of March, when Congress rises of necessity, and be assured I will not lose one possible moment in effecting it.

Although withdrawn from all anxious attention to political concerns, yet I will state my impressions as to the present war, because your letter leads to the subject. The essential grounds of the war were, 1st the orders of council; and 2d, the impressment of our citizens; (for I put out of sight from the love of peace the multiplied insults on our government and aggressions on our commerce, with which our pouch, like the Indian's, had long been filled to the mouth.) What immediately produced the declaration was, 1st the proclamation of the Prince Regent that he would never repeal the orders of council as to us, until Bonaparte should have revoked his decrees as to all other nations as well as ours; and 2d, the declaration of his minister to ours that no arrangement whatever could be devised, admissible in lieu of impressment. It was certainly a misfortune that they did not know themselves at the date of this silly and insolent proclamation, that within one month they would repeal the orders, and that we, at the date of our declaration, could not know of the repeal which was then going on one thousand leagues distant. Their determinations, as declared by themselves, could alone guide us, and they shut the door on all further negotiation, throwing down to us the gauntlet of war or submission as the only alternatives. We cannot blame the government for choosing that of war, because certainly the great majority of the nation thought it ought to be chosen, not that they were to gain by it in dollars and cents; all men know that war is a losing game to both parties. But they know also that if they do not resist encroachment at some point, all will be taken from them, and that more would then be lost even in dollars and cents by submission than resistance. It is the case of giving a part to save the whole, a limb to save life. It is the melancholy law of human societies to be compelled sometimes to choose a great evil in order to ward off a greater; to deter their neighbors from rapine by making it cost them more than honest gains. The enemy are accordingly now disgorging what they had so ravenously swallowed. The orders of council had taken from us near one thousand vessels. Our list of captures from them is now one thousand three hundred, and, just become sensible that it is small and not large ships which gall them most, we shall probably add one thousand prizes a year to their past losses. Again, supposing that, according to the confession of their own minister in Parliament, the Americans they had impressed were something short of two thousand, the war against us alone cannot cost them less than twenty millions of dollars a year, so that each American impressed has already cost them ten thousand dollars, and every year will add five thousand dollars more to his price. We, I suppose, expend more; but had we adopted the other alternative of submission, no mortal can tell what the cost would have been. I consider the war then as entirely justifiable on our part, although I am still sensible it is a deplorable misfortune to us. It has arrested the course of the most remarkable tide of prosperity any nation ever experienced, and has closed such prospects of future improvement as were never before in the view of any people. Farewell all hopes of extinguishing public debt! farewell all visions of applying surpluses of revenue to the improvements of peace rather than the ravages of war. Our enemy has indeed the consolation of Satan on removing our first parents from Paradise: from a peaceable and agricultural nation, he makes us a military and manufacturing one. We shall indeed survive the conflict. Breeders enough will remain to carry on population. We shall retain our country, and rapid advances in the art of war will soon enable us to beat our enemy, and probably drive him from the continent. We have men enough, and I am in hopes the present session of Congress will provide the means of commanding their services. But I wish I could see them get into a better train of finance. Their banking projects are like dosing dropsy with more water. If anything could revolt our citizens against the war, it would be the extravagance with which they are about to be taxed. It is strange indeed that at this day, and in a country where English proceedings are so familiar, the principles and advantages of funding should be neglected, and expedients resorted to. Their new bank, if not abortive at its birth, will not last through one campaign; and the taxes proposed cannot be paid. How can a people who cannot get fifty cents a bushel for their wheat, while they pay twelve dollars a bushel for their salt, pay five times the amount of taxes they . ever paid before? Yet that will be the case in all the States south of the Potomac. Our resources are competent to the maintenance of the war if duly economized and skillfully employed in the way of anticipation. However, we must suffer, I suppose, from our ignorance in funding, as we did from that of fighting, until necessity teaches us both; and, fortunately, our stamina are so vigorous as to rise superior to great mismanagement. This year I think we shall have learnt how to call forth our force, and by the next I hope our funds, and even if the state of Europe should not by that time give the enemy employment enough nearer home, we shall leave him nothing to fight for here. These are my views of the war. They embrace a great deal of sufferance, trying privations, and no benefit but that of teaching our enemy that he is never to gain by wanton injuries on us. To me this state of things brings a sacrifice of all tranquility and comfort through the residue of life. For although the debility of age disables me from the services and sufferings of the field, yet, by the total annihilation in value of the produce which was to give me subsistence and independence, I shall be like Tantalus, up to the shoulders in water, yet dying with thirst. We can make indeed enough to eat, drink and clothe ourselves; but nothing for our salt, iron, groceries and taxes, which must be paid in money. For what can we raise for the market? Wheat? We can only give it to our horses, as we have been doing ever since harvest. To-bacco? It is not worth the pipe it is smoked in. Some say whiskey; but all mankind must become drunkards to consume it. But although we feel, we shall not flinch. We must consider now, as in the Revolutionary war, that although the evils of resistance are great, those of submission would be greater. We must meet, therefore, the former as the casualties of tempests and earthquakes, and like them necessarily resulting from the constitution of the world. Your situation, my dear friend, is much better. For, although I do not know with certainty the nature of your investments, yet I presume they are not in banks, insurance companies, or any other of those gossamer castles. If in ground-rents, they are solid; if in stock of the United States, they are equally so. I once thought that in the event of a war we should be obliged to suspend paying the interest of the public debt. But a dozen years more of experience and observation on our people and government, have satisfied me it will never be done. The sense of the necessity of public credit is so univer-sal and so deeply rooted, that no other necessity will prevail against it; and I am glad to see that while the former eight millions are steadfastly applied to the sinking of the old debt, the Senate have lately insisted on a sinking fund for the new. This is the dawn of that improvement in the management of our finances which I look to for salvation; and I trust that the light will continue to advance, and point out their way to our legislators. They will soon see that instead of taxes for the whole year's expenses, which the people cannot pay, a tax to the amount of the interest and a reasonable portion of the principal will command the whole sum, and throw a part of the burdens of war on times of peace and prosperity. A sacred payment of interest is the only way to make the most of their resources, and a sense of that renders your income from our funds more certain than mine from lands. Some apprehend danger from the defection of Massachusetts. It is a disagreeable circumstance, but not a dangerous one. If they become neutral, we are sufficient for one enemy without them, and in fact we get no aid from them now. If their administra-tion determines to join the enemy, their force will be annihilated by equality of division among themselves. Their federalists will then call in the English army, the republicans ours, and it will only be a transfer of the scene of war from Canada to Massachusetts; and we can get ten men to go to Massachu-setts for one who will go to Canada. Every one, too, must know that we can at any moment make peace with England at the expense of the navigation and fisheries of Massachusetts. But it will not come to this. Their own peo-ple will put down these factionists as soon as they see the real object of their opposition; and of this Vermont, New Hampshire, and even Connecticut it-self, furnish proofs.

You intimate a possibility of your return to France, now that Bonaparte is put down. I do not wonder at it; France, freed from that monster, must again become the most agreeable country on earth. It would be the second choice of all whose ties of family and fortune give a preference to some other one, and the first of all not under those ties. Yet I doubt if the tranquility of France is entirely settled. If her Pretorian bands are not furnished with employment on her external enemies, I fear they will recall the old, or set up some new cause.

God bless you and preserve you in bodily health. Tranquility of mind depends much on ourselves, and greatly on due reflection "how much pain have cost us the evils which have never happened." Affectionately adieu.

CORREA DE SERRA, 1814, 14:221 - *TO DO WRONG IS A MELANCHOLY RESOURCE, EVEN WHERE RETALIATION RENDERS IT INDISPENSABLY NECESSARY.*

To Monsieur Correa de Serra[1]
Monticello, December 27, 1814

Dear Sir, Yours of the 9th has been duly received, and I thank you for the recipe for imitating purrolani, which I shall certainly try on my cisterns the ensuing summer. The making them impermeable to water is of great consequence to me. That one chemical subject may follow another, I enclose you two morsels of ore found in this neighborhood, and supposed to be of antimony. I am not certain, but I believe both are from the same piece, and although the very spot where that was found is not known, yet it is known to be within a certain space not too large to be minutely examined, if the material be worth it. This you can have ascertained in Philadelphia, where it is best known to the artists how great a desideratum antimony is with them.

You will have seen that I resigned the chair of the American Philosophical Society, not awaiting your further information as to the settlement of the general opinion on a successor without schism. I did it because the term of election was too near to admit further delay.

On the subject which entered incidentally into our conversation while you were here, when I came to reflect maturely, I concluded to be silent. To do wrong is a melancholy resource, even where retaliation renders it indispensably necessary. It is better to suffer much from the scalpings, the conflagrations, the rapes and rapine of savages, than to countenance and strengthen such barbarisms by retortion. I have ever deemed it more honorable and more profitable too, to set a good example than to follow a bad one. The good opinion of mankind, like the lever of Archimedes, with the given fulcrum, moves the world. I therefore have never proposed or mentioned the subject to any one.

I have received a letter from Mr. Say, in which he expresses a thought of removing to this country, having discontinued the manufactory in which he was engaged; and he asks information from me of the prices of land, labor, produce, etc., in the neighborhood of Charlottesville, on which he has cast his eye. Its neighborhood has certainly the advantages of good soil, fine climate, navigation to market, and rational and republican society. It would be

---

1 A lifelong friend and visitor to Monticello, Joseph Correa de Serra was a Portuguese diplomat, philosopher, intellectual and scientist. This letter reflects no small measure of candor with respect to war and various collateral issues (Schachner 1957, 931).

a good enough position too for the reestablishment of his cotton works, on a moderate scale, and combined with the small plan of agriculture to which he seems solely to look. But when called on to name prices, what is to be said? We have no fixed prices now. Our dropsical medium is long since divested of the quality of a medium of value; nor can I find any other. In most countries a fixed quantity of wheat is perhaps the best permanent standard. But here the blockade of our whole coast, preventing all access to a market, has depressed the price of that, and exalted that of other things, in opposite directions, and, combined with the effects of the paper deluge, leaves really no common measure of values to be resorted to. This paper, too, received now without confidence, and for momentary purposes only, may, in a moment, be worth nothing. I shall think further on the subject, and give to Mr. Say the best information in my power. To myself such an addition to our rural society would be inestimable; and I can readily conceive that it may be for the benefit of his children and their descendants to remove to a country where, for enterprise and talents, so many avenues are open to fortune and fame. But whether, at his time of life, and with habits formed for the state of society in France, a change for one so entirely different will be for his personal happiness, you can better judge than myself.

Mr. Say will be surprised to find, that forty years after the development of sound financial principles by Adam Smith and the economists, and a dozen years after he has given them to us in a corrected, dense and lucid form, there should be so much ignorance of them in our country; that instead of funding issues of paper on the hypothecation of specific redeeming taxes, (the only method of anticipating, in a time of war, the resources of times of peace, tested by the experience of nations,) we are trusting to tricks of jugglers on the cards, to the illusions of banking schemes for the resources of the war, and for the cure of colic to inflations of more wind. The wise proposition of the Secretary of War, too, for filling our ranks with regulars, and putting our militia into an effective form, seems to be laid aside. I fear, therefore, that, if the war continues, it will require another year of sufferance for men and money to lead our legislators into such a military and financial regimen as may carry us through a war of any length. But my hope is in peace. The negotiators at Ghent are agreed now on every point save one, the demand and cession of a portion of Maine. This, it is well known, cannot be yielded by us, nor deemed by them an object for continuing a war so expensive, so injurious to their commerce and manufactures, and so odious in the eyes of the world. But it is a thread to hold by until they can hear the result, not of the Congress of Vienna, but of Hartford. When they shall know, as they will know, that nothing will be done there, they will let go their hold, and complete the peace of the world, by agreeing to the *status ante bellum*. Indemnity for the past, and security for the future, which was our motto at the beginning of this war, must be adjourned to another, when, disarmed and bankrupt, our enemy shall be less able to insult and plunder the world with impunity. This will be after my time. One war, such as that of our Revolution, is enough for

one life. Mine has been too much prolonged to make me the witness of a second, and I hope for a *coup de grace* before a third shall come upon us. If, indeed,
Europe has matters to settle which may reduce this *hostis humani generis* to a
state of peace and moral order, I shall see that with pleasure, and then sing,
with old Simcon, *nunc dimittis Domine*. For yourself, *cura ut valeas, et me, ut amaris,
ama*.

JAMES MONROE, 1815, 14:226 ~ *PRIVATEERS WILL FIND THEIR OWN MEN AND MONEY. LET NOTHING BE SPARED TO ENCOURAGE THEM.*

To Colonel James Monroe
Monticello, January 1, 1815

Dear Sir, Your letters of November the 30th and December the 21st have
been received with great pleasure. A truth now and then projecting into the
ocean of newspaper lies, serves like headlands to correct our course. Indeed,
my skepticism as to everything I see in a newspaper, makes me indifferent
whether I ever see one. The embarrassments at Washington, in August last,
I expected would be great in any state of things; but they proved greater
than expected. I never doubted that the plans of the President were wise and
sufficient. Their failure we all impute, 1, to the insubordinate temper of Armstrong; and 2, to the indecision of Winder.[1] However, it ends well. It mortifies
ourselves, and so may check, perhaps, the silly boasting spirit of our newspapers, and it enlists the feelings of the world on our side; and the advantage of
public opinion is like that of the weather-gauge in a naval action. In Europe,
the transient possession of our capital can be no disgrace. Nearly every capital there was in possession of its enemy; some often and long. But diabolical
as they paint that enemy, he burnt neither public edifices nor private dwellings. It was reserved for England to show that Bonaparte, in atrocity, was an
infant to their ministers and their generals. They are taking his place in the
eyes of Europe, and have turned into our channel all its good will. This will
be worth the million of dollars the repairs of their conflagration will cost us.
I hope that to preserve this weather-gauge of public opinion, and to coun-
teract the slanders and falsehoods disseminated by the English papers, the
government will make it a standing instruction to their ministers at foreign
courts, to keep Europe truly informed of occurrences here, by publishing in
their papers the naked truth always, whether favorable or unfavorable. For
they will believe the good, if we candidly tell them the bad also.

But you have two more serious causes of uneasiness; the want of men
and money. For the former, nothing more wise or efficient could have been
imagined than what you proposed. It would have filled our ranks with regulars, and that, too, by throwing a just share of the burden on the purses of
those whose persons are exempt either by age or office; and it would have
rendered our militia, like those of the Greeks and Romans, a nation of war-

---

1 Secretary of War John Armstrong, who resigned, and General William Winder, commander of
U.S. forces in the capital region, were obvious and immediate targets of criticism after the
British burning of Washington (Stefanelli 2008).

riors. But the go-by seems to have been given to your proposition, and longer sufferance is necessary to force us to what is best. We seem equally incorrigible to our financial course. Although a century of British experience has proved to what a wonderful extent the funding on specific redeeming taxes enables a nation to anticipate in war the resources of peace, and although the other nations of Europe have tried and trodden every path of force or folly in fruitless quest of the same object, yet we still expect to find in juggling tricks and banking dreams, that money can be made out of nothing, and in sufficient quantity to meet the expenses of a heavy war by sea and land. It is said, indeed, that money cannot be borrowed from our merchants as from those of England. But it can be borrowed from our people. They will give you all the necessaries of war they produce, if, instead of the bankrupt trash they now are obliged to receive for want of any other, you will give them a paper promise funded on a specific pledge, and of a size for common circulation. But you say the merchants will not take this paper. What the people take, the merchants must take, or sell nothing. All these doubts and fears prove only the extent of the dominion which the banking institutions have obtained over the minds of our citizens, and especially of those inhabiting cities or other banking places; and this dominion must be broken, or it will break us. But here, as in the other case, we must make up our minds to suffer yet longer before we can get right. The misfortune is, that in the meantime we shall plunge ourselves in inextinguishable debt, and entail on our posterity an inheritance of eternal taxes, which will bring our government and people into the condition of those of England, a nation of pikes and gudgeons, the latter bred merely as food for the former. But, however these difficulties of men and money may be disposed of, it is fortunate that neither of them will affect our war by sea. Privateers will find their own men and money. Let nothing be spared to encourage them. They are the dagger which strikes at the heart of the enemy, their commerce. Frigates and seventy-fours are a sacrifice we must make, heavy as it is, to the prejudices of a part of our citizens. They have, indeed, rendered a great moral service, which has delighted me as much as any one in the United States. But they have had no physical effect sensible to the enemy; and now, while we must fortify them in our harbors and keep armies to defend them, our *privateers* are bearding and blockading the enemy in their own seaports. Encourage them to burn all their prizes, and let the public pay for them. They will cheat us enormously. No matter; they will make the merchants of England feel, and squeal, and cry out for peace.

I much regretted your acceptance of the War Department. Not that I know a person who I think would better conduct it. But, conduct it ever so wisely, it will be a sacrifice of yourself. Were an angel from heaven to undertake that office, all our miscarriages would be ascribed to him. Raw troops, no troops, insubordinate militia, want of arms, want of money, want of provisions, all will be charged to want of management in you. I speak from experience, when I was Governor of Virginia. Without a regular in the State, and scarcely a musket to put into the hands of the militia; invaded by two armies, Arnold's from the sea-board and Cornwallis' from the southward, when we were driven from Richmond and Charlottesville, and every member of my council fled from their homes, it was not the total destitution of means, but the mismanagement of them, which, in the querulous voice of the public, caused all our misfortunes. It ended, indeed, in the capture of the whole hostile force, but not till means were brought us by General Washington's army, and the French fleet and army. And although the legislature, who were personally intimate with both the means and measures, acquitted me with justice and thanks, yet General Lee has put all those imputations among the romances of his historical novel, for the amusement of credulous and uninquisitive readers. Not that I have seen the least disposition to censure you. On the contrary, your conduct on the attack of Washington has met the praises of every one, and your plan for regulars and militia, their approbation. But no campaign is as yet opened. No Generals have yet an interest in shifting their own incompetence on you, no army agents their rogueries. I sincerely pray you may never meet censure where you will deserve most praise, and that your own happiness and prosperity may be the result of your patriotic services.

Ever and affectionately yours,

P. H. WENDOVER, 1815, 14:279 – *I CONSIDER THE WAR [OF 1812]...*
AS 'MADE ON GOOD ADVICE,' THAT IS, FOR JUST CAUSES.

To P.H. Wendover[1],[2]
Monticello, March 13, 1815

Sir, Your favor of January the 30th was received after long delay on the road, and I have to thank you for the volume of discourses which you have been so kind as to send me. I have gone over them with great satisfaction, and concur with the able preacher in his estimate of the character of the belligerents in our late war, and lawfulness of defensive war. I consider the war, with him, as "made on good advice," that is, for just causes, and its dispensation as providential, inasmuch as it has exercised our patriotism and submission to order, has planted and invigorated among us arts of urgent necessity, has manifested the strong and the weak parts of our republican institutions, and the excellence of a representative democracy compared with the misrule of kings, has rallied the opinions of mankind to the natural rights of expatriation, and of a common property in the ocean, and raised us to that grade in the scale of nations which the bravery and liberality of our citizen soldiers, by land and by sea, the wisdom of our institutions and their observance of justice, entitled us to in the eyes of the world. All this Mr. McLeod has well proved, and from these sources of argument particularly which belong to his profession. On one question only I differ from him, and it is that which

---

1 This letter is endorsed "not sent."
2 Peter Hercules Wendover was a member of Congress from Representative from New York state (United States Congress 2008).

constitutes the subject of his first discourse, the right of discussing public affairs *in the pulpit.* I add the last words, because I admit the right in *general conversation* and in *writing;* in which last form it has been exercised in the valuable book you have now favored me with.

The mass of human concerns, moral and physical, is so vast, the field of knowledge requisite for man to conduct them to the best advantage is so extensive, that no human being can acquire the whole himself, and much less in that degree necessary for the instruction of others. It has of necessity, then, been distributed into different departments, each of which, singly, may give occupation enough to the whole time and attention of a single individual. Thus we have teachers of Languages, teachers of Mathematics, of Natural Philosophy, of Chemistry, of Medicine, of Law, of History, of Government, etc. Religion, too, is a separate department, and happens to be the only one deemed requisite for all men, however high or low. Collections of men associate together, under the name of congregations, and employ a religious teacher of the particular sect of opinions of which they happen to be, and contribute to make up a stipend as a compensation for the trouble of delivering them, at such periods as they agree on, lessons in the religion they profess. If they want instruction in other sciences or arts, they apply to other instructors; and this is generally the business of early life. But I suppose there is not an instance of a single congregation which has employed their preacher for the mixed purposes of lecturing them front the pulpit in Chemistry, in Medicine, in Law, in the science and principles of Government, or in anything but Religion exclusively. Whenever, therefore, preachers, instead of a lesson in religion, put them off with a discourse on the Copernican system, on chemical affinities, on the construction of government, or the characters or conduct of those administering it, it is a breach of contract, depriving their audience of the kind of service for which they are salaried, and giving them, instead of it, what they did not want, or, if wanted, would rather seek from better sources in that particular art or science. In choosing our pastor we look to his religious qualifications, without inquiring into his physical or political dogmas, with which we mean to have nothing to do. I am aware that arguments may be found, which may twist a thread of politics into the cord of religious duties. So may they for every other branch of human art or science. Thus, for example, it is a religious duty to obey the laws of our country; the teacher of religion, therefore, must instruct us in those laws, that we may know how to obey them. It is a religious duty to assist our sick neighbors; the preacher must, therefore, teach us medicine, that we may do it understandingly. It is a religious duty to preserve our own health; our religious teacher, then, must tell us what dishes are wholesome, and give us recipes in cookery, that we may learn how to prepare them. And so, ingenuity, by generalizing more and more, may amalgamate all the branches of science into any one of them, and the physician who is paid to visit the sick, may give a sermon instead of medicine, and the merchant to whom money is sent for a hat, may send a handkerchief instead of it. But notwithstanding this possible confusion of all sciences into one, common sense draws lines between them sufficiently distinct for the general purposes of life, and no one is at a loss to understand that a recipe in medicine or cookery, or a demonstration in geometry, is not a lesson in religion. I do not deny that a congregation may, if they please, agree with their preacher that he shall instruct them in Medicine also, or Law, or Politics. Then, lectures in these, from the pulpit, become not only a matter of right, but of duty also. But this must be with the consent of every individual; because the association being voluntary, the mere majority has no right to apply the contributions of the minority to purposes unspecified in the agreement of the congregation. I agree, too, that on all other occasions, the preacher has the right, equally with every other citizen, to express his sentiments, in speaking or writing, on the subjects of Medicine, Law, Politics, etc., his leisure time being his own, and his congregation not obliged to listen to his conversation or to read his writings; and no one would have regretted more than myself, had any scruple as to this right withheld from us the valuable discourses which have led to the expression of an opinion as to the true limits of the right. I feel my portion of indebtment to the reverend author for the distinguished learning, the logic and the eloquence with which he has proved that religion, as well as reason, confirms the soundness of those principles on which our government has been founded and its rights asserted.

These are my views on this question. They are in opposition to those of the highly respected and able preacher, and are, therefore, the more doubtingly offered. Difference of opinion leads to inquiry, and inquiry to truth; and that, I am sure, is the ultimate and sincere object of us both. We both value too much the freedom of opinion sanctioned by our Constitution, not to cherish its exercise even where in opposition to ourselves.

Unaccustomed to reserve or mystery in the expression of my opinions, I have opened myself frankly on a question suggested by your letter and present. And although I have not the honor of your acquaintance, this mark of attention, and still more the sentiments of esteem so kindly expressed in your letter, are entitled to a confidence that observations not intended for the public will not be ushered to their notice, as has happened to me sometimes. Tranquility, at my age, is the balm of life. While I know I am safe in the honor and charity of a McLeod, I do not wish to be cast forth to the Marats, the Dantons, and the Robespierres of the priesthood; I mean the Parishes, the Ogdens, and the Gardiners of Massachusetts.

I pray you to accept the assurances of my esteem and respect.

JAMES MADISON, 1815, 14:290 ~ PEACE AND HAPPINESS ARE PREFERABLE TO THAT FALSE HONOR WHICH, BY ETERNAL WARS, KEEPS THEIR PEOPLE IN ETERNAL LABOR, WANT, AND WRETCHEDNESS.

To the President of the United States (James Madison)
Monticello, March 23, 1815

Dear Sir, I duly received your favor of the 12th, and with it the pamphlet on the causes and conduct of the war, which I now return. I have read it with great pleasure, but with irresistible desire that it should be published. The reasons in favor of this are strong, and those against it are so easily gotten over, that there appears to me no balance between them. 1. We need it in Europe. They have totally mistaken our character. Accustomed to rise at a feather themselves, and to be always fighting, they will see in our conduct, fairly stated, that acquiescence under wrong, to a certain degree, is wisdom, and not pusillanimity; and that peace and happiness are preferable to that false honor which, by eternal wars, keeps their people in eternal labor, want, and wretchedness. 2. It is necessary for the people of England, who have been deceived as to the causes and conduct of the war, and do not entertain a doubt, that it was entirely wanton and wicked on our part, and under the order of Bonaparte. By rectifying their ideas, it will tend to that conciliation which is absolutely necessary to the peace and prosperity of both nations. 3. It is necessary for our own people, who, although they have known the details as they went along, yet have been so plied with false facts and false views by the federalists, that some impression has been left that all has not been right. It may be said that it will be thought unfriendly. But truths necessary for our own character, must not be suppressed out of tenderness to its calumniators. Although written, generally, with great moderation, there may be some things in the pamphlet which may perhaps irritate. The characterizing every act, for example, by its appropriate epithet, is not necessary to show its deformity to an intelligent reader. The naked narrative will present it truly to his mind, and the more strongly, from its moderation, as he will perceive that no exaggeration is aimed at. Rubbing down these roughnesses and they are neither many nor prominent, and preserving the original date, might, I think, remove all the offensiveness, and give more effect to the publication. Indeed, I think that a soothing postscript, addressed to the interests, the prospects, and the sober reason of both nations, would make it acceptable to both. The trifling expense of reprinting it ought not to be considered a moment. Mr. Gallatin could have it translated into French, and suffer it to get abroad in Europe without either avowal or disavowal. But it would be useful to print some copies of an appendix, containing all the documents referred to, to be preserved in libraries, and to facilitate to the present and future writers of history, the acquisition of the materials which test the truth it contains.

I sincerely congratulate you on the peace, and more especially on the *éclat* with which the war was closed. The affair of New Orleans was fraught with useful lessons to ourselves, our enemies, and our friends, and will powerfully influence our future relations with the nations of Europe. It will show them we mean to take no part in their wars, and count no odds when engaged in our own. I presume that, having spared to the pride of England her formal acknowledgment of the atrocity of impressment in an article of the treaty, she will concur in a convention for relinquishing it. Without this, she must understand that the present is but a truce, determinable on the first act of impressment of an American citizen, committed by any officer of hers. Would it not be better that this convention should be a separate act, unconnected with any treaty of commerce, and made an indispensable preliminary to all other treaty? If blended with a treaty of commerce, she will make it the price of injurious concessions. Indeed, we are infinitely better without such treaties with any nation.[1] We cannot too distinctly detach ourselves from the European system, which is essentially belligerent, nor too sedulously cultivate an American system, essentially pacific. But if we go into commercial treaties at all, they should be with all, at the same time, with whom we have important commercial relations. France, Spain, Portugal, Holland, Denmark, Sweden, Russia, all should proceed *pari passu.* Our ministers marching in phalanx on the same line, and intercommunicating freely, each will be supported by the weight of the whole mass, and the facility with which the other nations will agree to equal terms of intercourse, will discountenance the selfish higglings of England, or justify our rejection of them. Perhaps, with all of them, it would be best to have but the single article *gentis amicissimae,* leaving everything else to the usages and courtesies of civilized nations. But all these things will occur to yourself, with their counter-consideration.

Mr. Smith wrote to me on the transportation of the library, and, particularly, that it is submitted to your direction. He mentioned, also, that Dougherty would be engaged to superintend it. No one will more carefully and faithfully execute all those duties which would belong to a wagon master. But it requires a character acquainted with books, to receive the library. I am now employing as many hours of every day as my strength will permit, in arranging the books, and putting every one in its place on the shelves, corresponding with its order on the catalogue, and shall have them numbered correspondently. This operation will employ me a considerable time yet. Then I should wish a competent agent to attend, and, with the catalogue in his hand, see that every book is on the shelves, and have their lids nailed on, one by one, as he proceeds. This would take such a person about two days; after which, Dougherty's business would be the mere mechanical removal, at convenience. I enclose you a letter from Mr. Milligan, offering his service, which would not cost more than eight or ten days' reason able compensation. This is necessary for my safety and your satisfaction, as a just caution for the public. You know that there are persons, both in and out of the public councils, who will seize every occasion of imputation on either of us, the more difficult to be repelled in this case, in which a negative could not be proved. If you approve of it, therefore, as soon as I am through the review, I will give notice to Mr. Milligan, or any other person you will name, to come on immediately.

---

1 Jefferson was well aware that the framers of the American Constitution did not anticipate or desire the conclusion of many treaties. For this reason they made the process of treaty conclusion difficult, requiring that the president act only with the advice and consent of two-thirds of the Senators present, some even wishing to require adhesion of the House of Representatives or two-thirds majority of the entire Senate (Wright 1922, 246).

Indeed it would be well worth while to add to his duty, that of covering the books with a little paper, (the good bindings, at least,) and filling the vacancies of the presses with paper parings, to be brought from Washington. This would add little more to the time, as he could carry on both operations at once.

Accept the assurance of my constant and affectionate friendship and respect.

JOHN ADAMS, 1816, 14:393 - *A NATION UNITED CAN NEVER BE CONQUERED...THE OPPRESSORS MAY CUT OFF HEADS AFTER HEADS, BUT LIKE THOSE OF THE HYDRA, THEY MULTIPLY AT EVERY STROKE.*

To John Adams[1]
Monticello, January 11, 1816

Dear Sir, Of the last five months I have passed four at my other domicile, for such it is in a considerable degree. No letters are forwarded to me there, because the cross post to that place is circuitous and uncertain; during my absence, therefore, they are accumulating here, and awaiting acknowledgments. This has been the fate of your favor of November 13th.

I agree with you in all its eulogies on the eighteenth century. It certainly witnessed the sciences and arts, manners and morals, advanced to a higher degree than the world had ever before seen. And might we not go back to the era of the Borgias, by which time the barbarous ages had reduced national morality to its lowest point of depravity, and observe that the arts and sciences, rising from that point, advanced gradually through all the sixteenth, seventeenth and eighteenth centuries, softening and correcting the manners and morals of man? I think, too, we may add to the great honor of science and the arts, that their natural effect is, by illuminating public opinion, to erect it into a censor, before which the most exalted tremble for their future, as well as present fame. With some exceptions only, through the seventeenth and eighteenth centuries, morality occupied an honorable chapter in the political code of nations. You must have observed while in Europe, as I thought I did, that those who administered the governments of the greater powers at least, had a respect to faith, and considered the dignity of their government as involved in its integrity. A wound indeed was inflicted on this character of honor in the eighteenth century by the partition of Poland. But this was the atrocity of a barbarous government chiefly, in conjunction with a smaller one still scrambling to become great, while one only of those already great, and having character to lose, descended to the baseness of an accomplice in

---

1 Just as the end of the Revolutionary War sparked in the new nation a desire to incorporate its political beliefs into the Constitution, so did the coming of peace in 1815 inspire a new wave of American nationalism. Buried, at least for the moment, were old antagonisms. Political arties had disappeared, prosperity was on the rise, and peace prevailed. As Jefferson wrote in this letter to his old political foe, John Adams, "A nation united can never be conquered.... My temperament is sanguine. I steer my bark with hope in the head, leaving fear astern." It was indeed a time of optimism for America's leaders (McCardell 1979, 18).

the crime. France, England, Spain, shared in it only inasmuch as they stood aloof and permitted its perpetration.

How then has it happened that these nations, France especially and England, so great, so dignified, so distinguished by science and the arts, plunged all at once into all the depths of human enormity, threw off suddenly and openly all the restraints of morality, all sensation to character, and unblushingly avowed and acted on the principle that power was right? Can this sudden apostasy from national rectitude be accounted for? The treaty of Pillnitz seems to have begun it, suggested perhaps by the baneful precedent of Poland. Was it from the terror of monarchs, alarmed at the light returning on them from the west, and kindling a volcano under their thrones? Was it a combination to extinguish that light, and to bring back, as their best auxiliaries, those enumerated by you, the Sorbonne, the Inquisition, the Index Expurgatorius, and the knights of Loyola? Whatever it was, the close of the century saw the moral world thrown back again to the age of the Borgias, to the point from which it had departed three hundred years before. France, after crushing and punishing the conspiracy of Pilnitz, went herself deeper and deeper into the crimes she had been chastising. I say France and not Bonaparte; for, although he was the head and mouth, the nation furnished the hands which executed his enormities. England, although in opposition, kept full pace with France, not indeed by the manly force of her own arms, but by oppressing the weak and bribing the strong. At length the whole choir joined and divided the weaker nations among them. Your prophecies to Dr. Price proved truer than mine; and yet fell short of the fact, for instead of a million, the destruction of eight or ten millions of human beings has probably been the effect of these convulsions. I did not, in '89, believe they would have lasted so long, nor have cost so much blood. But although your prophecy has proved true so far, I hope it does not preclude a better final result. That same light from our west seems to have spread and illuminated the very engines employed to extinguish it. It has given them a glimmering of their rights and their power. The idea of representative government has taken root and growth among them. Their masters feel it, and are saving themselves by timely offers of this modification of their powers. Belgium, Prussia, Poland, Lombardy, etc., are now offered a representative organization; illusive probably at first, but it will grow into power in the end. Opinion is power, and that opinion will come. Even France will yet attain representative government. You observe it makes the basis of every Constitution which has been demanded or offered–of that demanded by their Senate; of that offered by Bonaparte; and of that granted by Louis XVIII. The idea then is rooted, and will be established, although rivers of blood may yet flow between them and their object. The allied armies now couching upon them are first to be destroyed, and destroyed they will surely be. A nation united can never be conquered. We have seen what the ignorant, bigoted and unarmed Spaniards could do against the disciplined veterans of their invaders. What then may we not expect from the power and character of the French nation? The oppressors may cut off heads after heads, but like those of the Hydra they multiply at every stroke. The recruits within a nation's own limits are prompt and without number; while those of their invaders from a distance are slow, limited, and must come to an end. I think, too, we perceive that all these allies do not see the same interest in the annihilation of the power of France. There are certainly some symptoms of foresight in Alexander that France might produce a salutary diversion of force were Austria and Prussia to become her enemies. France, too, is the neutral ally of the Turk, as having no interfering interests, and might be useful in neutralizing and perhaps turning that power on Austria. That a reacting jealousy, too, exists with Austria and Prussia, I think their late strict alliance indicates; and I should not wonder if Spain should discover a sympathy with them. Italy is so divided as to be nothing. Here then we see new coalitions in embryo, which, after France shall in turn have suffered a just punishment for her crimes, will not only raise her from the earth on which she is prostrate, but give her an opportunity to establish a government of as much liberty as she can bear—enough to ensure her happiness and prosperity. When insurrection begins, be it where it will, all the partitioned countries will rush to arms, and Europe again become an arena of gladiators. And what is the definite object they will propose? A restoration certainly of the *status quo prius*, of the state of possession of '89. I see no other principle on which Europe can ever again settle down in lasting peace. I hope your prophecies will go thus far, as my wishes do, and that they, like the former, will prove to have been the sober dictates of a superior understanding, and a sound calculation of effects from causes well understood. Some future Morgan will then have an opportunity of doing you justice, and of counterbalancing the breach of confidence of which you so justly complain, and in which no one has had more frequent occasion of fellow-feeling than myself. Permit me to place here my affectionate respects to Mrs. Adams, and to add for yourself the assurances of cordial friendship and esteem.

NOAH WORCESTER, 1816, 14:415 ~ *THE LOSS BY THE WAR MAY HAVE SECURED THE WEAKER NATION FROM LOSS BY FUTURE WRONG.*

To Reverend Noah Worcester[1]

Monticello, January 29, 1816

Sir, Your letter bearing date October 18th, 1815, came only to hand the day before yesterday, which is mentioned to explain the date of mine. I have to thank you for the pamphlets accompanying it, to wit, the Solemn Review, the Friend of Peace or Special Interview, and the Friend of Peace, No. 2; the first of these I had received through another channel some months ago. I have not read the two last steadily through, because where one assents to

---

1 One of the leaders of the American peace movement, Noah Worcester was the prime mover and corresponding secretary of the Massachusetts Peace Society. Worcester had served in the Revolution and was already fifty-six years old when, on Christmas Day of 1814, he released the one of the most effective pamphlets on the question ever written: *A Solemn Review of the Custom of War; Showing that War Is the Effect of Popular Delusion and Proposing a Remedy* (Allen 1930, 9).

propositions as soon as announced it is loss of time to read the arguments in support of them. These numbers discuss the first branch of the causes of war, that is to say, wars undertaken for the point of honor, which you aptly analogize with the act of dueling between individuals, and reason with justice from the one to the other. Undoubtedly this class of wars is, in the general, what you state them to be, "needless, unjust and inhuman, as well as anti-Christian." The second branch of this subject, to wit, wars undertaken on account of wrong done, and which may be likened to the act of robbery in private life, I presume will be treated of in your future numbers. I observe this class mentioned in the Solemn Review, p. 10, and the question asked, "Is it common for a nation to obtain a redress of wrongs by war?" The answer to this question you will of course draw from history. In the meantime, reason will answer it on grounds of probability, that where the wrong has been done by a weaker nation, the stronger one has generally been able to enforce redress; but where by a stronger nation, redress by war has been neither obtained nor expected by the weaker. On the contrary, the loss has been increased by the expenses of the war in blood and treasure. Yet it may have obtained another object equally securing itself from future wrong. It may have retaliated on the aggressor losses of blood and treasure far beyond the value to him of the wrong he had committed, and thus have made the advantage of that too dear a purchase to leave him in a disposition to renew the wrong in future. In this way the loss by the war may have secured the weaker nation from loss by future wrong. The case you state of two boxers, both of whom get a "terrible bruising," is apposite to this. He of the two who committed the aggression on the other, although victor in the scuffle, yet probably finds his aggression not worth the bruising it has cost him. To explain this by numbers, it is alleged that Great Britain took from us before the late war near one thousand vessels, and that during the war we took from her fourteen hundred. That before the war she seized and made slaves of six thousand of our citizens, and that in the war we killed more than six thousand of her subjects, and caused her to expend such a sum as amounted to four or five thousand guineas a head for every slave she made. She might have purchased the vessels she took for less than the value of those she lost, and have used the six thousand of her men killed for the purposes to which she applied ours, have saved the four or five thousand guineas a head, and obtained a character of justice which is valuable to a nation as to an individual. These considerations, therefore, leave her without inducement to plunder property and take men in future on such dear terms. I neither affirm nor deny the truth of these allegations, nor is their truth material to the question. They are possible, and therefore present a case which will claim your consideration in a discussion of the general question whether any degree of injury can render a recourse to war expedient? Still less do I propose to draw to myself any part in this discussion. Age and its effects both on body and mind, has weaned my attentions from public subjects, and left me unequal to the labors of correspondence beyond the limits of my personal concerns.

I retire, therefore, from the question, with a sincere wish that your writings may have effect in lessening this greatest of human evils, and that you may retain life and health to enjoy the contemplation of this happy spectacle; and pray you to be assured of my great respect.

NOAH WORCESTER, 1817, 18:298 ~ *[IT IS] MY DISPOSITION TO MAINTAIN PEACE UNTIL ITS CONDITION SHALL BE MADE LESS TOLERABLE THAN THAT OF WAR ITSELF.*

To Noah Worcester
Nov. 26, 1817

Sir, You have not been mistaken in supposing my views and feeling to be in favor of the abolition of war. Of my disposition to maintain peace until its condition shall be made less tolerable than that of war itself, the world has had proofs, and more, perhaps, than it has approved. I hope it is practi-cable, by improving the mind and morals of society, to lessen the disposition to war; but of its abolition I despair. Still, on the axiom that a less degree of evil is preferable to a greater, no means should be neglected which may add weight to the better scale. The enrolment you propose, therefore, of my name in the records of your society cannot be unacceptable to me. It will be a true testimony of my principles and persuasion that the state of peace is that which most improves the manners and morals, the prosperity and happiness of mankind; and although I dare not promise myself that it can be perpetually maintained, yet if, by the inculcations of reason or religion, the perversities of our nature can be so far corrected as sometimes to prevent the necessity, either supposed or real, of an appeal to the blinder scourges of war, murder, and devastation, the benevolent endeavors of the friends of peace will not be entirely without remuneration. I pray you to accept the assurance of my respect and consideration.

MARQUIS DE LAFAYETTE, 1817, 15:116 ~ *THE WAR [OF 1812] HAS DONE US... THIS GOOD... OF ASSURING THE WORLD, THAT ALTHOUGH ATTACHED TO PEACE...WE WILL MEET WAR WHEN IT IS MADE NECESSARY*

To Marquis de Lafayette
Monticello, May 14, 1817

Although, dear Sir, much retired from the world, and meddling little in its concerns, yet I think it almost a religious duty to salute at times my old friends, were it only to say and to know that "all's well." Our hobby has been politics; but all here is so quiet, and with you so desperate, that little matter is furnished us for active attention. With you too, it has long been forbidden ground, and therefore imprudent for a foreign friend to tread, in writing to you. But although our speculations might be intrusive, our prayers cannot but be acceptable, and mine are sincerely offered for the well-being of France. What government she can bear, depends not on the state of science, however exalted, in a select band of enlightened men, but on the condition of the gen-eral mind. That, I am sure, is advanced and will advance; and the last change of government was fortunate, inasmuch as the new will be less obstructive to the effects of that advancement. For I consider your foreign military oppressions as an ephemeral obstacle only.

Here all is quiet. The British war has left us in debt; but that is a cheap price for the good it has done us. The establishment of the necessary manufactures among ourselves, the proof that our government is solid, can stand the shock of war, and is superior even to civil schism, are precious facts for us; and of these the strongest proofs were furnished, when, with four eastern States tied to us, as dead to living bodies, all doubt was removed as to the achievements of the war, had it continued. But its best effect has been the complete suppression of party. The federalists who were truly American, and their great mass was so, have separated from their brethren who were mere Anglo men, and are received with cordiality into the republican ranks. Even Connecticut, as a State, and the last one expected to yield its steady habits (which were essentially bigoted in politics as well as religion), has chosen a republican governor, and republican legislature. Massachusetts indeed still lags; because most deeply involved in the parricide crimes and treasons of the war. But her gangrene is contracting, the sound flesh advancing on it, and all there will be well. I mentioned Connecticut as the most hopeless of our States. Little Delaware had escaped my attention. That is essentially a Quaker State, the fragment of a religious sect which, there, in the other States, in England, are a homogeneous mass, acting with one mind, and that directed by the Mother society in England. Dispersed, as the Jews, they still form, as those do, one nation, foreign to the land they live in. They are Protestant Jesuits, implicitly devoted to the will of their superior, and forgetting all duties to their country in the execution of the policy of their order. When war is proposed with England, they have religious scruples; but when with France, these are laid by, and they become clamorous for it. They are, however, silent, passive, and give no other trouble than of whipping them along. Nor is the election of Monroe an inefficient circumstance in our felicities. Four and twenty years, which he will accomplish, of administration in republican forms and principles, will so consecrate them in the eyes of the people as to secure them against the danger of change. The evanition of party dissensions has harmonized intercourse, and sweetened society beyond imagination. The war then has done us all this good, and the further one of assuring the world, that although attached to peace from a sense of its blessings, we will meet war when it is made necessary.

I wish I could give better hopes of our southern brethren. The achievement of their independence of Spain is no longer a question. But it is a very serious one, what will then become of them? Ignorance and bigotry, like other insanities, are incapable of self-government. They will fall under military despotism and become the murderous tools of the ambition of their respective Bonapartes; and whether this will be for their greater happiness, the rule of one only has taught you to judge. No one, I hope, can doubt my wish to see them and all mankind exercising self -government, and capable of exercising it. But the question is not what we wish, but what is practicable? As their sincere friend and brother then, I do believe the best thing for them, would be for themselves to come to an accord with Spain, under the guarantee of France, Russia, Holland, and the United States, allowing to Spain a nominal supremacy, with authority only to keep the peace among them, leaving them otherwise all the powers of self-government, until their experience in them, their emancipation from their priests, and advancement in information, shall prepare them for complete independence. I exclude England from this confederacy, because her selfish principles render her incapable of honorable patronage or disinterested co-operation; unless indeed, what seems now probable, a revolution should restore to her an honest government, one which will permit the world to live in peace. Portugal grasping at an extension of her dominion in the south, has lost her great northern province of Penambuco, and I shall not wonder if Brazil should revolt in mass, and send their royal family back to Portugal. Brazil is more populous, more wealthy, more energetic, and as wise as Portugal. I have been insensibly led, my dear friend, while writing to you, to indulge in that line of sentiment in which we have been always associated, forgetting that these are matters not belonging to my time. Not so with you, who have still many years to be a spectator of these events. That these years may indeed be many and happy, is the sincere prayer of your affectionate friend.

JOHN ADAMS, 1821, 15:333 - *THERE SHOULD BE A SCHOOL OF INSTRUCTION FOR OUR NAVY AS WELL AS ARTILLERY.*

To John Adams[1]
Monticello, September 12, 1821

Dear Sir, I am just returned from my other home, and shall within a week go back to it for the rest of the autumn. I find here your favor of August 20th, and was before in arrear for that of May 19th. I cannot answer, but join in, your question of May 19th. Are we to surrender the pleasing hopes of seeing improvement in the moral and intellectual condition of man? The events of Naples and Piedmont cast a gloomy cloud over that hope, and Spain and Portugal are not beyond jeopardy. And what are we to think of this northern triumvirate, arming their nations to dictate despotisms to the rest of the world? And the evident connivance of England, as the price of secret stipulations for continental armies, if her own should take side with her malcontent and pulverized people? And what of the poor Greeks, and their small chance of amelioration even if the hypocritical Autocrat should take them under the iron cover of his Ukazes. Would this be lighter or safer than that of the Turk? These, my dear friend, are speculations for the new generation, as, before they will be resolved, you and I must join our deceased brother Floyd. Yet I will not believe our labors are lost. I shall not die without a hope that light and liberty are on steady advance. We have seen, indeed, once within the records

1 While Jefferson's rapprochement with Adams was important to both men, it was especially important to Adams, who was gratified at being embraced as an equal by the man who had beaten him in 1800 and who had come to occupy a seat in the American pantheon alongside Washington and Franklin (Ferling 2004, 214).

of history, a complete eclipse of the human mind continuing for centuries. And this, too, by swarms of the same northern barbarians, conquering and taking possession of the countries and governments of the civilized world. Should this be again attempted, should the same northern hordes, allured again by the corn, wine, and oil of the south, be able again to settle their swarms in the countries of their growth, the art of printing alone, and the vast dissemination of books, will maintain the mind where it is, and raise the conquering ruffians to the level of the conquered, instead of degrading these to that of their conquerors. And even should the cloud of barbarism and despotism again obscure the science and liberties of Europe, this country remains to preserve and restore light and liberty to them. In short, the flames kindled on the 4th of July, 1777, have spread over too much of the globe to be extinguished by the feeble engines of despotism; on the contrary, they will consume these engines and all who work them.

I think with you that there should be a school of instruction for our navy as well as artillery; and I do not see why the same establishment might not suffice for both. Both require the same basis of general mathematics, adding projectiles and fortifications for the artillery exclusively, and astronomy and theory of navigation exclusively for the naval students. Berout conducted both schools in France, and has left us the best book extant for their joint and separate instruction. It ought not to require a separate professor.

A 4th of July oration delivered in the town of Milford, in your State, gives to Samuel Chase the credit of having "first started the cry of independence in the ears of his countrymen." Do you remember anything of this? I do not. I have no doubt it was uttered in Massachusetts even before it was by Thomas Paine. But certainly I never considered Samuel Chase as foremost, or even forward in that hallowed cry. I know that Maryland hung heavily on our backs, and that Chase, although first named, was not most in unison with us of that delegation, either in politics or morals, et *c'est ainsi que l'on ecrit l'histoire!*

Your doubt of the legitimacy of the word *gloriola*, is resolved by Cicero, who, in his letter to Lucceius expresses a wish *"ut nos metipsi vivi gloriola nostra perfruamur."* Affectionately *adieu.*

JOHN ADAMS, 1822, 15:372 – *A WAR BETWEEN [TWO DESPOTS] IS LIKE THE BATTLE OF THE KITE AND SNAKE. WHICHEVER DESTROYS THE OTHER LEAVES A DESTROYER THE LESS FOR THE WORLD.*

To John Adams
Monticello, June 1, 1822

It is very long, my dear Sir, since I have written to you. My dislocated wrist is now become so stiff that I write slow and with pain, and therefore write as little as I can. Yet it is due to mutual friendship to ask once in awhile how we do? The papers tell us that General Stark is off at the age of 93. Charles Thomson still lives at about the same age, cheerful, slender as a grasshopper, and so much without memory that he scarcely recognizes the members of his household. An intimate friend of his called on him not long since; it was difficult to make him recollect who he was, and, sitting one hour, he told him the same story four times over. Is this life?

"*With lab'ring step*
To tread our former footsteps? pace the round
Eternal?–to beat and beat
The beaten track? to see what we have seen,
To taste the tasted? o'er our palates to decant
Another vintage?"

It is at most but the life of a cabbage; surely not worth a wish. When all our faculties have left, or are leaving us, one by one, sight, hearing, memory, every avenue of pleasing sensation is closed, and athumy, debility and malaise left in their places, when friends of our youth are all gone, and a generation is risen around us whom we know not, is death an evil?

"*When one by one our ties are torn,*
And friend from friend is snatched forlorn,
When man is left alone to mourn,
Oh! then how sweet it is to die!
When trembling limbs refuse their weight,
And films slow gathering dim the sight,
When clouds obscure the mental light
'Tis nature's kindest boon to die! "

I really think so. I have ever dreaded a doting old age; and my health has been generally so good, and is now so good, that I dread it still. The rapid decline of my strength during the last winter has made me hope sometimes that I see land. During summer I enjoy its temperature, but I shudder at the approach of winter, and wish I could sleep through it with the dormouse, and only wake with him in spring, if ever. They say that Stark could walk about his room. I am told you walk well and firmly. I can only reach my garden, and that with sensible fatigue. I ride, however, daily. But reading is my delight. I should wish never to put pen to paper; and the more because of the treacherous practice some people have of publishing one's letters without leave. Lord Mansfield declared it a breach of trust, and punishable at law. I think it should be a penitentiary felony; yet you will have seen that they have drawn me out into the arena of the newspapers; although I know it is too late for me to buckle on the armor of youth, yet my indignation would not permit me passively to receive the kick of an ass.

To turn to the news of the day, it seems that the cannibals of Europe are going to eating one another again. A war between Russia and Turkey is like the battle of the kite and snake. Whichever destroys the other, leaves a destroyer the less for the world. This pugnacious humor of mankind seems to be the law of his nature, one of the obstacles to too great multiplication provided in the mechanism of the universe. The cocks of the hen yard kill one another up. Bears, bulls, rams, do the same. And the horse, in his wild state, kills all the young males, until worn down with age and war, some vigorous youth kills him, and takes to himself the harem of females. I hope we shall prove how much happier for man the Quaker policy is, and that the life of the feeder, is better than that of the fighter; and it is some consolation that the desolation by these maniacs of one part of the earth is the means of improving it in other parts. Let the latter be our office, and let us milk the cow, while the Russian holds her by the horns, and the Turk by the tail. God bless you, and give you health, strength, and good spirits, and as much of life as you think worth having.

JOHN ADAMS, 1822, 15:400 ~ *COLLISIONS...BETWEEN THE VESSELS OF WAR OF DIFFERENT NATIONS... BEGET WARS AND CONSTITUTE THE WEIGHTIEST OBJECTION TO NAVIES.*

To John Adams
Monticello, November 1, 1822

Dear Sir, I have racked my memory and ransacked my papers, to enable myself to answer the inquiries of your favor of October the 15th; but to little purpose. My papers furnish me nothing; my memory, generalities only. I know that while I was in Europe, and anxious about the fate of our seafaring men, for some of whom, then in captivity in Algiers, we were treating, and all were in like danger, I formed, undoubtingly, the opinion that our government, as soon as practicable, should provide a naval force sufficient to keep the Barbary States in order; and on this subject we communicated together, as you observe. When I returned to the United States and took part in the administration under General Washington, I constantly maintained that opinion; and in December, 1790, took advantage of a reference to me from the first Congress which met after I was in office, to report in favor of a force sufficient for the protection of our Mediterranean commerce; and I laid before them an accurate statement of the whole Barbary force, public and private. I think General Washington approved of building vessels of war to that extent. General Knox, I know, did. But what was Colonel Hamilton's opinion, I do not in the least remember. Your recollections on that subject are certainly corroborated by his known anxieties for a close connection with Great Britain, to which he might apprehend danger from collisions between their vessels and ours. Randolph was then Attorney General; but his opinion on the question I also entirely forget. Some vessels of war were accordingly built and sent into the Mediterranean. The additions to these in your time, I need not note to you, who are well known to have ever been. an advocate for the wooden walls of Themistocles. Some of those you added, were sold under an act of Congress passed while you were in office. I thought, afterwards, that the public safety might require some additional vessels of strength, to be prepared and in readiness for the first moment of a war, provided they could be preserved against the decay which is unavoidable if kept in the water, and clear of the expense of officers and men. With this view I proposed that they should be built in dry docks, above the level of the tide-waters, and covered with roofs. I further advised, that places for these docks should be selected where there was a command of water on a high level, as that of the Tyber at

Washington, by which the vessels might be floated out, on the principle of a lock. But the majority of the legislature was against any addition to the navy, and the minority, although for it in judgment, voted against it on a principle of opposition. We are now, I understand, building vessels to remain on the stocks, under shelter, until wanted, when they will be launched and finished. On my plan they could be in service at an hour's notice. On this, the finishing, after launching, will be a work of time.

This is all I recollect about the origin and progress of our navy. That of the late war, certainly raised our rank and character among nations. Yet a navy is a very expensive engine. It is admitted, that in ten or twelve years a vessel goes to entire decay; or, if kept in repair, costs as much as would build a new one; and that a nation who could count would gain new one in on twelve or fifteen years of peace, by burning its navy and building a time. Its extent, therefore, must be governed by circumstances. Since my proposition for a force adequate to the piracies of the Mediterranean, a similar necessity has arisen in our own seas for considerable addition to that force. Indeed, I wish we could have a convention with the naval powers of Europe, for them to keep down the pirates of the Mediterranean, and the slave ships on the coast of Africa, and for us to perform the same duties for the society of nations in our seas. In this way, those collisions would be avoided between the vessels of war of different nations, which beget wars and constitute the weightiest objection to navies. I salute you with constant affection and respect.

MARQUIS DE LAFAYETTE, 1823, 15:490 ~ *A NATION CANNOT BE CONQUERED WHICH DETERMINES NOT TO BE SO.*

To Marquis de Lafayette
Monticello, November 4, 1817

My Dear Friend, Two dislocated wrists and crippled fingers have rendered writing so slow and laborious, as to oblige me to withdraw from nearly all correspondence; not, however, from yours, while I can make a stroke with a pen. We have gone through too many trying scenes together, to forget the sympathies and affections they nourished.

Your trials have indeed been long and severe. When they will end, is yet unknown, but where they will end, cannot be doubted. Alliances, Holy or Hellish, may be formed, and retard the epoch of deliverance, may swell the rivers of blood which are yet to flow, but their own will close the scene, and leave to mankind the right of self-government. I trust that Spain will prove, that a nation cannot be conquered which determines not to be so, and that her success will be the turning of the tide of liberty, no more to be arrested by human efforts. Whether the state of society in Europe can bear a republican government, I doubted, you know, when with you, and I do now. An hereditary chief, strictly limited, the right of war vested in the legislative body, a rigid economy of the public contributions, and absolute interdiction of all useless expenses, will go far towards keeping the government honest and unoppressive. But the only security of all, is in a free press. The force of public opinion cannot be resisted, when permitted freely to be expressed. The agitation it produces must be submitted to. It is necessary, to keep the waters pure.

We are all, for example, in agitation even in our peaceful country. For in peace as well as in war, the mind must be kept in motion. Who is to be the next President, is the topic here of every conversation. My opinion on that subject is what I expressed to you in my last letter. The question will be ultimately reduced to the northernmost and southernmost candidate. The former will get every federal vote in the Union, and many republicans; the latter, all of those denominated of the old school; for you are not to believe that these two parties are amalgamated, that the lion and the lamb are lying down together. The Hartford Convention, the victory of Orleans, the peace of Ghent, prostrated the name of federalism. Its votaries abandoned it through shame and mortification; and now call themselves republicans. But the name alone is changed, the principles are the same. For in truth, the parties of Whig and Tory, are those of nature. They exist in all countries, whether called by these names, or by those of Aristocrats and Democrats, Cote Droite and Cote Gauche, Ultras and Radicals, Serviles, and Liberals. The sickly, weakly, timid man, fears the people, and is a Tory by nature. The healthy, strong and bold, cherishes them, and is formed a Whig by nature. On the eclipse of federalism with us, although not its extinction, its leaders got up the Missouri question, under the false front of lessening the measure of slavery, but with the real view of producing a geographical division of parties, which might insure them the next President. The people of the North went blindfold into the snare, followed their leaders for awhile with a zeal truly moral and laudable, until they became sensible that they were injuring instead of aiding the real interests of the slaves, that they had been used merely as tools for electioneering purposes; and that trick of hypocrisy then fell as quickly as it had been got up. To that is now succeeding a distinction, which, like that of Republican and Federal, or Whig and Tory, being equally intermixed through every State, threatens none of those geographical schisms which go immediately to a separation. The line of division now, is the preservation of State rights, as reserved in the Constitution, or by strained constructions of that instrument, to merge all into a consolidated government. The Tories are for strengthening the Executive and General Government; the Whigs cherish the representative branch, and the rights reserved by the States, as the bulwark against consolidation, which must immediately generate monarchy. And although this division excites, as yet, no warmth, yet it exists, is well understood, and will be a principle of voting at the ensuing election, with the reflecting men of both parties.

I thank you much for the two books you were so kind as to send me by Mr. Gallatin. Miss Wright had before favored me with the first edition of her American work; but her "Few Days in Athens," was entirely new, and has been a treat to me of the highest order. The matter and manner of the dialogue is strictly ancient; and the principles of the sects are beautifully and candidly explained and contrasted; and the scenery and portraiture of the interlocutors are of higher finish than anything in that line left us by the ancients; and like Ossian, if not ancient, it is equal to the best morsels of antiquity. I augur, from this instance, that Herculaneum is likely to furnish better specimens of modern than of ancient genius; and may we not hope more from the same pen?

After much sickness, and the accident of a broken and disabled arm, I am again in tolerable health, but extremely debilitated, so as to be scarcely able to walk into my garden. The hebetude of age, too, and extinguishment of interest in the things around me, are weaning me from them, and dispose me with cheerfulness to resign them to the existing generation, satisfied that the daily advance of science will enable them to administer the commonwealth with increased wisdom. You have still many valuable years to give to your country, and with my prayers that they may be years of health and happiness, and especially that they may see the establishment of the principles of government which you have cherished through life, accept the assurance of my affectionate and constant friendship and respect.

EPILOGUE

Thomas Jefferson died on July 4, 1826, and was buried beside his wife in the cemetery on the sloping hillside at Monticello. He had drawn the design and left the instructions for a plain obelisk of coarse stone to mark his grave and requested as his epitaph "the following inscription, and not a word more:"
Here was buried
Thomas Jefferson
Author of the Declaration of American Independence
of the Statute of Virginia for religious freedom
and Father of the University of Virginia.

He explained that "because by these, as testimonials that I have lived, I wish most to be remembered."[1]

Philosopher, diplomat, politician, inventor, writer, architect, and gardener, drawn from his numerous accomplishments, Thomas Jefferson is both an atypical and extraordinary individual — one who was clearly many things to many people. But, too, precisely because of these same collective endeavors, he has become so much a part of the nation's ongoing search for itself, so deeply implicated in the whole tapestry of American democracy, that succeeding generations are largely unable to see him clearly and objectively in his own life and time.[2]

From the very beginning, there was a clash between Jefferson, a firm believer in participatory democracy and in the republican form of government, and Alexander Hamilton, Washington's Treasury Secretary, who espoused a much more elitist form of government along imperial lines. The issues were

---

1 Cunningham 1987, 349.
2 Peterson 1975, vii.

fundamental in nature and Jefferson passionately resisted the Hamiltonian philosophy that proposed a presidency and a senate elected for life, in a plutocratic and aristocratic way, whereas only the representatives would have been elected for short terms. Hamilton was an admirer of the British monarchial empire, while Jefferson wanted a government modeled along the lines of the French republican ideas. In the end, domestically, successive American governments remained faithful to the Jeffersonian ideals of democracy, with each individual, rich or poor, having an equal voice in national affairs; while, with respect to foreign policy, the United States has supported international law and multilateral international cooperation, and rejected imperialism and colonialism as the foundation for international political order.[1]

To this end, Jefferson emerges as a seminal figure in American political thought. And although he was occasionally unrealistic about what the United States might achieve on its own, and even despite the pacifist reputation of his age, he did not take the view that war was an aberration, nor did he chose to ignore the interest of the state in security. On the contrary, Jefferson harbored a dominantly political perception of conflict. One in which a pragmatic view of foreign policy necessitated a pragmatic view of war and the selective application of violence. For example, while he disdained crusades, at the same time he could view war as the arbitrator of compromised rights. It would recur, Jefferson believed, because of the nature of man and states. Most of the time, war was an instrument of last resort, but occasionally, such as with the Barbary pirates or Spain, Jefferson could afford to be more aggressive and, like other statesmen in the age of limited war, he related the means at his disposal to the ends he wanted to achieve: a pragmatic view of foreign policy necessitated a pragmatic view of war.[2]

One final word about Jefferson, the man, is in place and may serve to narrow the focus with which to contemplate his thoughts. After a lengthy and unusual *Autobiography*, written at the age of seventy-seven, and with less indulgence in personalities than perhaps any other autobiography of the times, Jefferson appended a note in which he asked a simple question: "Is my Country the Better for my Having Lived at All?" The question is striking; most people, even if the notion would occur to them, would hesitate to express it, to bring forth into the light of print the results of a lifetime's activity. But Jefferson's sincerity and simplicity disarms, and one cannot help but to reads on to see what the man has to say in defense of himself.[3]

In the final analysis, it may be reasonable to argue that it is Jefferson who, by virtue of his writings, is most often associated with the American conscience and who carries the moral character of the nation on his back. But, if so, is it really possible for a historical figure to bear this type of symbolic burden and still remain simply a person, and not something more?[4]

---

1 Tremblay 2004.
2 Stuart 1976, 171.
3 Koch 1957, 189.
4 Wood 2006, 99-100.

The answer, one suspects, can be found in Jefferson's last letter, written but ten days prior to his death. Too old and infirm to leave Monticello, perhaps he sensed that this might be the last opportunity to register his personal stamp on the public understanding of just what the American Revolution had meant. The eloquent response was written to decline an invitation to travel to Washington, D.C., to attend a celebration commemorating the fiftieth anniversary of American independence. And although he was all but incapacitated by illness, he nonetheless labored over the reply with infinite care, correcting and revising his words with the same attention to detail that he had brought to the original draft of the Declaration of Independence. The result is one of the most inspired, and succinct, renditions of the Jeffersonian message in existence.[1]

Roger C. Weightman
Monticello, June 24, 1826

Respected Sir, The kind invitation I receive from you, on the part of the citizens of the city of Washington, to be present with them at their celebration of the fiftieth anniversary of American Independence, as one of the surviving signers of an instrument pregnant with our own, and the fate of the world, is most flattering to myself, and heightened by the honorable accompaniment proposed for the comfort of such a journey. It adds sensibly to the sufferings of sickness, to be deprived by it of a personal participation in the rejoicings of that day. But acquiescence is a duty, under circumstances not placed among those we are permitted to control. I should, indeed, with peculiar delight, have met and exchanged there congratulations personally with the small band, the remnant of that host of worthies, who joined with us on that day, in the bold and doubtful election we were to make for our country, between submission or the sword; and to have enjoyed with them the consolatory fact, that our fellow citizens, after half a century of experience and prosperity, continue to approve the choice we made. May it be to the world, what I believe it will be, (to some parts sooner, to others later, but finally to all,) the signal of arousing men to burst the chains under which monkish ignorance and superstition had persuaded them to bind themselves, and to assume the blessings and security of self-government. That form which we have substituted, restores the free right to the unbounded exercise of reason and freedom of opinion. All eyes are opened, or opening, to the rights of man. The general spread of the light of science has already laid open to every view the palpable truth, that the mass of mankind has not been born with saddles on their backs, nor a favored few booted and spurred, ready to ride them legitimately, by the grace of God. These are grounds of hope for others. For ourselves, let the annual return of this day forever refresh our recollections of these rights, and an undiminished devotion to them.

I will ask permission here to express the pleasure with which I should have met my ancient neighbors of the city of Washington and its vicinities,

---

1 Ellis 2001, 206.

with whom I passed so many years of a pleasing social intercourse; an intercourse which so much relieved the anxieties of the public cares, and left impressions so deeply engraved in my affections, as never to be forgotten. With my regret that ill health forbids me the gratification of an acceptance, be pleased to receive for yourself, and those for whom you write, the assurance of my highest respect and friendly attachments.

Th. Jefferson

Works Cited

Adams, Henry. 1930. *History of the United States of America During the Administration of Thomas Jefferson*. New York: A & C Boni.

Allen, Devere. 1930. *The Fight for Peace*. Appendix I: Conflicts Since the Beginning of the Organized Peace Movement. New York: Macmillan Co.

Barnes, William, and John Heath Morgan. 1961. *The Foreign Service of the United States: Origins, Development and Functions*. Department of State Publications, 96. Washington: Department of State, Bureau of Public Affairs, Historical Office.

Beeman, Richard R. 1972. *The Old Dominion and the New Nation, 1788-1801*. Lexington: University Press of Kentucky.

Berman, Eleanor Davidson. 1947. *Thomas Jefferson Among the Arts: An Essay in Early American Esthetics*. New York: Philosophical Library.

Bernstein, R.B. 2003. *Thomas Jefferson*. Oxford: Oxford University Press.

Binning, William C., Larry E. Esterly, and Paul A. Sracic. 1999. *Encyclopedia of American Parties, Campaigns, and Elections*. Westport, Conn: Greenwood Press.

Bolton, Herbert Eugene, and Thomas Maitland Marshall. 1920. *The Colonization of North America, 1492-1783*. New York: Macmillan Co.

Borden, Morton. 1971. *America's Eleven Greatest Presidents*. Rand McNally History Series. Chicago: Rand McNally.

Bowdoin College. "The Bowdoin Family History." *About Bowdoin*. http://www.bowdoin.edu. October 30, 2008.

Brands, H.W. 2000. *The First American: The Life and Times of Benjamin Franklin*. New York: Anchor Books.

Brodie, Fawn McKay. 1974. *Thomas Jefferson, An Intimate History*. New York: Norton.

Brooklyn Museum. 1917. *Early American Paintings; Catalogue of an Exhibition Held in the Museum of the Brooklyn Institute of Arts and Sciences, Brooklyn, February 3d to March 12th, 1917*.

Brown, Jerold E. 2001. *Historical Dictionary of the U.S. Army*. Westport, Conn: Greenwood Press.

Brown, Ralph H. 1943. *Mirror for Americans: Likeness of the Eastern Seaboard, 1810.* New York: American Geographical Society.

Brown, Stuart Gerry. 1954. *The First Republicans: Political Philosophy and Public Policy in the Party of Jefferson and Madison.* Syracuse: Syracuse University Press.

Caemmerer, H. Paul. 1932. *Washington, the National Capital.* Washington: U.S. G.P.O.

Carnahan, Burrus M. "Protecting Nuclear Facilities from Military Attack: Prospects After the Gulf War." *American Journal of International Law.* Vol.86, No.3 (1992).

Channing, Edward. 1906. *The Jeffersonian System, 1801-1811.* New York and London: Harper & Bros.

Clark, George Rogers, and Milo Milton Quaife. 2001. *The Conquest of the Illinois.* Shawnee Classics. Carbondale: Southern Illinois University Press.

Coe, Samuel Gwynn. 1928. *The Mission of William Carmichael to Spain.* Baltimore: The Johns Hopkins Press.

Columbia Encyclopedia 6th ed. 2007. "Genet, Edmond Charles Edouard." New York: Columbia University Press.

Creesy, Chuck. "Digital Monticello: The Revision of a Classic Typeface." *Association of American University Presses Exchange.* Winter (2003).

Cunningham, Noble E. 1987. In Pursuit of Reason: The life of Thomas Jefferson. Baton Rouge: Louisiana State University Press.

Currie, David P. 1999. *The Constitution in Congress: The Federalist Period 1789-1801.* Chicago: University of Chicago Press.

Davidson, Roger H., Susan Webb Hammond, and Raymond Smock. 1998. *Masters of the House: Congressional Leadership over Two Centuries.* Transforming American Politics. Boulder, Colo: Westview Press.

Davis, David Brion, and Steven Mintz. 1998. *The Boisterous Sea of Liberty: A Documentary History of America from Discovery Through the Civil War.* New York: Oxford University Press.

DeConde, Alexander. 1958. *Entangling Alliance; Politics and Diplomacy under George Washington.* Durham, N.C.: Duke University Press.

Downes, Paul. 2002. *Democracy, Revolution, and Monarchism in Early American Literature.* Cambridge, U.K.: Cambridge University Press.

Malone, Dumas. 1948. *Jefferson and His Time: Jefferson the Virginian.* Boston: Little, Brown.

Dupuy, R. Ernest, and Trevor Nevitt Dupuy. 1956. *Military Heritage of America.* McGraw-Hill Series in History. New York: McGraw-Hill.

Ellis, Joseph J. 1998. *American Sphinx: The Character of Thomas Jefferson.* New York, NY: Vintage Books.

_____. 2001. *Passionate Sage: The Character and Legacy of John Adams.* New York: Norton.

Farmer, Silas. 1890. *History of Detroit and Wayne County and Early Michigan.* Detroit: S. Farmer & Co. for Muncel & Co. (New York).

Ferling, John E. 2002. *Setting the World Ablaze: Washington, Adams, Jefferson, and the American Revolution.* Oxford: Oxford University Press.

_____. 2004. *Adams vs. Jefferson: The Tumultuous Election of 1800*. New York: Oxford University Press

_____. 2007. *Almost a Miracle: The American Victory in the War of Independence*. Oxford: Oxford University Press.

Foner, Philip Sheldon. 1976. *The Democratic-Republican Societies, 1790-1800: A documentary Sourcebook of Constitutions, Declarations, Addresses, Resolutions, and Toasts*. Westport, Conn: Greenwood Press.

Franklin, Benjamin and Brett F. Woods, 2006. *Letters from France: the Private Diplomatic Correspondence of Benjamin Franklin, 1776 - 1785*. New York: Algora.

Gerry, Elbridge, and Claude Gernade Bowers. 1927. *The Diary of Elbridge Gerry, Jr*. New York: Brentano's.

Greene, Francis V. 1911. The Revolutionary War and the Military Policy of the United States. New York: C. Scribner's Sons.

Greene, John C. 1984. *American Science in the Age of Jefferson*. Ames: Iowa State University Press.

Hagan, Kenneth J., and William R. Roberts. 1986. *Against All Enemies: Interpretations of American Military History from Colonial Times to the Present*. Contributions in Military Studies, no. 51. New York: Greenwood Press.

Hagy, Mark R. 1996. "Portrait of a Virginia Antifederalist: Theodorick Bland." *International Social Science Review*, 71: 3-13.

Hart, Gary. 2002. *Restoration of the Republic: The Jeffersonian Ideal in 21st-century America*. Oxford, UK: Oxford University Press.

Henderson, Dwight F. 1985.*Congress, Courts, and Criminals: The Development of Federal Criminal Law, 1801-1829*. Contributions in American History, no. 113. Westport, Conn: Greenwood Press.

Horsman, Reginald. 1962. *The Causes of the War of 1812*. Philadelphia: University of Pennsylvania Press.

Howard, Perry H. 1971. *Political Tendencies in Louisiana*. Baton Rouge: Louisiana State University Press.

Jameson, J. Franklin. 1898. *American Historical Review*. Vol. 3. London: MacMillan and Company.

Jefferson, Thomas, Joyce Oldham Appleby, and Terence Ball. 1999. *Thomas Jefferson, Political Writings*. Cambridge Texts in the History of Political Thought. New York: Cambridge University Press.

Jefferson, Thomas, Julian P. Boyd, L. H. Butterfield, Charles T. Cullen, and John Catanzariti. 1950. *Papers*. Princeton: Princeton University Press.

Kaplan, Lawrence S. 1967. *Jefferson and France: An Essay on Politics and Political Ideas*. New Haven: Yale University Press.

Kennedy, John Pendleton. 1849. *Memoirs of the life of William Wirt, Attorney General of the United States*. Philadelphia: Lea and Blanchard.

Kimball, Marie Goebel. 1947. *Jefferson, War and Peace, 1776 to 1784*. New York: Coward-McCann.

_____. 1950. *Jefferson: The Scene of Europe, 1784 to 1789*. New York: Coward-McCann.

Koch, Adrienne. 1950. *Jefferson and Madison: The Great Collaboration*. New York: Knopf.

_____. 1957. *The Philosophy of Thomas Jefferson*. Columbia Studies in American Culture, No. 14. Gloucester, MA: Peter Smith.

Langguth, A. J. 1988. *Patriots: The Men Who Started the American Revolution*. New York: Simon and Schuster.

Library of Congress. "The Thomas Jefferson Papers Timeline: 1743 -1827." *American Memory Collection*. http://lcweb2.loc.gov/ammem/collections/jefferson_papers/mtjtime1.html. November 4, 2008.

Lim, Elvin T. "Five Trends in Presidential Rhetoric: An Analysis of Rhetoric from George Washington to Bill Clinton,. *Presidential Studies Quarterly* 32, no. 2 (2002).

Marble, Annie Russell. 1907. *Heralds of American Literature: A Group of Patriot Writers of the Revolutionary and National Periods*. Chicago: University of Chicago Press.

Matloff, Maurice. 1996. *American Military History*. Vol.1. Conshohocken, PA: Combined Books.

McCaleb, Walter Flavius. 1936. *The Aaron Burr Conspiracy*. New York: Wilson-Erickson.

McCardell, John. 1979. *The Idea of a Southern Nation: Southern Nationalists and Southern Nationalism, 1830-1860*. New York: Norton.

Morris, Robert, Elmer James Ferguson, John Catanzariti, and Elizabeth M. Nuxoll. 1995. *The Papers of Robert Morris: 1781 - 1784*. Pittsburgh: University of Pittsburgh Press.

Mudge, Eugene Tenbroeck. 1939. *The Social Philosophy of John Taylor of Caroline: A Study in Jeffersonian Democracy*. New York: Columbia University Press.

National Archives of the United Kingdom. "George Hammond." *British Envoys to America, 1791-1891*. http://yourarchives.nationalarchives.gov.uk. October 19, 2008.

National Governors Association. "Benjamin Smith." *Governor's Information*. http://www.nga.org. October 30, 2008.

_____. "Robert Wright." *Governor's Information*. http://www.nga.org. October 30, 2008.

Newman, Edgar Leon, and Robert Lawrence Simpson. 1987. *Historical Dictionary of France from the 1815 Restoration to the Second Empire*. Historical Dictionaries of French History. New York: Greenwood Press.

Oliver, John William. 1956. *History of American Technology*. New York: Ronald Press Co.

Olson, James Stuart. 1992. *Historical Dictionary of the Spanish Empire, 1402-1975*. New York: Greenwood Press.

Patterson, Richard S. 1956. *The Secretaries of State: Portraits and Biographical Sketches*. Washington, DC: U.S. Government Printing Office.

Peterson, Merrill D. 1975. *Thomas Jefferson and the New Nation*.London: Oxford University Press.

Prucha, Francis Paul. 1984. *The Great Father: the United States Government and the American Indians*. Lincoln: University of Nebraska Press.

Republican Party of New York. 1809. *Address from the General Republican Committee of the City and County of New-York, to the Republican Electors*. New York: Republican Party.

Risjord, Norman K. 1978. *Chesapeake Politics, 1781-1800*. New York: Columbia University Press.

—————————. 1965. *The Old Republicans; Southern Conservatism in the Age of Jefferson*. New York: Columbia University Press.

Ritter, Abraham. 1860. *Philadelphia and Her Merchants*. Philadelphia: Private Edition.

Rutland, Robert Allen. 1955. *The Birth of the Bill of Rights, 1776-1791*. Chapel Hill: Published for the Institute of Early American History and Culture by the University of North Carolina Press.

Schachner, Nathan. 1957. *Thomas Jefferson: A Biography*. New York: T. Yoseloff.

Sears, Louis Martin. 1927. *Jefferson and the Embargo*. Duke University Publications. Durham, N.C.: Duke University Press

Smith, Frank. 1938. *Thomas Paine, Liberator*. New York: Frederick A. Stokes Company.

State Papers and Public Documents of the United States from the Accession of George Washington to the Presidency, Exhibiting a Complete View of Our Foreign Relations Since that Time: (1789-1818). Vol.10. 1819.

Stefanelli, Dana. 2008 Review of Herrick, Carole L., *August 24, 1814: Washington in Flames*. H-DC, H-Net Reviews. http://www.h-net.org/reviews/showrev. php?id=14256. November 1, 2008.

Steiner, George Albert. 1942. *Economic Problems of War*. New York: J. Wiley & Sons.

Stern, Gary M., and Morton H. Halperin. 1994. *The U.S. Constitution and the Power to go to War: Historical and Current Perspectives*. Contributions in Military Studies, no.150. Westport, Conn: Greenwood Press.

Strauss, Leo, and Joseph Cropsey. 1963. *History of Political Philosophy*. Chicago: Rand McNally.

Stuart, Reginald C. "Thomas Jefferson and the Function of War: Policy or Principle?" *Canadian Journal of History*. Vol.11, No.2 (1976).

Sturgis, Amy H. 2002. *Presidents from Washington through Monroe, 1789-1825: Debating the Issues in Pro and Con Primary Documents*. Westport, Conn: Greenwood Press.

Thomas, David Y. 1927. *One Hundred Years of the Monroe Doctrine*. New York: Macmillan.

Thomas Jefferson Foundation. "Timeline of Jefferson's Life." *Monticello, Home of Thomas Jefferson*. http://www.monticello.org/jefferson/timeline.html. November 2, 2008.

Tremblay, Rodrigue. "The Neo-Conservative Agenda: Humanism vs. Imperialism." Lecture, American Humanist Association, Las Vegas, NV, May 8, 2004.

Tucker, Robert W., and David C. Hendrickson. 1992. *Empire of Liberty: The Statecraft of Thomas Jefferson*. New York: Oxford University Press.

Turner, Frederick J. "The Origin of Genet's Projected Attack on Louisiana and the Floridas."*American Historical Review*. Vol.3, No.4 (1898).

Unger, Harlow G. 2002. *Lafayette*. New York: John Wiley & Sons.

United States Congress. *Biographical Directory of the United States Congress, 1774-present*. Washington, D.C.: The Congress. http://purl.access.gpo.gov/GPO/LPS21383. October 16, 2008.

United States Department of State. Office of the Historian. 2008. "The XYZ Affair and the Quasi-War with France, 1798-1800." http://www.state.gov/r/pa/ho/time/nr/16318.htm. October 26, 2008.

Valentine, Alan Chester. 1962. *Lord George Germain*. Oxford, England: Clarendon Press.

Varg, Paul A. 1964. *Foreign Policies of the Founding Fathers*. East Lansing: Michigan State University Press.

Wells, William V. 1888. *The Life and Public Services of Samuel Adams*. Vol.3. Boston: Little, Brown.

West's Encyclopedia of American Law. 2008. "William Wirt" http://www.answers.com/topic/william-wirt. October 31, 2008.

White House. "Thomas Jefferson." *Past Presidents*. www.whitehouse.gov/history/presidents/tj3.html. November 5, 2008.

White, Richard. 1983. *The Roots of Dependency: Subsistence, Environment, and Social Change Among the Choctaws, Pawnees, and Navajos*. Lincoln: University of Nebraska Press.

Wilson, Leonard. 1912. *Makers of America*. Vol. 2. Washington: B.F. Johnson, Inc.

Wilhite, Virgle Glenn. 1958. *Founders of American Economic Thought and Policy*. New York: Bookman Associates.

Wiltse, Charles Maurice. 1935. *The Jeffersonian Tradition in American Democracy*. Chapel Hill: University of North Carolina Press.

Wollery, William Kirk. 1927. *The Relation of Thomas Jefferson to American Foreign Policy, 1783-1793*. Baltimore: The Johns Hopkins Press.

Wood, Gordon S. 2006. *Revolutionary Characters: What Made the Founders Different*. New York: Penguin Books.

Wright, Quincy. 1922. *The Control of American Foreign Relations*. New York: Macmillan

Wright, Robert K., and Morris J. MacGregor. 1987. *Soldier-Statesmen of the Constitution*. CMH Pub, 71-25. Washington, DC: Center of Military History, U.S. Army.

INDEX